D0205030

ESSAYS ON THE INTELLECTUAL HISTORY OF ECONOMICS

JACOB VINER

Essays on the Intellectual History of Economics

EDITED BY

Douglas A. Irwin

PRINCETON UNIVERSITY PRESS
PRINCETON, NEW JERSEY

HB75
.V56
1991

Copyright © 1991 by Princeton University Press
Published by Princeton University Press, 41 William Street,
Princeton, New Jersey 08540
In the United Kingdom: Princeton University Press, Oxford

All Rights Reserved

not ref PF

Library of Congress Cataloging-in-Publication Data

Viner, Jacob, 1892–1970.
Essays on the intellectual history of economics / Jacob Viner ;
[compiled and] edited by Douglas A. Irwin.
p.   cm.
Includes index.
ISBN 0-691-04266-7 (alk. paper)
1. Economics—History. I. Irwin, Douglas A., 1962– .
II. Title.
HB75.V56   1991
330′.09—dc20   90-39761
                                                          CIP

This book has been composed in Times Roman

Princeton University Press books are printed on acid-free paper,
and meet the guidelines for permanence and durability of the
Committee on Production Guidelines for Book Longevity of the
Council on Library Resources

Printed in the United States of America by Princeton University Press,
Princeton, New Jersey

10 9 8 7 6 5 4 3 2 1

CONTENTS

612383

PART III   Review Articles

PART IV   Commencement Addresses

ACKNOWLEDGMENTS

SHORTLY AFTER Jacob Viner's death in 1970, a number of his friends and colleagues at Princeton sought to arrange publication of his principal essays on the history of economic thought. While this project apparently never advanced beyond early discussions, I was pleased to find that twenty years later interest among scholars in such a volume had not waned. In bringing together Viner's essays, I hope this collection serves as a lasting reminder of his scholarly contributions to intellectual history. I particularly hope that this volume introduces those unfamiliar with his work to the range and learning in his writings. This collection also provides a propitious opportunity to publish the text of five lectures Viner delivered in 1959 at a conference on "Economics and Freedom" at Wabash College.

In the preparation of this material, I am grateful for helpful discussions with and comments from many individuals, especially William Baumol, Jagdish Bhagwati, R.D.C. Black, Donald Dewey, Craufurd Goodwin, Daniel Hammond, and Jacques Melitz. I am particularly indebted to Arthur Bloomfield and Donald Winch for responding to my repeated requests for assistance. I also wish to thank Phillip Harth and Irwin Primer for providing the unpublished pages from Viner's introduction to Bernard Mandeville's *A Letter to Dion*.

The essays are republished here as they originally appeared, and they therefore contain inconsistencies in spelling, note format, and bibliographic style. The following publishers and institutions kindly granted permission to reprint material of Viner's that they had originally published: the University of Chicago Press, Princeton University Press, Oxford University Press, Cambridge University Press, the University of Toronto Press, Macmillan Publishing Company, Brown University, the Augustan Reprint Society, the American Economic Association, the Southern Economic Journal, and the Canadian Political Science Association. I thank the heirs of Jacob Viner (Arthur Viner and Ellen V. Seiler), the Princeton University libraries, the University of Toronto, and Wabash College for granting permission to publish or to quote from the unpublished papers of Jacob Viner.

Finally, I am grateful to Peter Kenen, the Director of the International Finance Section at Princeton University, for helpful advice and for providing generous financial assistance at an early stage of this project. Without the kind support of Ellen V. Seiler and the enthusiasm of Jack Repcheck, economics editor at Princeton University Press, this project would not have been completed.

Douglas A. Irwin
Washington, D.C.

ESSAYS ON THE INTELLECTUAL HISTORY OF ECONOMICS

INTRODUCTION

JACOB VINER ranks among the most distinguished economists and scholars of his generation.[1] Lionel Robbins, himself a great scholar in the history of economics, believed that Jacob Viner "was probably the greatest authority of the age in the history of economic and social thought."[2] Mark Blaug was less equivocal in judging Viner to be "quite simply the greatest historian of economic thought that ever lived."[3] Anyone familiar with Viner, either personally or through his writings, respects these claims as eminently justifiable. Indeed, only Joseph Schumpeter challenges Viner's reputation as this century's master of the history of economic thought.

Unlike Schumpeter, however, Viner did not leave behind a single *magnum opus* to stand as an enduring monument to his scholarly work in the history of economic thought. Instead, Viner's vast contribution to the history of thought has remained scattered in books and articles published over a period of half a century. This book aims to redress this state of affairs by collecting Jacob Viner's essay-length contributions to the intellectual history of economics, along with selected, previously unpublished material, into a single volume. The very appearance of this book, twenty-one years after Viner's death, testifies to the continuing significance of his scholarship.[4]

[1] See Fritz Machlup, "What the World Thought of Jacob Viner," *Journal of Political Economy* 80 (January–February 1972): 1–4.

[2] "Other names may come to the mind with achievements of comparable excellence in limited fields. But over the wide range of relevant literature from the sixteenth century onwards, he had no equal." Lionel Robbins, *Jacob Viner: A Tribute* (Princeton: Princeton University Press, 1970), pp. 6–7.

[3] Mark Blaug, *Great Economists since Keynes* (New York: Cambridge University Press, 1985), p. 256. Another recent assessment acclaims Viner's work in economic theory, "in addition to his perhaps even more distinguished work in the history of economics, where his accomplishments were almost without rival." Henry W. Spiegel, "Jacob Viner," in *The New Palgrave: A Dictionary of Economics*, eds. John Eatwell, Murray Milgate, and Peter Newman (New York: Stockton Press, 1987), 4:812.

[4] By one crude measure, attention to Viner's work has not diminished in the years since his death. The average annual number of citations of Viner's publications, taken from the *Social Science Citation Index*, shows remarkable consistency: 46 from 1971 to 1975; 78 from 1976 to 1980; 45 from 1981 to 1985; 46 from 1986 to 1988. References to Viner's seminal contributions to the study of

This collection opens with the text of five lectures Viner delivered at a Wabash College conference on "Economics and Freedom" in 1959. These previously unpublished lectures present a broad overview of economic and philosophical doctrines relating to freedom and commerce, a prominent theme in Viner's historical research.[5] Twelve of Viner's essays on the history of economic thought follow the lectures. Originally published at various times from 1927 to 1970, the essays cover a wide range of topics and demonstrate the breadth and depth of Viner's scholarship. Four review articles lend insight into Viner's assessment of work on topics that touched on his interests. Finally, two of Viner's commencement addresses on scholarship and learning, one previously unpublished, close out the volume.

This introduction aims to provide some background to the writings of Jacob Viner presented in this book. Little discussion of the lectures and essays themselves is needed, for anything written by Viner speaks clearly for itself. However, a brief commentary to set the stage for the essays—pointing out their significance when it may have been obscured by time, for example, or recording any change in Viner's position that may have occurred after publication—may assist the reader in fully appreciating Viner's contribution. Before discussing the Wabash lectures and the other essays in this light, a cursory sketch of Viner's career is provided to acquaint those unfamiliar with his work to him, after which Viner's distinctive approach to scholarship and the history of ideas is examined.

❀   ❀   ❀

Jacob Viner was born on May 3, 1892, in Montreal, Canada, shortly after his parents emigrated from Romania. Viner attended the Commercial and Technical High School in Montreal, and then attended McGill University, where he was a student of the economist and humorist Stephen Leacock.[6] Upon graduating from McGill in 1914, he went to Harvard University for two years of graduate training in economics.[7] Viner completed his doctoral dissertation, entitled *Canada's Balance of International Indebtedness, 1900–1914*, in 1922, under the supervision

---

Adam Smith's thought in publications commemorating the bicentennial of the *Wealth of Nations* partly account for the large figure in the second period.

[5] The publication of the lectures rounds out the appearance in print of manuscripts that Viner nearly completed but left unpublished at his death. See Fritz Machlup, "What Was Left on Viner's Desk," *Journal of Political Economy* 80 (March–April 1972): 353–64.

[6] Leacock wrote his dissertation at the University of Chicago under Thorstein Veblen on "The Doctrine of Laissez Faire," a topic that played a large role in Viner's future work. See Craufurd D. W. Goodwin, *Canadian Economic Thought: The Political Economy of a Developing Nation 1814–1914* (Durham: Duke University Press, 1961), pp. 190ff.

[7] Viner has been called "the most distinguished of the graduate students [in economics at Harvard] of this period." Edward S. Mason, "The Harvard Department of Economics from the Beginning to World War II," *Quarterly Journal of Economics* 97 (August 1982): 383–434.

of his mentor, Professor Frank W. Taussig. The dissertation won the David A. Wells prize and was published by Harvard University Press in 1924. Viner joined the faculty of the University of Chicago in 1916, but interrupted his teaching to work at the U.S. Tariff Commission under Taussig and at the U.S. Shipping Board during World War I. He then returned to Chicago, became a naturalized U.S. citizen in 1924, and was promoted to full professor in 1925. He also assumed the editorship (assisted by Frank H. Knight) of the *Journal of Political Economy*, which, under his guidance from 1928 to 1946, he brought "to the peak of its distinction."[8]

During the Great Depression, Viner actively promoted his views on economic policy. He advocated an expansionary fiscal policy by means of budget deficits, and criticized the sluggish response of monetary policy in the face of falling credit.[9] During this period he also became a valued government adviser, serving as a consultant to the Department of the Treasury (1935–39) and special assistant to Secretary Henry Morgenthau (1934, 1939, 1942). At various times during World War II and in the immediate postwar years, Viner served as adviser to the Department of State (1943–52) and the Board of Governors of the Federal Reserve System.

In 1946, Viner left Chicago to join the faculty at Princeton University. It has long been thought that Viner left the University of Chicago because of a controversy with Robert Hutchins, the president of the University, about the proper role of a university and its faculty. Viner explicitly denied this in his resignation letter to Hutchins, and apparently he moved for personal reasons.[10] At Princeton he became the third Walker Professor of International Finance in 1950, and he retired from teaching in 1960. He continued to do research and to write as a member of the Institute for Advanced Study at Princeton until his death on September 12, 1970.

Although he found public service—for limited periods at least—rewarding, Viner centered his career almost entirely around academic life. Viner was first and foremost a professor, having been a faculty member at Chicago and Princeton for more than forty years.[11] He taught or lectured at many other universities,

---

[8] William J. Baumol and Ellen V. Seiler, "Jacob Viner," *International Encyclopedia of the Social Sciences*, Vol. 18, *Biographical Supplement*, ed. David L. Sills (New York: Free Press, 1979), p. 783.

[9] See J. Ronnie Davis, *The New Economics and the Old Economists* (Ames: Iowa State University Press, 1971), pp. 39–47.

[10] See the letters to Robert Hutchins, January 24, 1946, and Martin Pierce, September 29, 1958, Jacob Viner papers, Princeton University. Viner sought to be close to his children, who had settled on the East Coast, and to benefit from the later retirement age at Princeton.

[11] Like Taussig, Viner is known to have been a tremendously stimulating teacher. Milton Friedman called Viner's price theory course "unquestionably the greatest intellectual experience of my

including Harvard, Yale, Stanford, Cambridge, the London School of Economics, the National University of Brazil, and the Graduate Institute of International Studies in Geneva. Recipient of thirteen honorary degrees from universities in America and Europe, he was also a member of several distinguished scholarly societies such as the American Academy of Arts and Sciences and the British Academy. In 1939, he was president of the American Economic Association, which in 1962 awarded him the prestigious Francis A. Walker medal.

Viner's major interest, one he maintained throughout his career, was in the theoretical and policy aspects of international economics. Even before his dissertation appeared in print, Viner completed *Dumping: A Problem in International Trade* (University of Chicago Press, 1923). Much later in his career he published *The Customs Union Issue* (Carnegie Endowment for International Peace, 1950). Both books were among the first systematic treatments of their subjects and each initiated a sizable literature in economics which, despite significant theoretical advances, continues to refer back to Viner's pioneering analysis. Viner's *International Economics* (Free Press, 1951) assembles many of his other contributions to international economics, focusing mainly on issues of international economic policy, while in *International Trade and Economic Development* (Free Press, 1953), he considered the relevance of classical trade theory as a guide to commercial policy under modern conditions.

His greatest achievement in the international field, however, is almost indisputably his *Studies in the Theory of International Trade* (Harper, 1937). The *Studies* thoroughly examined the leading theoretical contributions of mercantilist, classical, and early neoclassical inquiry into international economics. The book has been acclaimed both for its original contribution to the theory of international trade and payments and for its unparalleled treatment of the history and development of that theory. The book consists of two chapters on English foreign trade doctrine before Adam Smith, five chapters on nineteenth-century currency and banking controversies, and two final chapters on the gains from trade. It remains a standard reference to the mercantilist and classical theory of international trade.

Viner also made important contributions to other fields of economics, most notably price theory. His analysis of cost curves, originally published in 1931 under the title "Cost Curves and Supply Curves," is found in virtually every

---

life." *Lives of the Laureates*, eds. William Breit and Roger W. Spencer (Cambridge: MIT Press, 1986), p. 83; and Friedman's anonymous obituary notice "In Memoriam: Jacob Viner, 1892–1970," *American Economic Review* 61 (March 1971): 247–48. For other reminiscences, see Paul A. Samuelson, "Jacob Viner, 1892–1970," *Journal of Political Economy* 80 (January–February 1972): 5–11; Don Patinkin, *Essays On and In the Chicago Tradition* (Durham: Duke University Press, 1981); William J. Baumol, "Jacob Viner at Princeton," *Journal of Political Economy* 80 (January–February 1972): 12–15; Donald Winch, "Jacob Viner," *American Scholar* 50 (Autumn 1981): 519–25.

textbook on microeconomics today.[12] His original article contained a famous error, because Viner insisted that his draftsman, Y. K. Wong, draw a U-shaped, long-run average cost curve passing through the troughs of the short-run cost curves instead of forming a tangential envelope to them.[13] Viner also wrote on macroeconomic and monetary policy, methodology, economic development, and public finance. A good sample of the variety of his work is found in *The Long View and the Short* (Free Press, 1958), which contains many of Viner's essays on economic theory along with a bibliography of his publications from 1917 to 1957.

Viner's seminal work in international economics makes somewhat inaccurate the suggestion that he is best remembered for his writings on the history of economic thought. But his writings on this topic clearly stand out as one of his lasting contributions to economics.[14] Viner's attraction to the history of economic thought is evident early in his career. With the prominent exception of his essay on Adam Smith, however, Viner's initial work in the history of ideas was tied to his interest in the development of economic theory, especially—although not exclusively—international trade theory. Only after the appearance of the *Studies*, as his attention to theory gave way to policy, and particularly after he moved to Princeton, did he begin to pursue the history of economic and social thought as a subject unto itself. While this pursuit led him to treat the history of economic thought in an increasingly broad context, Viner never completely specialized in the subject. Even after he retired, when he had hoped to devote himself exclusively to such historical matters, Viner also wrote on monetary policy, the welfare state, and other contemporary economic issues.

By no means do the writings in this volume constitute the entire body of Jacob Viner's work in the intellectual history of economics. Five other contributions deserve mention. First, the *Studies* and his survey of classical trade theory in the *Encyclopedia of the Social Sciences* provide a detailed treatment of the evolution of the theory of international trade.[15] Second, Viner's *Guide to John Rae's Life*

[12] Reprinted with supplemental note in Jacob Viner, *The Long View and the Short* (Glencoe: Free Press, 1958), pp. 50–78.

[13] See Viner's supplementary note, and Samuelson, "Jacob Viner, 1892–1970," p. 9.

[14] Donald Winch provides an overview of Viner's work in this area in "Jacob Viner as Intellectual Historian," *Research in the History of Economic Thought and Methodology*, Vol. 1, ed. Warren J. Samuels (Greenwich: JAI Press, 1983), pp. 1–17.

[15] "International Trade: Theory," *Encyclopedia of the Social Sciences* Vol. 8, ed. E.R.A. Seligman (New York: Free Press, 1932), pp. 200–208. This neglected article provides a succinct yet comprehensive summary of the classical and early neoclassical theory of international trade and payments. Viner also penned an assessment of Frank Taussig's contributions to international economics that supplies insight into the state of theory in America at the turn of the century. "Professor Taussig's Contribution to the Theory of International Trade," *Explorations in Economics*, ed. Edward S. Mason (New York: McGraw-Hill, 1936), pp. 3–12.

of Adam Smith (A. M. Kelley, 1965)—which could almost stand as a short treatise on its own—remains an indispensable accompaniment to Rae's biography.
In addition, several short reviews by Viner of books on the history of economic
thought appear in *The Long View and the Short.*[16]

Two important manuscripts of Viner's on intellectual history were published
posthumously. His Jayne Lectures, delivered before the American Philosophical
Association in 1966, were published six years later as *The Role of Providence in
the Social Order* (Philadelphia: American Philosophical Society, 1972; Princeton: Princeton University Press, 1976). These lectures draw on Viner's wide
reading in eighteenth-century British economic and social thought. His book on
religion and economic thought, which he began in the mid-1950s but abandoned
in the mid-1960s, was later resurrected and published as *Religious Thought and
Economic Society* (Durham: Duke University Press, 1978). This work remains
somewhat curious, for although it represented a decade-long research agenda to
which Viner devoted tremendous time and energy, he never brought it to completion and very little of the research found its way into his other papers.[17] Familiarity with all of these works, and not just the essays in this volume, is essential for
anyone seeking to understand the full range of Viner's scholarly research in intellectual history.

❀   ❀   ❀

Jacob Viner's reputation as a great scholar is based on his wide knowledge and
objective treatment of the history of economic and social thought, especially that
of the eighteenth and nineteenth centuries. He continues to be admired both for
his broad understanding of the evolution of economic and social thought over the
centuries as well as for his detailed knowledge of specific issues and events. Donald Winch has noted that "Viner practiced many different forms of intellectual
history himself, examining individuals, schools, doctrines, periods, milieus, and
the filiation of concepts."[18] Indeed, the essays in this volume attest to Viner's
wide-ranging interests and to his skill in handling different types of material and
relating them to a common theme.

Vigorously rejecting the traditional confines of specialized academic research,

[16] Also absent from the present collection (on the grounds that they are not Viner writing on
intellectual history per se) are Viner's celebrated review of Keynes' *General Theory* and his later
reflections on that review. See "Mr. Keynes on the Causes of Unemployment," *Quarterly Journal
of Economics* 51 (November 1936): 147–67, reprinted in *The Long View and the Short*, pp. 85–102;
and "Comment on my 1936 Review of Keynes' *General Theory*," in *Keynes' General Theory: Reports of Three Decades*, ed. Robert Lekachman (New York: St. Martin's Press, 1964), pp. 257–66.

[17] The editorial introduction by Jacques Melitz and Donald Winch discusses why Viner never
completed the manuscript.

[18] Winch, "Jacob Viner as Intellectual Historian," p. 13.

Viner was a frequent practitioner of "trespassing"—working across the standard boundaries of inquiry into the subject matter of other disciplines. The waste from duplication that arises with trespassing, Viner believed, "is more than counterbalanced by the mutual stimulation of the overlapping disciplines which it tends to provide, and by the safeguards which it sets up against degeneration of the individual disciplines into formal and lifeless academic systems whose original organs of contact with the problems of real life and with the development of thought in other fields have become atrophied through more or less deliberate disuse."[19]

In notes prepared for a lecture titled "Why Study History of Economic Thought?" Viner distinguished between three methods of practicing the history of thought: accurate, descriptive reporting; evaluation as to the quality of analysis; and criticism based on the values of the critic.[20] Scrupulously avoiding the last category, Viner practiced a blend of descriptive reporting and evaluation for much of his career. In undertaking such an effort, Viner believed that description should be based on an accurate and objective reading of a work to ensure fairness to the author and interpretation based on internal consistency, rigor, relevance, and definitiveness of the treatment. Although he set strict standards of objectivity in the description and characterization of previous doctrine, this did not require neutrality so severe as to preclude evaluation or to prevent the arrival at a conclusion. A consequence of Viner's practice is that while one can always take issue with his conclusions—indeed, he relished scholarly debate—one can rarely question his fairness in handling the evidence used to support his case.

Such a combination of reporting and evaluation is clearly evident in the chapters of the *Studies,* for example, which examine early English trade doctrine. Viner's critical evaluation of mercantilism in these chapters reflects his attempt to achieve balance by countering and offsetting the favorable treatment of mercantilism by the German and English group of historical economists (or, in other places, the hostile treatment of the classical school by various parties). Viner achieved this by applying a different standard of evaluation than did the historical economists, namely, modern economic theory. In this context, Viner concluded that mercantilist economics did not appear as worthy of commendation as when judged by its contemporary relevance, the standard used by the historical economists.

The longer Viner worked as a historian of thought, the greater emphasis he placed on the unprejudiced and impartial reading of texts as an indispensible qual-

---

[19] Jacob Viner, *Studies in the Theory of International Trade* (New York: Harper & Bros., 1937), pp. 594–95.

[20] "Why Study History of Economic Thought?" Jacob Viner papers, Princeton University.

ity of an historian of thought and as an essential prerequisite to evaluation and criticism. An overriding obligation of the intellectual historian, he stated in his Jayne Lectures, is to be an objective reporter of the views of others, "yielding neither to favorable nor to unfavorable bias, nor to unmotivated carelessness." He warned that "even an approach to accuracy in reporting is an arduous and difficult art, calling for unintermitting self-discipline." Such attempts at dispassionate neutrality in dealing with conflicting ideas, he admitted, could "result in a lifeless, bloodless, anemic academic discipline, one which isolates ideas from human minds and passions." Most historians did not operate in this fashion, but "I confess that it comes reasonably close to how I have tried to operate" in practicing the art of intellectual history.[21] Yet Viner never viewed intellectual history as being quite as detached and austere as this implies. "It is possible," he continued, "to make more of the history of ideas than the mechanical compilation of annals or chronicles of autonomous ideas, all free, equal, and of no visible interest except to those perhaps mythical scholars, the old-fashioned antiquarians." Exploring the interplay of related or opposed ideas through time, distinguishing the different roles an idea can perform at various times and in various places, identifying how ideas can reflect the society in which they exist, "It is on the basis of some blend of these roles that I accept the history of ideas as a legitimate avocation for myself."[22]

So strongly did Viner believe that balanced reporting must precede evaluation or criticism that he sometimes felt it necessary to register his disapproval of the lack of care with which some treated historical scholarship, especially when lapses from impartial reporting led to misleading descriptions of previous thought. Although he respected John Maynard Keynes, for example, Viner took him to task for "seriously lacking in the unexciting but essential qualities for the intellectual historian of objectivity and of judiciousness."[23] Viner often did not dispute criticism or praise of older doctrine as long as serious effort was made to describe that doctrine accurately and fairly. While acknowledging the validity of many of Edwin Cannan's criticisms of English classical economics, for instance, Viner strongly objected to Cannan's disparagement of early English economists because "the picture which he gives of the nature of and the quality of the classical economists is . . . one-sided and inaccurate in its emphasis."[24] Undue bias

---

[21] Jacob Viner, *The Role of Providence in the Social Order* (Princeton: Princeton University Press, 1976), p. 2.

[22] Viner, *The Role of Providence*, p. 3.

[23] "Comment on my 1936 Review of Keynes' *General Theory*," p. 254.

[24] Viner wrote that Cannan's delight at exposing the blunders of classical economists "reminds one of George Eliot's Tom Tulliver, who, it may be remembered, was 'very fond of birds, that is of

could also reveal itself in attempts to use history to achieve a particular end. Viner defended the right of socialists and others to criticize the political doctrines of John Locke, but he refused to countenance what he felt were misrepresentations—intentional or otherwise—of Locke's views that gave strength to those criticisms. He identified several pitfalls that contributed to the misinterpretation of Locke: "reliance on second-hand reports of what Locke wrote or on partial, careless and hasty reading of original texts; failure to realize that some key terms used by Locke have undergone changes in meaning since his day; and lack of reasonable effort to keep biases under control."[25] Viner deeply felt that such negligence constituted a departure from the canons of historical scholarship, and such carelessness could easily awaken "the more combative side of [his] scholarly nature."[26]

Viner's trenchant review of Joseph Schumpeter's monumental *History of Economic Analysis* revealed much about his own approach to the history of economic ideas.[27] Viner admired the acumen of Schumpeter, whose "display of command of intellectual history is most impressive in its range and in its apparent depth." Although the book was "overambitious" and contained much that was "redundant, irrelevant, cryptic, strongly biased, paradoxical, or otherwise unhelpful or even harmful to understanding," Viner thought that it remained "by a wide margin, the most constructive, the most original, the most learned, and the most brilliant contribution to the history of the analytical phases of our discipline which has ever been made."

Yet Viner had serious reservations about the project, stemming chiefly from Schumpeter's biases. These biases "could take the form of exaggerated enthusiasm and praise as well as of undue disdain and contempt," although Viner conceded that Schumpeter was "basically generous" to those with whom he disagreed. Viner remained dismayed by Schumpeter's critical treatment of Adam Smith and David Ricardo and by his sympathetic treatment of the scholastics and

---

throwing stones at them.' " Review of Edwin Cannan, *A Review of Economic Theory*, in *Economica* No. 28 (March 1930): 74–84, reprinted in *The Long View and the Short*, pp. 395–405.

[25] "Life, Liberty, Property, and the State," Lecture IV of the Bryn Mawr Lectures (delivered in February–March 1956), p. 2, Jacob Viner papers, Princeton University. In a similar vein, Viner took issue with C. B. Macpherson's handling of Locke's property theory in *The Political Theory of Possessive Individualism* (see Chapter 16 below) and regretfully concluded that Macpherson's "apostolic mission" damaged his "scholarly endeavour," resulting in "a greater loss to learning than contribution to social salvation."

[26] This phrase was used by Jacques Melitz and Donald Winch to describe "Viner's careful use of historical evidence to construct a case against Weber and his followers" in a chapter on "Protestantism and the Rise of Capitalism" in *Religious Thought and Economic Society*, eds. Jacques Melitz and Donald Winch (Durham: Duke University Press, 1978), p. 8.

[27] The review of Joseph A. Schumpeter, *History of Economic Analysis* (New York: Oxford University Press, 1954) is reprinted in Chapter 14.

the mercantilists. The divergence may have been due to the fundamentally different approaches to the history of economic thought taken by Schumpeter and Viner. Schumpeter professed to be solely interested in tracing the development of analytical economics, whereas Viner's attention centered on the role of ideas in economics in a broader intellectual context.[28] Such differences were evident in Viner's dissent from Schumpeter's sharp distinction between means and ends, Schumpeter's position being that economic theory cannot assist in the choosing of ends. "Economic analysis, by exposing the source and the character of contradictions in a system of ends," Viner wrote, "can operate . . . to bring about a revision of an established set of ends . . . [or] . . . can conceivably show that the means requisite for the attainment of certain ends are not available, or are too costly in some sense, and may thus in effect force a revision of ends. . . . To deny any influence to economic analysis is to deny any role to reason in the formation by a sensible man of his system of ends."

Despite his passion for the history of thought, Viner maintained that he was agnostic as to the benefits of such study. "My own interest in the history of economic thought, intense though it is, is mainly of the 'idle curiosity' variety, and I try to refrain from claiming for it much more than curiosity-satisfying powers," he once observed.[29] Yet Viner strained to suppress his enthusiasm in "A Modest Proposal for Some Stress on Scholarship in Graduate Training," an erudite commencement address peppered with amusing anecdotes and quotations. Viner defined scholarship as "nothing more than the pursuit of broad and exact knowledge of the history of the workings of the human mind as revealed in written records." Viner excluded from scholarship, "as belonging to a higher order of human endeavor, the creative arts and scientific discovery." The essence of his modest proposal was the recommendation that graduate schools apply "some pressure or seduction" on students to become, in part, scholars. This pressure, Viner hastened to add, should be of second-order importance to pursuits that extend the frontiers of a discipline. Indeed, scholarship should neither detract from efforts to confront the pressing issues of the day nor become a haven for those who sought retreat from the problems in the world. "I concede that we don't want students and faculty unrestrainedly pursuing scholarship all over our universities while they have so much more urgent business to attend to." At the same time, he lamented the tendency of graduate schools to turn students into

[28] Winch briefly contrasts Schumpeter and Viner in "Jacob Viner as Intellectual Historian," pp. 8–9.

[29] Viner makes this claim in Chapter 16. Traces of Viner's influence can be detected in Donald Winch, "What Price the History of Economic Thought?" *Scottish Journal of Political Economy* 9 (November 1962): 193–204.

"trufflehounds . . . finely trained for a single small purpose and not much good for any other."

Thus, Viner advanced his proposal as a genuinely modest one, as he could not "claim much for the pursuit of scholarship for its own sake, either in material rewards for the scholar or in tangible benefit to the community." As for the pursuit of scholarship for scholarship's sake, Viner stated he would "refrain—not without effort—from subscribing to it" but "certainly do not venture to preach it." "All I plead on behalf of scholarship, at least upon this occasion, is that, once the taste for it has been aroused, it gives a sense of largeness even to one's small quests, and a sense of fullness even to the small answers to problems large or small which it yields, a sense which can never in any other way be attained, for which no other source of human gratification can, to the addict, be a satisfying substitute, which gains instead of loses in quality and quantity and in pleasure-yielding capacity by being shared with others—and which, unlike golf, improves with age."

That Viner derived personal enjoyment from the history of ideas was manifest in his love of books and libraries. Strict in his reliance on primary sources, Viner was renowned for his immense bibliographic knowledge. The Curator of Special Collections at the University of Chicago library once wrote to him: "I have a strong impression you must have read every economics text in the library from the frequency with which I see your signature on old book cards."[30] Even toward the end of his life, when he was ailing, Viner is still reported to have spent five hours a day reading and researching and to have devoted one day a week to the library.[31] Therefore, it is little wonder that Viner's writings resonate with a confidence that comes from independence of judgment arrived at after wide and thorough reading and unhurried reflection. At the same time, his ongoing attempts to canvass ever-greater amounts of obscure, primary literature created an obstacle to his bringing projects to completion.[32] Viner actively disseminated his knowledge in other ways, such as by responding quickly to other scholars' requests for

---

[30] Letter from Robert Rosenthal to Jacob Viner, May 21, 1969, Jacob Viner papers. Viner took a special interest in libraries and their collections and was often consulted by experts from the major research libraries for his opinions. In once quoting Francis Lieber's view, Viner probably endorsed it: "Libraries are the bridges over which civilization travels from generation to generation and from country to country, bridges that span over the widest oceans . . ." Francis Lieber to General Halleck, November 16, 1865, in *The Life and Letters of Francis Lieber* (Boston, 1882), p. 361.

[31] Winch, "Jacob Viner," p. 523.

[32] Viner was acutely aware of the difficulties of tracing the origin of an idea, as one could always go back further in time or look to other fields of inquiry from which hints of an idea had been borrowed. He once warned of "inadequate caution in the exercise of the hazardous pursuit of the discovery of the absolute priorities of doctrine" in James Angell's evaluation of early trade and monetary theory, but Viner himself enjoyed the chase too. "Angell's *Theory of International Prices*," *Journal of Political Economy* 34 (October 1926): 597–623, quote on p. 599.

bibliographic information and advising those producing modern editions of collected works of great thinkers. He likened these editions to great cathedrals because "they endow generations of mankind with treasures more precious than things purchaseable on the market place."[33]

Yet Viner endorsed the study of the history of thought for somewhat more profound reasons than personal edification and enjoyment. His aim in the *Studies*, which supplied a heavy dose of history to his discussion of international trade theory, was "to resurrect forgotten or overlooked material worthy of resurrection, to trace the origin and development of the doctrines which were later to become familiar, and to examine the claims to acceptance of familiar doctrine."[34] Another compelling reason for such study was the humbling effect it had in heightening one's awareness of the limitations of our knowledge. "If one should ask what profit, beyond the satisfaction of curiosity, knowledge of the history of ideas brings," he once put it, "I would not claim much more for it than that by helping us to understand the mental processes of our predecessors it helps us to attain humility with respect to the validity and the durability of our own ideas."[35] Yet one of the frustrations of scholarship as a "commitment to the pursuit of knowledge," he admitted, is that it is undertaken with the understanding that its objective may never be achieved. A good part of scholarship "takes the form of negative knowledge, of increasing awareness of the range and depth of our unconquered ignorance."[36] He once declined to comment on the substance of a former student's paper, but commended it with this observation: "I noted with admiration the fairness and the modesty with which you present your conclusions. Your care in avoiding over-statement and over-certitude is not exactly a fashionable virtue these days, but it is still a true one in my judgment."[37] One famous anecdote about Viner relates to his retort to Kelvin's dictum ("When you cannot measure . . . your knowledge is . . . meager . . . and . . . unsatisfactory . . .") as engraved on the Social Science Building at the University of Chicago: And when you *can* measure, Viner maintained, your knowledge is *still* of a meager and unsatisfactory kind.[38]

---

[33] See his review of a volume of John Stuart Mill's letters, reprinted below as Chapter 17.

[34] Viner, *Studies*, p. xiii.

[35] Viner, *The Role of Providence*, pp. 112–13.

[36] See his "Modest Proposal," reprinted below as Chapter 18. Viner also admitted this point: "Outside the quite extensive area where tautology rightly rules, certainty is beyond the reach of man, but for effectiveness in the life of action the false assurance that one has attained certainty is easy to achieve and is a great help and a great comfort." Viner, *The Role of Providence*, p. 3.

[37] Letter to C. Lowell Harriss, April 21, 1970, Jacob Viner papers.

[38] See Robert K. Merton, David L. Sills, and Stephen M. Stigler, "The Kelvin Dictum and Social Science: An Excursion into the History of an Idea," *Journal of the History of the Behavioral Sciences* 20 (October 1984): 319–31.

Viner continues to earn respect for his consistent efforts to meet high standards of scholarship. His particular approach to the history of thought made it unlikely, as Donald Winch has suggested, that he would initiate or influence any "school" of intellectual historians that would serve any purpose or motive other than careful and accurate scholarship, but he has taught many by his example. Yet Viner was also not free from occasional error, and he would not have wanted others to follow him blindly. Viner once counseled university graduates never to be "a disciple" and to entertain constantly the possibility that authorities may be wrong. Authorities may have to be accepted in certain cases, but always with an appreciation and awareness of "the possibility that new knowledge, new insights, new values may before long make [their] error evident."[39] For above all, Viner valued intellectual independence for himself and for others.

The Wabash Lectures

In June 1959, Viner delivered five lectures at a conference on Economics and Freedom at Wabash College in Crawfordsville, Indiana. "When I undertook to give those lectures at Wabash," Viner later recalled, "my assigned topic was foreign trade and commercial policy, but when I got to Wabash I soon realized that it was a conference on 'freedom' and I scrapped most of the material I had planned to use, and prepared notes for new lectures as I went along based in substantial part on material I had gathered for my Chicago lecture [The Intellectual History of Laissez Faire] and for a paper I am writing on the historical interrelations of 'moral theology' and economic thought."[40]

Though the subject matter of the conference caught him off guard, Viner succeeded in delivering a "little doctrinal tour through the ages," a journey which provides a succinct overview of the themes that dominated his life's work on the intellectual evolution of economic thought.[41] As such, the lectures provide a fitting introduction to the other essays in this volume. Viner's subject is nothing less than the evolution, from Graeco-Roman times to the period of classical economics, of mankind's continuous intellectual effort to understand the relationships between the individual, society, the state, and commerce. Numerous stops are made along the way to focus on transitions between major paradigms of thought and to ask what of previous doctrine was jettisoned, what was retained, and what new thinking was incorporated into the corpus of existing doctrine.

---

[39] See his address at the University of Toronto, reprinted below as Chapter 19.
[40] Letter to George J. Stigler, November 10, 1959, Jacob Viner papers.
[41] Machlup, "What Was Left on Viner's Desk," p. 358.

The first lecture, "Early Attitudes toward Trade and the Merchant," describes the hostility of Greek, Roman, and early Christian thinkers toward commerce. Viner also stresses the neglected doctrines of "universal economy" which emphasize the importance of trade in developing fraternity among the various peoples of the earth. In Viner's opinion, this doctrine "has claims to be the oldest and longest-lived economic doctrine we know of."

Lecture II, "The Nation-State and Private Enterprise," documents how the expansion of trade, along with the rise of a wealthy merchant class and its concomitant increase in political and economic influence, fostered a reassessment of the ethical views of commercial activity. Mercantilism emerged with the rise of the nation-state and owed little to theological doctrines of economics, except perhaps the zero-sum view of the gains from trade. Viner disputes the common belief that mercantilism sought as its only goal the enhancement of national power, stating instead that power and plenty were both objectives in mercantilist thinking. Viner also touches on his discoveries concerning the arcane manner of implementing government policy in seventeenth- and eighteenth-century England.

Lecture III, "The Emergence of Free-Trade and Laissez-Faire Doctrine," traces the origins of a systematic and principled advocacy of freedom to trade. Although the mercantilist literature contains pleas for commercial freedom, the pleas are made on behalf of interested parties who did not advocate free trade as a matter of principle or as based on a general theory suggestive of the beneficent effect of such freedom on society. Viner contests the view that economic freedom originated from the English common law. Doctrines favoring economic freedom can instead be traced to seventeenth-century thinkers, from Mandeville to the later Scottish moral philosophers, who sought to develop a theory which would indicate how private commercial activity stands in harmony with general public welfare and with private moral and ethical behavior.

Lecture IV, "Monopoly and Laissez Faire," considers how divergences from competition have forced advocates of laissez faire to modify their prescriptions. In the English literature, monopoly usually implied official restrictions on competition for the benefit of government corporations or private firms. Adam Smith associated such interference with fraud and waste and opposed it vigorously, but he went further in criticizing the collusive nature of businessmen. As anticompetitive government policies were redressed, the English classical economists minimized the importance of private monopoly left unaided by governmental interferences.

The final lecture, "The 'Economic Man,' or The Place of Economic Self-Interest in a 'Good Society,' " aims to correct misinterpretations about the role of self-interest in various systems of thought. In discussing various faulty conceptions of past doctrine, Viner denies that the economist has any special qualification for appraisal of types of economic systems and closes the lecture with this note of caution: "The modesty which it is incumbent upon us to manifest in due proportion should guard us against taking for granted that our qualifications in the field of ethics are of a distinctly higher order than those in the field of economics of our moral and clerical critics."

In the many years since these lectures were composed, intellectual historians of economics have probed different aspects of the themes that Viner considered, especially the emergence of favorable views of commerce which ultimately led to the laissez-faire doctrine.[42] But it is uncommon to find such a broad perspective in such a compact form. Lionel Robbins once observed that Viner "excelled both in exact bibliographical detail . . . and in the general sweep of perspective and appraisal."[43] The Wabash lectures testify to Viner's catholic interests, while the other essays in this book display his skill in handling the details without losing sight of broader influences. Indeed, many of the essays in this volume can be considered as an elaboration on the themes discussed in the lectures, a filling in of the particulars and a statement of qualifications. To these contributions, many of which were pathbreaking and influential in their respective areas, we now turn.

ADAM SMITH AND LAISSEZ FAIRE

Viner's earliest contribution to intellectual history was his essay "Adam Smith and Laissez Faire," presented to commemorate the one-hundred fiftieth anniversary of the *Wealth of Nations* in 1926. The major aim of the essay was to correct the view that Adam Smith was a doctrinaire proponent of laissez faire. Viner agreed that "there is no possible room for doubt" that Smith had "a strong presumption against government activity beyond its fundamental duties of protection against its foreign foes and maintenance of justice." Yet Viner catalogued a substantive list of Smith's advocacy, in places scattered throughout the *Wealth of Nations*, of government action which would improve upon the natural economic order. Viner summarily demolished the view that Smith was a dogmatic advocate of laissez faire; instead, Smith "saw a wide and elastic range of activity for government, and he was prepared to extend it even farther if government, by improving its standards of competence, honesty, and public spirit, showed itself entitled to wider responsibilities." To Viner, Smith was a great eclectic who took into account particular circumstance when counselling government intervention.

---

[42] See the editorial appendix following the Wabash lectures for references.
[43] Robbins, *Jacob Viner*, p. 7.

It is difficult today to appreciate fully how the essay advanced the study of Adam Smith. The essay dates from a period when not only Smith's economics but his policy recommendations were being stereotyped and viewed with displeasure.[44] Viner's essay played an important part in setting the record straight about Smith's role for the state in economic life. Indeed, the essay reoriented discussion of Smith's economic views so successfully and is now so much a part of our understanding of Smith that it has become "less revisionist than orthodox."[45] The central thesis of the essay has clearly stood the test of time: fifty years later a volume celebrating the bicentennial of the *Wealth of Nations* contains articles which describe Viner's article as a "masterly" and "classic" analysis of Smith's thought.[46]

The summary of the essay presented above neglects a theme that Viner develops in contrasting Smith's first book, the *Theory of Moral Sentiments*, with the *Wealth of Nations*. In the *Theory of Moral Sentiments*, human nature—consisting of self-interest, sympathy, and benevolence—and the external environment work in tandem to produce a harmonious natural order. The beneficent order in nature shows no serious flaws and operates to promote the welfare of mankind. Viner maintains that although traces of this approach appear in the *Wealth of Nations*, "on the points at which they come into contact there is a substantial measure of irreconcilable divergence between the *Theory of Moral Sentiments* and the *Wealth of Nations*, with respect to the character of the natural order." While there are tendencies and forces that act to bring harmony to the economic world, the lack of benevolence and sympathy along with divergences of interest make for a severely qualified harmony in the *Wealth of Nations*. A long list of exceptions to the doctrine of natural order in the economic world "demonstrate[s] beyond dispute the existence of a wide divergence between the perfectly harmonious, completely beneficent natural order of the *Theory of Moral Sentiments* and the partial and limited harmony in the economic order of the *Wealth of Nations*."

Viner attributes the divergence of the two books to their fundamentally different purposes. The *Theory of Moral Sentiments* was a philosophical book, in which, "failing to compare his conclusions with the facts, [Smith] saw no necessity for qualifying them." The *Wealth of Nations*, by contrast, was written with

---

[44] The milieu in which Viner's essay appeared is discussed in R. D. Collison Black, "Smith's Contribution in Historical Perspective," in *The Market and the State: Essays in Honour of Adam Smith*, eds. Thomas Wilson and Andrew S. Skinner (Oxford: Clarendon Press, 1976), pp. 42–63.

[45] James T. Kloppenberg, "The Virtues of Liberalism: Christianity, Republicanism, and Ethics in Early American Political Discourse," *Journal of American History* 74 (June 1987): 9–33, quote on p. 18, n. 11.

[46] Andrew S. Skinner and Thomas Wilson, eds., *Essays on Adam Smith* (Oxford: Clarendon Press, 1975).

an eye to the real world, where blemishes in the order appear: "The apparent discrepancies between the *Theory of Moral Sentiments* and the *Wealth of Nations* mark distinct advances of the latter over the former in realism and in application of the saving grace of common sense." For this reason, Viner believed the *Wealth of Nations* to be the better of the two books.

Viner did not base his case on the notion that Smith employs two separate men, a "sympathetic" man in the *Theory of Moral Sentiments* and an "economic" man in the *Wealth of Nations*. This idea was the original basis for the claim of a conflict between the two works—the "Adam Smith problem"—and is now rejected for its crucial misinterpretation of Smith's use of the term "sympathy." Viner's quite different focus is on the degree of natural harmony in the world as presented in the two books.[47] However, Viner later modified his view of the incompatibility of the two works in a 1968 contribution on Adam Smith to the *International Encyclopedia of the Social Sciences*. Viner admitted that many—including himself at "an early stage" of his study of Smith—"found these two works in some measure basically inconsistent." He now believed that Smith was working with two separate models which, by necessity, addressed different questions and which were in themselves incomplete. "Had he been able to complete his total system he would probably have demonstrated that the apparent inconsistencies were often not real ones, but were merely the consequences of deliberate shifts from one partial model to another." In Viner's opinion, David Hume's concept of "social distance"—that an individual's sentiments for others diminishes as the frame of reference moves outward from the family to neighbors to other fellow citizens—was key to reconciling in some degree the two books.[48]

Raphael and Macfie took this position one step further, maintaining in their

---

[47] See D. D. Raphael, *Adam Smith* (New York: Oxford University Press, 1985), pp. 86ff on Smith's use of the term "sympathy." Raphael also argues (pp. 91–92) that the five quotations from the *Theory of Moral Sentiments* which Viner used to support his position are not incompatible with the *Wealth of Nations* and suggests, contrary to Viner's view that one book is abstract and the other realistic, that the *Theory of Moral Sentiments* "relies, more than most of its genre, on examples from genuine experience, observed or gathered from works of history."

[48] See also Viner, *The Role of Providence*, pp. 80–84. "Re *T.M.S.*, I do not adhere now to everything I said about it in my 1926 lecture, although I still think I was substantially on the right track." Letter to A. L. Macfie, November 3, 1965, Jacob Viner papers. Viner also wrote that Smith dealt with only one man "who operates in two worlds, which impinge on him psychologically in different manners: first, the non-market world, the world of his family, his neighbors, his community and country, and second, the world of market transactions, of impersonality and anonymity, where the sense of justice is the only moral sentiment which has an important psychological role to play." Letter to A. L. Macfie, April 4, 1963, Jacob Viner papers. On this point see Russell Nieli, "Spheres of Intimacy and the Adam Smith Problem," *Journal of the History of Ideas* 47 (October–December 1986): 611–624.

introduction to the Glasgow edition of the *Theory of Moral Sentiments* that "the so-called 'Adam Smith problem' was a pseudo problem based on ignorance and misunderstanding."[49] Viner never quite went this far in dismissing the problems of reconciliation, but he clearly moved in that direction. "I would therefore still claim that it is not *easy* to reconcile *T.M.S.* and *W. of N.*, but I will not argue that there is logical contradiction between them," was as far as Viner went on the issue.[50] Viner recorded his change in view another way, originally writing that had Smith "been brought face to face with a complete list of the modifications to the principle of laissez faire to which he at one place or another granted his approval, I have no doubt that he would have been astounded at his own moderation." Viner later believed that "my list would not have disturbed" Smith because "his 'natural' did not always mean 'universal' " and he never excluded "the possible existence of exceptions of some importance to his general propositions."[51]

Viner's work on Smith assisted other scholars by providing numerous hints of important topics that deserved further attention. For example, he suggested that the concept of *jus naturale* in the writings of Grotius and Pufendorf "strongly influenced Smith's thinking" and that Smith's treatment of commutative justice in the *Theory of Moral Sentiments* "is especially important for a proper interpretation of the *Wealth of Nations*." This aspect of Smith's thought has since become a fruitful area of study by intellectual historians.[52] In addition, Viner's *Guide to John Rae's Life of Adam Smith* brought to light significant new material and urged scholars to correct errors that had been institutionalized by Rae's biography. Beginning with the discovery of detailed notes of Smith's lectures on jurisprudence and with the publication of *The Glasgow Edition of the Works and Correspondence of Adam Smith*, a project that Viner wholeheartedly encouraged from its inception but did not live to see completed, Viner's recommendations have been increasingly fulfilled as scholarship on Adam Smith has advanced markedly since the appearance of his *Guide*.

It has been the fashion in certain periods to downplay Smith's originality or

[49] "Introduction" to Adam Smith, *The Theory of Moral Sentiments*, eds. D. D. Raphael and A. L. Macfie (Oxford: Oxford University Press, 1976), p. 20. For a different view, see Laurence Dickey, "Historicizing the 'Adam Smith Problem': Conceptual, Historical, and Textual Issues," *Journal of Modern History* 58 (September 1986): 579–609, who cites Viner's earlier but not later opinion on the issue.

[50] Letter to A. L. Macfie, November 3, 1965, Jacob Viner papers.

[51] Below, p. 102, and letter to A. L. Macfie, November 3, 1965, Jacob Viner papers.

[52] Viner makes this point in Chapter 10. There is now a large literature examining the role of natural jurisprudence in Smith's thought. See, for example, Knud Haakonssen, *The Science of a Legislator: The Natural Jurisprudence of David Hume and Adam Smith* (New York: Cambridge University Press, 1981).

achievement. Viner never claimed that Smith was original in any specific point or insight in the *Wealth of Nations*: "On every detail, taken by itself, Smith appears to have had predecessors in plenty. On few details was Smith as penetrating as the best of his predecessors." From Viner's standpoint, Smith's major claim to fame was his doctrine that "economic phenomena were manifestations of an underlying order in nature, governed by natural forces" which "if left to its own course produc[es] results beneficial to mankind." Smith organized previously disperse elements of thought to create a logically coherent system "with the purpose of discovering the nature of the order which underlay its surface chaos." While acknowledging that Smith's economics had become antiquated, Viner was among those who "still acknowledge a strong influence of his writings on their system of values and gladly continue to do homage to his name."

Mandeville and Laissez Faire

Viner later pursued the development of the laissez-faire doctrine with reference to the work of the controversial social commentator Bernard Mandeville, whose *The Fable of the Bees* (1714) created a sensation for its irreverence in expounding an amoral theory of societal interactions. Viner's *Studies* briefly described Mandeville as a laissez-faire and individualist thinker who paved the way for Adam Smith.[53] Viner subsequently repudiated this position in a short introduction to a 1953 reprint of Mandeville's *A Letter to Dion* (1732), an introduction which became one of Viner's more widely debated contributions to intellectual history.

Viner maintains in the introduction to *Dion* that Mandeville's economic doctrine was "almost universally misinterpreted": "Many scholars, including economists who should know better, regard Mandeville as a pioneer expounder of laissez-faire individualism in the economic field and as such an anticipator of Adam Smith." On the contrary, Viner argues, Mandeville "was a convinced adherent of the prevailing mercantilism of his time" who "in contrast to Adam Smith, put great and repeated stress on the importance of the role of government in producing a strong and prosperous society, through detailed and systematic regulation of economic activity." Mandeville's phrase "Private Vices, Publick Benefits" was, according to Viner, commonly misconstrued to imply laissez faire, when in fact "Mandeville repeatedly stated that it was by 'the skilful Man-

[53] *Studies*, p. 99.

agement of the clever Politician' that private vices could be made to serve the public good, thus ridding the formula of any implication of laissez-faire.''[54]

At least two respected scholars of economic thought believed Viner to be mistaken in this interpretation of Mandeville. Nathan Rosenberg presents Mandeville not as an advocate of either intervention or laissez faire exclusively, but as one who suggested that sound political leadership could create a social and legal framework that would allow the individual pursuit of gain to generate public benefits. '' 'Dexterous Management' is not to be taken as the advocacy of a policy of continuous government intervention in domestic market processes,'' Rosenberg argues, ''rather, it is a way of stating that the welfare of society has been most advanced by the introduction and diffusion of laws and institutions which best utilize man's basic passions and which channel his energies into socially-useful activities.''[55] In a 1966 British Academy lecture, Friedrich Hayek agreed with Rosenberg, suggesting that Viner was misled by Mandeville's repeated use of the phrase ''dexterous management by which the skillful politician might turn private vices into public benefits'' to exaggerate the extent of his endorsement of intervention in economic affairs.[56]

Viner never published a reply to these points but responded to both Rosenberg and Hayek through personal correspondence. To Rosenberg, Viner refused to quarrel over whether Mandeville was an advocate of ''mercantilism'' or ''laissez-faire'' because the category he appropriately belonged to was a matter of degree and of one's definition of terms. He insisted, however, that it was a mistake to ''assign narrow limits to the range and scope of the interventionism covered by 'dexterous management.' '' As to his earlier statement in the *Studies*, Viner admitted: ''I unreservedly confess sin as of 1937. I can explain it, though not excuse it, by the fact that I had not then read Mandeville carefully except for specific foreign trade content, and that I allowed myself to be unduly influenced by Kaye. . . . I should have 'known better' even in 1937, but I should explain that my rebuke was directed only to those who had read Mandeville with some care and published their interpretation.''[57]

[54] In Chapter 14 below, Viner criticized Joseph Schumpeter for embracing the view that Mandeville was an early advocate of laissez faire, a view which Viner said was ''about as wrong as it could be.''

[55] Nathan Rosenberg, ''Mandeville and Laissez-Faire,'' *Journal of the History of Ideas* 24 (April–June 1963): 183–96, quote on p. 188. Rosenberg made a similar argument with reference to Adam Smith in his ''Some Institutional Aspects of the *Wealth of Nations*,'' *Journal of Political Economy* 68 (December 1960): 557–70.

[56] F. A. Hayek, ''Dr Bernard Mandeville,'' in *New Studies in Philosophy, Politics, Economics and the History of Ideas* (Chicago: University of Chicago Press, 1978), especially pp. 258–60.

[57] Letter to Nathan Rosenberg, July 23, 1963, Jacob Viner papers. The reference to Kaye is to F. B. Kaye's introduction to the Oxford edition (1924) of *The Fable of the Bees*. Kaye lauds Mande-

In reply to Hayek, Viner was unrepentant: "As things stand now, however, I see nothing to withdraw, to amend, or to justify, in what I have written about Mandeville except for one pre-1940 mistake, arising out of my following Kaye." Viner thought that "Mandeville's invocation of 'the wonderful power of political wisdom, by the help of which so beautiful a machine is raised from the most contemptible branches' breathes the spirit of his whole approach" and he could not understsand why Mandeville's phrase "dexterous management of the skilful politician" should be thought to have no meaning.[58]

Subsequent studies by other historians of thought have noted this controversy and have set forth different interpretations of Mandeville. One view is that Mandeville was a transitional figure whose thought encompassed both mercantilist and laissez-faire elements; another view denies that Mandeville should even be seriously considered as an economic theorist or thinker.[59] Indeed, both Viner and Hayek agreed that Mandeville's economic thought was undistinguished; for Viner it was "eccentric and archaic," for Hayek it was "rather mediocre, or at least unoriginal."[60] Both appreciated Mandeville not for his contribution to economics but for his literary skill and his insights into society. "Mandeville commands my admiration," Viner once stated, "partly for the evolutionary character of his conjectural history, but mainly for the skill, subtlety, and entertainment he demonstrates in his satirical efforts."[61] Regarding the former, Viner lent his qualified agreement to Hayek's praise of Mandeville's evolutionary theory of social institutions. As Viner explained to Rosenberg, Hayek "has emphasized and praised (rightly, I think) Mandeville's stress on the evolutionary character of major social institutions, but has derived from this (wrongly, I think) support for laissez-faire in general, and perhaps also interpreted it as evidence of Mandeville's laissez-faire thinking."[62]

---

ville as an important laissez-faire thinker who influenced Adam Smith. Viner attributed his failure to acknowledge his earlier error to the index of the *Studies*, which makes no reference to Mandeville.

[58] Letter to F. A. Hayek, January 23, 1967, Jacob Viner papers.

[59] Alfred F. Chalk, "Mandeville's *Fable of the Bees*: A Reappraisal," *Southern Economic Journal* 33 (July 1966): 1–16, first put forth the notion that Mandeville was a transitional figure, a view supported by Terence Hutchison, *Before Adam Smith: The Emergence of Political Economy, 1662–1776* (New York: Basil Blackwell, 1988), pp. 123–26. By contrast, M. M. Goldsmith, *Private Vices, Public Benefits: Bernard Mandeville's Social and Political Thought* (New York: Cambridge University Press, 1985), pp. 124ff, argues that Mandeville was "more a theorist of the spirit of capitalism than of its economic structure." See also Thomas A. Horne, *The Social Thought of Bernard Mandeville: Virtue and Commerce in Early Eighteenth-Century England* (New York: Columbia University Press, 1978), pp. 66ff.

[60] Letter to Gordon J. Vichert, December 2, 1969, Jacob Viner papers; and Hayek, "Dr. Bernard Mandeville," p. 250.

[61] Letter to Gordon J. Vichert, December 2, 1969, Jacob Viner papers.

[62] Viner first stated his agreement with Hayek in the Wabash lectures. His qualifications to Hayek's analysis were more clearly put elsewhere: "I admire as a great achievement Mandeville's evo-

As to Mandeville's entertainment value, Viner downplayed Mandeville's rigorist sincerity and reminded readers of the satirical aspect of his writings which F. B. Kaye ignored.[63] In addition, Viner noted Mandeville's intellectual debt to the Jansenists, particularly Pierre Nicole, which again had gone relatively unnoticed. Unfortunately, Viner's discussion of Nicole's influence on Mandeville was almost entirely excluded from the published introduction because of space limitations. The five excised pages, which discuss both the similarities and the differences in the thought of Nicole and Mandeville, are published here for the first time.

The Doctrine of Laissez Faire

Viner traced the development of the laissez-faire doctrine further in his Henry Simons lecture, "The Intellectual History of Laissez Faire," given at the University of Chicago Law School in 1959. Viner proposed to explore critically the "logical or rhetorical nature" of the arguments or the "art of persuasion" used to gain acceptance of laissez faire. In this essay as in his others, Viner equated laissez faire with the principles advocated by the Physiocrats and Adam Smith— namely, limiting governmental interference in society to establishing commutative justice, maintaining national defense, and creating certain public works inappropriate for private enterprise. This definition of laissez faire is compatible with Viner's other writings which demonstrate that Smith and others were not dogmatic adherents to laissez faire even though they accepted it as a general principle.

Viner first engaged in a wide-ranging discussion of the origins of the laissez-faire doctrine, following up on his remark in the *Studies* that "the antecedents of Smith's laissez-faire and free-trade views are probably rightly to be sought mainly in the philosophical literature . . . rather than in the earlier English economic literature."[64] Emerging as a unified doctrine only in the eighteenth century, the idea of laissez faire was woven from various elements of Graeco-Ro-

---

lutionary explanation of the process of development of social institutions. . . . But I fail to see the connection with 'liberty' which Hayek and you see. . . . The government of London, which Mandeville praised highly, was as much an evolutionary development for him as was language, but it included nevertheless a great mass of regulation and of officialdom, of 'interventionism.' . . . I see no theoretical or empirical ground for taking for granted that spontaneous or evolutionary development will necessarily or even preponderantly produce results which would or should be to my liking, even from a 'libertarian' point of view." Letter to Chiaki Nishiyama, June 23, 1961, Jacob Viner papers.

[63] Viner comments further on Mandeville's satire in Chapter 13. See also Phillip Harth, "The Satiric Purpose of *The Fable of the Bees*," *Eighteenth-Century Studies* 2 (Summer 1969): 321–40.

[64] *Studies*, p. 91.

man, Scholastic, common law, and mercantilist thought. In tracing its development, Viner stops at various points to correct common misperceptions: that the scholastic doctrine of "just price," for example, was meant to entail administered or regulated prices and not those arising from a competitive market, or that Hobbes had a particularly interventionist economic agenda for the centralized authority of Leviathan beyond the maintenance of domestic peace. Drawing on these varied sources, the Physiocrats and Adam Smith in their own eclectic manner developed a brand of laissez faire, each with a lengthy list of exceptions that was not fully integrated into their system.

Viner then shifted to a surprisingly personal critique of prominent themes in modern laissez-faire thinking. To the notion that laissez faire promotes liberty, Viner cautioned that liberties sometimes clash with each other or with other ideals. To the proposition that when freedom and regulation conflict it is best to err on the side of freedom, Viner suggested the alternative of forming a better-suited type of regulation instead of abandoning such action altogether. Although Viner was persuaded of an important link between laissez faire and competitive markets, his conviction was tempered by concerns about the prevalence of monopoly. About the laissez-faire presumption that an existing or a market-determined distribution of income was justifiable, Viner thought that ignoring calls for distributive justice was "glaringly unrealistic with respect to its chances of political success, and highly questionable also with respect to its more exalted criteria of merit."[65]

Although the essay critically reviewed the arguments used to support laissez faire, it did not necessarily constitute an endorsement by Viner of the alternative position. As he later put it: "I would want to leave clear, however, that I would have corresponding, and on the whole much more severe, criticisms to make [of] the historical arguments for extensive state-interventionism, and that such personal bias as I am conscious of as between full-fledged laissez faire and comprehensive interventionism is decidedly on the side of laissez faire. My position, as it has always been, is however, that neither of these provides an attractive program, and that it is in the area in between that the most attractive prospects lie."[66]

---

[65] However, he endorsed efforts to minimize the impact of redistribution on the market process and admitted that the post-World War II welfare state in England was, to his taste, overly concerned with distributive justice. See also Jacob Viner, "The United States as a 'Welfare State,' " in *The Nation's Economic Objectives*, ed. Edgar O. Edwards (Chicago: University of Chicago Press, 1964), pp. 151–67. Similar issues are discussed in Eugene Rotwein, "Jacob Viner and the Chicago Tradition," *History of Political Economy* 15 (Summer 1983): 265–80.

[66] Letter to P. R. Brahmananda, December 3, 1969, Jacob Viner papers. Viner always emphasized that criticism of a doctrine or opinion on his part did not necessarily constitute an endorsement of the alternatives. "I fear I have too often for the good of my reputation criticized arguments without disclaiming adherence to what the arguments were attacking, but I still think that, depending on the

Still, Viner's willingness to subject arguments favoring laissez faire to close scrutiny is evidenced well by his review of Friedrich Hayek's *The Constitution of Liberty* (1960). A recipient of the Nobel Memorial Prize in Economic Science in 1974 with a wide interest in philosophical and historical matters outside the discipline of economics, Hayek emerged as this century's foremost exponent of limited government. Although Viner admired Hayek's scholarship and eloquence, he had mixed feelings about Hayek's forays into political philosophy. As he once commented, "I admire a good deal of his work, and have no use for other parts of it."[67] These mixed feelings were evident in Viner's opinion of Hayek's celebrated *The Road to Serfdom* (1944): ". . . political criticism by scholars should always be in terms of a better alternative rather than of dogmas, no matter how appealing those dogmas be when stated in abstract terms. . . . I share, of course, Hayek's *stated* convictions, but I have never been at ease on political issues with Continental 'liberals,' who, I think, are almost always really of a different school, emotionally if not intellectually, than the old English liberalism which I find myself clinging to even as it appears to be vanishing from the world as a living faith."[68]

His comments on *The Constitution of Liberty* reflect this attitude as well. Viner found the political philosophy in the book too tendentious and categorical for his tastes, and he criticized Hayek's failure to explore adequately the conflicts and choices that need to be made between competing values. When Hayek turned to the application of his ideas to specific policies, however, Viner stated that "[w]ith much of it I am in substantial agreement; with some of it I am in full agreement." He thought Hayek's program for government to be extensive enough to make him unfit for the laissez-faire label and that advocates of extensive government intervention would do well to study Hayek's position.

MERCANTILISM

As already noted, much of Viner's early research in the history of economic thought complemented his work in the theory of international trade. For example, the first two chapters of the *Studies* on English theories of foreign trade before

---

circumstances, this is often the appropriate scholarly procedure. As has often enough been pointed out, many a correct conclusion has been supported by bad arguments, and I would add, it is generally wise to attack a bad argument even if one believes that its conclusion is correct, or, as often is or should be the case, if one is aware of ignorance as to the correctness of the conclusion." Letter to Paul A. Samuelson, August 27, 1959, Jacob Viner papers.

[67] Letter to Irwin Primer, March 26, 1969, Jacob Viner papers.

[68] Letter to Paul Douglas, June 3, 1945, Jacob Viner papers. See also Viner remarks on the book in the Wabash lectures.

Adam Smith, originally published as an article in 1930, undertook a searching examination of mercantilist trade doctrine. This work, "primarily an inventory of ideas, good and bad . . . classified and examined in the light of modern monetary and trade theory," was in part a reaction to the "state-building" interpretation, and the generally sympathetic treatment, of mercantilist doctrine by the German and English school of historical economists.[69] It was through his criticism that Viner hoped to provide a more balanced overall picture of mercantilist thought; had the historical economists scorned mercantilist thought, Viner might well have taken special pains to uncover and highlight the good in mercantilist analysis.

The appearance of an English translation of Eli Heckscher's landmark book *Mercantilism* in 1935 continued this criticial attention to mercantilist thought and policy. Viner clearly admired Heckscher's work, especially as it related to the history of economic policy, and called it "an absolutely indispensable guide."[70] But he was less convinced that Heckscher had clearly stated or had accurately characterized English mercantilist thought on the relationship between national power and economic wealth. Far from subordinating factors such as wealth to considerations of power, as he understood Heckscher to say, Viner insisted that both power and wealth were desired goals and were viewed as complementary and not competing ends of mercantilist policy.

In reply, Heckscher conceded that both "power" and "opulence" were always important goals of mercantilist economic policy. He reiterated, however, that greater significance was attached to power than to wealth, a ranking that was responsible for the "incessant commercial rivalries of the seventeenth and eighteenth centuries, which degenerated easily into military conflict."[71] With the subsequent rise of laissez faire, Heckscher argued, power gave way to wealth as the chief goal of economic policy.

In correspondence, Viner did "not deny that power was a more prominent objective of national policy in the 17th and 18th centuries than in the 19th. . . . All I dispute . . . is your argument that the mercantilists regarded power and prosperity as competing alternatives, as between which choice had to be made." With few exceptions, Viner insisted, "the English mercantilist literature treats

[69] Viner, *Studies*, p. 2.

[70] Eli F. Heckscher, *Mercantilism*, 2 vol. (London: Allen & Unwin, 1935, revised edition 1955). Viner's review is in *Economic History Review* 6 (October 1935): 99–101, reprinted in *The Long View and the Short*, pp. 407–10.

[71] Eli F. Heckscher, "Revisions in Economic History, V, Mercantilism," *Economic History Review* 7 (November 1936): 44–54, reprinted in D. C. Coleman, ed., *Revisions in Mercantilism* (London: Methuen, 1959), pp. 19–34.

power and prosperity as mutually supporting objectives . . . both were important objectives in their own right.''[72]

Viner expanded on this theme in his classic article, ''Power versus Plenty as Objectives of Foreign Policy in the Seventeenth and Eighteenth Centuries,'' which possibly ranks beside ''Adam Smith and Laissez Faire'' as his most influential essay in the history of ideas. Viner disputed the stereotype that mercantilism was a ''system of power'' that treated power as the sole goal of national policy and wealth as only a means to greater power. He believed that Heckscher made ''no important concession'' in his reply and, while again not disputing that ''mercantilists considered power as an end to itself . . . and that they considered wealth to be a means of power,'' he sought to examine whether mercantilists ''*ever* regarded power as the *sole* end of foreign policy, or ever held that considerations of plenty were *wholly* to be subordinated to considerations of power, or even whether they held that a choice has to be made in long-run national policy between power and plenty.'' Viner amassed an impressive array of textual evidence to support his contention that mercantilists believed that both wealth and power were ends to national policy and that each abetted the other. He concluded that ''it is much easier to show that power was not the sole objective of national policy in mercantilist thought than to explain how historians ever came to assert that it was.''

Viner's exposition of mercantilist objectives proved convincing. The chapter entitled ''Mercantilism as a System of Power'' in the revised edition of Heckscher's book was considerably changed in light of Viner's article.[73] Indeed, Viner's article quickly established itself as a standard reference on the topic, one whose influence extended beyond the fields of economic history and history of doctrine to research on the political economy of international relations. Viner had little to revise or withdraw twenty years later in his contribution ''Mercantilist Thought'' to the *International Encyclopedia of the Social Sciences*.

Mention should be made, however, of Viner's opinion of some prominent themes in the post-World War II treatment of mercantilism. Following Keynes' attempt to rehabilitate mercantilism in Chapter 23 of *The General Theory of Employment, Interest and Money*, some economists, including Joseph Schumpeter, have suggested that mercantilist economic thought did not deserve its poor repu-

---

[72] Letter to Eli Heckscher, June 24, 1938, Jacob Viner papers.

[73] A footnote inadvertently dropped from the chapter explicitly records this fact. See D. C. Coleman, *Revisions*, p. 100, n. 1. In an Addendum to the revised edition of *Mercantilism* (p. 359), Heckscher concedes that Viner's ''evidence impresses me as being sufficiently strong to make me abandon my original thesis on the issue. . . . I have come to the conclusion that the difference between the mercantilist position and that which succeeded it was a difference of degree and not a difference of kind,'' although Heckscher believed the difference to be a significant one.

tation. Viner never endorsed this position and always retained his low opinion of mercantilism. As he once put it, "I know of no scholar of even third-rate rank who made any contribution to it except that of lopping off one or more of its more obviously diseased branches."[74] In his *History of Economic Analysis*, Schumpeter paid tribute to Viner's contribution to the study of mercantilist and classical trade theory with glowing references to the *Studies*, but he questioned "whether Professor Viner is prepared to pass the same peremptory judgments on certain measures and arguments of our own time that are exactly similar to those of the mercantilist age." Viner replied that "events of recent decades have only strengthened rather than weakened my conviction of the faults, analytical, practical, utilitarian, of the mercantilist approach to international economic problems."[75]

Unfortunately, nowhere does Viner address at length the Keynesian interpretation of mercantilist thought, which states that the main objective of mercantilism was full employment and economic growth.[76] Viner continued to maintain that concern over the balance of trade was the distinguishing feature of mercantilist thought and that increased production and employment "was made to rest much more on the contribution it could make to a favorable balance of trade . . . than on an acceptance in principle of the desirability of a higher level of per capita consumption for the general public." Viner was also indifferent to exercises of this period attempting to minimize the differences between mercantilist and liberal thought. As he put it: "Even between extreme mercantilists and extreme advocates of laissez faire the difference in avowed general principle might consist only in that the mercantilist would stress the duty of intervention unless, by exception good reason existed for leaving things alone, while the laissez faire doctrinaire would insist that the government should leave things alone unless by exception special reasons existed why it should intervene."[77] By selection of specific issues, Viner did not think it difficult to make the moderate mercantilist appear as a moderate exponent of laissez faire.

Finally, because mercantilist doctrine was expounded and implemented in a multiplicity of ways, some scholars have argued that the term "mercantilism" itself is vacuous.[78] The charge, however, applied more to mercantilist policy than

[74] See Chapter 9 below.

[75] Schumpeter, *History of Economic Analysis*, p. 336, n. 4. Viner replies in his review of Schumpeter's book.

[76] See, for example, William D. Grampp, "The Liberal Elements of English Mercantilism," *Quarterly Journal of Economics* 66 (November 1952): 465–501.

[77] See below, p. 212 and p. 265.

[78] See, for example, D. C. Coleman, "Mercantilism Revisited," *Historical Journal* 23 (December 1980): 773–91.

to mercantilist economic thought, where Viner devoted his attention, and he refused to abandon the term. Although he once admitted that broad descriptions of
mercantilism ''are almost necessarily half-truths or empty,'' Viner later wrote
that he could not see how ''mercantilism as a term designating a distinguishable
body of doctrines and governmental practices is more vulnerable to the charge of
imprecision than the general run of terms used by social scientists for such purposes. . . . It is sometimes the same economic historians who object to the term
'mercantilism' as empty of content in the absence of a matching body of doctrine
who insist that the body of doctrine and of practices to which the label has been
applied had in its prime a degree of suitability approaching the miraculous to the
contemporary needs of mankind.''[79]

ENGLISH CLASSICAL ECONOMICS

In his work on international trade and price theory, Viner claimed as his intellectual ancestors the English classical and, to a lesser extent, neoclassical economists.[80] Although he repeatedly demonstrated an interest in the English classical
economists, Viner never wrote a treatise on their economic thought in general. In
the 1940s, Viner published two articles on English political economy that, in
retrospect, appear to mark a new direction for his research in the history of economics. In contrast to much of his previous work, these articles, on Alfred Marshall and on Jeremy Bentham and John Stuart Mill, contain virtually no discussion of economic theory. In both articles, Viner declines as ''not part of my
assignment'' any analysis of the economics of Mill or Marshall. Instead, the discussion is entirely on the ethical or philosophical foundations of their economic
thought and on their theory of the individual and the state. At times Viner almost
descends into a reductionist view according to which the economic thought of
Mill and Marshall largely reflected a strict utilitarian upbringing or the prevailing
Victorian beliefs.

The fiftieth anniversary of Alfred Marshall's *Principles of Economics* was the
occasion for Viner to pen an assessment of the great Victorian economist. He was
eminently qualified to provide a view of Marshall because Viner was in part a

---

[79] Viner, *Studies*, p. 2, and below, p. 228.

[80] While Viner has often been described as a neoclassical economist, Joseph Dorfman with good
reason called Viner a ''twentieth-century Ricardian.'' Joseph Dorfman, *The Economic Mind in American Civilization*, Vol. 5, *1918–1933* (New York: Viking Press, 1959), pp. 480ff. Curiously, Viner
never wrote at length on Ricardo's economic thought, perhaps because for much of his career he was
awaiting Piero Sraffa's edition of Ricardo's collected works, or because Ricardo's thought, unlike
that of Smith, Bentham, and J. S. Mill, was not enriched by a philosophical background.

Marshallian economist. His renowned course in price theory, Economics 301 at the University of Chicago, was heavily based on Marshall, and his published work in price theory reflected a Marshallian approach. But in this assessment Viner eschewed reflection on Marshall's economics in favor of examining his political and ethical beliefs, as Marshall came to economics from ethics and mathematics. From ethics, Marshall inherited a Benthamite view which was softened by the Victorian rhetoric of "moral earnestness." Although mathematically trained, Marshall used evolutionary biology to motivate economic theory, leading him, Viner suggests, to doubt the usefulness of mathematics in economics. As much as he admired Marshall, Viner thought him slightly antiquated and believed that "[b]oth the Victorian complacency with respect to the present and the Victorian optimism with respect to future progress are now utterly inappropriate."

Eight years later, on the occasion of the two-hundredth birthday of Bentham and the one-hundred fiftieth anniversary of Mill's *Principles of Political Economy*, Viner wrote on the intellectual relationship of these two men. This article also contains slight mention of economic theory and focuses on utilitarian thought. Noting the reliance of contemporary economics on utilitarian thinking, Viner justifies his long discussion of the doctrine by suggesting that knowing one's premises in economics and their sources may be beneficial. Viner discusses Bentham's program of reform and its underpinnings in utilitarian thought and disputes the common notion that a conflict exists between Bentham's approach to government and his economic doctrines. The latter, Viner notes, did not approach laissez faire, but allowed for a wide range of government activities to close the gap between private and public interest.

Viner then traces John Stuart Mill's early adherence to Benthamite utilitarianism, his rebellion against its more austere features and his attraction to romantic and sentimental schools of thought, and his later return (with qualifications) to the utilitarian flock. Viner dismisses Mill's sympathetic treatment of socialism as "in large degree platonic, for in no major concrete instance did Mill actually commit himself to the desirability of a specific drastic change." Mill's romantic period, however, softened his economic doctrine to accommodate a wider range of considerations in human actions and "enabled him to carry on a sustained liaison with socialist ideas and interventionist economic programmes almost wholly within the classical school boundaries of laissez faire and economic individualism."[81]

Toward the end of the essay, Viner returns to the theme of laissez faire, defending the English classical economists against charges that they were staunchly

---

[81] This point is made in Chapter 17.

opposed to all government intervention in the economy. "[L]ike all the other major classical economists except perhaps Senior—who was not a Benthamite," Viner maintained, "J. S. Mill gave only a very qualified adherence to laissez-faire. It was for him only a rule of expediency, always subordinate to the principle of utility, and never a dogma."[82] Viner clearly took pains to demonstrate in many of his writings that Smith and nineteenth-century English economists were not dogmatic adherents to laissez faire. In making this defense and in providing an objective exposition of classical thinking (or a sympathetic critique of laissez faire and utilitarianism), Viner was acting to save the economists and adherents to their doctrines from misinterpretation. Such defense was urgently required in the 1930s and thereafter when classical thought had generally acquired a bad reputation and was, in some circles, bastardized. This loss of appreciation for—at times debasement of—classical thought occurred partly because many intellectuals during and after the Great Depression believed in the necessity of social and economic planning and other forms of government control. This attitude contributed to a questioning of the motives and interests of the classical economists and put those sympathetic to classical theories on the defensive. In pointing out the active role for government in classical thought, Viner was probably also attempting to provide balance against other economists who sought to invoke the classical prescription of laissez faire to support their views. Thus, Viner was a key figure in rescuing classical thought from being hopelessly distorted to serve the ideological purposes of various parties.[83]

THE DISCIPLINE OF ECONOMICS IN PERSPECTIVE

As a respected and admired elder statesman of the economics profession in the 1950s and 1960s, Viner was frequently called upon to dispense some of his vast knowledge of the history of economics and to put broad trends in economic think-

[82] The Manchester School, for example, linked political economy with laissez faire, a tie vigorously denied by many classical economists. Viner's conclusion is supported in Edward R. Kittrell, " 'Laissez Faire' in English Classical Economics," *Journal of the History of Ideas*, 27 (October–December 1966): 610–20. In addition, see Arthur J. Taylor, *Laissez Faire and State Intervention in Nineteenth Century Britain* (London: Macmillan, 1972).

[83] Lionel Robbins, in his *The Theory of Economic Policy in English Classical Political Economy* (London: Macmillan, 1952; 2nd ed., 1978), played an instrumental role in this effort. Robbins wrote the book because "I had been increasingly disturbed by the crudity and wrongheadedness of many contemporary conceptions . . . in regard to the famous classical system. . . . I felt more and more that the classical system in general, misrepresented almost beyond belief, was being used as a convenient Aunt Sally by any writer or speaker who wished to set his *soi-disant* enlightened views against a background of black reaction." Robbins, *Autobiography of an Economist* (London: Macmillan, 1971), p. 226.

ing into perspective. One such example is his short talk " 'Fashion' in Economic Thought." Viner defined fashion as a prevalent but short-lived framework of economic analysis, noting that "the history of economics as a discipline is to quite a large extent a history of fashion in economic thinking." Viner did not believe that fashion was a bad thing for economics. Economic theory, in method of attack and in choice of problem to address, Viner suggests, has always been closely linked to the problems of the world, and he ventures the opinion that economics probably has followed more often than it has led public opinion. "Economics is not sufficiently an autonomous discipline to be able to go far in its own way with respect to goals, to objectives, or to methods of analysis." When it has, Viner says, these internally generated fashions are difficult to explain.

At one point Viner recalls the observation that economics has never had a good press. He expands on this thought in his "The Economist in History," given as the Richard T. Ely address before the American Economic Association in 1962. Here Viner provides an amusing look at the views of economics and economists expressed throughout history by those outside the profession, such as Thomas Carlyle's quip that "Of all the quacks that ever quacked, political economists are the loudest," and Theodore Roosevelt's dictum that advocacy of free trade "seems inevitably to produce fatty degeneration of the moral fibre." Viner's insight reveals why critics of the classical economists focused their bitter if amusing attacks on the economist's methodology: ". . . no lay public is normally concerned with the manner in which intellectuals reach their conclusions unless it objects strongly to the conclusions. . . . By attacking the methodology [critics] could lessen the appeal of the conclusions without opening themselves as much to charges of self-interested partisanship."

Viner also explains how satire contributed to the downfall of the Physiocrats in France and how the Physiocrats' lack of humor only added to their plight: "The solemnly serious tones of the replies brought only additional peals of laughter." "It seems always to have been true that the only effective rejoinder to clever satire . . . is comparably clever countersatire," Viner sagely observes, "but it is not characteristic of sects to recruit wits to their ranks."

EIGHTEENTH-CENTURY ENGLISH THOUGHT

Viner soon returned to the topic of economics and satire, one of his favorite themes, this time concentrating his attention on the Augustan age of satire. Viner had considerable interest in eighteenth-century English thought and appears at one point to have considered writing a book on the subject.[84] Although the book never came to fruition, material from it later appeared in his piece on satire, in another article published just before his death, and in his Jayne lectures.

When Viner examined the modern literature on eighteenth-century English satire, he discovered that satirists were treated with reverence, as possessors of truth heaping ridicule on fools who deserved such a fate. Viner advanced an alternative view, that satire could be employed by those with good or bad intentions and that an ancient doctrine associating satire and laughter with sin handicapped retaliation in kind by the religious establishment. In fact, Viner found only two instances in which satire was used against satire: in exclusively literary settings, and in controversies between literary Anglicans and deists (or free thinkers). He noted the standard problems besetting interpretation of satire, such as discerning its intended purpose or deciding at which points the author was being earnest or ironic. The sophistication of the audience is an important element in the success of satire, and he pointed out that "Satire is a two-edged weapon; if misunderstood, the wrong edge may cut." Edmund Burke's *A Vindication of Natural Society* (1756), in Viner's judgment, was a case in point: its exaggerated attack on government was taken literally by many readers. But, Viner wryly adds, to be explicit about one's purpose, as when Swift added a preface explaining his intent in one work, must be "a humiliating thing, I should think, for a satirist to have to do."

Viner concluded that the amount of satire of any importance in economics debates was meager, although he commended Voltaire's critique of the Physiocrats as "one of the few major satirical achievements in the history of economic thought." He also found one author who in 1716 opposed labor-saving devices in a manner that anticipated Frédéric Bastiat's early nineteenth-century "A Petition from Manufacturers of Candles," a clever, *reductio ad absurdum* plea for protection against ruinous and unfair competition from the sun.[85] However, most of the Augustan satirists aimed their pointed prose at manners and customs, not at economic and political institutions, and the reforms they sought were to be achieved by changing individual behavior, not by restructuring institutions. Satirists had a conservative tendency and never made the step from "ridicule of social inequality not resting on differences in merit to advocacy of the legislative abolition of inequality."

Viner's "Man's Economic Status" was his penultimate publication and was similar in some respects to the Augustan satire article. This tour of eighteenth-

---

[84] See Machlup, "What Was Left on Viner's Desk," p. 361.

[85] Frédéric Bastiat, *Economic Sophisms*, trans. Arthur Goddard (Princeton: D. van Nostrand, 1964), pp. 56–60.

century English upper-class attitudes toward the poor describes contemporary opinions on education, equality, debt, charity, the poor laws, and other issues. What struck Viner about the century was how "inert and inept" government was administratively and how social thought was rife with "a dominating complacency with respect to the eighteenth-century *status quo*." One senses Viner's unease and concern that the complacency was too securely entrenched and the society was too languid and uncaring in its attitude. For while "the England of the century we are discussing has always impressed me as a nearly perfect gentleman's utopia," he found very little evidence from the literature of the period reflecting a recognition of the desirability of social change or a concern for the plight of the poor and laboring classes. Like Adam Smith, Viner's sympathies were clearly with these people.[86]

Despite his feelings, Viner strove to maintain balance: "I resist deliberately and determinedly . . . giving expression to any urge I may be subject to to assert obligations of the eighteenth century to conform to your—or to my—standards of social justice, of freedom, of beauty." Viner neither offered an apologia for the defects of the century nor criticized the century for its faults, "for in moral matters," Viner wrote, "I am a historical relativist of what is perhaps a peculiar kind. I believe that each century except one's own has a right to its abuses, but that no century has an obligation to condemn, to praise, or to offer apologies for, another century's lapses from perfection."[87]

[86] As he once explained, "I would not trade the free market system for any alternative I have ever heard of. But no human institution works acceptably . . . without some patching and trimming. . . . My concern is largely limited to those to whom fortune has been harsh—broken families, children in slum areas or with incompetent or inadequate parents, underprivileged minority groups, and such like. To such I would have the state be generous, both on grounds of humanity, and to give them a reasonable chance of becoming useful citizens. That about covers the extent of my social-reform program, but it is, I believe, a sizeable job, very incompletely accomplished, even in our rich U.S.A." Letter to W. A. Paton, February 13, 1956, Jacob Viner papers.

[87] See below, p. 302.

PART I

The Wabash Lectures

1

FIVE LECTURES ON ECONOMICS AND FREEDOM

Delivered at Wabash College, Crawfordsville, Indiana
June 1959

LECTURE I

Early Attitudes toward Trade and the Merchant

There are surprisingly ancient origins for some of the modern ideas with respect to the nature and functions of trade, domestic and international.

Among the Greek and the Roman philosophers hostile or contemptuous attitudes towards trade and the merchant were common, based in the main on aristocratic and snobbish prejudice, and with no or naive underpinning of economic argument. Thus Aristotle maintained that trade was an unseemly activity for nobles or gentlemen, a "blameable" activity. He insisted that wealth was essential for nobility, but it must be inherited wealth. Wealth was also an essential need of the state, but it should be obtained by piracy or brigandage, and by war for the conquest of slaves, and should be maintained by slave-workers.

It was a commonplace of Greek and Roman thought, destined to be absorbed in the Christian tradition, that trade was either by its inherent nature, or through the temptations it offered to those engaged in it, pervasively associated with fraud and cheating, especially, according to Cicero, if it were "small," or retail trade. Horace decried trade as "unnatural" and "impious."

Foreign trade, or "sea-trade," was especially frowned upon by Cicero as involving in some way danger to the public weal, and by the elder Pliny as resulting in a drain of gold to India, a complaint destined to become a major aspect of mercantilist thought of the seventeenth and eighteenth centuries.

The early Christian Fathers on the whole took a suspicious if not definitely hostile attitude toward the trade of the merchant or middleman, as being sinful or conducive to sin, essentially as involving either necessarily or commonly fraud or exploitation or violation of charity. They relied in large part on Biblical texts, as, for instance, the association in *Ecclesiasticus*, XXVI 29, of trade with sin: "A merchant shall hardly keep himself from doing wrong; and an huckster shall not be freed from sin"; or the New Testament account of the ejection by Jesus of traders from the temple, interpreted as a condemnation of trade itself, and not merely as a condemnation of its practice at a wrong time and in a wrong place. An interesting instance was the emphasis by St. Augustine and others on a verse of the Psalms (LXXI.15) as mistranslated in the Septuagint, and in the early Latin translations from the Septuagint, to read: "Because I have not known *trading*, [*negotiationem*], I will enter into the powers of the Lord."

In obedience to this apparent text, St. Augustine advises: "Let Christians amend themselves; let them not trade." He is troubled, however, and presents with apparently some sympathy the objection of a trader that it is not trading itself but its fraudulent pursuit which is to be condemned and that the trader could not escape the temptation to sin merely by turning to a craft such as shoemaking, where he would be tempted to lie as to when the shoes would be finished and to cheat by poor workmanship. Or if he turned to farming, he might sin by desiring a crop failure so that he could sell from his store at a high price to the famished poor.

For the early Christian Fathers, as for the pagan philosophers, it was the element in trade of the pursuit of a middleman's profit which they found specially objectionable, as demonstrating "avarice," and therefore "sin." St. Augustine referred elsewhere to an actor who told his audience that what they all wished for was the opportunity to buy cheap and sell dear. St. Ambrosius commented that Joshua was able to order the sun to stand still, but that he would have found it a more formidable task to subdue the pursuit of gain. St. Chrysostom, in a passage which was to continue to have influence into the Middle Ages and beyond because of its citation in Gratian's authoritative *Decretals*, said: "In chasing from the Temple sellers and buyers, the Lord signified the merchant almost never, and even never, can be pleasing to God. That is why no Christian should be a merchant; if he wishes to be one, let him be chased out of the church of God."

Underlying this condemnation of trade was an implicit economic analysis which failed to see any possible counterpart in service to the buyer or the community for the gain of a merchant selling at a higher price than that at which he had bought. This came nearest to being made explicit in a passage of St. Jerome, destined to have a lasting influence: "All riches proceed from sin. No one can gain without another man losing."

"If sin has not been committed by the actual proprietor of wealth, the wealth is the product of sin committed by his ancestors."

As in the case of Cicero and the elder Pliny, a number of the early Christian Fathers found foreign or "sea" trade especially objectionable from a moral point of view. Because sea-trade involved unusual hazards, addiction to it demonstrated a special degree of avarice. Since necessaries were always available nearby, sea trade meant catering to the sinful desire for luxury. Sea trade, moreover, carried with it special moral risks, contamination by contact with pagans, the absence of home discipline and consequently susceptibility to temptation to practice adultery, and so forth.

If these Fathers had been asked, How could society do without middlemen merchants? it seems clear that they would have answered somewhat as follows: In the absence of avarice and of a desire for luxuries, the material needs of society could be met without recourse to middlemen through the practice of subsistence agriculture, or through the exchange on a barter basis or its equivalent of the products of agriculture and of the crafts, or through voluntary sharing of surpluses.

This is, however, only one side of the story of early attitudes towards trade, the side which is familiar to modern scholars and theologians.

There was another trend of thought, important in classical pagan and in early Christian thought, but which has been for the most part overlooked, or assumed to have originated in much later times by modern scholars. This other doctrine substitutes eulogy for condemnation with respect at least to *overseas* trade. This is the doctrine which has been labelled the doctrine of "Universal economy," a phase of the more general doctrine of the "universalism" of mankind. In its earliest form it is naturalistic, or at least without express supernatural or teleological reference. Thus Euripides, in his *Suppliants*, makes Theseus say: "Each country provides for itself what its climate refuses to it by maritime expeditions of its vessels." The historian, Florus, in the time of Augustus, says: "Suppress commerce and you tear apart the bonds of the human race." And Plutarch says:

[The sea] has rendered sociable and tolerable our existence which, without this, would have been fierce and without commerce, by making available through mutual assistance what otherwise would have been lacking, and by bringing into existence, through the exchange of goods, community and friendship.

To Libanius, a fourth century professor, although he was a pagan, is probably due a large part of the credit for the entrance of the doctrine into the Christian tradition, to remain a part of it until very recent times. Among his students were at least two of the Christian Fathers, St. Basil and St. John Chrysostom. He seems to have been the first to give the doctrine a theological flavor and thus to make it attractive to the religious-minded. He was the first to give, in germ at least, an express support of the doctrine in terms of what might be regarded as economic analysis. In the 17th Century, Grotius, in stating the doctrine, with due reference to Libanius, made it known to and authoritative for latitudinarian and rationalistic Protestantism, as well as for the Enlightenment in general. Libanius' statement was as follows:

> God did not accord all things to all parts of the earth, but he has divided his gifts among different countries, so that peoples should have need one of the other, in order that from their mutual dependence they should be led to maintain society (community) together. Thus He has brought commerce into existence as a means available to all the world of enjoying in common all things wherever they were produced.

The economist will see that if "all things" in this passage of Libanius is interpreted to cover climate, resources, human aptitudes, as well as products, it leads logically to a doctrine of free trade based on international division of labor. In fact, it did over the years undergo such development, and I think the doctrine thus has claims to be the oldest and longest-lived economic doctrine we know of. Its original function in the Christian tradition, however, was not to describe on an objective basis the rationale of economic process, still less, to praise commerce, but instead to serve as evidence of the providential design of the universe, and of the universal brotherhood of man as part of that design. It was only much later, beginning with Grotius, Vittoria, and Suarez, that it was invoked as a support to a legal doctrine of freedom of the seas and of the right of strangers to carry on commerce in all regions—though not necessarily on the basis of what we now call "free trade." It was apparently not until the nineteenth century, when Cobden, for example, insisted that "free trade was the international law of God," that it was invoked in support of the doctrine that *all* artificial barriers to foreign trade were both *morally* and *economically* evil.

None of the Christian Fathers, and none of the medieval scholastics, seem to have noticed the existence side-by-side of these two doctrines apparently completely contradictory of each other, one of which treated commerce as sinful or close to sin, and the other of which treated commerce as one of the temporal instruments by which Providence promoted its benevolent design on behalf of mankind. It would be interesting if an instance could be found of a writer who maintained both doctrines. St. Thomas Aquinas has been credited with the universal economy doctrine, although I have so far failed to find a confirmatory text. What is clear, however, is that, under the influence of Aristotle, St. Thomas does, at times at least, deal suspiciously with trade. At one point, following Aristotle almost word for word with reference to the relation of trade to nobility, he stops short, however, where Aristotle says that trade is "blameable." Trade, Aquinas says, is in itself not virtuous, or evil. It can become licit if directed to a legitimate end, such as maintenance of one's household (as distinguished presumably from pursuit of enrichment); acquisition of means to be used in relief of the poor; and the rendering of a service to the community. At another point, however, he recommends that foreign trade be kept to a minimum, so as not to cater to luxury, so as not to bring dangerous contacts with foreign ideas and customs, and on the metaphysical ground that self-sufficiency and order of moral merit are positively correlated, one of the many instances where the propensity to find a hierarchical ordering of merits or virtue by classes has had only obfuscation as its product.

Later scholastics occasionally expressed hostility to specific effects of or aspects of foreign trade. It was often impracticable to enforce on foreign merchants or on dealers in foreign merchandise the canonist or civil law regulations or percepts with respect to "just price," either because foreigners were not subject to local jurisdiction or because the variability of conditions in foreign trade and the lack of necessary information made ascertainment of the "just" price impossible. Usury was believed to be specially associated with foreign trade transactions, concealed in foreign exchange operations or in bottomry contracts. Some of the scholastics were uneasy about marine insurance, since it seemed to involve rejection of the decrees of Providence. With the advent of Colonial expansion, there was associated with foreign trade systematic cruelty to and enslavement of natives, the slave-trade, and the notorious avarice of some of the conquistadors and colonial merchants. All of this gave concern to some of the scholastics.

On the other hand, the Renaissance, especially in its Italian manifestations, brought new attitudes with respect to the dignity of the merchant, his usefulness to society, and the general legitimacy of the moderate pursuit of wealth through commerce, provided the merchant who thus attained riches used it with taste, with liberality, and with concern for the welfare and the magnificence of his city. Perhaps most significant, there were now for the first time great merchants, powerful, cultured, educated, and able and willing to speak out effectively on behalf of their role in society. To some extent, there was a corresponding change of attitude on the part of some of the leading Italian scholastics of the period, notably in Florence and in Venice, reflecting, no doubt, the influence of a new kind of environment where merchants were also the rulers, the aristocrats, the patrons of the Church and of the arts, and able spokesmen for their own interpretation of the place of commerce and of wealth in a well-governed society. In general, however, the theologians continued to regard commerce, the pursuit of gain, and business activity in general, as dangerous to morality and to religion, and to be uncertain of or indifferent to their role in contributing to the temporal welfare of mankind.

No one has succeeded in tracing any link between scholastic theology or economics and mercantilism, and some scholars of repute have positively denied any link in the sense that scholastic doctrine provided the mercantilists with any elements of doctrine, or that any important scholastics expounded mercantilist doctrine themselves. In general, the universalistic as distinguished from nationalist orientation of the Catholic Church and its traditions, and the traditional theological suspicion of the merchant and of commerce, kept Catholic doctrine free from important entanglements with mercantilism.

On one point, however, there was an intellectual link, fortuitous but nevertheless of some practical importance, between the economic doctrines of the Church and mercantilism. The doctrine that one man's gain is another man's loss which some theologians had expounded was taken over by mercantilism and transformed into the doctrine that one country's gain was another country's loss, as well as into its converse, that one country's loss was another country's gain. Out of this doctrine evolved the doctrines of the essential rivalry, instead of harmony, between the economic interests of nations, and the belief that the use of power to gain wealth, including its use to impoverish rival countries, was a rational and often more effective program for the promotion of a country's economic welfare than the pursuit of efficiency in production and the sharing between countries through peaceful competition of the mutual benefits of friendly trade. There was here, of course, the sharpest of conflicts between the doctrine of the universal economy and mercantilist doctrine. The doctrine of the universal economy, as I have pointed out, had been absorbed into Christian doctrine.

It was not, however, until the period of the Enlightenment, and largely under secular auspices, that it was used in a frontal attack against mercantilism. Meanwhile, mercantilists who could not ignore the doctrine of universal economy were ingenious enough to find ways of invoking it in defense of nationalistic restrictions on commerce. For instance, since Providence had assigned to England wool as its special resource, it must have intended also that the processing of the wool should be an English vocation; it was therefore in keeping with, rather than in conflict with divine will, that by export prohibitions and other devices, England should prevent its wool from going abroad in its raw form. One should never underestimate the ingenuity of the human mind in finding bad uses for good arguments—or good uses for bad arguments—and many an originator of an idea, whether good or bad, would have been astounded and shocked if he could have foreseen the strange uses to which it was destined to be put. The doctrine of a universal economy provides only one example of many.

LECTURE II

The Nation-State and Private Enterprise

The emergence of mercantilist economic doctrine was a phase of the emergence of nationalism and the nation-state. My major concern in this lecture will therefore be with certain phases of mercantilism in its relation to private free enterprise.

Mercantilism was a body of economic and political doctrine formulated to serve an essentially new type of community organization, the nation-state, with precise boundaries, and with objectives, loyalties, and recognized moral obligations largely confined to these boundaries. As a matter of historical association rather than of logical affinity, it was also adapted, especially in the maritime countries, to new types of economic institution: the large-scale market, the large-scale business association, and the emergence of powerful merchants, influential on government and on public opinion. Earlier there had predominated first the feudal system, with its rural orientation, and its substantial independence of other than very local trade. Later, the modern town as a trading and fabricating center had grown in importance, independent of feudal authority and traditions, possessed of substantial powers of self-government, and directed by or responding to a commercial, non-aristocratic, non-feudal, oligarchy, the "bourgeois" or burgher class. Above the feudal manor and the late medieval town had been, on the Continent, the "universal" or non-national Holy Roman Empire and the even more universal Catholic Church. Loyalties were to the Church, to princes, feudal lords, cities, to some extent to the Holy Roman Empire, but not to national political organizations of "peoples" or "nations." One of the tasks falling to the new kind of political organization, the nation-state, was that of formulating the proper relations between government and business, between national objectives and the ambitions and ends of the "merchants."

Although modern scholars, under German influence, commonly interpret mercantilist policy as having had as its sole ultimate goal the building up of national power, this seems to me basically wrong. The mercantilists sought for their nations, as ultimate ends, both power and plenty, and believed that each was a prerequisite for the attainment of the other. They developed, on Machiavellian lines, a nationalistic ethic, where, as against other peoples outside the national boundaries, "raison d'état," or the national interest, would be the predominant criterion for policy, so that, in case of conflict of ends, moral obligation would not transcend the national boundaries. This was a sharp break with previous European attitudes, and especially with Christian thought as far as Christendom was concerned. It had, however, its analogies in earlier times, as in the case of ancient Israel, in relation to the Gentiles; of Athens or Rome in relation to the "barbarians"; or of medieval Christendom in relation to Islam. Within the Christian world, that is, within Europe, mercantilism constituted a sharp break with scholastic thought. There seems not to have been a contemporary literature clearly recognizing and discussing this, and the first extensive examination of the moral implications of mercantilism came only with the eighteenth century enlightenment, and predominantly outside orthodox Catholicism. In their silent struggle for dominance over men's minds and practices, nationalism proved a stronger force than Catholic universalism, while for fortuitous historical reasons Protestantism became itself a subordinate phase of nationalism where it was not a weak minority sect. "Gallicanism," in the Catholic Church, Erastianism in Protestantdom, weakened or eliminated, in the field of politics at least, the universalism of mediaeval Christianity and allowed nationalism to take its place.

Mercantilism developed with respect to "power" a static theory, a theory of its existence in a constant aggregate quantity, so that what one country gained in power another country must lose. By a seemingly plausible but largely misplaced analogy, this theory was extended also to wealth, and, with more validity in an age of "hard" money, to money. Thus "balance of power" and "balance of trade" were analyzed as if they were not only closely-related in fact but closely similar as analytical concepts. With the additional element of identification or near-identification of money and wealth, it became prevailing doctrine that international commerce was a contest for larger shares of a given world stock of money, that the prosperity of a country depended on its relative share of the world's monetary stock, that success in commerce required military strength and military strength was dependent on wealth, and that the normal politico-economic relations of countries were therefore those of a state of war or near-war, that trade was a contest in which only one party could be the gainer, and that in large part trade and war were similar activities, using somewhat different means to serve identical ends.

This was of course both a basically erroneous body of doctrines and a body of doctrines hostile to the peace and the prosperity of the world. It nevertheless still has defenders, even among economists, and especially economic historians who seem often to be unwilling or unable to distinguish between historical "explanation" and historical "justification." It must be conceded also that there were elements of "truth" in the sense of internal logical consistency and of external relevance to legitimate objectives, in the mercantilist doctrine, and that later free-trade and pacifist critics of mercantilism often ignored or denied these valid elements of the doctrine, and in rejecting it root-and-branch committed themselves to doctrine correspondingly fallacious in kind if not in degree, because correspondingly unqualified and unbalanced.

In the field of power it is correct to say that power is relative, not absolute, and that therefore what A gains in power must be at the expense of some B. In the field of wealth, it is not correct to hold that wealth is static or has definitely prescribed limits, and it is not correct to say that one man's or one country's gain must be another man's or another country's loss. But one country's gain *can* be, *may* be another country's loss, and if power is used as a gain-getting instrument, as a substitute for mutually-beneficial commerce, the more powerful country, or the country which uses its power more skilfully and assiduously, may succeed in getting wealth by subtraction from a previous holder of it. By capturing booty in war, by piracy, by monopolizing trade routes, by capturing and selling or exploiting slaves, by monopolizing by force against potential rivals an export market or a source of valuable imports, it was wholly possible in theory and to some extent realizable in practice for a country by its use of power to enrich itself through impoverishing another country or other countries.

In the absence of a high degree of flexibility of prices, and in a period of growing population and growing prevalence of a market-economy over a subsistence economy, steady growth of the national stock of "money" was an essential requirement of steady maintenance of national prosperity, and, except for the output of local gold and silver mines, the national stock of money metals could be augmented only via a "favorable balance of trade." Here, however, both the mercantilists and modern commentators, sympathetic and unsympathetic, have failed to see that there were available even before the days of paper money and of "bank money" ways in which countries without gold and silver mines and without favorable balances of trade could reconcile economic growth with a constant or even shrinking national stock of the precious metals.

By "debasement" of the national metallic currency through increased use of base alloys; by depreciation "or raising" the currency by making a given coin of unaltered content represent a larger number of monetary units of account; by decreasing the seigniorage rate, i.e. reducing the proportion of the metal presented for coinage which the mint retained for coining on its own behalf; by reducing the extent to which the normal deterioration of the coinage through wear-and-tear, clipping, and "sweating," was replaced at government expense through recoinage; and by lowering the minimum standards of tolerance as legal tender of deteriorated coins; and, finally, by inducing by one device or another a greater flow of the national stock of monetary metals into the monetary circulation and out of "hoards" and supplies of silver and gold "plate"; by these means a government could in practice bring about a larger monetary stock in terms of the standard monetary units, such as "pounds sterling" or "louis" or "thaler," even when the national stock of the monetary metals remained constant or was shrinking. Even if the nominal foreign exchange rates, in terms of equal metallic units of specified precious metals, were, within the limits of the shipping points, perforce constant, there could because of the factors stated, and also by appropriate regulations of the foreign exchange markets, be flexibility of the *effective* exchange rates, or the rates at which units of the national currencies actually in circulation at standard rates of debt-paying-capacity, actually exchanged for each other in international transactions. It is only through overlooking these various possibilities, therefore, that mercantilists and modern commentators on mercantilism have often argued as if it were a matter of fact that in the absence of domestic mines a country could avoid deflation while achieving economic growth only by having a surplus of exports over imports, or a "favorable" balance of trade. They often overlooked also that throughout much of the mercantilist period the monetary problem, whether recognized as such or not, was one of avoiding sharp inflation rather than one of avoiding deflation.

"Tampering with the currency," however, was for most of the mercantilist period and for most countries, because of legal traditions, popular resentment, moral scruples, and lack of technical know-how, not a normal and respectable practice, and was resorted to chiefly in times of extreme financial crisis, or by unscrupulous monarchs at inexpedient times from the point of view of an intelligently-appraised national interest. If the possibility of using currency devices be abstracted from, and if the substantial absence of healthy types of price-flexibility in the markets be conceded to have been characteristic of the age, a logical defence of some types of mercantilist trade regulation could be based not only on nationalist but even on cosmopolitan grounds.

But the common assumption that because under certain circumstances a certain degree of trade regulation can be justified on analytical and practical grounds is of itself a valid defense of mercantilist thought, is erroneous and leads rather to a forceful criticism of it, since it is a pervasive characteristic of mercantilist literature that it advocates *permanent* restrictions of various kinds on foreign trade without reference to a maximum degree of restriction which is desirable, or to the conditions required to be present if such restriction is to be defensible. An analogous case would be if the practice of unrestrained and persistent inflation were defended on the ground that expansion of the money-supply and a rise in prices are beneficial during the downward phase of a business cycle. It is paradoxical that economic historians frequently in this essentially unhistorical manner defend mercantilism in general by appeal to historical episodes where the use of mercantilist devices was (fortuitously or otherwise) temporarily associated with conditions of downward-pressure on the price-structure.

In any case, the mercantilist devices of a non-force type used persistently included such practices as duties on or prohibitions of import and export; subsidies, direct and indirect, to export; regulations, intended to be restrictive of import of commodities, governing currency and foreign-exchange transactions; and restrictions on interest and wage levels intended to foster exports or to facilitate domestic competition with imports. When combined with these devices there were added the noncommercial instruments of mercantilist policy: "trade wars"; conquest and monopolization of colonial areas; monopolization by force of trade-routes and open-seas fisheries; monopolization by force of the slave-trade; and so forth, it seems difficult to me to understand how so many scholars, including economists, can defend mercantilism not only on strictly national grounds but as sensible and appropriate doctrine even from a non-nationalistic point-of-view. I must repeat, however, that disapproval of mercantilism from both national and cosmopolitan points of view should not be carried to the extent of adopting an opposite error: that of the complete harmony of real economic interest between countries.

In my first lecture, I gave some account of the doctrine of "universal economy," perhaps more appropriately to be labelled the doctrine of "economic universalism" and I stated that it continued to be widely expounded from ancient times through the Middle Ages to the modern age. There would appear to be a sharp and irreconcilable conflict between economic universalism and mercantilism, and economic universalism had attained so general and unquestioned acceptance as maxim that it must have been an embarrassment to mercantilists.

There is not much concrete evidence, however, of such embarrassment. Many mercantilists made no reference to the doctrine, perhaps as deliberate avoidance. None, as far as I know, attacked it or expressly disassociated themselves from it. Some mercantilists expressly invoked it as an argument against specific restrictions of trade or specific types of resort to force as an instrument of gain, while refraining from reference to it when arguing for other types of mercantilist practice of which they approved. Thus Montchretien, who was a convinced advocate of restrictions on import of *commodities*, was hostile to restrictions on the movement of *merchants*, and appealed to the doctrine of economic universalism as condemnatory of such restrictions. John Campbell while arguing for import and export duties, appealed to the economic universalism argument against absolute prohibitions of import or export, which would constitute "a kind of breach of the law of nations." It was used by mercantilists, as for example by Edward VI of England in 1553, in connection with his sending a mission of exploration to the

Far East, as an argument why countries should not be permitted (or would not be justified) in maintaining closed frontiers to trade. Perhaps the most interesting use of the argument by mercantilists was the one I referred to in my first lecture, whereby by a subtle distortion the argument was made to serve trade-restrictionist purposes. From the many available texts, I cite from a tract by Daniel Defoe in which he attributes, with approval, the argument to Henry VII of England:

> Henry VII justly inferred that Heaven having been so bountiful to England as to give her the wool, as it were, in a peculiar grant, exclusive of the whole world, it was a mere rebellion against His Providence, and particularly ungrateful to His Bounty, that the English nation should reject the offer, give away the blessing, and by an unaccountable neglect send their wool abroad to be manufactured, and even buy their own cloth of the Flemings with ready money.

Here the doctrine is used as an argument for the preemption of manufacturing by the countries which produce the raw materials. It has been used also as an argument for the preemption of manufacturers by countries in temperate zones, or by "advanced" countries. It has been charged in recent times by economists writing on behalf of the underdeveloped countries that economists in the English classical school have in essence invoked a static law of comparative costs as if Providence had permanently assigned to England manufacturing and to the underdeveloped countries the extractive industries. I cannot find any confirmation of this in the writings of the English classical school, but I can find something very close to it in, of all places, the major work of the historically most important critic of the English classical school in the field of international trade doctrine, Friedrich List. In his *The National System of Political Economy*, he writes:

> A country of the torrid zone would make a very fatal mistake, should it try to become a manufacturing country. *Having received no invitation to that vocation from nature*, it will progress more rapidly in riches and civilization if it continues to exchange its agricultural productions for the manufactured products of the temperate zone.

In the regulation of foreign trade, the mercantilist countries used a variety of administrative devices. In a number of countries, state trading-monopolies were established with respect to particular commodities, and especially minerals where the country in question was an important source of world-supply, notably, the Swedish tar monopoly and the Papal alum monopoly, in which latter case excommunication was used as a weapon against those who turned from the Papal source to the Turkish infidels for their supplies; or with respect to trade-areas, as in the case of the Portuguese colonial trade under Pombal, and of French, German, and other state-owned trading companies.

In England and Holland recourse was had to privately-owned and managed but state-chartered and state-regulated companies with monopoly privileges, and with varying degrees of subordination of the individual members (or share-owners) of the company to the company as a whole in the conduct of commercial operations. The British and the Dutch East Indies Companies, the British Muscovy and Royal African Companies, the South Seas Company, are famous instances.

English individual merchants, though convinced and extreme mercantilists, could in the name of "free trade" consistently oppose violently either state-operated monopolies or state-chartered monopolies into which they could not obtain entrance, or could not obtain entrance on terms satisfactory to themselves. As a result, there is an abundance of English pleas for "free-trade" throughout two centuries before Adam Smith was to make the first English systematic case for free trade in the sense in which we understand the term today. What "free-trade" meant as a rule before the days of Adam Smith was either freedom of trade from state-owned or state-chartered monopolies, or freedom of any merchant of good standing to enter a chartered or "regulated" trading-company on equal terms with other members, but without opposition to the operation of the company as a whole on monopoly principles.

The English mercantilist businessman was for obvious reasons violently opposed to state-owned and state-operated monopolies, and often expressed his opposition in terms of a plea for "freedom." Adam Smith, *per contra*, maintained that where monopoly was necessary or desirable, it was preferable that the monopoly should be a state-owned and state-operated one rather than a private one, and cited in support of his position the superior record of the state-owned Portuguese East India Company as compared to the privately-owned British East India Company.

In England after 1660, mercantilism was associated with an extraordinarily large degree of private enterprise. Although the statute books were heavy with regulatory legislation, there was a minimum of national governmental machinery for the enforcement of this legislation. It was something like a police state without official policemen; a meddlesome government without a bureaucracy. This paradox was accomplished by a really extraordinary combination of devices which, I believe, you will be troubled to find descriptions of in the textbook histories of England or accounts of its eighteenth century government.

Routine governmental functions were "farmed" or contracted out to private enterprise: handling of the public debt, to the Bank of England; some taxes to private tax-farmers; government printing to private printers.

Other services which elsewhere were governmental were in England partially or completely left in the hands of franchised businessmen operating for profit: lighthouses and rescue and salvage work, to Trinity House; supply to the army of food, uniforms, etc. left in the hands of the officers, who thus recouped themselves for having to buy their commissions; officers and crews of the navy, and providers and outfitters of ships, paid in whole or in part from their earnings in prize-money; high officials of the mint paid in whole or in part by the privilege of using mint facilities in refining and assaying precious metals for their private customers; operation of the prisons chartered to private individuals operating for a profit derived from sale of food and privileges to the prisoners.

The administration of justice and the execution of other "public" functions was decentralized and left to local volunteer, unsalaried, and unprofessional "officials," who either rendered these services without remuneration as a service to the community, or who found their remuneration in various perquisites and opportunities for profit, legitimate or otherwise, associated with their functions.

The detection of offenses against the law, protection against potential offenders, the detention and prosecution of offenders, was left as a field for private enterprise, so that there were no "policemen"; guards and watchmen were privately hired and paid, crime was detected and prosecuted by volunteer "informers" who obtained their pay through a share in the penalties imposed by the court; vagrants and beggars were apprehended by local landlords or farmers, in order either to expel them from the locality and thus bring about a lowering of the "poor rates," or to get first call on their forced labor at strictly regulated rates of pay; and so forth.

Statues wherever practicable were so framed as to make it to the interest of injured parties to carry out the tasks of identification, apprehension, and prosecution of the offenders.

While France and England, therefore, were about equally "mercantilistic," there were striking differences in the administrative aspects of French "Colbertisme" and what, for England, might be called "government regulation through private enterprise." This peculiar combination of free enterprise, of a bureaucracy of minimal proportions, and nevertheless of comprehensive state regulation of industry and commerce, has led to a widespread confusion of the English eighteenth century system of government outside the area of collection and administration of customs duties with genuine "laissez faire," with "economic freedom," and with "liberalism."

This system did not arise accidentally, but responded to the wishes of the ruling classes. These wanted regulation of trade and industry in a mercantilistic spirit. They disliked, however, personal contact with officialdom; they wanted cheap government; they feared the consequences for parliamentary sovereignty of an extensive body of highly-paid officials, under executive or monarchial control; they had no confidence in either the integrity or the efficiency of the typical official or "placeman"; they were aware that the patronage made possible by the availability of government jobs was generally used as a political instrument in elections and in the subornation of members of parliament.

In 1753 the Government submitted to Parliament what as far as is now known was an innocent bill to take a census of population and of employment, which failed of passage because of strong opposition. The grounds for opposing the bill were stated by one opponent, William Thornton, in terms which reveal how extraordinarily strong the hostility to *administration* could be among persons who were not hostile to legislation:

> Our enemies abroad are the Spaniards and the French, and our enemies at home are place-men and tax-masters; and I should ill deserve the confidence placed in me by my constituents, if I should concur to increase the knowledge or the power of either, which has, with equal assiduity and perseverance been employed against us.

If the Englishman before Adam Smith demanded "freedom" or "liberty," it was not something abstract or general but a particular collection of specific "freedoms" or "liberties." In the field of government, it was freedom from monarchial prerogative; from a powerful bureaucracy; from personal contact with uniformed officialdom. It was *not* freedom from regulatory legislation enacted by Parliament with "due process of law," and administered either by unpaid local magistrates or by judicial process in the courts of the realm. An Englishman like William Thornton could, without any consciousness of inconsistency, and probably also without any inconsistency in fact, violently oppose the "inquisition" of a census-taker while advocating laws to regulate exports and imports, to set maximum prices or maximum or minimum wages, or to prescribe the minimum width to which woolen cloth could be woven or the minimum width of the rims of wagon-wheels, or to prohibit combinations of workers or of employers.

LECTURE III

The Emergence of Free-Trade and Laissez-Faire Doctrine

In my treatment in this lecture of the emergence of doctrines of "economic freedom," I will confine myself to intellectual history, thus evading any attempt to tackle the difficult problem of tracing the influence on analysis or convictions of external material circumstances, or of "social forces." I of course would not presume to claim that the doctrines of free trade, and of laissez faire in general, were a product of pure thought, independent of change in environment and especially of changes in technology and in social structure. A crude form of determinism I will deny, however, namely that the free-trade doctrine—or the doctrine of laissez faire—arose merely or even predominantly because there evolved a social group or class whose felt interest was in free trade and who spoke or found spokesmen to hire on behalf of this doctrine. This is speculatively conceivable, and in some degree has visible historical substantiation. But I can trace no significant personal vested interest in free trade of any of its prominent exponents or of their immediate circles of friends, relatives, or occupational associates: the physiocrats, Adam Smith, the Manchester School, the neo-classical economists, English and American. All of these sought the support of interested groups, but none of them was, as far as I can determine, a member of an interested group.

The history of free-trade doctrine is largely a history of a phase of laissez-faire doctrine, but they are not to be identified with each other too closely. For economists, free trade has often been merely one important application of a general principle of non-interference beyond more-or-less specified narrow limits of government with private enterprise. But some of the more vehement exponents of laissez faire in general, notably American businessmen in the nineteenth century, and their legal spokesmen, were extreme protectionists and interventionists when tariff policy was in question. This was also, I believe, true of the Careys, or of the "Philadelphia School" of American economists. Nor need this be accepted as *prima facie* demonstration of intellectual confusion or inconsistency, unless it is logically absurd to refrain from carrying every general proposition to its "logical" conclusion. It can be made intellectually respectable to adhere to laissez faire on internal matters and to protection in the foreign trade field by distinguishing between a "national" and a "cosmopolitan" point of view and arguing that while the benefits and the costs of internal laissez faire all accrue to members of the nation, none of the benefits and much of the costs of protection accrued to foreigners. It is important, therefore, in appraising the analytical quality of doctrine in this field to determine as best one can whether its exponents are arguing from a national or a cosmopolitan point of view.

It is possible also to adhere with intellectual consistency to both internal laissez faire and protection while taking a cosmopolitan or universalist point of view if one can find significant and relevant differentia because of technical or institutional factors between internal economic process and the character of economic transactions which cross national boundaries: for example, free competition internally, the predominance of monopoly abroad; low income levels at home, higher income levels abroad, and an income-levelling tendency of the application of protection by low-income countries. The association of free trade with "freedom" moreover is not necessarily one of identity, as note the attempt of England, in its free-trade period, to impose free trade, successfully in the case of India and the Crown Colonies, unsuccessfully in the case of Canada and the Australian colonies, by the exercise of its imperial dominance.

In tracing the evolution of doctrines of economic freedom, it is necessary to take certain precautions lest there result distortion of history. Changes in the uses of terms must be explored, and the dangers of describing the thought of an earlier period by means of later terms or concepts unknown to them must be guarded against. Care must be taken lest the dominant thought of a period by misinterpreted on the basis of unrepresentative texts or writers. For instance, while the terms "liberty" and "freedom," or their equivalents in other languages were widely used from ancient times, no attempt ever seems to have been made until the eighteenth century to give them a general or "abstract" meaning in the economic, or, for that matter, in the political field. When concrete and specific issues were under discussion, reference was normally to specific "liberties" or "freedoms," not to "liberty" in general or "freedom" in general. Even when specific "liberties" were being discussed, it was commonly explained even by their enthusiastic exponents that it was "liberty within the law," not an unqualified liberty to do as one pleases, which would be "license," that was being advocated. It was, even with reference to specific liberties, liberty from specified actual or potential exercise of authority rather than liberty from all external authority that often and perhaps generally was advocated. Of the notion of adding specific liberties to each other so as to obtain a maximum quantity of liberty in general, I can find no clear trace before the eighteenth century.

When the term "freedom" was used in England it meant the freedom of Englishmen from non-English authority or from monarchical or ecclesiastical authority, not freedom from all authority. It often meant rejection of a mild exercise of authority by a disliked agency in order to submit without complaint to a more severe but accepted agency of coercion. There is little convincing evidence, I believe, that advocacy of specific liberties from specific coercive agencies for specific groups or categories of persons was historically, markedly elastic or extensible to other coercive agencies or to members of other groups of persons. Protestant sects, for example, were for several centuries advocates of religious freedom for themselves. I am not convinced that the common opinion is correct that this led them in thought or in practice to be advocates of political freedom in general, of economic freedom in general, or even of religious freedom in general, except accidentally as their own religious freedom seemed to them to be attainable only by the conquest of other kinds of freedom for themselves or by the extension to other sects of the religious freedom they sought for themselves. The common association of religious freedom with political and economic freedom and all of them with Protestantism seems to me of highly questionable historical validity.

In the same way I would question the association which some scholars make between the ''common law'' and ''economic freedom,'' or the broader and more philosophic theory, as expounded notably by Professor Hayek, that of the association of economic freedom with the possibility of the gradual evolution of social cohesion and social institutions from the spontaneous and atomistic initiative of countless individuals, not only without original blueprints and comprehensive master-plans, but without systematic guidance or moulding or constraint by formal agencies of government.

It is true of English common law, as I suppose also of continental customary law and of local or ''vulgar'' Roman law, that it escaped systematic and formal codification by any central authority. ''Government,'' whether absolute monarch or a statute-making council or legislature of some kind, either substantially left the existing common law without interference beyond providing the power to support the magistrates in its enforcement, or, if government did go beyond this, it was, almost by definition, substituting another kind of law, official decree or legislative statute, for the common law, even if it claimed only to be ''declaring'' rather than ''making'' the law. But it seems to be the historical fact that in England statutory law was important from late medieval times on, that common law was residual law in the sense that it operated only in the area which the statute-making authorities chose not to cover, and that even in that residual area statute law provided guides and analogies which were freely drawn on by the magistrates applying common law.

Also, it is true that, in the main, the body of common law grew by a cumulative, gradual, and unplanned process of building precedent on precedent, in England these ''precedents'' consisting of actual cases, or perhaps more accurately of reports and recollections of actual cases, on the Continent of the opinions and hypothetical cases expounded by judicial scholars who were not necessarily and not generally practicing magistrates.

What I question is that it has been or can be demonstrated by historical evidence that the common law was predominantly governed, in principle or in practice, by a general hostility to governmental intervention in economic process, or that it can be convincingly argued that spontaneous, unplanned, gradual development of social institutions is necessarily more conducive to "economic freedom" in the sense of freedom from governmental regulation than is planned and systematic legislation.

The thesis that the common law has inherent in it a marked bias against governmental intervention in the economic field can be plausibly supported for England, I believe, only by a partial selection of evidence, aside perhaps from the special period 1600 to 1640, where unpopular government aroused opposition from common law lawyers as part of a general popular opposition, and where the unpopularity of government was in large part owing to the fact that it was using novel agencies and novel procedures to impose novel types and degrees of constraint on the economic activities of private individuals.

The common law lawyer inevitably has a professional jealousy of other forms of law-making than through court decision invoking past court decisions. In the Stuart period, law was not only being promulgated without the normal recourse to Parliament, on the basis of monarchical prerogative, but new courts had been established which decided cases without appeal either to statutes or to past court decisions. It was in this period that Sir Edward Coke appealed to the common law as a traditional barrier to the interference by government with the economic and other "freedoms" of the individual. It seems now to be generally agreed, however, that Coke distorted and misinterpreted the past common law tradition to make it seem strongly favorable to what we would now call economic liberalism. Moreover, even to Coke, "liberty" in the common law sense was a very much narrower, a very much more specific and limited obstacle to government action, than the "liberty" or "freedom" of nineteenth century liberal thought. It was a maxim of Coke himself that "the common law will rather suffer a private injury than a public inconvenience," and common law lawyers no less than bureaucrats or legislators were fully adept at discovering public inconveniences. It was not, moreover, against parliamentary statutes but against royal prerogative and newfangled courts that in the Stuart period common law lawyers joined with others in doing battle on behalf of freedom, although it was in this period that legal force seemed first to have been claimed, a claim never to be successful in English legal history, for the doctrine that there was a body of "fundamental law," a "higher law," which magistrates could evoke against even statutes of Parliament enacted with "due process of law."

For there to be an inherent bias in the common law in favor of ''freedom'' or ''liberty'' of the individual as against government in general, certain conditions are prerequisite:

(a) there must be conflict or tension between the ''people'' or an influential class or group thereof and the regular state agencies on matters in which specific individual ''liberties'' or ''freedoms'' are involved;

(b) the friction or tension arises out of an attempt of government to cancel or to restrict the ''liberties'' or ''freedoms'' which this group or class had habitually enjoyed;

(c) the loyalties or subjective commitments of the judges and lawyers are to these ''freedoms'' or ''liberties''—or to the group enjoying or seeking to enjoy them—rather than to the agencies of government seeking to abolish them;

(d) what the relevant group or class wants is the protection of old or the establishment of new liberties for its own members, not the suppression of old liberties of members of other groups or classes nor the establishment at the expense of its own members of new liberties for other groups or classes.

Only when all of these conditions are met will the common law lawyers be found unambiguously on the side of ''freedom.''

Hayek, in his argument for the possibility of spontaneous and unplanned evolution of complex social institutions, not requiring governmental initiation or systematic regulation for their existence, rightly cites Mandeville's examples of the development of language and of the art of ship-building. Mandeville's exposition was truly a pioneer and a brilliant one; the evolution of common law could plausibly be cited as an additional illustration, if a sharp distinction could rightly be made between law-making by the common law courts and ''governmental'' law-making, which would, as a minimum, presumably require the assumption that it was not ''government'' which selected the magistrates and that ''government'' exercised no disciplinary power over them. But Mandeville cannot be appropriately cited in support of the application to all and especially to economic institutions of this theory of spontaneous generation and development, without the involvement of government, of needed and complex social institutions. For Mandeville applied his theory to the evolution of the governmental regulative machine itself, to explain why, for example, the extremely complex system of governmental regulation which was needed to keep a great city like London going could have evolved without need of inventive geniuses, of comprehensive blue-prints, and of extensive advance planning.

The credit for pioneer formulation of a *general* doctrine of economic freedom from governmental regulation, as distinguished from selective advocacy of specific "freedom," belongs to the physiocrats and to Adam Smith, and in neither case do I see important indebtedness either to a common law tradition or to earlier doctrines of general freedom. As is always the case, however, they built up their general case for laissez faire with the help of detailed items of doctrine or analysis which had been expounded by earlier writers. Their originality consisted largely in building up a case for economic "freedom" in a generalized sense from earlier arguments for a varying but always limited and selective schedule of specific or particular "freedoms." The most important earlier sources on which they built were, I believe, social philosophies which without discussing expressly the appropriate economic functions of government analyzed the elements in the physical and the social order of nature which tended toward a self-operating and beneficial pattern of social behavior of mankind, notably Cumberland, Shaftesbury, and Hutcheson, who emphasized the non-egoistic, cooperative instincts and sentiments of man, and Mandeville and others who stressed the extent to which considerations of self-interest entered into patterns of socially-useful mutual exchange of services on a contractual basis. I should point out, however, that in the case of Mandeville, as in the case of the Jansenist, Pierre Nicole, from whom he borrowed, the emergence of public virtue or benefit from self-interested activity, or "private vices," could be relied upon to occur on a large scale only if government restricted, guided, bribed individuals in conformity with a pattern which would channel their activity into paths in harmony with the public good. In Mandeville's language, "private vices" are "public virtues" only "when skilfully managed by the able politician."

Another important source from which the physiocrats and Adam Smith probably drew indirectly, and which in any case created receptivity in the minds of the public for their laissez-faire doctrines, was the rise of the large-scale merchant, with ability to formulate, or to find talent able and willing to formulate for him, a reasoned exposition of his useful role in society if left largely or wholly to his own devices. The Renaissance magnates of Florence and Venice provide some notable examples, but I will limit myself to citing from a brief prepared by Konrad Peutinger, the able jurist who served the sixteenth century German family of great merchants, the Fuggers. In 1530, the municipal council of Nurenberg proposed to the German Diet the enactment of an ordinance directed mainly against the Fuggers which, among other things, would limit the number of partners, the amount of capital used, and the number of branches, to be permitted to any one business firm. In his brief attacking this proposal, Peutinger defended the social usefulness and the legitimacy not only of private enterprise, but of large-scale private enterprise. I will paraphrase the more interesting and relevant portions of his lengthy brief.

When merchants sell grain at a higher price than that at which they bought it, this does not mean that they are a monopoly, or that they are doing something unlawful; every merchant seeks to sell his wares at as high a price as possible and he does not thereby violate any law.

Large-scale trade reduces the cost per unit and thus reduces prices. It is true that many firms had failed and that others had undergone heavy losses. But this was nothing new and had nothing to do with monopoly. No man was compelled to invest his money in such enterprises; what a man does of his free will cannot be imputed as an injury inflicted by someone else: *unde volenti nil fit injuria*. With respect to the proposed provision that maximum prices should be set for all commodities, this would be counter to the common law and would bring damage to German trade. The agreements needed with foreign states, so that German merchants could buy foreign goods within the price-limits fixed, would not be obtainable. The provision would be unenforceable for such commodities as spices, wine, grain, whose prices vary with the harvests and with the quantities brought to the Lisbon market. No German would pursue a trade where extra gains were prohibited, but losses were possible. If as a result Germans would be forced out of overseas trade, profits would go to foreigners while prices in Germany would be higher. It is not possible for Germans to establish a monopoly, and such a strait jacket on trade would involve a greater menace to the welfare of individuals and of the community than would a monopoly.

Every man, be he priest or laic, prince, gentleman or burgher, wholesale or retail merchant, peasant or whatever else, has the right to seek his enrichment in an honorable way, to manage his estate so as to make it yield income, and in general to pursue his own self-interest, especially as it serves also the common good that a land should have rich inhabitants.

To require as was proposed annual reports to make sure that the permitted maximum capital was not exceeded would violate all trade customs, under which no one is required to reveal to a stranger his profits or losses. No large-scale merchant has the time to spare to make such reports.

The merchant often hazards not only money and estate, but his life; at least as much as do those who acquire wealth by less active means. The trade gains of firms are a benefit not only to themselves, but also to many others, above all to the princes and landlords, who (indirectly) derive more benefit from large-scale trade than do the merchants directly engaged in it, but who have no losses to bemoan.

It would therefore be inexcusable to place obstacles before the activities of men who have the ambition in accordance with the precepts of God, of honor and of law, to increase their estate and by enlarging their investments to raise in lawful manner their personal incomes.

This is, you will agree, quite modern-sounding, and provides rich material for a generalized laissez-faire doctrine. It is not, however, itself laissez-faire doctrine. From its content, its context, and other statements by Peutinger and by the Fuggers, we know that it was not governmental regulation in general or in principle which was being objected to, but specific forms or degrees of it, and not ''freedom'' which was being defended, but specific forms and degrees of it.

I turn now to an English author who is often cited as one of the sources of English laissez-faire doctrine, but is even more often cited as an early exponent of the totalitarian state, Thomas Hobbes. I do not think it is difficult to explain how Hobbes came to be for some the arch type of the totalitarian and for others a pioneer exponent of liberal doctrine. Hobbes was an exponent of centralization of coercive power, of its monopolization by the sovereign. That is why he is regarded by many as an exponent of totalitarianism. But, like the later physiocrats, who were greatly influenced by him, he wanted power centralized in order to minimize its use, in order that no one except the sovereign should be in a position to exercise coercion over individuals. The sovereign should exercise the power under his command only for legitimate purposes and to the minimum degree consistent with the realization of such purposes. In all his many writings there is very little advocacy of any use by the sovereign of his power except for national defense and to assemble, and so-to-speak to put under lock-and-key so that it would not be used, any segments of power which might otherwise be available for use by Church, by private armies, or by particular social groups. That is why some scholars have perceived in Hobbes an exponent of liberalism.

For the physiocrats, the role of the state is also primarily to collect and monopolize all the available power, so that it should not be used. The economic order, if left alone, would through the mutual harmony of self-interest of individuals work with optimum benefit to society, with the major function of government to educate the people so that they would see the merits of a self-operating economy.

In Adam Smith's system as applied to the social behavior in general of mankind, the beneficial outcome of laissez faire results from the social instincts imbedded in human nature, as well as from the ''moral sentiments'': sympathy for others, the desire for social approval, the dictates of conscience, and, to a minor extent, benevolence towards others. In the economic market-place, as described in the *Wealth of Nations*, the beneficial outcome of laissez faire is ascribed to other factors than instincts and social sentiments. Within the family, in relations with one's friends and one's immediate neighbors, in one's operations as a patriotic citizen of one's country, the instincts, the social sentiments, conscience, patriotism, suffice to produce a good society. In the market, however, one is dealing as with strangers; to use later terminology, the market is "anonymous." The social sentiments, therefore, are not aroused into action, and man behaves in response to calculating, rational self-interest. Fortunately, however, the nature of economic process is such, it involves such a high degree of harmony of interests between the individuals participating in it, that, provided only that government enforces the rules of justice, it need do little else to assure a flourishing economy.

It is not clear that Adam Smith believed that laissez faire would maximize the wealth of a nation in terms of a theoretically conceivable maximum. What is clear is that subject to a vaguely-defined list of qualifications, economic society left to its autonomous operation would produce a higher level of economic welfare than would accrue if government, inefficient, ignorant, and profligate, as in practice it was, should try to direct or regulate it. Beyond, moreover, its material benefits, it is clear that for Adam Smith laissez faire had ethical or moral value in that it left to the individual unimpaired the "liberty" to which he had a natural right. It is quite probable, therefore, that Adam Smith would have rejected an extensive program of state regulation of economic enterprise even if he had believed that the wealth of nations could thereby be augumented.

LECTURE IV

Monopoly and Laissez Faire

Modern advocates of an approach to laissez faire recognize that whatever rationale it has rests on the assumption that economic society under laissez faire would be, or could be made to be substantially competitive. Towards the monopolistic aspects of modern society they take various attitudes. Some look upon them as serious obstacles to economic welfare, and would have an otherwise laissez-faire state vigorously suppress all important manifestations of monopoly that are not for special reasons to be accepted. Others maintain that government itself is, directly or indirectly, the major support of monopoly and that in a laissez-faire economy monopoly, with minor exceptions, would not be able either to establish or to maintain itself in the absence of government support. Others while expressing in principle hostility to monopoly deny its practical importance and contend that in the main moderate elements of monopoly can be tolerated without serious loss, or even with benefit, in a predominantly competitive, laissez-faire economy; like the competitive "economic man," the monopolistic firm, without intending it, is as if guided by an invisible hand, serving the public interest. A sketch of the history of attitudes toward monopoly may be of interest in connection with this issue.

The concept of monopoly as the exclusive or almost exclusive control over the supply of a commodity or service by a single firm or person and of such control giving its possessor arbitrary power over the price of the monopolized commodity is ancient. Monopoly power is frequently referred to in the classical Greek literature, and in ancient Rome there was specific legislation against it. The term itself, in its Latin form, *monopolium*, is also ancient. The word "monopoly" apparently made its first appearance in the English language around 1600, but the idea was much older, and in the original Latin version of More's Utopia (1516) not only does the term *monopolium* appear as meaning control over the supply of a commodity by a single seller or association of sellers, but also the term *oligopolium*, as meaning control over supply by a small number of sellers operating independently. Becher, an Austrian cameralist of the seventeenth century, distinguished between: *monopolium*, control by a single person; *propolium*, a small number of sellers acting independently; and *polypolium*, a large number of competing sellers, or an approximation of our concept of "atomistic competition."

While logical distinctions between degrees of monopoly or competition were thus not wholly absent in older times, there was of course a good deal of loose and imprecise verbal and analytical usage, and also a good deal of misplaced precision of terminology. I will confine my comments to English usage, although similar practice occurred on the Continent. The term "monopoly" was frequently applied to any trade where there was a legal or a legally-sanctioned restriction on entry, as in the case of the English "regulated companies," even if, aside from a general code of behavior involving protection to buyers rather than the reverse, the members competed freely with each other. In form, and to some degree in practice, such a "regulated company" could represent the substitution of self-regulation for formal law, common, or administrative, or statutory, intended to protect buyers against abuse or fraud or monopolistic exploitation. Even the restrictions on entry into such companies, moreover, were often mild and incomplete, since membership of any regulated company or "guild" often gave the right to practice the trade or craft of any other guild, though not the right to participate in guild-management.

Until the time of the classical school, it seems to have been the usual practice to restrict the term "monopoly" to either government monopolies or private monopolies operating under official charter or sanction of some sort. The English classical school, however, used the term with both extreme narrowness and extreme looseness, but found little manifestation of the fact of monopoly in the strict sense in actual practice. They tended to define "monopoly," expressly or by implication, narrowly, so as to restrict it to control by a single seller or organized group of sellers, and to leave unexamined the phenomena lying between perfect monopoly and perfect competition. On the other hand, they sometimes applied the term monopoly to specific practices which might lead to the establishment of monopoly power, but need not necessarily do so, such as "forestalling" and "regrating." As in earlier times also, they applied the term "monopoly" to a situation where a single country was the sole source of supply of a commodity, i.e., a "national monopoly," even if there was full competition between the individual sellers. They applied the term also to a situation where a commodity, or factor of production, or service, had, or was believed to have, what we now call "zero elasticity of supply," so that a higher price would not bring out a larger quantity. The chief usage of this kind was in connection with land, so that land-rent was spoken of as if it were a monopoly revenue. Similar usage was followed in connection with old masters, or antiquarian books or manuscripts.

There was also a general failure on the part of the classical school, when dealing with monopoly, to recognize the restraint on the power of a monopolist to raise price indefinitely arising out of the existence of a higher-than-unity elasticity of demand on the part of potential buyers. Express recognition of this limitation on the monopolist's power seems first to have come with Galiani in the eighteenth century. Rigorous mathematical demonstration of it was first achieved by Cournot, in France, in 1838, and by Charles Ellet, in the United States, in 1839, and no instance of such demonstration seems to have occurred in England before the 1870's.

The attitude towards monopoly in its strict sense, and especially towards private monopoly, was almost invariably hostile in the literature of ancient Greece and Rome, in the theological and canonist texts of the Middle Ages, and in early English common law. The resort by the Stuarts to the grant of monopoly franchises and "patents" to raise revenue without need of resort to Parliament and to reward friends intensified the hostility of Englishmen, and especially of the common law lawyers, to monopolies. The grant of charters to joint-stock or to "regulated" companies was also regarded with suspicion as facilitating the establishment of monopoly. Parliament insisted on such grants being made only by individual Acts of Parliament, with each charter containing specific restrictions on the kind of activity to be permitted and on the size of the company, to guard against the danger of monopoly, and with the charters requiring Parliamentary renewal at stated intervals.

For companies operating in foreign trade there was less opposition to the legalization of the exercise of monopoly power. It was argued that any exercise of monopoly power would be at the expense of foreigners. English merchants operating abroad, it was claimed, both needed to be carefully regulated so as not to discredit English businessmen in general or otherwise do injury to English national interests, and to be given unity and cohesion in their dealings with foreign authorities and in their rivalry with foreign monopolies. As far as the merchant class was concerned, it seems clear that it was favorable to the organization of foreign trade on a monopoly basis and that, with only rare exceptions, the merchants who did object had a personal vested interest arising out of their exclusion from membership in such companies or from particular objections to the mode of management of these companies. Then, as perhaps always, merchants were hostile mainly to monopolies which they were excluded from or could not enter on their own terms.

In England the chartered companies operating in foreign trade were all private and, subject to the limitations of their charters and to the general statutory restrictions on trade and on transactions in bullion applicable to all alike, were left unregulated and free from inspection or supervision by government as far as day-to-day operations were concerned. Their mode of operation, however, usually came up for searching examination and criticism, in Parliament and outside, when charters came up for renewal. The criticisms were in large part directed to alleged violation of English mercantilistic legislation, or to the conduct of trade in conflict with national trade objectives, but there were also charges of unduly restrictive conditions of entry and of unfair competition with and persecution of non-members.

The only economic activity of the government in foreign territory was the operation of the mail service, as part of the Royal Prerogative. When by a decision of the Privy Council in 1627 merchants were permitted to operate an independent foreign post a high government official (Sir John Coke) objected on the ground that private post would mean uncensored post and that this was ''unfit a time . . . to give libertie to everie man to write and send what hae list. . . .'' But this was a special case, and until Adam Smith no one seems to have questioned the wisdom of the practice of leaving the government as well as the trade of some overseas colonies—as notably in the case of the East Indies Company—in the hands of a private company.

On the Continent, the role of the government in the management and operation of the great chartered companies went much further than in England, although varying from company to company. What was generally true was that each such company operated on monopolistic principles, and that even when, as in Holland, except for the Dutch East Indies Company, there were no chartered companies, the merchants in particular trades organized themselves quietly into cartels and price-rings. What competition there was in the international trade of the mercantilist-period was confined largely, though far from wholly, to competition between national trading companies, who, as far as they could, used force, their own or that of their governments, to maintain as exclusive control as they could over the trade of specific territories and over specific trade-routes.

The superiority in general of a market in which competition prevailed over a monopolistically-controlled one was often at least implied whenever a specific monopoly was under attack, and in their writings the physiocrats presented substantially along its modern lines the positive case for competition. Adam Smith, however, was the first economist to make monopoly in general a major target, and to bring against it the full weight of such command of economic analysis as he possessed.

Adam Smith intensely disliked monopoly in all its forms, and chiefly because he regarded them as inevitably attaining or seeking monopoly power, he disliked all large-scale companies. The large-scale company, he held, can be efficient only when its activities can be confined to routine operations. Even then it is objectionable unless the large-scale operation has greater utility than the small-scale or unless greater capital is needed than can be collected by an ordinary copartnership.

Where monopoly was needed, and especially where, as in the case of India, trade needed to be combined with the exercise of governing power, Adam Smith preferred a government-owned and government-operated monopoly company, such as the Portuguese East India Company, to a privately-owned and managed one, such as the British East Indies Company.

Adam Smith carried his dislike of monopoly to extreme lengths, and it runs through his repeated scathing remarks about businessmen, and their monopolizing tendencies.

He, for example, in 1774, in a letter to Dr. Cullen, opposed restricting the practice of medicine to those holding university degrees or passing required examinations, on the ground that these restrictions would be used as sources of revenue to the institutions involved, or as means of raising the fees which could be charged, but without relieving the public from dependence on the reputation of practitioners and on their own good judgment for protection against quackery and incompetence. Dr. Cullen, who had argued for some measure of regulation of entrance into the profession, replied to Smith's argument that it was an illusion that the ordinary lay individual could judge of the merits of a medical man, but we do not know whether Smith replied, or what his reply would have been.

In one field of commerce, however, the internal corn trade, where opinion in general was most disposed to share his belief in the prevalence and the evil of a monopolizing tendency, Smith displayed a marked scepticism. It was here, he said, of all trades that monopoly is least possible of organization, because of the great size of the industry, the great number of dealers, and their general geographical dispersion. He also clearly believed that rural landlords and farmers were of all economic groups least disposed to seek monopoly profits, and that therefore their cooperation could not be obtained by would-be organizers of a corn-trade monopoly.

The English classical school followed Adam Smith in their dislike of and condemnation of monopoly. They extended, however, to almost the whole range of industry and trade Smith's argument re the corn-trade that the size of the task, the number of persons involved, and their dispersion over space, made the establishment of an enduring monopoly a practical impossibility. They incidentally applied this reasoning also to the question of the possibility of raising wages through the formation of trade-unions.

The general position of the classical school in this respect is accurately and compactly stated in the following quotation from David Buchanan:

> No body of traders ever can frame an effectual combination against the public, as all such engagements are broken by the partial interest of the individual concerned. No trader will keep up his prices for the profit of others; he will always sell when

it suits his own convenience, and upon this principle accordingly is founded all this rivalship of trade.

It seems to me that the later verdict that this was substantially erroneous reasoning is valid. Even in the corn-trade and high transportation costs of the period made a regional monopoly much less difficult to establish, at least temporarily, than Adam Smith supposed. It seems clear also that Adam Smith and his followers argued excessively from the tacit assumption that a monopoly which was temporary only or which was not "perfect" in the modern sense could not yield appreciable monpoly revenue. In any case, we now know that, apparently without exception, every English industry of the time whose history has been studied was riddled with price-rings or equivalent arrangements, often only on a regional basis but sometimes on a national basis. There is no *a priori* reason for assuming that these were predominantly or universally of negligible effect, and the fact that their practice was so widespread provides an empirical presumption that they brought to their practitioners in some significant degree the realization of their price-raising objectives.

To this scepticism of the English classical school about the possibility of monopoly must undoubtedly be attributed in significant part the absence of any anti-monopoly legislation in nineteenth-century England. On the other hand, it was the continued fear of monopoly when the scale of enterprise was large which was responsible for the withholding of general statutory sanction for the incorporation of limited-liability joint-stock companies without limitation as to scale of operations until after the middle of the century, and the classical economists of the time were divided as to the wisdom of this repeal of the ancient restrictions on "big business." It is quite clear that the general public was confused by the combination in the doctrine of the classical school of a pronounced condemnation in principle of monopoly and a refusal to recognize its existence in fact; a confusion well-expressed by a cartoon of the time which showed one of the marchers in a street-demonstration carrying a banner reading: "No Monopoly!" and another carrying a banner reading: "No Competition!"

LECTURE V

The "Economic Man," or The Place of Economic Self-Interest in a "Good Society"

Whatever school of social thought modern economists, moral philosophers, political scientists, or theologians, belong to, it has long seemed to me that they predominantly begin with radical misinterpretations of the thought of earlier schools of social thought with respect to the role of economic self-interest either in the world as it is in fact or in an ethically ideal world. In this lecture I will endeavor to make a minor contribution toward correction of these misinterpretations by means of a historical sketch of doctrine with respect to the role of economic self-interest in society, but the limitations of a single lecture will force me to restrict myself to comment on a selected number of high-spots in this history.

The worldly "prudent" man, the man who pursues only his self-interest, temporally-conceived so as to exclude concern for his religious salvation in another world, and somewhat narrowly conceived psychologically so that self-interest and "selfishness" become synonymous or nearly so, is an ancient concept. Until the eighteenth century it was regarded by practically all schools of social thought as a realistic concept, applicable to all mankind except for the occasional "saint." In the Christian tradition, especially in its Augustinian phase, it was associated intimately with the doctrines of the fall of man and of original sin, and in pre-Christian pagan thought it was associated with the myth of an original "Golden Age" which had passed away. Some of the early Christian Fathers combined the two myths, the one of the virtuous couple in the Garden of Eden before the fall, and the other of a golden age in which human society lived without avarice, rivalry, malice, or ambition. As they contrasted the sinful state of man in their own time with a flawless original state from which he had fallen, the pagan myth had the useful function of leaving scope for social analysis of the relations of men with each other in an ideal community larger than a single pair.

The "economic man," or the man for whom his economic interests are the sole or predominant interests, is, and has almost always been, the most common form or variant of the worldly prudent man, but there have been times when other forms of self-interest have received emphasis. "Avarice," *avaritia*, is a key term in the history of social doctrine, and this to us would suggest a strictly economic interpretation. It needs to be borne in mind, however, that "avarice" has often been given a broader meaning than a yearning—or an excessive yearning—for material possessions, for wealth, or for income. It has relevantly been noted, for instance, that avarice is likely to manifest itself, among aristocrats as ambition for status, prestige, power, among scholars and clergymen as vanity and pride, and only or chiefly among merchants or businessmen as lust for money and material possessions. But it has been mainly with respect to economic morale and the social consequences of economic behavior that there has been continuing interest from ancient times in the analysis of the moral status and social results of "avarice." Horace speaks ironically of the anxious flight of the merchant from any threat of impoverishment. Virgil speaks of the *auri socra fames* characteristic of much of mankind. The *fames insatiabilis mercatorum*, the insatiable hunger of the *merchant* for wealth, was a stereotype of the early Christian Fathers and of their medieval successors.

There has always been, even within the sphere of economic avarice, a tendency for theologians and poets and aristocrats to draw a class-line as between different manifestations of economic ambition, and to look with special scorn on the economic objectives of small-scale merchants. The merchant who confined himself to substantial transactions and who spent his earnings lavishly tended to escape harsh criticism in ancient Greece and Rome, and in Renaissance Italy. In England, there was—and continues to be—a tendency to look with approval, or to overlook the special forms which "avarice" could systematically take on the part of a wealthy landed-aristocracy, while the penny-pinching of the small retail merchant or the struggling master-craftsmen was looked upon with disgust. I know of no form of economic ambition which is less romantic when observed objectively than the dowry-practices of the English landed-aristocrats of past centuries. A few years ago I was told by the steward of a great and ancient East-Anglian estate that one of its masters said of his male ancestors that "they never let their love light except where the land lay." Even Adam Smith contrasted the financial behavior of great landlords, marked by "childish vanity" as in his judgment it was, not unfavorably with those of merchants and artificers, governed by "their own pedlar principle of turning a penny where a penny was to be got," and here as elsewhere he seemed strangely to overlook the fact that penny-grabbing and penny-pinching have psychologically at least a different significance for those to whom pennies are objectively important than for those to whom they are only subjectively so. In the appraisal of the economic activity of the middle classes there has always been a tendency for moralists and aristocrats to allow their verdicts to be subtly influenced by unconscious class-snobbery or intellectual arrogance.

The ascription to human nature along Augustinian lines of extreme subjection to material and selfish ends reached its highest, or most extreme, point in Calvinism in the Protestant tradition, and in Jansenism in the Catholic tradition. Paradoxically, it was adopted whole-heartedly, though with cynical intent, by the "libertine" or free-thinkers of the sixteenth to eighteenth centuries, from Montaigne, Charron, La Rochefoucauld on to Hobbes, Bayle and Mandeville. It was also adopted, as a matter of fact and without cynical or religious intent, by the mercantilists as a fundamental premiss of their economic analysis.

Hobbes, the Jansenists (especially Nicole and Domat), Mandeville, and the mercantilists in general drew from this belief as to the selfish nature of man and the worldly character of his objectives the conclusion that it was the major role of government to regulate, coerce, and bribe men, so that they would use the energy and drive which their selfish ends gave them in such patterns of behavior as, from at least a temporal point of view, would produce a flourishing and prosperous society. For Hobbes the major social end was peace, and in his view only a strong state, with a monopoly of power, could channel human activity in such manner as to produce internal peace, with prosperity as a valuable by-product. Nicole, not uninfluenced by Hobbes, drew the same conclusion, but given his Augustinian theology, he did not regard the end-result with the same enthusiasm as did Hobbes. The discipline imposed by a strong state could produce a society which looked at from outside would display harmony, mutual help, peace, and prosperity. But since the selfish motivation underlying it all was sinful, because it did not have *caritas*, or love of God, as its sole objective, such a society was rotten at heart, and all who participated in it on its own terms were doomed to eternal damnation. Mandeville, a libertine in both the technical and the popular sense, masquerading in Calvinist or Jansenist clothes, pretended to reach the same conclusions as those of Nicole, but it seems clear to me, as it did to all of his contemporaries though to few of his modern commentators, that it was the prosperity and the peace, and not the eternal damnation, which he took seriously.

The mercantilists took over the psychological doctrine that man was a selfish, or at least a self-regarding animal; they followed the unanimous opinion of their predecessors that out of individual selfishness unless regulated and disciplined by a superior authority, there could not come social prosperity; they accepted without scrutiny the proposition that for individuals (though not for governments or princes) the sole or predominant self-regarding interest were material or economic in character; they accepted man's selfish nature as a fact, without special interest in appraising it in moral or religious terms; they saw in an active and powerful government the only force strong enough and motivated soundly enough to harness all of this selfish energy to a desirable social, that is, national, set of objectives.

Beginning in the late seventeenth century but attaining importance as an influence only in the eighteenth and nineteenth centuries, opposition to this line of thought appeared on both theological and economic grounds, and out of this opposition emerged, by a complicated intellectual process, the laissez-faire doctrines of the physiocrats, of Adam Smith, of the English classical school, of the Manchester School, of their Continental and American nineteenth-century offshoots, and I suppose also of the present-day group which is sometimes on the Continent given, and which perhaps has accepted the label of "Neo-Liberals."

The Physiocrats arrived at their laissez-faire doctrine by way of a strange blend of a special species of providentialism, of Hobbsism, and of some fresh and important economic analysis of the co-ordinating, harmonizing, and organizing function of free competition. There was a providential harmonious and self-operating *physical* order of nature which, under appropriate social organization and sound intellectual perception, could be matched in its providential character, in its automatism, and in its beneficence, in the *social* order of nature. Through proper education this would become "evident" (in the Cartesian sense of the word) to all men; by *reasonable* men what was the "evident" course of behavior to follow in the social interest would be seen also to be the proper course of behavior in their own individual interest. It was the role of the economists to perceive and to expound, to government and to the public, the nature of the "evident" truth. It was the role of government, through its Hobbesian monopoly of power, its "legal despotism," to bring about, with the help of the economists, the general acceptance of the "evident" doctrine, and to suppress inconsistent or hostile action on the part of ignorant or malicious individuals, of monopoly groups, and of unfriendly foreign countries. Beyond this, the normal operation of free competition would suffice, without further state intervention, to produce in the social order that harmony, mutual cooperation, and efficiency manifest in the physical order of nature.

In England the important intellectual developments which prepared the ground for the formulation of an economic doctrine of laissez faire consisted for the most part of contributions by moral philosophers and theologians, contributions whose major objective often was to rebut Hobbes, even though on strictly economic matters Hobbes was probably less of a state-interventionist than were many of those who opposed him on theological and moral issues. The major ethical doctrines presented in order to rebut Hobbes were in the eighteenth century distinguished as the "selfish" and the "sentimental" schools, and both of these schools provided ingredients for the laissez-faire doctrine in its mature nineteenth century form.

The "selfish school" consisted predominantly of a long succession of Cambridge University theologians, to whose doctrine there was given in the nineteenth century the appropriate enough label of "theological utilitarianism." Although they were not deeply concerned with the question of "sin" in the Augustinian or Calvinist or Jansenist sense, to serve their purpose of demonstrating an important social function for the belief in immortality and in future rewards and punishments, or in other words for orthodox religion, they attacked Hobbes' stress on the role of the state—or of the policeman—in moralizing society. On the other hand, to rebut the optimistic account of human nature given by the sentimental school, which seemed to make unnecessary either a strong police force or reliance on religion, with its promise of hope for future rewards and threat of future punishments as needed agents of moral discipline, they retained and even accentuated the pessimistic appraisal of human nature when left to its own devices presented by the Augustinian tradition within the Church and by Hobbes and the libertines outside it. The big names in this school are Waterland, Edmund Law, and Paley. It is not clear that they exerted any important influence on economic thought, although Malthus was in this tradition and the doctrine of "moral restraint" which he expounded as the *moral* solution—though in his mind not probably a practically efficacious one—of the problem of excess population was probably a product of this tradition. The connection with laissez faire of this school is a tenuous one—by stressing the theological sanctions for good social behavior they directed attention away from, though without expressly denying, the need for extensive social discipline applied by government.

The sentimental school had much greater importance for laissez-faire doctrine. It was launched in the seventeenth century, as a reply to Hobbes, by theologians of deist tendencies or by laymen of even more doubtful religious orthodoxy, of whom Lord Shaftesbury was most prominent. The essence of their doctrine for present purposes was the stress on the social sentiments, on the non-rationalistic social instincts and affections of men, which led them to serve their fellowmen out of sympathy and fellow-feeling. Francis Hutcheson, the teacher of Adam Smith at Glasgow, was a member of this school, and the "moral sentiments" of Adam Smith's *Theory of Moral Sentiments* were essentially the sympathy, the benevolence, and "the moral sense" which were the key elements in the social philosophy of Shaftesbury and of Hutcheson.

It is necessary to mention one other line of doctrine formulated in rebuttal of Hobbes, the doctrine of Bishop Richard Cumberland, which influenced the Physiocrats and Adam Smith. Cumberland argued that the social order was so constituted that there was essential harmony between rational self-interest and the common good, and that even in the absence of government, or of hope for future rewards and fear of future punishment, rational men would constitute a good society—though not as good as if religious and political sanctions for good social behavior were also operative. It needs to be noted that while the sentimental school relied on instincts for good social behavior, Cumberland put his emphasis on the rationality of men and the rationality of good behavior.

Adam Smith, for his social system as a whole, drew from all these sources in an eclectic manner. For his theory of society outside the market place, for the explanation of man's behavior in his family, towards his friends and neighbors, and as a citizen of his country, Adam Smith stressed the Shaftesburian "moral sentiments," sympathy, benevolence, propriety, desire for public approval and for self-approval. For the market-place, he relied on the Cumberlandian rationality of good behavior and on the efficient functioning as an economic organizer of free competition, where he probably borrowed from the Physiocrats. I believe that the explanation of Smith's divergent treatment of social behavior inside and outside the market-place is that he assumed that in the market-place social relations were basically mechanical or "anonymous," so that the social sentiments were insufficiently strong as a disciplinary force, and self-interest, moderated by an inner sense of justice as well as by politically-enforced justice, would be the dominant psychological force. In both spheres, however, except for the enforcement of justice, and except for a few functions which private initiative could not or would not perform, society would as a rule best achieve its potentialities if left alone by government. It should always be remembered, however, that Adam Smith tried not to be a "man of system," and that were it not for his qualifications, he would have been a simpler, less human, and, in my opinion, less wise a man.

I come at last to the laissez-faire doctrine and the "economic man" concept of the English classical school. It should by now be obvious that both are evolutions from the earlier thought whose history I have been sketching. I will concern myself, therefore, not with these affiliations but with the differences in content or in emphasis of the English classical school doctrine from those of its intellectual ancestors. In the first place, their doctrine was thoroughly secularized, and they felt no need to invoke Adam Smith's "invisible hand" to explain how men in serving their individual interest efficiently would best serve the common interest. In the second place, although their doctrine was close to Cumberland's in its reliance on rationalistic motivation, where Cumberland argued that men would see that by best serving the common interest they were simultaneously best serving their individual interest, they, like Adam Smith, while adopting the common good as their own good philosophically-speaking, did not attribute this perception or concern to the ordinary man in his economic behavior, and regarded the common good as an incidental and not consciously-intended end-result of the self-interested pursuit of the private good, brought about by the inherent *modus operandi* of free competition. Third, for analytical purpose, instead of relying on the real man psychologically-speaking as they saw him, they invented a construct, the economists' "economic man," who as an abstraction, corresponded closely to Adam Smith's whole man or real man as Smith saw him when he was operating in the market-place. But the classical school did not present the "economic man" as more than a somewhat distant approximation to the real man even as he behaved in the market-place. In order to accept this as a useful abstraction, they had only to believe that it was sufficiently close to reality to provide a substantially correct over-all account of the behavior of the competitive market under laissez faire, but to be prepared to qualify their analysis whenever it was observed that the behavior of the real man was substantially different.

It seems reasonably clear that Adam Smith regarded human behavior *in the market-place* as both in fact and ideally corresponding to that of the later construct of the "economic man," although the landed gentry were in his opinion not smart enough quite to achieve this standard, and although it was for Smith only a utilitarian or efficiency ideal, and aesthetically or sentimentally was rather revolting to him. For the English classical school the "economic man" was, even as far as routine economic behavior was concerned, neither ideal nor real. This is of course not the usual interpretation, especially on the part of non-economists, who almost invariably treat the "economic man" as wholly unreal but as presented by the classical economists as wholly real. But the classical economists did not really believe that even in the market-place men acted only from self-interest, nor did they believe that economic interest, the maximization of income or the minimization of unpleasant effort, was the sole form of self-interest. If they erred through lack of realism, as I believe they did, it was: that they relied too much on an abstraction as making relevant theorizing possible without resort to more than a minimum of systematic observation; that even for their abstract "economic man" they took too much for granted that he would have a clear and simple and accurate knowledge of what his economic interests were; and that they thought they knew well enough for their analytical purposes how to draw a sharp line between the economic interests to which the "economic man" could be assumed to confine his concern and the non-economic interests which he should or would disregard.

Lionel Robbins has perhaps more fully than anyone else demonstrated how much deeper and wider was the psychological motivation of real man as seen by the classical school economists than the psychology attributed by them for analytical purposes to the "economic man." This applies also the accounts of human nature given by other writers, earlier, contemporary, and later, to whom has been attributed by modern scholars belief in the reality of the "economic man." Hobbes, for instance, while he insisted that man was selfish also insisted that his economic objectives were subject to the limitations imposed by the rivalry of other objectives: "The business of the World," he said, "consisteth in nothing else but a perpetual contention for Honor, Riches, and Authority," and he was well aware that these could be conflicting objectives. Bentham is commonly reputed to have expounded the doctrine that man behaves only in response to selfish interests. I think that if he had been allowed to give his own definition of "selfish interest," he would have agreed, but it would have been a definition of very wide inclusiveness. In any case, he repeatedly emphasized that men sought more things than wealth. At one point, he listed Hobbes' three major objectives of man: "wealth, the love of reputation and the love of power" as having "efficient power over the human heart." At another point he objected to the exclusion in English law of the evidence of "interested" parties, on the ground that it treated pecuniary interest as the only important source of biased testimony. "Love, properly so-called, the love of power, friendship, hate, and all the other passions of the human heart, seem to have been reckoned undeserving of the same precautions. Pecuniary interest is apparently the only interest whose influence they recognize. This is a fragment of the barbarism of ancient times." Evan Bastiat, who gave to the laissez-faire doctrine a form more extreme, more unqualified, than ever manifested itself in English economics, nevertheless explained that political economy was deliberately abstracting a part from the whole of human nature, and that it applied this abstraction, the "economic man," only to that part of human activity where transactions occurred between men who were unacquainted with each other and who owed each other only justice. Political economy dealt only with the cold domain of personal interest, and left to its sister, ethics, the attractive region where religious sentiment, paternal and maternal tenderness, filial piety, love, friendship, patriotism, charity, politeness, and conscience reigned.

The critic, of course, might object that Bastiat had not correctly located the boundary line between these two regions, or might even deny that there were two regions distinguishable in the manner in which Bastiat in his writings in general distinguished them. This is of course the major criticism of laissez-faire doctrine which humanitarian and religious authors have made, and it is one which economists as such have no particular qualifications to appraise, provided the criticism does not consciously or unconsciously embody, economic analysis or economic criteria of moral appraisal. It is no answer at all that freedom is a moral good, and that therefore "economic freedom," in a laissez-faire sense, is a moral good, since there are freedoms and freedoms, counteracting, interdependent, complementary, and rival, and the place of economic freedom in the general system of freedoms, and of "freedom" in the general system of values, is a problem for investigation, and for value-judgments in the light of such investigation, not an autonomous categorical imperative. The attack on laissez faire of the economic planner who accepts economic efficiency in some relevant sense as his criterion for appraisal is another matter. Here the laissez faire economist can find adequate weapons of defense in his own professional armory and in his own observations and measurements of economic phenomenon, if one may assume that these dialectical weapons have only single cutting edges.

Modern laissez-faire exponents have abandoned appeal to a providentially-designed pattern of mutual harmony of interests. When they are discreet and sophisticated, they confine their ethical argument to the proposition that economic freedom is of itself a moral good, to be preserved and pursued when this does not involve too great a cost in the sense of loss of other goods, including other types of freedom, and they make their case rest predominantly on the presentation of argument and empirical evidence of the superior *economic* efficiency of a free-market free-competition economy to other forms of economic organization of society. To me it does not seem that the economist as economist has professional qualifications for undertaking more responsibility or claiming more authority than this in the area of appraisal of different possible patterns of relation of the individual to the state and of the state to the individual. The modesty which it is incumbent upon us to manifest in due proportion should guard us against taking for granted that our qualifications in the field of ethics are of a distinctly higher order than those in the field of economics of our moralist and clerical critics.

EDITORIAL APPENDIX TO THE
WABASH LECTURES

The Wabash lectures, found among the Jacob Viner papers at Princeton University, consist of thirty-two single-spaced, typed pages, but contain no footnotes or references. The purpose of this appendix is to indicate some of the primary and secondary sources Viner may have consulted in writing the lectures. Although it is clearly an enormous task to determine Viner's source in every instance, many references could be found either in his other writings or from material among his other papers at Princeton. The editor has taken the liberty of adding additional references to recent secondary sources that contribute to Viner's discussion. This appendix is by no means exhaustive or complete, nor does it pretend to have duplicated all the references Viner would have made had he supplied his own sources. All omissions and errors are the responsibility of the editor and not Jacob Viner.

LECTURE I: EARLY ATTITUDES TOWARD TRADE AND THE MERCHANT

The attitude of ancient Greek thinkers toward commerce is discussed in Johannes Hasebroek, *Trade and Politics in Ancient Greece* (London: G. Bell & Sons, 1933).

Viner surveys Christian views on commerce in his *Religious Thought and Economic Society* (Durham: Duke University Press, 1978), pp. 34–38. See also Raymond De Roover, "Scholastic Attitudes Toward Trade and Entrepreneurship," in his *Business, Banking, and Economic Thought*, ed. Julius Kirshner (Chicago: University of Chicago Press, 1974), pp. 336–45.

St. Augustine's dictum "let them not trade" is in *A Select Library of the Nicene and Post-Nicene Fathers of the Christian Church*, ed. Philip Schaff, Vol. VII, *Saint Augustin: Exposition on the Book of Psalms* (New York: Brown Bros., 1888), p. 320.

On the concept of the universal economy, Viner once recommended Ernst Oberfohren, *Die Idee der Universalökonomie* (Jena: Verlag von Gustav Fischer, 1915) for coverage of the French literature from 1600 to 1800 (Bodin to Physiocrats). Viner discusses the doctrine in Chapter 2 of his Jayne lectures, *The Role of Providence in the Social Order* (Princeton: Princeton University Press, 1976).

What Euripides makes Theseus say in the *Suppliants* depends on the translation, of which there are many. One translation that is close to Viner's version appears in *The Complete Greek Tragedies*, eds. David Grene and Richard Lattimore, Vol. IV, *Euripides* (Chicago: University of Chicago Press, 1958), p. 142, lines 210–11.

The quote from Libanius is in his *Orations* (III), quoted in Hugo Grotius, *De Jure Belli Ac Pacis Libri Tres* (1625), *The Law of War and Peace*, trans. Francis W. Kelsey (Oxford: Clarendon Press, 1925), II.II.13.5, pp. 199–200. Grotius (ibid., p. 199, n. 3) also quotes from Florus and Plutarch, giving original citations to *Epitome Rerum Romanarum* and *Whether Water or Fire is More Useful*, respectively.

Numerous references to the providential aspects of free trade may be found in Richard Cobden, *Speeches on Questions of Public Policy*, 2 vols., eds. J. Bright and J. E. Thorold Rogers (Oxford: Oxford University Press, 1868).

Grotius and other natural law thinkers are discussed in Richard Tuck, *Natural Rights Theories* (Cambridge: Cambridge University Press, 1979).

For St. Thomas Aquinas' views on commerce, see *On Kingship, to the King of Cyprus*, trans. Gerald B. Phelan (Toronto: Pontifical Institute of Mediaeval Studies, 1949), (II, 3) pp. 74–78.

The transition from scholastic to mercantilist doctrine is covered in Raymond De Roover, "Scholastic Economics: Survival and Lasting Influence from the Sixteenth Century to Adam Smith," *Quarterly Journal of Economics* 69 (May 1955): 161–90.

The use of the universal economy doctrine by mercantilists in the case of England and its wool trade is discussed by Viner in *Studies in the Theory of International Trade* (New York: Harper & Bros., 1937), pp. 100ff.

Lecture II: The Nation-State and Private Enterprise

Several sources provide background to mercantilist doctrine: the first two chapters of Viner's *Studies*, Viner's essays on "Power versus Plenty" and "Mercantilist Thought" reprinted in this volume, and Eli Heckscher's *Mercantilism* (London: George Allen & Unwin, 1935; rev. ed. 1955). Joyce O. Appleby, *Economic Thought and Ideology in Seventeenth Century England* (Princeton: Princeton University Press, 1978) provides an overview from the perspective of an historian.

Viner mentions Antoyne Montchrétien, *Traicté de l'Oeconomie Politique* (Rouen, 1615), which is discussed further in Nannerl O. Keohane, *Philosophy and the State in France* (Princeton: Princeton University Press, 1980), pp. 163–68.

Viner also refers to John Campbell's enormous two-volume *Political Survey of Britain* (London, 1774) and to Daniel Defoe's obscure *Of Royall Education*, ed. Karl D. Bülbring (London: D. Nutt, 1895).

The quote by Friedrich List is from the introduction to his *The National System of Political Economy* (Philadelphia: Lippincott, 1856), p. 75.

William Thornton made his statement opposing a census in Parliament in 1753, as recorded in *The Parliamentary History of England*, Vol. XIV, 1747–1753 (London: T. C. Hansard, 1813), pp. 1318–22, 1322–30, 1355–60, quote at 1319.

Lecture III: The Emergence of Free-Trade and Laissez-Faire Doctrine

Hayek discusses common law and economic freedom in *The Constitution of Liberty* (Chicago: University of Chicago Press, 1960), especially chapters 11 and 15.

The distortion of common law in favor of freedom is discussed in Donald O. Wagner, "Coke and the Rise of Economic Liberalism," *Economic History Review* 2 (October 1935): 30–44, and William Letwin, "English Common Law Concerning Monopolies," *University of Chicago Law Review* 21 (Spring 1954): 355–85.

Hayek considers Mandeville and evolutionary institutions in *Individualism and Economic Order* (Chicago: University of Chicago Press, 1948), especially in the first essay, "Individualism: True and False."

Antecedents of Adam Smith's economic perspective are treated in Richard F. Teichgraeber III, *'Free Trade' and Moral Philosophy: Rethinking the Sources of Adam Smith's Wealth of Nations* (Durham: Duke University Press, 1986) which concentrates on Hutcheson and Hume; and in Milton L. Myers, *The Soul of Modern Economic Man: Ideas of Self-Interest, Thomas Hobbes to Adam Smith* (Chicago: University of Chicago Press, 1983), which discusses Cumberland, Shaftesbury, and Hutcheson. Links between Mandeville and Smith are explored in Thomas A. Horne, "Envy and Commercial Society: Mandeville and Smith on 'Private Vices, Public Benefits,'" *Political Theory* 9 (November 1981): 551–69.

Raymond De Roover, "Monopoly Theory prior to Adam Smith: A Revision," *Quarterly Journal of Economics* 65 (November 1951): 492–524, discusses Konrad Peutinger and makes reference to P. Hecker, "Ein Gutachten Conrad Peutingers in Sachen der Handelsgesellschaften," *Zeitschrift des Historischen Vereins für Schwaben und Neuburg* 2 (1875): 188–216.

Hobbes' economics is discussed in Aaron Levy, "Economic Views of Thomas Hobbes," *Journal of the History of Ideas* 20 (October 1954); 589–95, and William Letwin, "The Economic Foundations of Hobbes' Politics," in *Hobbes and Rousseau: A Collection of Critical Essays*, eds. Maurice Cranston and Richard S. Peters (Garden City: Anchor-Doubleday, 1972), pp. 143–64.

On the Physiocrats, see Henry Higgs, *The Physiocrats* (London: Macmillan, 1897); and Martin Albaum, "The Moral Defenses of the Physiocrats' Laissez Faire," *Journal of the History of Ideas* 16 (April 1955): 179–97.

Adam Smith's views can be found in *An Inquiry into the Nature and Causes of the Wealth of Nations* (1776; Glasgow Edition of Smith's works, 1976); and Viner's essay "Adam Smith and Laissez Faire" reprinted in this volume.

LECTURE IV: MONOPOLY AND LAISSEZ FAIRE

Usage of the terms monopoly and oligopoly are in Sir Thomas More's *Utopia* (1516) and Johann Joachim Becher's *Politische Discurs* (1667).

Limitations on the power of monopolies are recognized in Ferdinando Galiani, *Della Moneta* (Napoli, 1750); Antonie Augustin Cournot, *Researches into the Mathematical Principles of the Theory of Wealth* (1st ed. in French, 1838; English 1897); and Charles Ellet, *An Essay on the Laws of Trade* (Richmond, 1839). See Viner's review of Raymond Sachot, *Les Prix de Monopole d'aprés les Doctrines et dans les faits* in the *Journal of Political Economy* 36 (June 1928): 411–12, and C. D. Calsoyas, "The Mathematical Theory of Monopoly in 1839: Charles Ellet, Jr.,'' *Journal of Political Economy* 58 (April 1950): 162–70.

Scholastic views of monopoly are treated in Raymond De Roover, "Monopoly Theory Prior to Adam Smith," *Quarterly Journal of Economics* 65 (November 1951): 492–524, and Joseph Höffner, *Wirtschaftsethik und Monopole* (Jena, 1941).

On Sir John Coke, see Dorthea Coke, *The Last Elizabethan: Sir John Coke, 1563–1644* (London: John Murray, 1937).

Adam Smith's views on monopoly are presented in *The Wealth of Nations*. Viner cites a letter from Smith to Dr. Cullen, which appears in *The Correspondence of Adam Smith*, eds. E. C. Mossner and I. S. Ross, 2nd ed. (Oxford: Clarendon Press, 1987), pp. 173–79.

The quotation from David Buchanan is from his edition of Adam Smith's *Wealth of Nations* (Edinburgh: Oliphant, Waugh, & Innes, 1814), p. 100.

LECTURE V: THE "ECONOMIC MAN," OR THE PLACE OF ECONOMIC SELF-INTEREST IN A "GOOD SOCIETY"

An introduction to some of the issues discussed here can be found in Leslie Stephens, *A History of English Thought in the Eighteenth Century* (London: Smith-Elder, 1876).

Viner further discusses Richard Cumberland, *De Legibus Naturae Disquisitio Philosophia* (1672), *A Treatise of the Laws of Nature*, trans. John Maxwell (London: R. Phillips, 1727), in his Jayne lectures. See also Milton L. Myers, *The Soul of Modern Economic Man: Ideas of Self-Interest, Thomas Hobbes to Adam Smith* (Chicago: University of Chicago Press, 1983).

See Lionel Robbins, *The Theory of Economic Policy in English Classical Political Economy* (London: Macmillan, 1952), on the philosophical assumptions behind classical analysis.

Bentham discusses why rules of evidence should not exclude testimony from interested parties in *The Works of Jeremy Bentham*, ed. John Bowring, Vol. 7, *Rules of Judicial Evidence* (1827) (New York: Russell and Russell, 1962) book IX, chapter III, pp. 397–400.

Frédéric Bastiat discusses political economy and "economic man" in *Economic Harmonies* [1850], trans. W. Hayden Boyers, ed. George B. de Huszar (Princeton: D. van Nostrand, 1964), pp. 25ff.

PART II

Major Essays

2

ADAM SMITH AND LAISSEZ FAIRE

I. The Harmonious Order of Nature

An endeavor to make a just appraisal of Adam Smith's original contributions to economic doctrine would even today be a task of extraordinary difficulty.[1] On the one hand, what was serviceable in his doctrines has become so thoroughly incorporated in our modern thinking that we discover it upon the slightest provocation in whatever we may read that was written before his day, and we are especially prone to make a virtue of obscurity in his predecessors by taking it for granted that it conceals premature insight rather than unduly prolonged lack of it. On the other hand, there is always great danger lest what we credit to a writer as priority of doctrine may not in reality be merely an indecent exposure of our own ignorance concerning his predecessors. There is much weight of authority and of evidence, however, that Smith's major claim to originality, in English economic thought at least, was his detailed and elaborate application to the wilderness of economic phenomena of the unifying concept of a co-ordinated and mutually interdependent system of cause and effect relationships which philosophers and theologians had already applied to the world in general. Smith's doctrine that economic phenomena were manifestations of an underlying order in nature, governed by natural forces, gave to English economics for the first time a definite trend toward logically consistent synthesis of economic relationships, toward "system-building." Smith's further doctrine that this underlying natural order required, for its most beneficient operation, a system of natural liberty, and that in the main public regulation and private monopoly were corruptions of that natural order, at once gave to economics a bond of union with the prevailing philos-

Lecture delivered at the University of Chicago on Jan. 21, 1927, in a series commemorative of the one-hundred and fiftieth anniversary of the publication of the *Wealth of Nations*. Reprinted from the *Journal of Political Economy* 35 (April 1927):198–232.

[1] References to Adam Smith's writings are to the following editions: *History of Ancient Physics*, and *Theory of Moral Sentiments*, in "Essays Philosophical and Literary by Adam Smith" (Ward, Lock & Co., London, n.d.); *Wealth of Nations*, Cannan edition; *Lectures*, Cannan, editor.

ophy and theology, and to economists and statesmen a program of practical reform.

Smith was *the* great eclectic. He drew upon all previous knowledge in developing his doctrine of a harmonious order in nature manifesting itself through the instincts of the individual man. The oldest source in which he expressly finds an approach to his own views is in the science of the classical philosophers: "In the first ages of the world . . . the idea of an universal mind, of a God of all, who originally formed the whole, and who governs the whole by general laws, directed to the conservation and prosperity of the whole, without regard to that of any private individual, was a notion to which [the Ancients] were utterly strangers . . . [but] as ignorance begot superstition, science gave birth to the first theism that arose among those nations, who were not enlightened by divine Revelation."[2]

The Roman *jus naturale*, through Grotius and Pufendorf, strongly influenced Smith's thinking. The Renaissance emphasis on the individual, the naturalistic philosophy of Shaftesbury, Locke, Hume, Hutcheson, the optimistic theism of the Scotch philosophers, the empiricism of Montesquieu, were more immediate and more powerful influences. Science, philosophy, theology, psychology, history, contemporary observation of facts—all of them were made to produce, under Smith's capable management, an abundance of evidence of the existence of an order in nature in which beneficent intentions toward mankind could be discerned. If Smith at times showed more catholicity than scientific discrimination in what he accepted as supporting evidence, if some of this evidence appeared upon close scrutiny to be conjectural, contradictory, irrelevant, or inconclusive, the rightness of argument, the power of his exposition, the attractiveness of his conclusions served to overwhelm the captious critic and to postpone closer scrutiny to a later day.

Smith's major claim to fame, as I have said, seems to rest on his elaborate and detailed application to the economic world of the concept of a unified natural order, operating according to natural law, and if left to its own course producing results beneficial to mankind. On every detail, taken by itself, Smith appears to have had predecessors in plenty. On few details was Smith as penetrating as the best of his predecessors. There had been earlier pleas for freedom of internal trade, freedom of foreign trade, free trade in land, free choice of occupations, free choice of place of residence. Some philosophers, notably Shaftesbury and Smith's own teacher, Hutcheson, had already extended to economic phenomena, though sketchily, the concept of an underlying natural order manifesting itself through the operation of physical forces and individual psychology. But Smith

---

[2] *History of Ancient Physics*, pp. 391, 392.

made an original forward step when he seriously applied himself to the task of analyzing the whole range of economic process with the purpose of discovering the nature of the order which underlay its surface chaos. Claims have been made for the Physiocrats, but the evidence indicates that Smith had already formulated his central doctrine before he came into contact with them or their writings. As early as 1755 Smith had publicly asserted his claim to priority, as against some unnamed rival, in applying to the economic order the system of natural liberty. In doing so, he cited a lecture, delivered in 1749, which even in the fragment which has survived contains the essence of his fully developed doctrine, as expounded in the *Wealth of Nations*. It even uses as English equivalent of the very phrase ''laissez faire,'' which the Physiocrats were soon to make the war cry of the system of natural liberty.

> Projectors disturb nature in the course of her operations on human affairs, and it requires no more than to *leave her alone* and give her fair play in the pursuit of her ends that she may establish her own designs. . . . Little else is required to carry a state to the highest degree of affluence from the lowest barbarism but peace, easy taxes, and a tolerable administration of justice; all the rest being brought about by the natural course of things. All governments which thwart this natural course, which force things into another channel, or which endeavour to arrest the progress of society at a particular point, are unnatural, and, to support themselves, are obliged to be oppressive and tyrannical.[3]

In his *Theory of Moral Sentiments*, Smith develops his system of ethics on the basis of a doctrine of a harmonious order in nature guided by God, and in an incidental manner applies his general doctrine with strict consistency to the economic order. In his later work, the *Wealth of Nations*, Smith devotes himself to a specialized inquiry into the nature of the economic order. It is a commonplace among the authorities on Adam Smith that it is impossible fully to understand the *Wealth of Nations* without recourse to the *Theory of Moral Sentiments*. The vast bulk of economists, however, who have read the *Wealth of Nations* without reading the *Theory of Moral Sentiments*, have not regarded Smith's masterpiece as an obscure book, as one especially hard to understand. On the other hand, the very authorities who are most emphatic in asserting the need of reference to the *Theory of Moral Sentiments* to understand the *Wealth of Nations*, once they embark upon their self-imposed task of interpreting the latter in the light of the former, become immersed in difficult problems of interpretation for which scarcely any two writers offer the same solution. The system of individual liberty is much in evidence among the interpreters of Smith, but that natural harmony which should also re-

---

[3] John Rae, *Life of Adam Smith*, London, Macmillan & Co., 1895, pp. 62–63. Italics mine.

sult is strikingly lacking. The Germans, who, it seems, in their methodical manner commonly read both the *Theory of Moral Sentiments* and the *Wealth of Nations*, have coined a pretty term, *Das Adam Smith Problem*, to denote the failure to understand either which results from the attempt to use the one in the interpretation of the other. I will endeavor to show that the difficulties of the authorities result mainly from their determination to find a basis for complete concordance of the two books, and that there are divergences between them which are impossible of reconciliation even by such herioc means as one writer has adopted of appeal to the existence in Smith's thought of a Kantian dualism. I will further endeavor to show that the *Wealth of Nations* was a better book because of its partial breach with the *Theory of Moral Sentiments*, and that it could not have remained, as it has, a living book were it not that in its methods of analysis, its basic assumptions, and its conclusions it abandoned the absolutism, the rigidity, the romanticism which characterize the earlier book.

II. The "Theory of Moral Sentiments"

In the *Theory of Moral Sentiments*, Smith develops the doctrine of a beneficent order in nature, manifesting itself through the operation of the forces of external nature and the innate propensities implanted in man by nature. The moral sentiments, self-interest, regulated by natural justice and tempered by sympathy and benevolence, operate in conjunction with the physical forces of nature to achieve the beneficent purposes of Nature. Underlying the matter-of-fact phenomena of human and physical nature is benign Nature, a guiding providence, which is concerned that natural processes shall opperate to produce the "happiness and perfection of the species." Smith is unfortunately far from explicit as to just how Nature makes certain that nature shall not betray the former's intentions, though he does say that Nature dictates to man the laws which he shall follow.[4] It seems, however, that the essence of Smith's doctrine is that Providence has so fashioned the constitution of external nature as to make its processes favorable to man, and has implanted *ab initio* in human nature such sentiments as would bring about, through their ordinary working, the happiness and welfare of mankind. the many titles by which this beneficent Nature is designated must have taxed severely the terminological resources of the Scotch optimistic theism. Among them are: "the great Director of nature."[5] "the final cause,"[6] "the Author of nature,"[7] "the

---

[4] *Theory of Moral Sentiments*, p. 75.

[5] *Ibid.*, p. 71 n.

[6] *Ibid.*, p. 80.

[7] *Ibid.*, p. 96.

great Judge of hearts,"[8] "an invisible hand,"[9] "Providence,"[10] "the divine Being,"[11] and, in rare instances, "God."[12] Smith definitely commits himself to the theism of his time. The harmony and beneficence to be perceived in the matter-of-fact processes of nature are the results of the design and intervention of a benevolent God.

> The idea of that divine Being, whose benevolence and wisdom have, from all eternity, contrived and conducted the immense machine of the universe, so as at all times to produce the greatest possible quantity of happiness, is certainly of all the objects of human contemplation by far the most sublime. . . . The administration of the great system of the universe, . . . the care of the universal happiness of all rational and sensible beings, is the business of God and not of man. To man is allotted a much humbler department, but one much more suitable to the weakness of his powers, and to the narrowness of his comprehension; the care of his own happiness, of that of his family, his friends, his country.[13]
>
> Thus self-preservation, and the propagation of the species, are the great end which Nature seems to have proposed in the formation of all animals. . . . But though we are . . . endowed with a very strong desire of those ends, it has not been intrusted to the slow and uncertain determinations of our reason to find out the proper means of bringing them about. Nature has directed us to the greater part of these by original and immediate instincts. Hunger, thirst, the passion which unites the two sexes, the love of pleasure, and the dread of pain, prompt us to apply those means for their own sakes, and without any consideration of their tendency to those beneficent ends which the great Director of nature intended to produce by them.[14]

Society can get along tolerably well even though beneficence is absent and self-interest and justice alone operate. "Society may subsist among different men, as among different merchants, from a sense of its utility, without any mutual love or affection; and though no man in it should owe any obligation, or be bound in gratitude to any other, it may still be upheld by a mercenary exchange of good offices according to an agreed valuation." Beneficence "is the ornament which embellishes, not the foundation which supports, the building. . . . Justice, on the contrary, is the main pillar that upholds the whole edi-

---

[8] *Ibid.*
[9] *Ibid.*, p. 163.
[10] *Ibid.*, p. 163.
[11] *Ibid.*, p. 210.
[12] *Ibid.*, pp. 80, 97.
[13] *Ibid.*, p. 210.
[14] *Ibid.*, p. 71 n.

fice." "Society may subsist, though not in the most comfortable state, without beneficence; but the prevalence of injustice must utterly destroy it."[15]

There are no serious flaws in the harmonious operation of natural forces, even in the economic order, where self-interest, which is ordinarily a virtue, but if not regulated by justice may degenerate into vice, is the most powerful of the impulses to action:

> If we consider the general rules by which external prosperity and adversity are commonly distributed in this life, we shall find, that notwithstanding the disorder in which all things appear to be in this world, yet even here every virtue naturally meets with its proper reward, with the recompense which is most fit to encourage and promote it; and this too so surely, that it requires a very extraordinary concurrence of circumstances entirely to disappoint it. What is the reward most proper for encouraging industry, prudence, and circumspection? Success in every sort of business. And is it possible that in the whole of life these virtues should fail of attaining it? Wealth and external honours are their proper recompense, and the recompense which they can seldom fail of acquiring.[16]

The poorer classes have little if any ground for complaint as to their lot in life, and no reason to seek to improve it except by methods which contribute to the general welfare of society. "In the middling and inferior stations of life, the road to virtue and that to fortune . . . are, happily, in most cases, very nearly the same. . . . The good old proverb, therefore, that honesty is the best policy, holds, in such situations, almost always perfectly true."[17] Beneficent Nature so operates the machinery behind the scenes that even inequality in the distribution of happiness is more apparent than real:

> [The rich] are led by an invisible hand to make nearly the same distribution of the necessaries of life, which would have been made, had the earth been divided into equal portions among all its inhabitants, and thus without intending it, without knowing it, advance the interest of the society, and afford means to the multiplication of the species. When Providence divided the earth among a few lordly masters, it neither forgot nor abondoned those who seemed to have been left out in the partition. These last, too, enjoy their share of all that it produces. In what constitutes the real happiness of human life, they are in no respect inferior to those who would seem so much above them. In ease of the body and peace of the mind, all

[15] *Ibid.*, p. 79.
[16] *Ibid.*, p. 146.
[17] *Ibid.*, 58.

the different ranks of life are nearly upon a level, and the beggar, who suns himself by the side of the highway, possesses that security which kings are fighting for.[18]

Smith concedes that the processes of nature operate at times with what, by man's standards, are results so unjust that they arouse our indignation:

> Fraud, falsehood, brutality, and violence . . . excite in every human breast such scorn and abhorrence, that our indignation rouses to see them possess those advantages which they may in some sense be said to have merited, by the diligence and industry with which they are sometimes attended. The industrious knave cultivates the soil, the indolent good man leaves it uncultivated. Who ought to reap the harvest? Who starve, and who live in plenty? The natural course of things decides it in favour of the knave; the natural sentiments of mankind in favour of the man of virtue.[19]

This is a familiar dilemma of the optimistic theology, but Smith is precluded from adopting the familiar solution that "the ways of the Lord are inscrutable" by the fact that he is at the moment engaged in the task of formulating with great precision and assurance just what the ways of the Lord are. A contemporary economist of Adam Smith, Josiah Tucker, who was also by the necessity of his profession a theologian, when faced with an apparent conflict between the processes of nature and the "fundamental Principle of Universal Benevolence" found an ingenious solution in the conclusion a priori that there must be something wrong in the appearance of things: "I conclude *a priori*, that there must be some flaw or other in the preceding Arguments, plausible as they seem, and the Appearance of Things at first Sight makes for this Conclusion . . . the Fact itself cannot be so."[20] Smith also succeeded in keeping his theory alive when the force of conflicting fact seemed to threaten to destroy it, but his method was more gentle to the facts. Man has been given by nature one standard by which to judge it, but nature has retained another and different standard for itself. "Both are calculated to promote the same great end, the order of the world, and the perfection and happiness of human nature."[21] Only an inordinately exacting critic would suggest that this solution is not wholly satisfactory, since Smith can have logically reached it only by applying to nature its own standard, which it was not appropriate for man to use. But if this solution does not satisfy, Smith has another one. If we despair of finding any force upon earth which can check the triumph of

---

[18] *Ibid.*, p. 163.
[19] *Ibid.*, pp. 147–148.
[20] *Four Tracts* (Glocester, 1774), p. 12.
[21] *Theory of Moral Sentiments*, p. 148.

injustice, we "naturally appeal to heaven, and hope that the great Author of our nature will himself execute hereafter what all the principles which he has given us for the direction of our conduct prompt us to attempt even here; that he will complete the plan which he himself has thus taught us to begin; and will, in a life to come, render to every one according to the works which he has performed in this world."[22] If, judged by men's standards, the order of nature does not result in perfect justice on earth, we apparently have two alternative explanations: either that man's standards are an inadequate basis for appraisal, or that there is opportunity in a future state for redress of the injustices of the present one.

What we have, therefore, in the *Theory of Moral Sentiments* is an unqualified doctrine of a harmonious order of nature, under divine guidance, which promotes the welfare of man through the operation of his individual propensities. Of these, self-interest is the most important one, in so far as economic life is concerned, though it is subject to the regulations of natural justice, to which it must conform. "In the race for wealth, for honours, and preferments, he may run as hard as he can, and strain every nerve and every muscle, in order to outstrip all his competitors. But if he should jostle, or throw down any of them, the indulgence of the spectators is entirely at an end. It is a violation of fair play, which they cannot admit of."[23] In economic matters, benevolence plays but a minor role. There is no express formulation of a principle of laissez faire, and no explicit condemnation of governmental interference with individual initiative; but it is quite clearly implied that self-interest, if regulated by justice, which may be natural justice, but is likely to be more effective if it is administered by a magistrate, is sufficient to attain the ends of Nature in the economic world. There is convincing evidence from other sources that Smith was already an exponent of the system of natural liberty.

III. The System of Natural Liberty in the "Wealth of Nations"

Traces of the general doctrine expounded in the *Theory of Moral Sentiments*, that there is a beneficent order in nature which, if left to take its own course, will bring to mankind maximum happiness and prosperity, are undoubtedly to be discovered in the *Wealth of Nations*. Traces of every conceivable sort of doctrine are to be found in that most catholic book, and an economist must have peculiar theories indeed who cannot quote from the *Wealth of Nations* to support his spe-

---

[22] *Ibid.*, p. 149.
[23] *Ibid.*, p. 76.

cial purposes. But it can be convincingly demonstrated, I believe, that on the points at which they come into contact there is a substantial measure of irreconcilable divergence between the *Theory of Moral Sentiments* and the *Wealth of Nations*, with respect to the character of the natural order.

In the first case, the emphasis in the *Theory of Moral Sentiments* upon a benevolent deity as the author and guide of nature is almost, though not quite, completely absent in the *Wealth of Nations*. There are only a few minor passages in the later work which can be adduced as supporting evidence of the survival in Smith's thought of the concept of a divinity who has so shaped economic process that it operates necessarily to promote human welfare: an incidental allusion to "the wisdom of nature";[24] a remark that with respect to smuggling the laws of the country had "made that a crime which nature never meant to be so";[25] and a more famous passage, the main reliance of those who would completely reconcile the doctrines expounded in the two works, in which Smith repeats the phrase "the invisible hand" which he had used in the *Theory of Moral Sentiments*.[26] The only explicit reference to God is one which could have given but scant comfort to the natural theology of his time: "Superstition first attempted to satisfy this curiosity [about natural phenomena], by referring all those wonderful appearances to the immediate agency of the gods. Philosophy afterward endeavoured to account for them from more familiar causes, or from such as mankind were better acquainted with, than the agency of the gods."[27] To the extent that Smith in the *Wealth of Nations* does expound a doctrine of a harmonious order in nature, he accounts for it, as a rule, and perhaps even invariably, by reference to "more familiar causes [and] to such as mankind were better acquainted with, than the agency of the gods." The significance for our purposes of this virtual disappearance from the *Wealth of Nations* of the doctrine of an order of nature designed and guided by a benevolent God is that it leaves Smith free to find defects in the order of nature without casting reflections on the workmanship of its Author.

To some extent Smith makes use of this freedom. In both works he finds an inherent harmony in the order of nature, whereby man, in following his own interests, at the same time and without necessarily intending it serves also the general interests of mankind. In the *Theory of Moral Sentiments*, this harmony, as I have shown, is represented as universal and perfect. In the *Wealth of Nations*, this harmony is represented as not extending to all elements of the economic order, and often as partial and imperfect where it does extend. Where harmony does prevail, it is as a rule a sort of average or statistical harmony, revealing itself

[24] *Wealth of Nations*, II, 172.
[25] *Ibid.*, II, 381.
[26] *Ibid.*, I, 421.
[27] *Ibid.*, II, 256.

only in the general mass of phenomena and leaving scope for the possibility that natural processes whose general effect is beneficial may work disadvantageously in individual cases or at particular moments of time. As a rule, though not invariably, Smith qualifies his assertions of harmony by such phrases as "in most cases," "the majority," "in general," "frequently." For example, the exercise of common prudence is a prerequisite if the system of natural liberty is to operate harmoniously, and "though the principles of common prudence do not always govern the conduct of every individual, they always influence that of *the majority* of every class or order."[28] "It is advantageous to the great body of workmen . . . that all these trades should be free, though this freedom may be abused in all of them, and is more likely to be so, perhaps, in some than in others."[29] Drawbacks "tend not to destroy, but to preserve, what it is *in most cases* advantageous to preserve, the natural division and distribution of labour in the society."[30]

There are a number of well-known passages in the *Wealth of Nations* in which Smith asserts the existence of a more-or-less complete harmony between the general interests of society and the particular interests of individuals.

It is not from the benevolence of the butcher, the brewer, or the baker, that we expect our dinner, but from their regard to their own interest. We address ourselves, not to their humanity but to their self-love, and never talk to them of our own necessities but of their advantages. . . .[31] Every individual is continually exerting himself to find out the most advantageous employment for whatever capital he can command. It is his own advantage, indeed, and not that of the society, which he has in view. But the study of his own advantage naturally, or rather necessarily leads him to prefer that employment which is most advantageous to the society. . . .[32] As every individual, therefore, endeavours as much as he can both to employ his capital in the support of domestic industry, and so to direct that industry that its produce may be of the greatest value; every individual necessarily labours to render the annual revenue of the society as great as he can. He generally, indeed, neither intends to promote the public interest, nor knows how much he is promoting it. By preferring the support of domestic to that of foreign industry he intends only his own security; and by directing that industry in such a manner as its produce may be of the greatest value, he intends only his own gain, and he is in this, as in many other cases, led by an invisible hand to promote an end which was no part of his intention. . . . [33] The natural effort of every individual to better

[28] *Ibid.*, I, 278. Italics mine.
[29] *Ibid.*, I, 456.
[30] *Ibid.*, II, 1–2. Italics mine.
[31] *Ibid.*, I, 16.
[32] *Ibid.*, I, 419.
[33] *Ibid.*, I, 421.

his own condition, when suffered to exert itself with freedom and security, is so powerful a principle, that it is alone, and without any assistance, not only capable of carrying on the society to wealth and prosperity, but of surmounting a hundred impertinent obstructions with which the folly of human laws too often incumbers its operations; though the effect of these obstructions is always more or less either to encroach upon its freedom, or to diminish its security.[34]

But whereas in the *Theory of Moral Sentiments* such general statements as these comprise the main substance of the doctrine of a harmonious order in the economic world, in the *Wealth of Nations* they play a much more modest rôle. Though Smith in the *Wealth of Nations* frequently makes general statements intended apparently to apply to the entire universe, he has always before him for consideration some concrete problem, or some finite section of the universe. In no instance does Smith rely heavily upon his assertions as to the existence of harmony in the natural order at large to establish his immediate point that such harmony exists within the specific range of economic phenomena which he is at the moment examining. Such demonstration he accomplishes primarily by means of reference to the nature of these specific phenomena, by appeal to some self-evident principles of human psychology, by citation of historical object lessons, or by inference from contemporary experience. The general statements, though they may, as has been asserted, reveal the secret basis of Smith's conclusions, are given the appearance of mere obiter dicta, thrown in as supernumerary reinforcements to an argument already sufficiently fortified by more specific and immediate data. Smith's argument for the existence of a natural harmony in the economic order, to be perserved by following the system of natural liberty, is, in form at least, built up by detailed inference from specific data and by examination of specific problems, and is not deduced from wide-sweeping generalizations concerning the universe in general. What were the secret mental processes of Adam Smith whereby he really reached his conclusions it seems at this late date somewhat difficult to talk about with any degree of assurance.

Nowhere in the *Wealth of Nations* does Smith place any reliance for the proper working of the economic order upon the operation of benevolence and sympathy, the emphasis upon (the latter of) which was the novel feature in the account of human nature presented in the *Theory of Moral Sentiments*.* In the *Wealth of Nations*, benevolence is not merely as a rule left out of the picture of the economic order; when mentioned, it is with the implication that it is a weak reed upon which to depend. "By pursuing his own interest he frequently promotes that of the society more effectually than when he really intends to promote it. I

* The words in parenthesis are needed as a clarification of the original text. J.V.
[34] *Ibid.*, II, 43.

have never known much good done by those who affected to trade for the public good. It is an affectation, indeed, not very common among merchants, and very few words need be employed in dissuading them from it."[35] The only other instance in which Smith concedes the possible operation of benevolence in the economic world he also does not take too seriously:

> Whatever part of the produce . . . is over and above this share, he [i.e., the landlord] naturally endeavours to reserve to himself as the rent of his land, which is evidently the highest the tenant can afford to pay in the actual circumstances of the land. Sometimes, indeed, the liberality, more frequently the ignorance, of the landlord, makes him accept of somewhat less than this portion. . . . This portion, however, may still be considered as the natural rent of land, or the rent for which it is naturally meant that land should for the most part be let.[36]

The consequences of the intervention of liberality apparently are not "natural," are not in accordance with the intent of nature! Smith shows little faith in the prevalence of benevolence in the economic sphere. "Man has almost constant occasion for the help of his brethren, and it is in vain for him to expect it from their benevolence only. . . . It is not from the benevolence of the butcher, the brewer, or the baker, that we expect our dinner, but from their regard to their own interest."[37] "The late resolution of the Quakers in Pennsylvania to set at liberty all their negro slaves, may satisfy us that their number cannot be very great. Had they made any considerable part of their property, such a resolution could never have been agreed to."[38] Even the college professor cannot be expected to expend much energy in teaching effectively, cannot even be depended upon to teach at all, if it is not made to his interest to do so.[39] In the case of the clergy, the situation seems even more desperate. If they are endowed, they become indolent, and their zeal and industry become impaired. If, on the other hand, they are dependent upon voluntary contributions for their support, they become too zealous. He quotes from his skeptical friend Hume:

> . . . This interested diligence of the clergy is what every wise legislator will study to prevent; because, in every religion except the true, it is highly pernicious. . . . Each ghostly practitioner, in order to render himself more precious and sacred in the eyes of his retainers, will inspire them with the most violent abhorrence of all other sects, and continually endeavour, by some novelty, to excite the languid devotion of his audience. No regard will be paid to truth, morals, or de-

[35] *Ibid.*, I, 421.
[36] *Ibid.*, I, 145.
[37] *Ibid.*, I. 16.
[38] *Ibid.*, I, 365.
[39] *Ibid.*, II, 250 ff.

cency in the doctrines inculcated. Every tenet will be adopted that best suits the disorderly affections of the human frame. Customers will be drawn to each conventicle by new industry and address in practising on the passions and credulity of the populace.[40]

Smith laid little stress even in the *Theory of Moral Sentiments* upon the importance of benevolence in the economic order. But writers who have labored under a sense of obligation to find a basis for reconciliation of the *Wealth of Nations* with the *Theory of Moral Sentiments* have nevertheless discovered a problem in the insignificant rôle assigned to benevolence in the *Wealth of Nations*. Buckle's solution of the problem was that in the *Wealth of Nations* Smith was deliberately abstracting from all principles of human nature except self-interest, whereas in the *Theory of Moral Sentiments* he aimed at a complete picture of human nature. Not a trace of evidence is discoverable, however, that Smith in the *Wealth of Nations* was aware that he was abstracting selected elements from the totality of human nature. It awaited a later and keener mind, Ricardo, to discover the possibilities of the technique of deliberate abstraction in the field of economics. A more ingenious attempt at reconciliation rests, in part, on the identification of self-interest as used in the *Wealth of Nations* with rational pecuniary interest, with a desire for more wealth, and by demonstrating that Smith takes into account other motives than the rational desire for more wealth, claims to demonstrate that Smith did not exclude all principles but self-interest from the economic sphere. But self-interest meant to Smith not only the desire for wealth, but self-love in all its possible manifestations. "It is the interest of every man to live as much at his ease as he can."[41] "Avarice and ambition in the rich, in the poor the hatred of labour and the love of present ease and enjoyment," envy, malice and resentment,[42] all of these are manifestations of self-interest; the agreeableness, the ease or hardship, the cleanliness or dirtiness, the honorableness or dishonorableness, of the different employments are all factors affecting the attractiveness to labor of different occupations, as well as the wages paid: "Honour makes a great part of the reward of all honourable professions."[43] Smith distinguishes also between what a man is interested in and what is to his interest. Man is sometimes ignorant of the latter. "But though the interest of the labourer is strictly connected with that of the society, he is incapable either of comprehending that interest, or of understanding its connexion with his own."[44] It is what a

[40] *Ibid.*, II, 276.
[41] *Ibid.*, II, 250.
[42] *Ibid.*, II, 203.
[43] *Ibid.*, I, 102.
[44] *Ibid.*, I, 249.

man regards as his interest, even though mistakenly, that controls his actions. But every possible impulse and motive to action is included under self-interest except a deliberate intention to promote the welfare of others than one's self.

From his examination of the operation of self-interest in specific phases of the economic order and of the consequences of government interference with the free operation of self-interest, Smith arrives at an extensive program for the extension of the system of natural liberty through the abolition of existing systems of governmental regulation, though he nowhere brings the several items in that program together. Four main reforms are advocated. Free choice of occupations is to be established through the abolition of the apprenticeship regulations and settlement laws; free trade in land, through the repeal of laws establishing entails, primogenitures, and other restrictions on the free transfer of land by gift, devise, or sale; internal free trade, where such does not already prevail, by the abolition of local customs taxes; and most important of all, free trade in foreign commerce, through the abolition of the duties, bounties, and prohibitions of the mercantilistic régime and the trading monopolies of the chartered companies. These various restrictions and regulations are objectionable either because they operate to keep commerce, labor, or capital from following the channels in which they would otherwise go, or because they attract to a particular species of industry a greater share of the factors than would ordinarily be employed in it. In all of these cases there is close harmony, under the system of natural liberty, between the interests of individuals and the public interest, and interference by government, instead of promoting, hinders, though it does not necessarily prevent, the attainment of prosperity.

In England all of this program has been achieved, and in so far as such things can be traced to their source, the influence of the *Wealth of Nations* was an important factor in bringing about the reforms. That they were genuine reforms most economists will admit, though even in England there is no longer the unanimity there once was on these matters. It is a somewhat ironical coincidence that the least important plank in Smith's program, the reform of the English law of property, should be in process of final achievement only as the permanence of the greatest of his victories, the establishment of free trade in foreign commerce, faces its first serious threat in sixty years.

IV. FLAWS IN THE NATURAL ORDER

The foregoing is familiar matter. What is not so familiar, however, is the extent to which Smith acknowledged exceptions to the doctrine of a natural harmony in the economic order even when left to take its natural course. Smith, himself, never brought these together; but if this is done, they make a surprisingly comprehensive list and they demonstrate beyond dispute the existence of a wide divergence between the perfectly harmonious, completely beneficent natural order of the *Theory of Moral Sentiments* and the partial and limited harmony in the economic order of the *Wealth of Nations*. Masters and workmen have a conflict of interest with respect to wages, and the weakness in bargaining power of the latter ordinarily gives the advantage in any dispute to the former.[45] Masters, traders, and apprentices, on the one hand, and the public on the other, have divergent interests with respect to apprenticeship rules.[46] The interest of merchants and manufacturers is in high profits, which are disadvantageous to the public.[47] Merchants and manufacturers have interests opposed to those of the farmers and landlords,[48] and of the general public.[49] "People of the same trade seldom meet together, even for merriment and diversion, but the conversation ends in a conspiracy against the public, or in some contrivance to raise prices. It is impossible indeed to prevent such meetings, by any law which either could be executed, or would be consistent with liberty and justice."[50] The corn-dealer, on the whole, performs a useful service, but because of his "excess of avarice" he does not perform it perfectly.[51] The merchant exporter sometimes finds it to his interest, when dearth prevails both at home and abroad, "very much [to] aggravate the calamities of the dearth" at home by exporting corn.[52] Men commonly overestimate their chances of success in risky ventures, with the consequence that too great a share of the nation's stock of capital goes into such ventures.[53] It being the custom to pay attorneys and clerks according to the number of pages they had occasion to write, their self-interest led them "to multiply words beyond all necessity, to the corruption of the law language of, I believe, every court of justice in Europe."[54] Private initiative cannot be trusted to take proper care of the roads.[55] Division of labor operates to impair the intelligence, enterprise, martial courage, and moral character of the laborers,[56] though division of labor is itself

---

[45] *Ibid.*, I, 68–69.
[46] *Ibid.*, I, 125.
[47] *Ibid.*, I, 100; II, 112 ff.
[48] *Ibid.*, I, 129.
[49] *Ibid.*, I, 250.
[50] *Ibid.*, I, 130.
[51] *Ibid.*, II, 26.
[52] *Ibid.*, II, 40.
[53] *Ibid.*, II, 64–65.
[54] *Ibid.*, II, 213.
[55] *Ibid.*, II, 217.
[56] *Ibid.*, II, 267.

"the necessary, though very slow and gradual, consequence of a certain propensity in human nature . . . the propensity to truck, barter, and exchange one thing for another."[57] In old countries, "rent and profit eat up wages, and the two superior orders of people oppress the inferior one."[58] This is only a partial list of the defects in the natural order, even when left to take its own course, which Smith points out, though it would suffice to provide ammunition for several socialist orations. This is a far cry from the account given in the *Theory of Moral Sentiments* of a perfectly harmonious order of nature, operating under divine guidance, to promote its "great end, the order of the world, and the perfection and happiness of human nature."

In the *Theory of Moral Sentiments* Smith started out with a few general propositions about the nature of the universe which any educated Scotchman of his day would have vouched for as self-evident truths; and following them wherever they led him, he picked up en route a few more self-evident truths about the nature of human nature, and finally reached conclusions of the sort we have examined. Failing to compare his conclusions with the facts, he saw no necessity for qualifying them, and no reason for reexamining his premises. Unfortunately, these premises were in special need of careful scrutiny, for they were all drawn from a peculiar class of axioms which urgently require, but are incapable of, proof. In his earlier work Smith was a purely speculative philosopher, reasoning from notions masquerading as self-evident verities. In the *Wealth of Nations* Smith made use of a rich harvest of facts gathered by personal observation at home and abroad, by conversation and correspondence with many keen and intelligent observers of the current scene, by wide reading in a miscellany of sources, from law books to travelers' tales. With this factual material Smith kept close contact, and he never departed from it for long. He still, it is true, retained his flair for resounding generalizations of heroic range. There is a long-standing feud between sweeping generalization and run-of-the-mill factual data, and when Smith brought them together he did not always succeed in inducing altogether harmonious relations. But Smith's strength lay in other directions than exactly logical thinking, and he displayed a fine tolerance for a generous measure of inconsistency. It is to his credit that when there was sharp conflict between his generalization and his data, he usually abandoned his generalization.

There would be little ground for insistence upon reconciliation between the *Theory of Moral Sentiments* and the *Wealth of Nations* if it were simply a case of comparing one book written in 1757 with another written in 1776. It may not be as common as it should be for a man in his full maturity to advance beyond the

---

[57] *Ibid.*, I, 15.
[58] *Ibid.*, II, 67.

level of his first book; but it surely is not a rare phenomenon requiring to be explained out of existence. In every respect which is of concern to the economist as such, with the possible exception of his treatment of benevolence, the apparent discrepancies between the *Theory of Moral Sentiments* and the *Wealth of Nations* mark distinct advances of the latter over the former in realism and in application of the saving grace of common sense. But in the last year of his life Smith made extensive revisions of and additions to the *Theory of Moral Sentiments*, without diminishing in any particular the points of conflict between the two books. This would make it seem that in Smith's mind, at least, there was to the last no consciousness of any difference in the doctrines expounded in the two books. Though we grant this, however, are we obliged to accept his judgement and to strain interpretations in order to find consistency prevailing where inconsistency appeareth to reign supreme? I think not. There persisted within the *Wealth of Nations*, through five successive editions, many, and to later eyes obvious, inconsistencies. When Smith revised his *Theory of Moral Sentiments* he was elderly and unwell. It is not altogether unreasonable to suppose that he had lost the capacity to make drastic changes in his philosophy, but had retained his capacity to overlook the absence of complete co-ordination and unity in that philosophy.

V. The Functions of Government

Adam Smith, as has been shown, recognized that the economic order, when left to its natural course, was marked by serious conflicts between private interests and the interests of the general public. This would seem to suggest that there was an important sphere in which government interference with private interests might promote the general welfare. In his one deliberate and comprehensive generalization dealing with the proper functions of the state, Smith made it clear, however, that he would narrowly restrict the activities of government. "According to the system of natural liberty, the sovereign has only three duties to attend to; . . . first, the duty of protecting the society from the violence and invasion of other independent societies; secondly, . . . the duty of establishing an exact administration of justice; and, thirdly, the duty of erecting and maintaining certain public works and certain public institutions."[59] Even here, however, he grants to government a somewhat more extensive range of proper activities than in many scattered dicta throughout the remainder of the book, where he was primarily condemning some specific governmental activity and was not really giving serious consideration to the wider problem of the proper range of governmental ac-

[59] *Ibid.*, II, 184–185.

tivity. Smith had himself undermined what is ordinarily regarded as his principal argument for laissez faire, by demonstrating that the natural order, when left to take its own course, in many respects works against, instead of for, the general welfare. How can his adherence, notwithstanding, to a policy of narrow limitation of the functions of government be explained?

The *Wealth of Nations*, though it was from one point of view only a segment of a larger and systematic treatise on social philosophy, was at the same time a tract for the times, a specific attack on certain types of government activity which Smith was convinced, on both a priori and empirical grounds, operated against national prosperity, namely, bounties, duties, and prohibitions in foreign trade; apprenticeship and settlement laws; legal monopolies; laws of succession hindering free trade in land. Smith's primary objective was to secure the termination of *these* activities of government. His wider generalizations were invoked to support the attack on *these* political institutions. Everything else was to a large degree secondary. Smith made many exceptions to his general argument for laissez faire. But his interest as a reformer and a propagandist was not in these exceptions. He nowhere gathered together in orderly fashion the exceptions which he would have made to his general restriction of government activity to protection, justice, and the maintenance of a few types of public works and public institutions. When considering in general terms the proper functions of government, he forgot all about these exceptions. If he had been brought face to face with a complete list of the modifications to the principle of laissez faire to which he at one place or another had granted his approval, I have no doubt that he would have been astounded at his own moderation. I once heard a president of a state bankers' association at the afternoon session of its annual convention make the theme of his presidential address the unmitigated iniquity of government interference with business and the necessity of more businessmen in government in order that they should see to it that there was less government in business. In the evening of the same day he introduced to the audience the state commissioner of banking as one to whom the bankers were deeply indebted, because by promoting the enactment of sound regulations governing the entrance into the banking field and the practice of banking he had secured the suppression of irresponsible and fraudulent banking, to the benefit of the solid and respectable bankers there assembled and of the general public. He was as sincere in the evening as he had been that afternoon. Not only was Smith fully capable of this type of inconsistency, but there is in the *Wealth of Nations* an almost exact parallel of this modern instance.[60]

There is no possible room for doubt, however, that Smith in general believed that there was, to say the least, a strong presumption against government activity

---

[60] Cf. *ibid.*, II, 307.

beyond its fundamental duties of protection against its foreign foes and maintenance of justice. In his *Lectures*, Smith had said: "Till there be property, there can be no government, the very end of which is to secure wealth [i.e., to make wealth secure], and to defend the rich from the poor,"[61] following closely Locke's dictum that "Government has no other end but the preservation of property." In the *Wealth of Nations* he was more guarded: "Civil government, so far as it is instituted for the security of property, is in reality instituted for the defence of the rich against the poor, or of those who have some property against those who have none at all."[62] What were the considerations which brought Smith to his laissez faire conclusions? His philosophical speculations about a harmonious order in nature undoubtedly made it easier for him to reach a laissez faire policy, though I believe that the significance of the natural order in Smith's economic doctrines has been grossly exaggerated. But was not government itself a part of the order of nature, and its activities as "natural" as those of the individuals whom it governed? Smith is obscure on this point, and an adequate answer to this question, if possible, at all, would require a detailed examination of Smith's position in the evolution of political theory, especially with respect to the origin of government and the character of the state of nature in the absence of government. It is clear, however, that to Smith the activities of government in the maintenance of justice are an essential part of the order of nature in its full development, and that such activities are not interferences with the system of natural liberty.

In the *Theory of Moral Sentiments* there is a vague passage which seems to suggest that government itself is an agency of the order of nature, and to imply that all of its activities may, therefore, be as "natural" as those of individuals.[63] In the *Wealth of Nations*, Smith is a little more precise. He draws a definite line between those activities of government which are, and those which are not, in accord with the natural order, on the basis of empirical data. Government activity is natural and therefore good where it promotes the general welfare, and is an interference with nature and therefore bad when it injures the general interests of society. Whether in particular circumstances it works well or ill is to be determined only by examination of the character of those circumstances, though in most cases such examination may be expected a priori to reveal that it works badly.

This general presumption against government intervention in the affairs of mankind was itself largely the product of direct inference from experience. Against those particular activities of government which he subjected to special

---

[61] *Lectures*, p. 15.

[62] *Wealth of Nations*, II, 207.

[63] *Theory of Moral Sentiments*, pp. 163–64.

attack, viz., mercantilistic regulations, settlement and apprenticeship laws, legal monopolies, Smith thought he had specific objections, drawn from the results of their operation, sufficient to condemn them. Aside from protection and justice, these were the important activities of the governments of his day. In condemning them he was not far from condemning all the main types of government activity, aside from justice and protection, which were prominently in the public view. To justify these activities, it was necessary, Smith believed, to credit government with better knowledge of what was to a man's interest than the ordinary man himself was endowed with. This Smith could not concede. The standards of honesty and competence of the governments of his day with which Smith was acquainted were unbelievably low, moreover, not only in comparison with what they are today in England, Germany, and the Scandinavian countries, but apparently even in comparison with earlier periods in English political history. Smith had encountered few instances in which government was rendering intelligent and efficient service to the public welfare outside of the fields of protection and justice. The English government of his day was in the hands of an aristocratic clique, the place-jobbing, corrupt, cynical, and class-biased flower of the British gentry, who clung to the traditional mercantilism not so much because of a strong faith that it met the problems of a growing trade struggling to burst its fetters, but because they did not know anything else to do. Even when Smith was prepared to admit that the system of natural liberty would not serve the public welfare with optimum effectiveness, he did not feel driven necessarily to the conclusion that government intervention was preferable to laissez faire. The evils of unrestrained selfishness might be better than the evils of incompetent and corrupt government.

In this connection, Smith has, indeed, a lesson to teach the "new economics" of the present day, which is peddling antique nostrums under new trademarks, and which has substituted for the answer to all economic problems of the classically trained parrot, "demand and supply," the equally magical phrase, "social control." If the standards of public administration are low, progress from a life regulated by the law of demand and supply to a life under the realm of social control may be progress from the discomforts of the frying-pan to the agonies of the fire.

It is the highest impertinence and presumption, therefore, in kings and ministers, to pretend to watch over the oeconomy of private people, and to restrain their expence, either by sumptuary laws, or by prohibiting the importation of foreign luxuries. They are themselves always, and without any exception, the greatest spendthrifts in the society. Let them look well after their own expence, and they may safely trust private people with theirs. If their own extravagance does not ruin the state, that of their subjects never will.[64] . . . The violence and injustice of the rulers of mankind is an ancient evil, for which, I am afraid, the nature of human affairs can scarce admit of a remedy.[65]

Where, by exception, good government made its appearance, Smith was ready to grant it a wider range of activities.

> The orderly, vigilant, and parsimonious administration of such aristocracies as those of Venice and Amsterdam, is extremely proper, it appears from experience, for the management of a mercantile project of this kind. But whether such a government as that of England; which, whatever may be its virtues, has never been famous for good oeconomy; which, in time of peace, has generally conducted itself with the slothful and negligent profusion that is perhaps natural to monarchies; and in time of war has constantly acted with all the thoughtless extravagance that democracies are apt to fall into; could be safely trusted with the management of such a project, must at least be a good deal more doubtful.[66]

Smith believed, moreover, that there were evils involved in the economic order which it was beyond the competence of even good government to remedy. To repeat a useful quotation: "People of the same trade seldom meet together, even for merriment and diversion, but the conversation ends in a conspiracy against the public, or in some contrivance to raise prices. It is impossible indeed to prevent such meetings, by any law which either could be executed, or would be consistent with liberty and justice."[67] We have tried, in this country, to abolish Gary dinners by law. Whether we have succeeded seems still to be open to argument.

So much for the negative aspects of Smith's theory of the function of the state. Let us examine now what concessions he made to the possibilities of the promotion of human welfare through govermental action. Smith conceded that it was the duty of the goverment to provide protection against external foes, and on the ground of their necessity for defense, he approved of commercial regulations which on purely economic grounds he would condemn. "The act of navigation is not favourable to foreign commerce, or to the growth of that opulence which can arise from it. . . . As defence, however, is of much more importance than opulence, the act of navigation is, perhaps, the wisest of all the commercial regulations of England."[68] In the same spirit, Smith mildly supported bounties on

[64] *Wealth of Nations*, I, 328.
[65] *Ibid.*, I, 457.
[66] *Ibid.*, II, 303.
[67] *Ibid.*, I, 130.
[68] *Ibid.*, I, 429.

manufactures necessary for defense, which would not otherwise be produced at home.[69]

Smith assigned to government also "the duty of establishing an exact administration of justice."[70] Unfortunately, Smith never succeeded in carrying out his original plan of writing a treatise on jurisprudence, and the scattered materials in the *Wealth of Nations* and the meager outline in the *Lectures* are insufficient to give us a trustworthy judgement as to what he would include under "justice." His own definition in the *Wealth of Nations*, "the duty of protecting, as far as possible, every member of the society from the injustice or oppression of every other member of it," if broadly interpreted, would assign to government the task of a major reconstruction of the economic order, since Smith, as has been shown, recited many phases of it in which injustice and oppression prevailed. It seems clear, however, that Smith, like later and more doctrinaire exponents of laissez faire, took for granted the inevitability of private property and class conflict, and understood by justice the whole legal and customary code of his time dealing with indivudual rights, privileges, and obligations under that system of economic organization. It is also likely that Smith failed to see how far acceptance of even the prevailing code of justice carried him from a simple order of nature in which natural justice automatically emerges from the harmony of individual interests, independently of governmental machinery and sanctions. Punishment and enforcement of redress after the act in case of dishonesty, violence, fraud, clearly would be included under the "administration of justice." Smith would, perhaps, include as a proper phase of this function such preventive measures as would tend to give security against the perpetration of dishonesty, extortion, and violence. In any case, he does not oppose such regulations, though his *Lectures* indicate that he would include them under "police" rather than "justice."[71] "The institution of long apprenticeships can give no security that insufficient workmanship shall not frequently be exposed to public sale. When this is done it is generally the effect of fraud, and not of inability; and the longest apprenticeship can give no security against fraud. Quite different regulations are necessary to prevent this abuse. The sterling mark upon plate, and the stamps upon linen and woollen cloth, give the purchaser much greater security than any statute of apprenticeship."[72] Unqualified adherence to the principle of *caveat emptor* was apparently not a necessary implication of Smith's laissez faire doctrines. Enforcement of contracts is specified as an important function of government,[73] and a law oblig-

---

[69] *Ibid.*, II, 23.

[70] *Ibid.*, II, 185.

[71] *Lectures*, 154, ff.

[72] *Wealth of Nations*, I, 123–124.

[73] *Ibid.*, I, 97.

ing masters to pay wages in money rather than in kind is justifiable as a protection to the workers against fraud. "It imposes no real hardship upon the masters. It only obliges them to pay that value in money, which they pretended to pay, but did not always really pay, in goods."[74] "Where there is an exclusive corporation, it may perhaps be proper to regulate the price of the first necessary of life."[75] Protection of slaves against violence by their masters is approved of both as in accord with common humanity and as promoting the productivity of slave labor.[76] Smith recognized the existence of a higher social justice, which may override the "natural liberty" of the individual, but he would invoke it sparingly. Regulations of paper money banking "may, no doubt, be considered as in some respect a violation of natural liberty. But those exertions of the natural liberty of a few individuals, which might endanger the security of the whole society, are, and ought to be, restrained by the laws of all governments; of the most free, as well as of the most despotical. The obligation of building party walls, in order to prevent the communication of fire, is a violation of natural liberty, exactly of the same kind with the regulations of the banking trade which are here proposed."[77] but "To hinder . . . the farmer from sending his goods at all times to the best market, is evidently to sacrifice the ordinary laws of justice to an idea of public utility, to a sort of reasons of state; and act of legislative authority which ought to be exercised only, which can be pardoned only in cases of the most urgent necessity."[78] We have here, perhaps, the germ of that later maxim of convenient vagueness, that every individual should be protected in his natural rights, but only to the extent to which they do not interfere with the natural rights of others. There is no evidence that Smith would include as a proper phase of the administration of justice any drastic revision of the content of these rights.

There remains to be considered the third government function: "erecting and maintaining certain public works and certain public institutions, which it can never be for the interest of any individual, or small number of individuals, to erect and maintain; because the profit could never repay the expense to any individual or small number individuals, though it may frequently do much more than repay it to a great society."[79] Smith here clearly assigns to the government a duty of promoting the general welfare other than in connection with protection and justice, if the means to do so are within the power of the government, but not within the power of individuals. What the relationship of this function is to the

[74] *Ibid.*, I, 143.
[75] *Ibid.*, I, 144.
[76] *Ibid.*, II, 88.
[77] *Ibid.*, I, 307.
[78] *Ibid.*, II, 41–42.
[79] *Ibid.*, II, 185.

natural order Smith does not discuss in the *Wealth of Nations*. The attention given to it by Smith has been attributed to the influence of the Physiocrats. In the *Theory of Moral Sentiments* there is one passage which appears to praise such institutions, but may have been intended in a satirical sense:

> The same principle, the same love of system, the same regard to the beauty of order, of art and contrivance, frequently serves to recommend those institutions which tend to promote the public welfare. . . . It is not commonly from a fellow-feeling with carriers and waggoners that a public-spirited man encourages the mending of high roads. When the legislature establishes premiums and other encouragements to advance the linen or woollen manufactures, its conduct seldom proceeds from pure sympathy with the wearer of cheap or fine cloth, and much less from that with the manufacturer or merchant. The perfection of police, the extension of trade and manufactures, are noble and magnificent objects. . . . They make part of the great system of government, and the wheels of the political machine seem to move with more harmony and ease by means of them. . . . All constitutions of government, however, are [ought to be?] valued only in proportion as they tend to promote the happiness of those who live under them.[80]

In the *Lectures*, the only relevant passage is a passing reference under the general heading of "Police" to what may be regarded as a detailed phase of this function of government, the promotion of cleanliness, presumably of the streets.[81]

In the *Wealth of Nations* the discussion lacks somewhat in breadth, perhaps because it is merely incidental to Smith's discussion of the financial aspects of government. The public works and public institutions in this class, says Smith, "are chiefly those for facilitating the commerce of the society, and those for promoting the instruction of the people."[82] He nowhere purports to give a complete list of the public works proper to government, but he mentions highways, bridges, canals, and harbors. In discussing the propriety of particular projects, however, he completely ignores the criterion he had laid down at the beginning of his discussion, namely, the impossibility of their being conducted profitably as private enterprises. The only reason he gives for his approval of government maintenance of the highways is that private management would not have a sufficient incentive to maintain them properly, and therefore could not be trusted to do so.[83] He apparently approves of government operation of canals, though he

[80] *Theory of Moral Sentiments*, pp. 163–64.
[81] *Lectures*, p. 154.
[82] *Wealth of Nations*, II, 214.
[83] *Ibid.*, II, 217.

grants that they can be left safely in private hands,[84] and that they can be profitably managed by joint-stock companies.[85]

The modern issue of the propriety of government participation in commerce and industry is dealt with by Adam Smith almost solely from the viewpoint: Can the government make a net revenue out of it? He takes coinage for granted as a government function without considering any possible alternative. He apparently approves of government operation of the post-office, but if so, the only ground given is the ability of the government to manage it with successful financial results.[86] He in general disapproves of government ventures into business, but solely on the ground that the government is a poor trader and a poor manager. The public domain, except what may be needed for parks, should be disposed of, because the sovereign is a poor farmer and forester. Smith apparently could not read German, and makes no references to German literature. Knowledge of the success of some of the German principalities in managing the public domain, and in other phases of public administration, would perhaps have lessened Smith's opposition to government ventures into industry. The modern advocate of laissez faire who objects to government participation in business on the ground that it is an encroachment upon a field reserved by nature for private enterprise cannot find support for this argument in the *Wealth of Nations*.

Of government "institutions," other than public works, intended to facilitate commerce, Smith opposes legal monopolies in general, though he concedes the validity of a temporary monopoly when a trading company undertakes, at its own risk and expense, to establish a new trade with some remote and barbarous nation, and he indicates that he approves for the same reason of the institutions of patent and copyright.[87]

Smith supports the participation of the government in the general education of the people, because it will help prepare them for industry, will make them better citizens and better soldiers, and happier and healthier men in mind and body. Public education is made necessary to check as far as may be the evil effects on the standards, mentality, and character of the working classes of the division of labor and the inequality in the distribution of wealth.[88] Here once more Smith draws a picture of the economic order under the system of natural liberty which is quite different from that beatific state which he dreamed about in the *Theory of Moral Sentiments*.

It is quite probable that Smith overlooked some current activities of govern-

[84] *Ibid.*, II, 216–217
[85] *Ibid.*, II, 247.
[86] *Ibid.*, II, 303.
[87] *Ibid.*, II, 245.
[88] *Ibid.*, II, 267 ff.

ment to which he would have given his approval if they had been called to his attention. The absence, for instance, in the *Wealth of Nations* of any discussion of poor relief as a public function has often been commented upon, and is generally regarded as having been due to oversight. But we have not yet revealed the full extent to which Smith showed himself prepared to depart from a rigid policy of laissez faire. The one personal characteristic which all of his biographers agree in attributing to him is absent-mindedness, and his general principle of natural liberty seems to have been one of the things he was most absent-minded about. We have already seen that in his more systematic discussion of the functions of government, Smith made important concessions to the possibility of government promotion of the general welfare through public works and institutions. In stray but frequent moments of intimate contact with facts apparently hostile to the principle of natural liberty, Smith conveniently forgot the principle and went beyond the limits set in his formal discussion to the proper activities of government. In arguing for the duty of government to support educational institutions which promote the martial spirit of the people, Smith incidentally concedes that "it would deserve its most serious attention to prevent leprosy or any other loathsome and offensive disease, though neither mortal nor dangerous, from spreading itself among them,"[89] from which it may reasonably be inferred that he would even more strongly support public action taken to prevent the spread of dangerous diseases, and thus would include public hygiene among the proper functions of government. In many instances Smith supported government restrictions on private initiative where neither justice nor defense was involved, and where the sole aim was to improve upon the direction which private initiative gave to the investment of capital, the course of commerce, and the employment of labor. He supported the compulsory registration of mortgages,[90] and he wrote approvingly of colonial laws which promoted agricultural progress by checking the engrossing of land.[91]

To the great indignation of Jeremy Bentham, he approved of the prevailing restriction of the maximum rate of interest to 5 per cent, on the ground that if a higher rate were current, "the greater part of the money which was to be lent, would be lent to prodigals and projectors, who alone would be willing to give this high interest. . . . A great part of the capital of the country would thus be kept out of the hands which were most likely to make a profitable and advantageous use of it, and thrown into those which were most likely to waste and destroy it.[92] We may be inclined to agree with Bentham that this is an inadequate

[89] *Ibid.*, II, 272.
[90] *Ibid.*, II, 347.
[91] *Ibid.*, II, 73.
[92] *Ibid.*, I, 338.

defense of the usury laws, but what makes it significant for our purposes is that it involves an admission on Smith's part that the majority of investors could not be relied upon to invest their funds prudently and safely, and that government regulation was a good corrective for individual stupidity.

Smith also makes several concessions to the mercantilistic policy of regulation of the foreign trade. He admits that there are circumstances under which export restrictions on corn may be warranted;[93] he approves of a moderate export tax on wool on the ground that it would produce revenue for the government and at the same time would afford an advantage over their foreign competitors to the British manufacturer of woolens;[94] he favors moderate taxes on foreign manufactures, which would still give to domestic workmen "a considerable advantage in the home market."[95]

Smith recommended that rents in kind should be taxed more heavily than money rents, because "such rents are always more hurtful to the tenant than beneficial to the landlord."[96] He would tax rent from leases which prescribe to the tenant a certain mode of cultivation more heavily than other rent, in order to discourage the practice of making such leases, "which is generally a foolish one."[97] He would tax at more favorable rates the landlord who cultivates a part of his own land, because it is of importance that the landlord, with his greater command of capital and his greater willingness and capacity to try experiments, should be encouraged to take an active part in agriculture.[98] He would penalize by heavier taxation the landlord who capitalizes a part of the future rent, because this is usually the expedient of a spendthrift, is frequently hurtful to landlord and tenant, is always hurtful to the community.[99] Shortly thereafter, however, Smith returns to laissez faire: "The principal attention of the sovereign ought to be to encourage, by every means in his power, the attention both of the landlord and of the farmer; by allowing both to pursue their own interest in their own way, and according to their own judgement; . . ."[100]

Smith gives a little support to the use of the taxing power as what would now be called "an instrument of social reform." He approves of a tax on the retail sale of liquor so adjusted as to discourage the multiplication of little alehouses,[101]

---

[93] *Ibid.*, II, 41.

[94] *Ibid.*, II, 152.

[95] *Ibid.*, II, 367. Smith may, however, have supported such taxes as an alternative to the existing higher taxes and prohibitions of import, and not as preferable to free import.

[96] *Ibid.*, II, 316.

[97] *Ibid.*

[98] *Ibid.*

[99] *Ibid.*, II, 315.

[100] *Ibid.*, II, 318.

[101] *Ibid.*, II, 337.

and of a heavy tax on distilleries as a sumptuary measure against spirituous liquors, especially if accompanied by a reduction in the tax on "the wholesome and invigorating liquors of beer and ale."[102] He supports heavier highway tolls upon luxury carriages than upon freight wagons, in order that "the indolence and vanity of the rich [be] made to contribute in a very easy manner to the relief of the poor."[103] He asserts that "the gains of monopolists, whenever they can be come at [are] certainly of all subjects the most proper for taxation.[104] The modern single-taxer finds support for his cause in Smith's argument for the special taxation of land values. "Ground-rents, so far as they exceed the ordinary rent of land, are altogether owing to the good government of the sovereign. . . . Nothing can be more reasonable than that a fund which owes its existence to the good government of the state, should be taxed peculiarly, or should contribute something more than the greater part of other funds, towards the support of the government."[105] He lends mild support to the principle of progressive taxation: "It is not very unreasonable that the rich should contribute to the public expence, not only in proportion to their revenue, but something more than in that proportion."[106]

Though there is nowhere in Smith's writings a general discussion of the possibilities of voluntary co-operation, he makes clear that he did not hope for much good from it. Making a reasonable inference from past experience, but a bad forecast of the subsequent trend, he saw in the joint-stock company very limited promise even for money-making purposes.[107] It was his verdict that the corporate guilds had failed to promote good workmanship.[108] Exception being made for the Scottish Presbyterian church, he saw even in religious associations much to blame.[109] About the only types of voluntary association in which Smith saw a high degree of effectiveness in accomplishing their purposes were associations of merchants and manufacturers to exploit the consumer and of masters to exploit the worker.

Adam Smith was not a doctrinaire advocate of laissez faire. He saw a wide and elastic range of activity for government, and he was prepared to extend it even farther if government, by improving its standards of competence, honesty, and public spirit, showed itself entitled to wider responsibilities. He attributed

102 *Ibid.*, II, 375.
103 *Ibid.*, II, 216.
104 *Ibid.*, II, 377.
105 *Ibid.*, II, 329.
106 *Ibid.*, II, 327.
107 *Ibid.*, II, 246.
108 *Ibid.*, I, 131.
109 *Ibid.*, II, 273 ff.

great capacity to serve the general welfare to individual initiative applied in competitive ways to promote individual ends. He devoted more effort to the presentation of his case for individual freedom than to exploring the possibilities of service through government. He helped greatly to free England from the bonds of a set of regulatory measures which had always been ill advised and based on fallacious economic notions, but he did not forsee that England would soon need a new set of regulations to protect her laboring masses against new, and to them dangerous, methods of industrial organization and industrial technique. Smith was endowed with more than the ordinary allotment of common sense, but he was not a prophet. But even in his own day, when it was not so easy to see, Smith saw that self-interest and competition were sometimes treacherous to the public interest they were supposed to serve, and he was prepared to have government exercise some measure of control over them where the need could be shown and the competence of government for the task demonstrated. His sympathy with the humble and the lowly, with the farmer and the laborer, was made plain for all to see. He had not succeeded in completely freeing himself from mercantilistic delusions, and he had his own peculiar doctrinal and class prejudices. But his prejudices, such as they were, were against the powerful and the grasping, and it was the interests of the general masses that he wished above all to promote, in an age when even philosophers rarely condescended to deal sympathetically with their needs. He had little trust in the competence or good faith of government. He knew who controlled it, and whose purposes they tried to serve, though against the local magistrate his indictment was probably unduly harsh. He saw, nevertheless, that it was necessary, in the absence of a better instrument, to rely upon government for the performance of many tasks which individuals as such would not do, or could not do, or could do only badly. He did not believe that laissez faire was always good, or always bad. It depended on circumstances; and as best he could, Adam Smith took into account all of the circumstances he could find. In these days of contending schools, each of them with the deep, though momentary, conviction that it, and it alone, knows the one and only path to economic truth, how refreshing it is to return to the *Wealth of Nations* with its eclecticism, its good temper, its common sense, and its willingness to grant that those who saw things differently from itself were only partly wrong.

3

MARSHALL'S ECONOMICS, IN RELATION
TO THE MAN AND TO HIS TIMES

MALTHUS ONCE SAID with reference to Senior's lectures on population, that "it was among the disadvantages of public lectures, that the lecturer sometimes though he was called upon to say something new, where there was nothing new to be said." Malthus, it may be ventured, would have been willing to concede that he had contributed substantially to placing Senior in that position by having himself previously said most of what was worth saying about population. Asked to speak to the Association on Marshall as part of the celebration of the fiftieth anniversary of the publication of his *Principles*, I find myself very much in the position Malthus thought Senior was in.

My own plight I attribute mainly to four factors: First, so much of what knowledge I may have about Marshall has been gained through the years from the late Dr. Taussig's writings, teaching, and conversation that I can no longer separate what I have learned for myself from what I have derived from him. Secondly, the fifty years and more of published commentary on Marshall's *Principles* have made it difficult to find fresh cause for praise or complaint. Third, the admirable *Memorials of Alfred Marshall*, 1925, edited by Pigou, and containing penetrating and enlightening contributions by Keynes, Edgeworth, and Pigou on the relation of Marshall's personality and social philosophy to his economics, has so thoroughly exploited the biographical data available even to insiders that not much scope is left to those who had never seen nor heard Marshall in the flesh nor had an opportunity to draw on the rich fund of oral Cambridge tradition. What would be ordinarily a substitute, published letters, are also unavailable except for the few published in the *Memorials*. Finally, Mr. Schumpeter has kindly made available to me in advance a generous-sized abstract of his paper on the pure theory aspects of Marshall's *Principles*, with the consequence that I cannot easily, without resort to plagiarism, fill out what I can find to say within my own assignment by encroachment on his. If, then, what I say should sound unduly familiar and

Reprinted from the *American Economic Review* 31 (June 1941): 22–35.

commonplace, solace must be sought in the also familiar and commonplace reflection that on the subject of Marshall what is new is highly unlikely at this late date also be both true and significant. I will deal in turn with the influence on Marshall's economics of his political views, of his moral philosophy, and of some of his methodological predilections.

I

Marshall was in many respects a highly representative late Victorian intellectual. He was a Victorian "liberal" in his general orientation toward social problems, as probably also in the narrower partisan sense. English economics was throughout the nineteenth century intimately bound up with English politics, and throughout the century English economists had, probably without any important exception, political affiliations or preferences which influenced and were influenced by their economic doctrines. It is possible to ascertain with some degree of assurance the political affiliations of the earlier economists from their economic writings, but this requires an examination of their position with respect to issues which, though of minor importance for economics, sharply divided the various political groupings. On the major economic issues of the nineteenth century which were also important political issues, notably, foreign trade policy, the treatment of the poor, and the economic rôle of the state, there was much overlapping of position as between the political parties, at least during the first half of the century. By the middle of the century all the political parties as parties had accepted, or had ceased to contest, the free trade doctrine which stemmed from Adam Smith and which all the major economists except Malthus enthusiastically supported. By the late 1830's there was opposition only from one wing of the Tories and from the extreme radicals to the principle of confining relief to the able-bodied poor on the basis of "less eligibility"; that is, of granting it only in such unattractive form that the incentives to industry, thrift, and prudential control of the birthrate should not be undermined, a principle developed with almost complete agreement by the classical economists on the strength of Smithian individualism, Benthamite-Malthusian population theory, and the Malthusian-Ricardian law of diminishing returns, plus in all probability a large dose of unconscious puritanism. The period from 1800 to 1850 was, whatever party was in power, fairly consistently a period of piecemeal legislative repeal, item by item, of the mass of legislation restrictive of domestic freedom of enterprise which had survived on the statute books from the mercantilist period, and this trend also was aided and abetted by all the classical economists from the Benthamites, at one extreme, to the most conservative Whigs, like Malthus and Senior, at the other. On the major political issues of the first half of the century, therefore, while there might be a question as to whether the classical economists were determining the historical trend, or merely riding it, it is clear that they were not fighting it. It can now be seen, if it was not then possible to do so, that what conflict there then was between legislators and economists turned for the most part on the pace, and not on the general direction, of the legislative activity.

Even the Tory party, whose basic political philosophy seemed to be that all institutions were evil when new and irreproachable when aged, was moving, though slowly, reluctantly, and with misgivings and internal dissension, on the paths mapped out for it by the anti-Tory economists. It is in fact a paradox in the history of the relations of economics and politics in early nineteenth century England that the one political movement of importance which the historians most unitedly ascribe to the influence of the economists, the advocacy of extreme *laissez-faire* by the Manchester School, was the only one which the leading economists felt impelled expressly to denounce as going counter to, or at least beyond, the teachings of political economy. In so far as the dogmatic *laissez-faire* position of the Manchester School found in its own day, aside from the tariff question, any adherents among the ranks of economists, these were Continental or American economists. John Stuart Mill, Senior, Cairnes, McCulloch, Torrens, Longfield, the only English economists of note of the period, all sharply dissociated themselves from some at least of the doctrines of the Manchester School and denied its pretensions to support from the "principles of political economy." The classical economists did espouse *laissez-faire*, but a *laissez-faire* avowedly subject to qualification and requiring specific justification in each case of potential application.

* The Manchester School, in any case, had but a brief period of power. The growing information—and exaggeration—about working and living conditions in the factory towns, the steadily increasing political power of the working classes even under the restricted suffrage of the Reform Act of 1832, and the widespread humanitarian reaction against the doctrine of governmental impotence to remedy unmerited distress, made support of governmental inaction as a policy increasingly dangerous politically to any party which committed itself too strongly to it. With the establishment by the second Reform Act of 1867 of very nearly complete adult male suffrage, it became necessary for both the aristocratic Conservative or Tory party and the by-now predominantly middle-class Liberal party, if either were to gain or retain power as against the other, and if a third and "subversive" working-class party, as strong as or stronger than they, was not to come into being, to woo the working classes by support of a policy of wider govern-

mental activity in relief of distress and poverty. Social reform through legislation thereafter became respectable political doctrine for both parties, and reform legislation in fact obtained active support alternately or simultaneously from both major parties during the remainder of the century.

During the period of Marshall's youth, John Stuart Mill was the only economist of great public eminence, and Mill, who in his own youth had been one of the original Benthamites, had in his intellectual development absorbed something from almost every major humanitarian and utopian current of his time while managing substantially to retain most of the form and much of the substance of the sterner doctrines of the Bentham-James Mill-Ricardo circle under whose discipline he had been brought up to a too-precocious maturity. With his too-catholic blending of the dour individualism and the unrelenting *a priori* political democracy of the classical school, the utopianism of the Owenites and the St. Simonians, the patriarchal humanitarianism of Wordsworth and Coleridge, and the new misgivings as to the workings of political democracy and social equalitarianism in actual practice as revealed in the United States, John Stuart Mill was the connecting link with respect to political presuppositions for Marshall, as for many later economists in England (and also in the United States), between the classical school of the 1820's and the late-Victorian neoclassical economics. It is substantially true that from the 1870's on all English economic *theorists* of any note were, although with varying degrees of certitude and enthusiasm, political liberals of the John Stuart Mill type. It incidentally seems also to be substantially true that all the English economic *historians* of note were conservative, imperialist, anti-democratic, in their political tendencies, or else went far beyond the liberals in their advocacy of radical social and economic reforms.

The data available on Marshall's political opinions are scanty and scattered. They suffice, however, to support the following summary of the substance and content of his political liberalism as being probably correct as far as it goes:

(1) Marshall was a believer in political democracy, meaning by it essentially universal (male) suffrage, decisions reached by free discussion and by majority vote, and an electorate educated at public expense. In the Benthamite tradition, he held these beliefs not on natural rights grounds, but on the utilitarian ground that they were essential for good government.

(2) Marshall was an individualist in most of the many senses of the term. His ultimate criterion for appraising the social value of any polity was the nature of its probable impact upon the character and well-being of *individuals*. His appraisals of policies and trends were always in terms of what they did for individuals, singly or in groups, and never in terms of their contribution to the prestige or power of an idealized "state" distinguishable from its people. His hope for social

progress rested primarily on the capacity for industry, thrift, enterprise, voluntary coöperation, and "economic chivalry," of enlightened individuals, and he had limited, though some, faith in the possibilities of betterment through restrictive or coercive legislation or through the direct exercise of governmental enterprise in the economic field.

(3) Marshall also was essentially a political equalitarian in the Bentham-J. S. Mill sense. He not only wished every (male) adult to count as one and only as one in the machinery of political democracy, but he believed, with the English classical school, that in so far as there were significant differences in the capacities and the economic status of the different social classes these class differences were for the most part not due to biological differences in innate capacity or character as between individuals but were due instead to environmental differences, to inequality of opportunity: "the poverty of the poor [was] the chief cause of that weakness and inefficiency which are the cause of their poverty."[1]

(4) Basically, Marshall's political doctrines carried the hallmark also of Victorian complacency and gentility. While he recognized the problem of poverty as a major one, he never revealed any doubt that it could be substantially resolved within the limits of British parliamentary democracy and of a free enterprise economy. He was impatient alike with theories of economic history which treated economic and social progress as if it was in any sense inevitable or automatic, and with pessimistic theories which treated it as impossible, or as impossible without revolutionary political changes. He was confident that if only there were sufficient goodwill ("economic chivalry") and economic understanding substantial progress would in fact occur, and he evidently had faith in the effectiveness of sound moral preaching to produce the goodwill and of sound Cambridge economics to produce the understanding. The progress he sought, moreover, was not to be merely a matter of more goods, but of access to and liking for a more leisurely and more refined life for *all* the people, so that even hod-carriers could be gentlemen. The stamp of the political doctrines is perceptible throughout his economic writings.

II

Marshall is said by his biographers to have come to economics from ethics. But his early interest in ethics arose out of his search for a guide to his conscience rather than from an intellectual interest in the metaphysical aspects of moral phi-

---

[1] "The Present Position of Economics" (1885), in A. C. Pigou, ed., *Memorials of Alfred Marshall* (London, Macmillan, 1925), p. 155

losophy. In his younger days at Cambridge as student and teacher the conflict waged hot between utilitarian and idealistic theories of ethics, but there is no evidence that Marshall ever took real interest in this controversy or believed that it had immediate significance for his economics. It would be more accurate, I think, on the basis of the available evidence, to say that Marshall came to economics from his morals, from his zeal to make a contribution to the social betterment of man. Of the many passages in his writings which reveal Marshall's conviction that it is the duty of educated men to strive for the improvement of social conditions, and that a sound and moralized economics is a valuable instrument to this end, and his self-dedication to economics in this spirit, the following are representative:

> Is there not a great fund of conscientiousness and unselfishness latent in the breasts of men, both rich and poor, which could be called out if the problems of life were set before them in the right way, and which would cause misery and poverty rapidly to diminish?[2]

> It will be my most cherished ambition, my highest endeavour, to do what with my poor ability and my limited strength I may, to increase the numbers of those, whom Cambridge, the great mother of strong men, sends out into the world with cool heads but warm hearts, willing to give some at least of their best powers to grappling with the social suffering around them; resolved not to rest content till they have done what in them lies to discover how far it is possible to open up to all the material means of a refined and noble life.[3]

> . . . I have devoted myself for the last twenty-five years to the problem of poverty, and . . . very little of my work has been devoted to any inquiry which does not bear on that.[4]

I see no grounds for questioning either Marshall's complete sincerity in this connection, or the conformity of his life as a whole—which of course does not mean the whole of his life in every detail—to his announced principles. The moral earnestness with which Marshall regarded the rôle of economics and his own rôle as an economist was thoroughly Victorian, was altogether in keeping with the spirit of his times in liberal educated circles. If, in so far as simple formulae ever have validity when applied to the thought of a generation, late eighteenth century thought can be said to have reflected enlightenment without

---

[2] Lecture by Marshall (1883) quoted in "In Memoriam: Alfred Marshall," by Pigou, *op. cit.*, p. 83.

[3] "The Present Position of Economics" (1885), *ibid.*, p. 174.

[4] Alfred Marshall, "Minutes of Evidence taken before the Royal Commission on the Aged Poor, June 5, 1893," *Official Papers* (London, Macmillan for the Royal Economic Society, 1926), p. 205.

zeal, light without warmth, and our present-day world to exhibit zeal without enlightenment, heat without light, then it may be remembered that the late Victorian age in which Marshall reached maturity was the age of "sweetness *and* light," of reason tempered—some would say alloyed—by pity.

There are genuine differences in tone here between the Benthamite economists of the 1820's and Marshall. In one of the passages I have cited, Marshall spoke of the need for "cool heads but warm hearts." Bentham and his followers laid more stress on the dangers than on the benefits which might result from warm-heartedness. The Benthamites had, as much as Marshall, dedicated their lives to the betterment of the conditions of the mass of mankind, and Marshall, like the Benthamites, believed that charity and goodwill unguided and unrestrained by "sound" general principles could do more harm then good. But Bentham's circle believed that acquaintance with sound principles was more urgently needed than goodwill. In Marshall's case this does not seem to be true, for Marshall seems on the whole to have been more fearful of too little stress on the heart than of too little exercise of the mind. There is a passage in Marshall's writings which is interesting not only because of its bearing on this point but also because it is the only passage in all of Marshall's writings in which I have been able to detect the slightest taint of humor—and even here it may well have been unconcious:

G. Possibilities of Discrimination
[between worthy and unworthy]

. . . .

9. Patience in bearing other people's sufferings is as clear a duty as patience in bearing one's own, but it may be carried too far.[5]

John Stuart Mill was here again the connecting link between the Benthamites and Marshall. Under the influence largely of Wordsworth, he had reacted against his father's and Bentham's social philosophy as unduly cold and hard, and as lacking the moderating element obtainable from giving a larger rôle to "feeling." Mill introduced into the main line of English economic thought the sentimentality, the heart-throbbing, which Bentham, James Mill, Ricardo, McCulloch, Malthus, and Senior had carefully avoided. John Stuart Mill had thus made it more difficult for the humanitarians and the tear-evoking novelists to accuse the economists of having made it possible to freeze one's heart and yet live at peace with one's conscience. When Bagehot wrote, in a not wholly facetious vein, that "no real

---

[5] "Royal Commission on the Aged Poor (1893), Memorandum and Evidence offered to the Commissioners by Professor Alfred Marshall. (i) Preliminary Memorandum. A. Preliminary Statement." *Ibid.*, pp. 202–3.

Englishman in his secret soul was ever sorry for the death of a political economist; he is much more likely to be sorry for his life," it was not economists like
J. S. Mill or Marshall whom he had in mind. In any case, once Marshall had
become the leading British economist it ceased to be a common charge against
economics that "it dires up the hearts and the imaginations of the most who
meddle with it" (Miss Lucy Aikin), or that all that it asked of men "is that they
should harden their hearts" (Robert Southey); and the question whether humane
men could be devotees of the dismal science had ceased to be a live one.

While it could be argued that these were more largely differences in mode of
expression as between the Benthamites and Marshall, corresponding merely to
changes in verbal style, than differences in substance, it seems clear that Marshall's lesser willingness to be patient about the immediate woes of the poor led
him actively to seek means of reconciliation between advocacy of relief of distress on humanitarian grounds and adherence to the Benthamite principle that it
was urgent to preserve unimpaired by excessive charity the capacity for and the
will to practice self-help on the part of the poor. To take one instance: the classical
economists, in appraising the claims of the aged poor to generous relief, held
that, as old age was a foreseeable contingency, in general provision for it should
be regarded as an individual responsibility. They drew no distinction between
absence of reserves for old age due to expenditures on gin, on the one hand, and
to expenditures on the education, nutrition and health of children, on the other.
Marshall expressly refused to follow them on this point:

> Too much stress is often laid both from the ethical and from the economical point
> of view on those forms of thrift which result in material provision for sickness and
> old age, in comparison with those forms which benefit the coming generation.
>
> This is greatly due to the influence exerted on the administrations of poor-relief
> and charity by the economic and social philosophy of the early years of this cen-
> tury.[6]

When Marshall spoke of the task of economics to search for methods of opening up to all "the material means of a refined and noble life," he again used
language which the Benthamites would not have found to their taste. Bentham
would have spoken instead in terms of making available greater provision for the
poor, without setting limits as to the amount to be desired of such increase in
provision or inquiring as to its contribution to the refinement or ennobling of the
life of the poor, provided only it contributed to their happiness. To Bentham, or
so he claimed at least, "pushpin was equal to poetry" if they produced equal

[6] *Ibid.*, p. 202.

quantities of happiness, and he and his followers carefully avoided resort to any criterion for appraisal of the use which men made of their resources except its effect on their own, or their neighbors', or their children's happiness.

Here again John Stuart Mill was the connecting link between the strict utilitarianism of the early classical school, on the one hand, and the Victorian stress on refinement and nobility of Marshall, on the other hand; for Mill had diluted the Benthamite doctrine by insisting that over and above the purely quantitative differences between utilities there was a hierarchy of higher-and-lower, nobler-and-less-noble utilities which should be taken into account. Whatever may be the merits of this issue, and it is one on which there still seems to be as much room for inconclusive debate as there was when it was first raised, for Marshall the choice in favor of Mill as against Bentham was a convenient one. It not only put him in accord with the dominant ethical thought in the Cambridge of his time, but it also enabled him to retain an evangelistical note in his economics even after he had on intellectual grounds eliminated it from his theology.

Marshall, however, never explicitly discussed these ethical issues, and in fact sought deliberately to avoid being entrapped into open discussion thereof and into formal statement of his position by using as colorless and irenic terms as were available to express the ethical implications and presuppositions of his economics. Without surrendering or completely concealing his position, he thus succeeded fairly well in escaping the necessity of ever having to defend it.

III

Marshall came to economics also from mathematics. Educated at Cambridge, noted for its emphasis on the educational and disciplinary value of rigorous training in mathematics, he attained high distinction in that field as a student. He taught mathematics before he taught economics. He had not only distinct aptitude but also great liking for mathematical forms of reasoning. It is clear, however, that he had grave mistrust of the consequences of unrestrained employment of formal mathematics in economic analysis. One factor in this distrust was probably a lurking puritan suspicion of the morality of any highly pleasurable activity: the formulation and solution of economic problems in mathematical, and especially graphical, terms yielded him so much intellectual and aesthetic delight that it for that reason alone became somewhat suspect to him as a worthy occupation. Mathematics, and especially graphs, were Marshall's fleshpots, and if he frequently succumbed to their lure it was not without struggle with his conscience. It can also be said for Marshall that when he did succumb he not only frequently warned his readers not to take his mathematical adventures too seriously but shielded them from the young and the susceptible by confining them to footnotes and appendices where, as he rightly anticipated, only the hardened sinners already beyond further corruption would prolongedly gaze. Marshall also was anxious for a wide audience, and the fact that the bulk of his potential readers were both unable and unwilling to read economics in mathematical form no doubt was an additional consideration.

But Marshall had other and presumably better reasons for misgivings as to the effect on economics of the extensive use of mathematics. First, the mathematical approach required rigorous abstraction, whereas Marshall thought that the economist must strive to account for the concrete. Secondly, although this may not be wholly a different consideration, Marshall believed that economics must become more complicated and more biological in character, whereas mathematical economics tended toward excessive simplification and sought its prototype rather in mechanics than in biology.

Marshall from the first had a live sense of the complexity and variability of the interrelations between economic phenomena, and of the biological rather than mechanical nature of these interrelations. During his early years at Cambridge, as student and as teacher, the influence of Darwin and of Huxley was strong. Cambridge was becoming a center for distinguished work in the biological sciences, challenging in intellectual prestige to some extent the traditional academic aristocracies of theology, philosophy, the classics, and mathematics and the physical sciences. While I know of no evidence that Marshall was ever a serious student of biology, and I have been unable to find that there was any personal intimacy between Marshall and the distinguished Cambridge biologists, physiologists, pathologists, psychologists, and so forth of his time, biological ideas were then very much in the air, and could be absorbed without special effort. In any case, Marshall saw in biological rather than in mechanical modes of thought the most suitable instruments of economic analysis. ". . . in the later stages of economics, when we are approaching nearly to the conditions of life, biological analogies are to be preferred to mechanical, other things being equal. . . . The Mecca of the economist is economic biology rather than economic dynamics."[7]

The biological sciences have in fact proved least tractable of all the natural sciences to abstract mathematical analysis, for largely the same reasons, I suppose, which in all probability led Marshall, and others, to see but a limited scope for the fruitful use of mathematics in economic theory: (1) great complexity of the problems; (2) significant variables too great in number for their separate analysis and yet not great enough in number to make reliance upon technical proba-

---

[7] "Distribution and Exchange" (1898), *Memorials*, pp. 317–18

bility theory without specific analysis of particular variables a safe procedure; (3) the absence of reversibility in the interactions of variables; (4) the restricted scope for completely controlled experiment; (5) the absence of that complete indifference of the investigator to the material with which he is working and to the nature of his results which is the only reliable guarantee of scientific objectivity which we can have.

Devotees of the mathematical approach to economic problems frequently claim for that approach that the alternative non-symbolic method, or the "literary method" as they too generously put it, is too imprecise and clumsy a tool for the exposition in all their complexity of the relationships between economic variables, with the implication that it is the complexity of economic problems, rather than their simplicity, which establishes a necessary and fruitful field for the use of mathematics. Marshall, both in his formal writings and in his letters of warning to his disciples against overindulgence in mathematics, seems to me to have taken exactly the reverse view, although not in so many words; namely: that non-symbolic language and simple statistical methods alone had the elasticity to deal with the infinite detail and variability of concrete economic phenomena; that resort to mathematics, unless confined to a preliminary stage of economic investigation, involved a greater degree of surrender of this elasticity than it was wise to accept; and that only the relatively simple propositions in economics could be expressed in mathematical form, and even then only at the cost of artificial and often serious further simplification. It must have been the complexities of the biological as distinguished from the mechanical aspects of economic problems which Marshall had in mind, for I cannot see how he could have intended to deny that, whatever the degree of complexity of the mechanical type economic problems may involve, they can be handled better with than without the aid of mathematics.

There was still another element leading Marshall to cry down the value of the mathematical method. Marshall, at least in his frequent moralizing moods, placed no high value on economic analysis as a good in itself, as a cultural pursuit or a substitute for chess. Writing to Edgeworth in 1902, he said:

> In my view "theory" is essential. No one gets any real grip of economic problems unless he will work at it. But I conceive no more calamitous notion than that abstract, or general, or "theoretical" economics was "economics" proper. It seems to me an essential but a very small part of economics proper: and by itself sometimes even—well, not a very good occupation of time.[8]

From this and other passages it can be inferred that Marshall, believing as he did that it was "pure theory" which lent itself most fully to mathematical expo-

[8] Letter by Marshall to Professor F.Y. Edgeworth (1902), *ibid.*, p. 437

sition, that for economics to be a serviceable instrument of human betterment it must be extended to include consideration of the concrete detail not readily or at all amenable to abstract mathematical treatment, and that the attraction of mathematics led some economists to neglect the concrete detail and to confine themselves to pure theorizing, minimized the usefulness of mathematics to economics in order to check the tendency toward what he regarded as undue abstraction.[9]

I am no mathematician myself, and I try always to remember and to profit from Edgeworth's merited reproof to an Italian economist who had had the temerity to question the usefulness of Edgeworth's application of the mathematical method to taxation problems: "The withers of the mathematician are not wrung by these commonplaces. The use of the method is not necessarily attended with an exaggeration of its importance. The inability to use it is not a qualification for appreciating its usefulness." Professional mathematicians have assured me, moreover, that the uninitiated can have no conception of the feats which can be performed by the aid of the elastic, the precise, the versatile, and the delicate apparatus of the modern higher mathematics. Although they have also upon occasion suggested to me that economists are pressing it to perform false miracles, I venture no disclaimer, therefore, of whatever general or specific claims for their method mathematical economists may make, provided they are confined to mathematical claims beyond my understanding or ability to test. But non-mathematical economists with an inferiority-complex—which today includes, I feel certain, very nearly all non-mathematical economists—may be pardoned, perhaps, if they derive a modest measure of unsanctified joy from the spectacle of the great Marshall, a pioneer in mathematical economics himself, disparaging the use of mathematics in economics, and counting as wasted effort the mastery of any other economist's mathematical symbols. If, as seems doubtful, Marshall's warnings served to dissuade any budding Cambridge economic geniuses with aptitude for mathematics from acquiring an abundant command of its techniques, they no doubt served economics ill rather than well. But if they helped to check the descent of economics to the status of an unwanted foundling on mathematics' doorstep, they did render a useful service.

If Marshall's puritan conscience led him to disparage the method from which he undoubtedly derived the greatest intellectual excitement and joy, even that over-scrupulous conscience occasionally took a holiday. Marshall recognized

---

[9] Cf. J. M. Keynes, "Alfred Marshall, 1842–1924," ibid., p. 37: ". . . Marshall was too anxious to do good. He had an inclination to undervalue those intellectual parts of the subject which were not directly connected with human well-being or the condition of the working classes or the like, although indirectly they might be of the utmost importance, and to feel that when he was pursuing them he was not occupying himself with the Highest. . . . When his intellect chased diagrams and Foreign Trade and Money, there was an evangelical moraliser of an imp somewhere inside him, that was so ill-advised as to disapprove."

that the instruments for a general ethical calculus were lacking, but he claimed that the institution of money provided an adequate basis for calculations of *economic* satisfaction and sacrifice: "The pure science of Ethics halts for lack of a system of measurement of efforts, sacrifices, desires, etc., fit for her wide purposes. But the pure science of Political Economy has found a system that will subserve her narrower aims."[10]

Marshall was well aware and repeatedly acknowledged that the monetary unit represented substantially different quantities of satisfaction and of sacrifice for rich and for poor, respectively. It would seem that this was an insuperable barrier to the use of market prices as a measurement of such satisfaction and sacrifice as between different persons, and that, with his acceptance of the problem of poverty as the major problem for economics, Marshall would have felt obliged to recognize that even for a calculus of economic happiness no satisfactory instruments of measurement were available. His zeal for quasi-quantitative analysis and for reaching value-judgements overcame, however, his other scruples, and he adopted an analytical procedure which operated to distract attention from the necessity of making full allowance for the inequality in the distribution of wealth and income in reaching such value-judgements. In a passage in his *Principles* which has not escaped unfavorable notice by others, Marshall offered what must be regarded as a glaringly weak defense of this procedure:

> On the whole, . . . it happens that by far the greater number of the events with which economics deals affect in about equal proportions all the different classes of society; so that if the money measures of the happiness caused by two events are equal, there is not in general any very great difference between the amounts of the happiness in the two cases.[11]

Marshall was here setting up a screen between himself and his readers, on the one hand, and the problem of poverty on the other, in order to be free to engage, without too sharp pangs of conscience, in what was for himself a delectable intellectual activity. This was not Marshall at his best, however, nor even the normal Marshall, and there have been few of us who have made conscience be our guide as to subjects of investigation and methods of analysis as steadily and as consistently as did Marshall.

I do not regard it as part of my function to render a definite appraisal of Marshall as man or as economist. In any case, those aspects of Marshall's work with which I have dealt are not really matters for appraisal, and narration and descrip-

---

[10] "Mr. Mill's Theory of Value" (1876), *ibid.*, p. 126.
[11] Alfred Marshall, *Principles of Economics*, 6th ed., p. 131

tion are all that is called for. That Marshall was a great figure, one of the greatest, in the history of our discipline, and that without being by any means flawless he nevertheless fully earned his status, I would strongly argue if I knew of sufficient dissent from significant quarters and on significant grounds to give any point to such argument.

But Marshall is now long dead, and the rule "De mortuis non nisi bonum" is a required rule of morals or of good manners only for men very recently dead. There would be no point therefore in treating Marshall, whether the man or his work, with special tenderness or reserve. He had, beyond doubt, his weaknesses on both counts, including some with which he may have infected his followers, so that we regard them as points of strength. I am sure also that even his virtues are not be to admired by us to the point of slavish imitation. Each generation should—and will—work out its own economics, borrowing from, reacting from, improving upon, retrograding from, that of the preceding generation. Marshall's economics is now distinctly that of a generation which is past, and is increasingly *not* that of our own. For one thing, it is essentially the economics of a society assumed to be free and to have its economic affairs conducted by free individuals. Freedom, whether of the economic system as such, or of individuals, has over a large part of the earth's surface either never existed or been suppressed. The appropriate economics of the day is, moreover, the economics of war and preparation for or against war, *Wehrwirtschaft*, and Marshall here has only very limited guidance to offer.

It was a characteristic of Victorian, including Marshallian, public utterances that they typically ended on a double note, of assurance, on the one hand, of continuance into the future of all the well-established institutions and cherished values of the Victorian age, and of promise, on the other hand, of continued betterment of the social conditions of mankind. Both the Victorian complacency with respect to the present and the Victorian optimism with respect to future progress are now utterly inappropriate. As a social philosopher, Marshall is not yet merely a period piece. If he should become so in the near future, it would properly be a matter for concern, but not for surprise.

4

POWER VERSUS PLENTY AS OBJECTIVES
OF FOREIGN POLICY IN THE
SEVENTEENTH AND EIGHTEENTH
CENTURIES

IN THE SEVENTEENTH and eighteenth centuries economic thought and practice were predominantly carried on within the framework of that body of ideas which was later to be called "mercantilism." Although there has been almost no systematic investigation of the relationship in mercantilist thought between economic and political objectives or ends in the field of foreign policy, certain stereotypes have become so prevalent that few scholars have seriously questioned or examined their validity. One of these stereotypes is that mercantilism was a "system of power," that is, that "power" was for mercantilists the sole or overwhelmingly preponderant end of foreign policy, and that wealth, or "plenty," was valued solely or mainly as a necessary means to attaining or retaining or exercising power. It is the purpose of this paper to examine in the light of the available evidence the validity of this interpretation of mercantilist thought and practice. Tracing the history of ideas, however, always runs to many words, and limitations of space force me to confine myself, even with respect to bibliographical references, to samples of the various types of relevant evidence. That the samples are fair ones I can only attest by my readiness in most cases to expand them indefinitely.

The pioneer historians of mercantilism were nineteenth-century German scholars, predominantly Prussians sympathetic to its economic and political philosophy, and especially to its emphasis on state interests as opposed to the private interests of citizens. The interpretation of mercantilism by Schmoller as primarily a system of state-building is familiar, and commonly accepted by economic his-

Reprinted from *World Politics* 1 (October 1948): 1–29.

torians.[1] A similar stress on the political aspects of mercantilist commercial policy is common in the German writings. The proposition that the mercantilists sought a favorable balance of trade, wealth, and the indefinite accumulation of the precious metals solely as means to power seems first to have been launched by Baron von Heyking, who indeed claims priority for his interpretation.[2] Schmoller similarly interpreted the uncorrupted mercantilism of Prussia and of the non-maritime countries in general, but he maintained that the "imperialism" of the maritime powers was a debased mercantilism, characterized by an unscrupulous use of military power to promote ultimate commercial ends, and half-condemned it on that ground.[3]

This distinction betwen "pure" mercantilism, a "Staatsmerkantilismus," which can obtain its full development only in an absolute monarchy, and the mercantilism of countries where the commercial classes are influential and the state has to serve and to reconcile private economic interests, is also made much of by a later German writer, Georg Herzog zu Mecklenburg Graf von Carlow. For "pure" mercantilism, the ruling principle is not economic but the promotion of the power of the state.[4] In general, however, the historians have not distinguished between the mercantilism of the absolute and the constitutional states, and where they have dealt at all with the questions of the ultimate aims of mercantilism they have almost invariably asserted that these were solely or preponderantly political, although only too often with ambiguity or even outright self-contradiction, and almost invariably without presentation of substantial evidence.

[1] I suspect, nevertheless, that it is highly questionable. The economic unification of the nation-state appears mostly to have occurred before the advent of mercantilism, as in England, or after its decay, as in France, Spain, Russia, Switzerland, Italy, the United States, or the British Dominions, if the national unification of tariffs or other significant criteria are applied. Even Colbert promoted regional as well as national self-sufficiency. As Moritz Bonn has commented (*Journal of Political Economy*, LIV [1946], 474), "A parochialist like Gustav Schmoller naturally deduced his impressions of mercantilism from the policies of primitive Prussia."

[2] *Zur Geschichte der Handelsbilanztheorie*, Berlin 1880, Ch. 2, "Die Beziehungen der Theorie der Handelsbilanz zur Theorie des politischen Gleichgewichtes." The claim for priority is on p. 43. This chapter is a pioneer and valid demonstration of the existence of a close relationship between mercantilist balance-of-trade and balance-of-power theorizing and policy, but there is not a trace of valid demonstration in it that wealth considerations were made wholly subservient to power considerations.

[3] See his *Umrisse and Untersuchungen*, Leipzig, 1898, especially Ch. I, "Das Merkantilsystem in seiner historischen Bedeutung," pp. 42–60; see also "Die englische Handelspolitik des 17. und 18. Jahrhunderts," in *Jahrbuch für Gesetzgebrung, Verwaltung, und Volkswirtschaft*, XX (1899), 1211–1241. F. Brie, *Imperialistische Strömungen in der Englischen Literatur*, 2nd ed., Halle, 1928, p. 68, characterized English mercantilism of the eighteenth century, along Schmollerian lines, as "kaufmännisch gefärbte Imperialismus."

[4] *Richelieu als merkantilistischer Wirtschaftspolitiker und der Begriff des Staatsmerkantilismus*, Jena, 1929, pp. 198ff.

A case in point is William Cunningham, the English economic historian. His predominant interpretation of English mercantilism was that it sought power rather than or much more than plenty, and that it valued plenty solely or mainly as an instrument or support or power, although he easily slipped, in this as in other analytical issues, into ambiguity if not hopeless contradiction.[5] An English economic historian sympathetic to mercantilism, W.A.S. Hewins, regarded this interpretation as unfair to the mercantilists, and offered the following rendition of Cunningham's position to indicate its inacceptability:

> . . . one might almost imagine him [i.e., Cunningham] saying: "The mercantile system is concerned with man solely as a being who pursues national power, and who is capable of judging the comparative efficacy of means to that end. It makes entire abstraction of every other human passion or motive, except those which may be regarded as perpetually antagonising principles to the pursuit of national power—viz. neglect of shipping and aversion to a fish diet. The mercantile system considers mankind as occupied solely in pursuing and acquiring national power."[6]

All the German and English economic historians who found in mercantilism the complete subordination of economic to political considerations seem to have been themselves sympathetic to the subordination of the individual to the state and to the exaltation of vigorous nationalism characteristic of mercantilism, and to have been hostile to nineteenth century liberalism and its revolt against the residues of mercantilist legislation. Where this was combined, as in Schmoller and Cunningham, with a dislike of the rise of the bourgeois and his values to dominance over politics, to attribute to the mercantilists the conception of power

[5] Cf., for contradiction with the view that power was the predominant objective, *The Growth of English Industry and Commerce in Modern Times*, Vol. II, *In Modern Times, Part I*, Cambridge, 1903, p. 459: "From the Revolution till the revolt of the colonies, the regulation of commerce was considered, not so much with reference to other elements of national power, or even in its bearing on revenue, but chiefly with a view to the promotion of industry." Cf. also, *The Wisdom of the Wise*, Cambridge, 1906: "In the pre-scientific days the end which men of affairs kept in view, when debating economic affairs, was clearly understood; the political power of the realm was the object they put before them, . . ." (p. 21) "We recognize [today] that the defence of the realm is essential to welfare, but we are no longer so much concerned about building up the power of the country, or so ready to engage in aggressive wars *for the sake of commercial advantage*, as Englishmen were in the eighteenth century." (p. 22) The italics are mine. The contradiction the italicized words seem to indicate may not be real, since Cunningham may have had in mind that the "commercial advantages" were sought for the sake of their contribution to British power, but such exposition, ambiguous, if not contradictory, is so common in the literature that it provides of itself a justification for an article such as the present one.

[6] In a review of Cunningham's *Growth of English Industry and Commerce* in *The Economic Journal*, II (1892), 696. Cunningham, in a reply to Hewins and other reviewers, ibid., IV (1894), 508–16, permitted this interpretation of his position to pass without comment, although it must have been obvious to him that Hewins regarded it as a *reductio ad absurdum*.

as the sole or preponderant end of national policy was to praise rather than to blame them.

Eli Heckscher, the great Swedish economic historian and the outstanding authority on mercantilism today, follows the standard interpretation of the mercantilist objectives, but clearly to add to their shame rather than to praise them. Heckscher is an outstanding liberal, and individualist, a free-trader, and clearly anti-chauvinist. When to the section of his great work dealing with the foreign policy of the mercantilists he gives the heading "Mercantilism as a System of Power."[7] and applies it to mercantilism in general and not only to the mercantilism of the absolute monarchies or of the non-maritime countries, he is reinforcing the indictment of it which he makes on other grounds, for to him "power" is clearly an ugly name for an ugly fact. More systematically, more learnedly, and more competently than anyone else, he supports his thesis that the mercantilists subordinated plenty to power. His argument calls therefore for detailed examination if this proposition is to be questioned.

Heckscher really presents an assortment of theses, ranging from the proposition (1) that for mercantilists—whether for most, or many, or only some, not being made very clear—power was the sole ultimate end of state policy with wealth merely one of the means to the attainment of power, through the "eclectic" thesis (2) that power and plenty were parallel ends for the mercantilists but with much greater emphasis placed on power than was common before or later, to the concession (3) that mercantilists occasionally reversed the usual position and regarded power as a means for securing plenty and treated purely commercial considerations as more important than considerations of power. His central position, however, and to this he returns again and again, is that the mercantilists expounded a doctrine under which all considerations were subordinated to considerations of power as an end in itself, and that in doing so they were logically and in their distribution of emphasis unlike their predecessors and unlike the economists of the nineteenth century.

It is difficult to support this account of Heckscher's position by direct quotation from his text, since he presents it more by implication and inference from mercantilist statements than by clear-cut and explicit formulation in his own words. That mercantilists according to Heckscher tended to regard power as the sole end is to be inferred by the contrasts he draws between the position he attributes to Adam Smith—wrongly, I am sure—that "power was certainly only a means to the end" of "opulence,'' and the "reverse" position of the mercantilists,[8] the "reverse," I take it, being the proposition that wealth was only a means

---

[7] *Mercantilism*, translated by Mendel Shapiro, 2 vols., London, 1935, II, 13–52.
[8] *Ibid.*, II, 17.

to power. That there is something special and peculiar to mercantilism in conceiving power as an end in itself underlies all of Heckscher's exposition, but the following passages come nearest to being explicit. "The most vital aspect of the problem is whether power is conceived as an *end in itself*, or only as a means for gaining something else, such as the well-being of the nation in this world or its everlasting salvation in the next."[9] This leaves out of account, as an alternative, Heckscher's "eclectic" version, where both power and plenty are ends in themselves. On John Locke's emphasis on the significance for power of monetary policy, Heckscher comments, with the clear implication that the injection into economic analysis of considerations of power is not "rational," that it is "interesting as a proof of how important considerations of power in money policy appeared even to so advanced a rationalist as Locke."[10]

Heckscher later restated his position in response to criticisms, but it seems to me that he made no important concession and indeed ended up with a more extreme position than at times he had taken in his original exposition.

> The second of the aims of mercantilist policy . . . —that of power—has met with a great deal of criticism from reviewers of my book. . . . I agree with my critics on that point to the extent of admitting that both "power" and "opulence" . . . have been, and must be, of importance to economic policy of every description. But I do not think there can be any doubt that these two aims changed places in the transition from mercantilism to *laissez-faire*. All countries in the nineteenth century made the creation of wealth their lode-star, with small regard to its effects upon the power of the State, while the opposite had been the case previously.[11]

The evidence which Heckscher presents that the mercantilists considered power as an end in itself and as an important end, and that they considered wealth to be a means of power need not be examined here, since there is no ground for disputing these propositions and, as far as I know, no one has ever disputed them. That the mercantilists overemphasized these propositions I would also not question. Nor will I enter into extended discussion of the rationality of these concepts beyond stating a few points. In the seventeenth and eighteenth centuries, colonial and other overseas markets, the fisheries, the carrying trade, the slave trade, and

---

[9] *Ibid.*, II, 16.

[10] *Ibid.*, II, 47.

[11] "Revisions in Economic History, V, Mercantilism," *The Economic History Review*, VII (November 1936), 48. The foreign policy implications of the nineteenth century economics, I believe, need investigation as much as do the aims of mercantilism. Until such investigation is systematically made, comparisons with mercantilism are liable to be misleading with respect to the true position of both bodies of doctrine.

open trade routes over the high seas, were all regarded, and rightly, as important sources of national wealth, but were available, or at least assuredly available, only to countries with the ability to acquire or retain them by means of the possession and readiness to use military strength.

In the seventeenth and eighteenth centuries also, "power" meant not only power to conquer and attack, and the prestige and influence which its possession gave, but also power to maintain national security against external attack. "Power as an end in itself" must, therefore, be interpreted to include considerations of national security against external aggression on the nation's territory and its political and religious freedom. Given the nature of human nature, recognition of power as an end in itself was therefore then neither peculiar nor obviously irrational unless there is rational ground for holding that the promotion of economic welfare is the sole sensible objective of national policy to which every other consideration must be completely subordinated.

There remains, therefore, to be examined only whether Heckscher has demonstrated that mercantilists *ever* regarded power as the *sole* end of foreign policy, or ever held that considerations of plenty were *wholly* to be subordinated to considerations of power, or even whether they ever held that a choice has to be made in long-run national policy between power and plenty.

Despite his wide knowledge of the mercantilist literature, Heckscher fails to cite a single passage in which it is asserted that power is or should be the *sole* end of national policy, or that wealth matters *only* as it serves power. I doubt whether any such passage can be cited, or that anyone ever held such views. The nearest thing to such statements which Heckscher does cite are statements maintaining that wealth is a means of power and is important as such, unaccompanied by express acknowledgment that wealth is also important for its own sake. In almost every case he cites, it is possible to cite from the same writer passages which show that wealth was regarded as valuable also for its own sake. The passage of this type which Heckscher most emphasizes is a "passing remark" of Colbert in a letter: "Trade is the source of finance and finance is the vital nerve of war." Heckscher comments that Colbert here "indicates clearly the relationship between means and ends."[12] But argument from silence is notoriously precarious, and if it were to be pressed would work more against than for Heckscher's thesis, since there is a great mass of mercantilist literature in which there is no mention whatsoever, and no overt implication, of considerations of power. Colbert does not here indicate that the relationship was a one-way one. To make a significant point Heckscher would have to show that Colbert would not also have subscribed

[12] *Mercantilism*, II, 17.

to the obverse proposition that strength is the vital nerve of trade and trade the source of finance.

Of all the mercantilists Colbert is the most vulnerable, since he carried all the major errors of economic analysis of which they were guilty to their most absurd extremes both in verbal exposition and in practical execution, and since, either as expressing his own sentiments or catering to those of his master, Louis XIV, he developed more elaborately than any other author the serviceability to power of economic warfare, the possibilities of using military power to achieve immediate economic ends, and the possibilities of substituting economic warfare for military warfare to attain national ends. Even in his case, however, it is not possible to demonstrate that he ever rejected or regarded as unimportant the desirability for its own sake of a prosperous French people or the desirability of guiding French foreign policy, military and economic, so as to augment this prosperity. In many of his official papers he is obviously catering to Louis XIV's obsession with power and prestige, or perhaps to a conventional fashion of *pretending* that a great monarch would be so obsessed,[13] so that there is no reason to reject, as unrepresentative of his genuinely-held views, such passages as the following:

> . . . comme toutes les alliances entre les grands rois ont toujours deux fins principales, l'une leur gloire particulière et quelquefois la jonction de leurs intérêts, soit pour conserver, soit pour acquérir . . . et l'autre les avantages de leurs sujets . . . Et quoyque, dans l'ordre de le division, celuy de l'avantage de leurs sujets soit le dernier, il est néanmoins toujours le premier dans les esprits de bons princes. . . .
>
> Les avantages de leurs sujets consistent à les maintenir en repos au dedans et à leur procurer par le moyen du commerce, soit plus de facilités de vivre aux nécessiteux, soit plus d'abondance aux riches.[14]

[13] Cf. the following passage in his famous "Mémoire au Roi sur les Finances" of 1670: "Il est certain, Sire, que Vostre Majesté . . . a dans son esprit et dans toute sa nature la guerre par préférence à toute autre chose. . . . Vostre Magesté pense plus dix fois à la guerre qu'elle ne pense à ses finances." *Lettres Instructions et Mémoires de Colbert*, P. Clément, ed., Paris, 1870, VII, 252. This long memoir is a plea to the king to look to his economic policy, including economic warfare, as an essential instrument for attaining his ends. Even in the case of Louis XIV, himself, it is easy to show from his writings that the prosperity of his people, while no doubt inexcusably underemphasized, was a matter of some concern to him for its own sake.

[14] "Dissertation sur la question: quelle des deux alliances de France ou de Hollande peut estre plus avantageuse à l'Angleterre," March, 1669. *Lettres*, VI, 261. A letter of Colbert to Louis XIV in 1681 contains the following passage: "Ce qu'il y a de plus important, et sur quoi il y a plus de réflexions à faire, c'est la misére très-grande des peuples." C. Dareste de la Chavanne, *Histoire de l'Administration en France*, Paris, 1848, II, 258.

Certain peculiar features of mercantilist economic analysis—features incidentally which modern apologists for mercantilist economics such as Lipson seem strangely to avoid discussing—do seem to imply a disregard on the part of mercantilists for economic welfare.[15] What was apparently a phase of scholastic economics, that what is one man's gain is necessarily another man's loss, was taken over by the mercantilists and applied to countries as a whole.

They incorporated this with their tendency to identify wealth with money, and with their doctrine that, as far as money was concerned, what mattered was not the absolute quantity but the relative quantity as compared with other countries. Since the quantity of money in the world could be taken as constant, the quantity of wealth in the world was also a constant, and a country could gain only at the expense of other countries. By sheer analogy with the logic of military power, which is in truth a relative matter, and with the aid of the assumption of a close relationship between "balance of power" and "balance of trade," which, however, they failed intelligently to analyze, the mercantilists were easily led to the conclusion that wealth, like power, also was only a relative matter, a matter of proportions between countries, so that a loss inflicted on a rival country was as good as an absolute gain for one's own country. At least one mercantilist carried this doctrine to its logical conclusion that plague, war, famine, harvest failure, in a neighboring country was of economic advantage to your own country.[16] On such doctrine, Adam Smith's trenchant comment is deserved, although he exaggerates its role in mercantilist thought and practice:

> By such maxims as these, however, nations have been taught that their interest consisted in beggaring all their neighbours. Each nation has been made to look with an invidious eye upon the prosperity of all the nations with which it trades, and to consider their gain as its own loss. Commerce, which ought naturally to be, among nations, as among individuals, a bond of union and friendship, has become the most fertile source of discord and animosity. The capricious ambition of kings and ministers has not, during the present and the preceding century, been more fatal to the repose of Europe, than the impertinent jealousy of merchants and manufacturers. The violence and injustice of the rulers of mankind is an ancient evil, for which, I am afraid, the nature of human affairs can scarce admit of a remedy. But the mean rapacity, the monopolizing spirit of merchants and manufacturers, who neither are, nor ought to be, the rulers of mankind, though it cannot perhaps

---

[15] See Ephraim Lipson, *The Economic History of England*, Vols. II–III, "The Age of Mercantilism," 3rd edition, London, 1943.

[16] Theodor Ludwig Lau, *Aufrichtiger Vorschlag*, 1719, as reported in Walther Focke, *Die Lehrmeinungen der Kameralisten über den Handel*, Erlangen (dissertation), 1926, p. 59.

be corrected, may very easily be prevented from disturbing the tranquillity of any body but themselves.[17]

Heckscher cites mercantilist doctrine such as Adam Smith here criticizes as evidence that the mercantilists were not interested in economic welfare for its own sake, but subordinated it to considerations of power. Adam Smith's assumption that the exposition of such doctrine was confined to merchants to the exclusion of statesmen (or philosophers) is invalid. But in so far as it was expounded by merchants, it is scarcely conceivable that these were so different from merchants at other times that they were governed more by chauvinist patriotism than by rapacity. The significance of such doctrine is not that those who adhered to it placed power before plenty, but that they grossly misunderstood the true means to and nature of plenty. What they were lacking in was not economic motivation but economic understanding.

What then is the correct interpretation of mercantilist doctrine and practice with respect to the roles of power and plenty as ends of national policy? I believe that practically all mercantilists, whatever the period, country, or status of the particular individual, would have subscribed to all of the following propositions: (1) wealth is an absolutely essential means to power, whether for security or for aggression; (2) power is essential or valuable as a means to the acquisition or retention of wealth; (3) wealth and power are each proper ultimate ends of national policy; (4) there is long-run harmony between these ends, although in particular circumstances it may be necessary for a time to make economic sacrifices in the interest of military security and therefore also of long-run prosperity.

The omission of any one of these four propositions results in an incorrect interpretation of mercantilist thought, while additions of other propositions would probably involve internal dispute among mercantilists. It is to be noted that no proposition is included as to the relative weight which the mercantilists attached to power and to plenty, respectively. Given the general acceptance of the existence of harmony and mutual support between the pursuit of power and the pursuit of plenty, there appears to have been little interest in what must have appeared to them to be an unreal issue. When apparent conflict between these ends did arise, however, differences in attitudes, as between persons and countries, did arise and something will be said on this matter later.

That plenty and power were universally regarded as each valuable for its own sake there is overwhelming evidence, in the contemporary writings of all kinds, and what follows is more or less a random sampling of the available evidence. In

---

[17] *Wealth of Nations*, Cannan, ed., London, 1904, I, 457–58.

the text accompanying and interpreting the Frontispiece of Michael Drayton's poem, *Polyolbion*, 1622, there is the following passage:

> Through a Triumphant Arch, see Albion plas't,
> In Happy site, in Neptunes arms embras't,
> In Power and Plenty, on hir Cleevy Throne

In Barbier d'Aucour's *Au Roy sur le Commerce, Ode*, 1665,[18] an early French equivalent of *Rule Britannia*, appear the following lines:

> Vos vaisseaux fendant tous les airs,
> Et cinglant sur toutes les Mers,
> Y porteront vostre puissance;
> Et ce Commerce plein d'honneur,
> Fera naistre dans vostre France,
> Un flus et reflus de bon-heur.

Montchrétien opens his book with this passage: "Ceux qui sont appellez au gouvernement des Estats doyvent en avoir la gloire, l'augmentation et l'enrichissement pour leur principal but."[19] Another Frenchman, writing in 1650 says:

> Deux choses sont principalement necessaires pour rendre un Estat florissant; c'est assavoir le Gouvernement, & le Commerce; & comme sans celuy-là il est impossible qu'il puisse longtemps subsister; de mesme sans celuy-cy on le voit manquer de mille sortes de choses importantes à la vie, & il est impossible que les peuples acquierent de grandes richesses.[20]

John Graunt, in 1662, states that "the art of governing, and the true politiques, is how to preserve the subject in peace, and plenty."[21] An anonymous English writer, in 1677, declares that: "The four main interests of a nation are, religion, reputation, peace, and trade. . . ."[22] William III, in his declaration of war

---

[18] The citation from D'Aucour in the text is made from a reprint extracted from J. Carnandet, *Le Trésor des Pièces Rares . . . de la Champagne*, Paris, 1863–1866. D'Aucour was a tutor of Colbert's son. F. C. Palm, *The Economic Policies of Richelieu*, Urbana, 1920, pp. 178–79, quotes from an earlier *Ode à . . . Richelieu*, in much the same vein by Jean de Chapelain (1595–1624), which similarly stresses power and plenty.

[19] *Traicté de l'œconomie politique* [1615], Th. Funck-Brentano ed., Paris, 1889, p. 11.

[20] Cited from Ch. Vailart dit St. Paul, *Histoire du Ministère d'Armand . . . Duc de Richelieu*, Paris, 1650, I, 332.

[21] *Natural and Political Observations made upon the Bills of Morality* [London, 1662], Johns Hopkins University Reprint, Baltimore, 1939, p. 78.

[22] *The Present State of Christendom, and the Interest of England, with Regard to France* [1677], in *The Harleian Miscellany*, London, 1810, VIII, 106.

against France in 1689, gives as one of the reasons that Louis XIV's "forbidding the importation of a great part of the product and manufactures of our Kingdom, and imposing exorbitant customs upon the rest, are sufficient evidence of his design to destroy the trade on which the wealth and safety of this nation so much depends."[23] In the preamble of 3 and 4 Anne, cap. 10, are the following words: "The Royal Navy, and the navigation of England, wherein, under God, the wealth, safety, and strength of this Kindgom is so much concerned, depends on the due supply of stores necessary for the same."[24] An English pamphlet of 1716 on the relations with Russia, after describing the Czar as "a great and enterprizing spirit, and of a genius thoroughly politic" attributes to him and his people "an insatiable desire of opulency, and a boundless thirst for dominion."[25] William Wood, a noted mercantilist writer, refers to the English as "a people . . . who seek no other advantages than such only as may enlarge and secure that, whereby their strength, power, riches and reputation, equally encrease and are preserved. . . ."[26] Bernard Mandeville discusses how "politicians can make a people potent, renown'd and flourishing."[27] An anonymous English writer states in 1771 that:

"Nature, reason and observation all plainly point out to us our true object of national policy, which is commerce; the inexhaustible source of wealth and power to a people."[28] In an undated memoir of Maurepas to Louis XVI, on the commerce of France, occur the following passages: "Le commerce est la source de la félicité, de la force et de la richesse d'un état. . . . La richesse et la puissance sont les vrais intérêts d'une nation, et il n'y a que le commerce qui puisse procurer l'une et l'autre."[29]

Such evidence as the foregoing that in the age of mercantilism wealth and power were both sought for their own sakes could easily be multiplied many fold. In English literature of the period of all kinds, from poetry to official documents, the phrases "power and plenty," "wealth and strength," "profit and power," "profit and security," "peace and plenty," or their equivalents, recur as a constant refrain. Nor is there any obvious reason, given the economic and political conditions and views of the seventeenth and eighteenth centuries, why power *and*

---

[23] As cited in *Mercator, or Commerce Retrieved*, No. 1, London; May 26, 1713.

[24] Cited in G. S. Graham, *Sea Power and British North America 1783–1820*, Cambridge Mass., 1941, p. 143.

[25] *The Northern Crisis; or Impartial Reflections on the Policies of the Czar* [London, 1716], as reprinted in Karl Marx, *Secret Diplomatic History of the Eighteenth Century*, London, 1899, p. 32.

[26] *Survey of Trade*, 2nd ed., London, 1719, Dedication, pp. iv–v.

[27] *The Fable of the Bees* [6th ed., 1731], F. B. Kaye ed., Oxford, 1924, I, 185.

[28] *Considerations on the Policy, Commerce and Circumstances of the Kingdom*, London, 1771, as quoted in the preface to G. S. Graham, *British Policy and Canada, 1774–1791*, London, 1930.

[29] *Mémoires du Comte de Maurepas*, Paris, 1792, III, 195.

plenty should not have been the joint objectives of the patriotic citizen of the time, even if he had freed himself from the mercantilist philosophy. Adam Smith, though not a mercantilist, was speaking for mercantilists as well as for himself when he said the "the great object of the political economy of every country, is to increase the riches and power of that country."[30]

In all the literature I have examined, I have found only one passage which is seriously embarrassing for my thesis, not because it subordinates in extreme fashion economic to political considerations, but for the reverse reason. The passage, in an anonymous and obscure pamphlet of 1754, whose authorship I have been unable to determine, is as follows:

> You want not, Gentlemen, to be informed by me, that commerce is the nearest and dearest concern of your country. It is what should be the great object of public attention in all national movements, and in every negotiation we enter into with foreign powers. Our neighbours on the continent may, perhaps, wisely scheme or quarrel for an augmentation of dominions; but *Great Britain, of herself, has nothing to fight for, nothing to support, nothing to augment but her commerce*. On our foreign trade, not only our wealth but our mercantile navigation must depend; on that navigation our naval strength, the glory and security of our country.[31]

It is much easier indeed to show that power was not the sole objective of national policy in mercantilist thought than to explain how historians ever came to assert that it was. The evidence they cite in support of this proposition is not only extremely scanty but is generally ambiguous if not wholly irrelevant to their thesis. It would be extremely difficult, I am sure, for them to cite even a single passage which unmistakably rejects wealth as a national objective worth pursuing for its own sake or unconditionally subordinates it to power as an ultimate end. It is only too probable that there has been operating here that intellectual "principle of parsimony" in the identification of causes which, whatever its serviceability in the natural science, has in the history of social thought worked only for ill.

Cunningham and Heckscher[32] make much of a passage of Francis Bacon's

[30] *Wealth of Nations*, Cannan, ed., London, 1904, I, 351.

[31] *Mercator's Letters on Portugal and its Commerce*, London, 1754, p. 5. The italics are not in the original text.

[32] Heckscher refers to this as "a very characterisitic passage" (*Mercantilism*, II, 16), but I find it difficult to cite a duplicate, whether from Bacon's writings or in the period generally. See also Heckscher, "Revisions in Economic History, V, Mercantilism," *Economic History Review*, VII (November 1936), 48: "I think Cunningham was right in stressing the famous saying of Bacon about Henry VII: 'bowing the ancient policy of this Estate from consideration of plenty to consideration of power.'"

made famous by modern scholars in which he speaks of King Henry VII "bowing the ancient policy of this estate from consideration of plenty to consideration of power" when in the interest of the navy he ordered that wines from Gascony should be imported only in English bottoms. As a fifteenth century measure, this falls outside the period of present interest, but Bacon, no doubt, put much of his own ideas, perhaps more than of Henry VII's, in his *History of the Reign of King Henry the Seventh*. It is relevant, therefore, that Bacon speaks of Henry VII as conducting war for profit, and attributes to him even over-developed economic objectives. In 1493, Henry VII had declared an embargo on all trade with the Flemish provinces because the pretender, Perkin Warbeck, was being harbored there. The embargo after a time "began to pinch the merchants of both nations very sore, which moved them by all means they could devise to affect and dispose their sovereigns respectively to open the intercourse again." Henry VII, no longer apprehensive about Warbeck, was receptive. "But that that moved him most was, that being a King that loved wealth and treasure, he could not endure to have trade sick, nor any obstruction to continue in the gate-vein, which disperseth that blood," and by the *intercursus magnus* of 1495–96 with the Archduke of Austria he negotiated the end of the trade war.[33]

Not so frequently stated as that power and plenty are properly joint objectives of national policy but undoubtedly a pervasive element in the thought of the period is the proposition that they are also harmonious ends, each reinforcing and promoting the other. The idea is expressed in the maxim attributed to Hobbes: "Wealth is power and power is wealth."[34] There follow some passages in which the idea is spelled out somewhat more fully: "Foreign trade produceth riches, riches power, power preserves our trade and religion."[35] "It is evident that this

---

[33] See *The Works of Francis Bacon*, James Spedding, ed., London, 1858, VI, 95–96; 172–73. Cf. also *Considerations touching a War with Spain* [1624] in *The Works of Francis Bacon*, Philadelphia, 1852, II, 214, where he says that: "whereas wars are generally causes of poverty or consumption . . . this war with Spain, if it be made by sea, is likely to be a lucrative and restorative war. So that, if we go roundly on at the first, the war in continuance will find itself." On the other hand, in his *Essays or Counsels* [2nd ed., 1625], *Works*, London, 1858, VI, 450–51, he makes what appears to be a clear-cut statement that the prestige of power ("grandeur") is more important than plenty.

[EDITOR'S NOTE: Viner later clarified that the word used—"greatness," not "grandeur"—was actually in Bacon's essay "Of the True Greatness of Kingdoms and Estates." He also admitted that there is no "clear-cut" statement in this essay, but "only a pervasive implication, that military strength and military prowess are the most distinguished or praiseworthy aims of national policy. Perhaps I conceded too much in assuming that when Bacon uses the terms 'true greatness' he necessarily means by it what should be most sought after." Letter to Eli Heckscher, October 29, 1951, Jacob Viner papers.]

[34] J. E., Barker, *Rise and Decline of the Netherlands*, London, 1906, p. 194.
[35] Josiah Child, *A Treatise concerning the East India Trade*, London, 1681, p. 29.

Kingdom is wonderfully fitted by the bounty of God Almighty, for a great pro-
gression in wealth and power; and that the only means to arrive at both, or either
of them, is to improve and advance trade. . . .''[36] "For as the honesty of all
governments is, so shall be their riches; and as their honour, honesty, and riches
are, so will be their strength; and as their honour, honesty, riches, and strength
are, so will be their trade. These are five sisters that go hand in hand, and must
not be parted.''[37] "Your fleet, and your trade, have so near a relation, and such
mutual influence upon each other, they cannot well be separated; your trade is the
mother and nurse of your seamen; your seamen are the life of your fleet, and your
fleet is the security and protection of your trade, and both together are the wealth,
strength, security and glory of Britain.''[38]

"By trade and commerce we grow a rich and powerful nation, and by their
decay we are growing poor and impotent. As trade and commerce enrich, so they
fortify, our country."

"The wealth of the nation he [the 'Patriot King'] will most justly esteem to be
his wealth, the power his power, the security and the honor, his security and
honor; and by the very means by which he promotes the two first, he will wisely
preserve the two last.''[39]

De la marine dépendent les colonies, des colonies le commerce, du commerce la
faculté pour l'Etat d'entretenir de nombreuses armées, d'augmenter la population
et de fournir aux enterprises les plus glorieuses et les plus utiles.[40]

George L. Beer has commented, with particular reference to the statement
from Lord Haversham quoted above, that "The men of the day argued in a circle

---

[36] *Ibid., A New Discourse of Trade*, 4th ed. (ca. 1690), Preface, p. xliii.

[37] Andrew Yarranton, *England's Improvement by Sea and Land*, London, 1677, p. 6.

[38] Lord Haversham in the House of Lords, November 6, 1707, *Parliamentary History of England*, VI, 598. Cf. also James Whiston, *A Discourse of the Decay of Trade*, London, 1693. p. 3:

"For, since the introduction of the new artillery of powder guns, &c., and the discovery of the
wealth of the Indies, &c. war is become rather an expense of money than men, and success attends
those that can most and longest spend money: whence it is that prince's armies in Europe are
become more proportionable to their purses than to the number of their people; so that it uncon-
trollably follows that a foreign trade managed to the best advantage, will make our nation so
strong and rich, that we may command the trade of the world, the riches of it, and consequently
the world itself. . . . Neither will the pursuing these proposals, augment the nation's wealth and
power only, but that wealth and power will also preserve our trade and religion, they mutually
working for the preservation of each other. . . ."

[39] Lord Bolingbroke, "The Idea of a Patriot King," in *Letters on the Spirit of Patriotism*, London, 1752, pp. 204, 211.

[40] Petit, a colleague of the French Foreign Minister, Choiseul, in 1762, as cited by E. Daubigny,
Choiseul et la France d'Outre-Mer après le Traité de Paris, Paris, 1892, p. 176.

of sea power, commerce and colonies. Sea power enabled England to expand and to protect her foreign trade, while this increased commerce, in turn, augmented her naval strength."[41] Circular reasoning this may have been, but it was not, logically at least, a "vicious circle," since under the circumstances of the time it was perfectly reasonable to maintain that wealth and power mutually supported each other, that they were, or could be made, each a means to the augmentation of the other.[42]

In contending that by the mercantilists power and plenty were regarded as coexisting ends of national policy which were fundamentally harmonious, I do not mean that they were unaware that in specific instances economic sacrifices might have to be made in order to assure national security or victory in an aggressive war. But as a rule, if not invariably, when making this point they showed their belief that such economic sacrifices in the short run would bring economic as well as political gains in the long run. The selfishness from a patriotic point of view of taxpayers resisting wartime impositions for armament or for war was always a problem for statesmen in the age of mercantilism, and sometimes the parsimony of monarchs was also a problem. It was also necessary at times for statesmen to resist the pressure from merchants to pursue petty commercial ends which promised immediate economic gain but at the possible cost of long-run military security and therefore also of long-run national prosperity. The mercantilist, no doubt, would not have denied that if necessity should arise for choosing, all other things would have to give way to considerations of the national safety; but his practice might not rise to the level of his principles, and his doctrine would not lead him to recognize that such choice was likely to face him frequently. It is not without significance that it was an anti-mercantilist economist, Adam Smith, and not the mercantilists, who laid down the maxim that "defence is more important than opulence." A typical mercantilist might well have replied that ordinarily defense is necessary to opulence and opulence to effective defense, even if momentarily the two ends might appear to be in conflict.

---

[41] *The Old Colonial System, 1600–1754*, New York, 1912, I, 16.

[42] Edmond Silberner, *La Guerre dans la Pensée Economique du XVIe au XVIIIe Siècle*, Paris, 1939, concentrates on the search for attitudes toward war, idealizing or pacific, rather than on the motivations of foreign policy, but it presents a rich collection of extracts from the contemporary literature which in so far as it is pertinent to the present issue is, I believe, wholly confirmatory of my thesis. Cf. also, by the same author, *The Problem of War in Nineteenth Century Economic Thought*, Princeton, 1946, p. 286: "In the protectionist view, there is a reciprocal action between the economic and war: industrialization facilitates the conduct of war, and military victories increase the possibilities of industrialization and of economic prosperity. This point of view recalls that of the mercantilists: wealth increases power, and power augments wealth." The thesis presented in the text above is also supported not only by the title but by the contents, if I understand his Italian aright, of Jacopo Mazzei's article, "Potenza Mezzo di Ricchezza e Ricchezza Mezzo di Potenza nel Pensiero dei Mercantilisti," *Rivista Internazionale di Scienze Sociali*, XLI (January 1933), 3–19.

Queen Elizabeth was notoriously parsimonious and one of her diplomatic agents, Buckhurst, in reasoning with her in 1587 when the safety of England against the menace from Spain appeared to call for rearmament, anticipated Adam Smith's maxim:

And alwaies when kinges and kingdomes do stand in dout of daunger, their saftie is a thing so far above all price of treasure, as there shold be no sparing to bring them even into certenty of assurans.

He accordingly advised Elizabeth to:

unlock all your cofers and convert your tresure for the advauncing of worthy men and for the arming of ships and men of war, that may defend you, sith princes' treasures serve only to that end and lie they never so fast nor so full in their chests, can no waies so defend them.[43]

Statesmen frequently found it necessary to warn against endangering political ends by unwise pursuit of temporary or petty commercial gains in response to pressure from business interests. This was especially true in connection with the relations between England and France during the Seven Years' War, which to many contemporaries seemed to be conducted with too much attention to economic considerations of minor importance. Just before the outbreak of the conflict, when it was still being debated whether the issue between the two countries should be settled by economic or military means, Lord Granville was reported as "absolutely against meddling with trade—he called it, vexing your neighbours for a little muck."[44] And in the face of the struggle itself, Mirepoix, the French Ambassador to England, is said to have commented "that it was a great pity to cut off so many heads for the sake of a few hats."[45] In the course of controversy over the Newfoundland fisheries after the ending of hostilities, in 1763, Choiseul appealed to Halifax: "mais pour l'amour de Dieu, ne laissons pas des querrelles de pêcheurs dégénérer en querrelles de nations."[46]

To some extent this point of view may have been a reflection of a certain disdain for trade in general which was beginning to affect the aristocratic class

[43] "Correspondentie van Robert Dudley Graaf van Leycester," Part II, *Werken uitgiven door het Historisch Genootschap*, Utrecht, 3rd Series, No. 57 (1931), pp. 239, 240.

[44] *The Diary of the Late George Bubb Dodington*, new ed., London, 1784, pp. 344–45.

[45] [William Knox], *Helps to a Right Decision*, London, 1787, p. 35; cf. also a slightly different version in *Letters Military and Political from the Italian of Count A. Algorotti*, Dublin, 1784, p. 129. The hats were involved, of course, because beaver skins were the main prize of the American fur trade, and the hair from these skins was the basic raw material for the men's hats of the time.

[46] Cited in *Mélanges d'histoire offerts à M. Charles Bémont*, Paris, 1913, p. 655.

who conducted the foreign relations of the time. It would be a mistake, however, to explain it in terms of basic disregard for economic considerations, rather than as belief that the pursuit of temporary and minor economic benefits should not be permitted to dominate foreign policy. Such is the position of John Mitchell, who makes clear elsewhere that "power and prosperity" are the proper ends of policy:

> It is well known, that our colonies in America are rather more under the tuition and influence of the merchants in Britain, than the government perhaps, and that all public measures relating to them are very much influenced by the opinions of our merchants about them. But the only things that they seem to attend to are the profits of trade. . . . This, it is true, is necessary to be considered likewise, but it is not the only thing to be attended to. The great thing to be considered by all states is power and dominion, as well as trade. Without that to support and protect our trade, it must soon be at an end.[47]

While mercantilist doctrine, moreover, put great stress on the importance of national economic interests, it put equally great stress on the possibility of lack of harmony between the special economic interests of the individual merchants or particular business groups or economic classes, on the one hand, and the economic interest of the commonwealth as a whole, on the other. Refusal to give weight to *particular* economic interests, therefore, must never be identified with disregard for the national economic interest as they conceived it, in interpreting the thought of the mercantilists. In human affairs, moreover, there is always room for divergence between dogma and practice, between principles and the actual behavior of those who profess them. It is doctrine, and not practice, which is the main concern here. The task of ascertaining how much or how little they corresponded in the age of mercantilism, and what were the forces which caused them to deviate, is the difficult duty of the historian, in whose hands I gladly leave it.

It was the common belief in France, however, that commercial objectives and particular commercial interests played a much greater role in the formulation and

---

[47] *The Contest in America between Great Britain and France*, London, 1757, Introduction, p. xvii. Cf. also *A Letter to a certain Foreign Minister, in which the grounds of the present war are truly stated*, London, 1745, p. 6: "That we receive great benefits from trade, that trade is a national concern, and that we ought to resent any attempt made to lessen or to injure it, are truths well known and out of dispute, yet sure the British people are not to be treated like a company of merchants, or rather pedlars, who, if they are permitted to sell their goods, are to think themselves well off, whatever treatment they may receive in any other respect. No, surely, the British nation has other great concerns besides their trade, and as she will never sacrifice it, so she will never endure any insult in respect to them, without resenting it as becomes a people jealous of their honour, and punctual in the performance of their engagements."

The occasion for this outburst was a Prussian "rescript" insisting that Britain should not intervene in quarrels between German states, since they had nothing to do with British commerce.

administration of British than of French foreign policy, and some Englishmen would have agreed. There was universal agreement, also, that in "Holland" (*i.e.*, the "United Provinces"), where the merchants to a large extent shared directly in government, major political considerations, including the very safety of the country or its success in wars in which it was actually participating, had repeatedly to give way to the cupidity of the merchants and their reluctance to contribute adequately to military finance. Whether in the main the influence of the commercial classes, where they had strength, worked more for peace or for war seems to be an open question, but there appears little ground for doubt that with the merchants, whether they pressed for war or for peace, the major consideration was economic gain, either their private gain, or that of their country, or both.

The material available which touches on these strands of thought is boundless, and there can here be cited only a few passages which give the flavor of contemporary discussion. We will begin with material relating to the influence of the merchant and of commercial considerations on British policy.

Sir Francis Bacon, in reporting a discussion in Parliament, in the fifth year of James I's reign, of the petition of the merchants with regard to their grievances against Spain, makes one of the speakers say that: "although he granted that the wealth and welfare of the merchant was not without a sympathy with the general stock and state ["estate?"] of a nation, especially an island; yet, nevertheless, it was a thing too familiar with the merchant, to make the case of his particular profit, the public case of the kingdom." The troubles of the merchants were partly their own fault: they so mismanaged their affairs abroad that "except lieger ambassadors, which are the eyes of kings in foreign parts, should leave their sentinel and become merchants' factors, and solicitors, their causes can hardly prosper." Wars were not to be fought on such minor issues. Another speaker was more sympathetic to the merchants, who were "the convoy of our supplies, the vents of our abundance, Neptune's almsmen, and fortune's adventurers." Nevertheless, the question of war should be dealt with by the King and not by Parliament, presumably because the merchants wielded too much influence there. Members of Parliament were local representatives with local interests; if they took a broader view it was accidental.[48]

Allies or potential allies of England sometimes were troubled by England's supposed obsession with commercial objectives as making her an unreliable ally where other interests were involved. In September, 1704, a minister of the Duke of Savoy issued a memorial which the English representative at that Court reported as holding that England and Holland, "the maritime powers (an injurious

---

[48] *The Works of Sir Francis Bacon*, Philadelphia, 1852, II, 193–99.

term, I think, which goes into fashion) were so attentive to their interests of trade
and commerce, that, perhaps, they would . . . abandon the common interests of
Europe'' in the defeat of France in the war then under way.[49] When Pitt declared
to Catherine the Great of Russia that no Russian conquest could give offense to
England, she was skeptical, and replied: "The acquisition of a foot of territory
on the Black Sea will at once excite the jealousy of the English, whose whole
attention is given to petty interests and who are first and always traders.[50]

Montesquieu and Quesnay both thought that in England, unlike France and
other countries, the interests of commerce predominated over other interests:

> D'autres nations font céder des intérêts de commerce à des intérêts politiques; celle
> ci [i.e. England] a toujours fait céder ses intérêts politiques aux intérêts de son
> commerce.[51]
> . . . en Angleterre . . . où les lois du commerce maritime ne se prêtent point aux
> lois de la politique; où les intérêts de la glèbe et de l'État sont subordonnés aux
> intérêts des négociants; où le commerce des productions de l'agriculture, la pro-
> priété du territoire et l'État même ne sont regardés que comme des accessoires de
> la métropole, et la métropole comme formée de négociants.[52]

The history of British policy and practice with respect to enemy trade and to
trade with the enemy during war provides abundant and occasionally startling
evidence that considerations of plenty did not always automatically give way to
considerations of power. There is much in British history, as in the history of
Holland, of France, and of Spain, to support the statement of Carl Brinkmann
that: "The history of war trade and trade war is a rich mine of interest to the
economic and social historian just for the peculiar ways in which the autonomy
of business connexions and traditions is seen cutting across even the sternest decrees and tendencies of political *ultima ratio*."[53]

[49] *The Diplomatic Correspondence of the Right Hon. Richard Hill*, London, 1845, I, 479; see
also II, 751.

[50] Cited by Edward Crankshaw, *Russia and Britain*, New York, no date (ca. 1943), pp. 45–46.

[51] Montesquieu, *De l'Espirit des Lois*, Book XX, Ch. 7.

[52] *Oeuvres Économiques et Philsophiques de F. Quesnay*, Auguste Oncken, ed., Paris, 1888, p.
429. Quesnay is referring here specially to Britain's policy with respect to the trade of the colonies.
Adam Smith's comment on the monopolistic aspects of this policy was more acid: "To found a great
empire for the sole purpose of raising up a people of customers, may at first sight appear a project fit
only for a nation of shopkeepers. It is, however, a project altogether unfit for a nation of shopkeepers;
but extremely fit for a nation whose government is influenced by shopkeepers." *Wealth of Nations*,
Cannan, ed., II, 114.

[53] *English Historical Review*, XXXIX (April 1924), 287. There is not space here to elaborate on
this theme, but reference to one striking instance will serve to bring out the nature of the evidence
available. In the 1740's, during the War of the Austrian Succession, English marine insurance companies insured French vessels against capture at sea by the British navy, and Parliament, after pro-

That in Holland commercial interests predominated was taken for granted in both France and England when foreign policy was formulated. Thurloe commented, in 1656, that all proposals "of alliances of common and mutual defense, wherein provision was to be made for the good of the Protestant religion" failed "in respect the United Provinces always found it necessary for them to mingle therewith the consideration of trade. . . . The Hollanders had rather His Highness [Oliver Cromwell] be alone in it than that they should lose a tun of sack or a frail of raisins."[54] A French naval officer, writing to Colbert with reference to the failure of the Dutch to provide the fleet which they had promised for the Levant, said that he was not at all surprised: "les Hollandais n'agissent en cette occasion que par leur propre intérêt; et comme ils ont peu ou point de bâtiments en Levant, et qu'en leur pays ils ne regardent qu'au compte des merchands, ils n'ont garde d'envoyer et de faire la dépense d'une escadre de ce côté-là."[55]

In the summary given in Cobbett's *Parliamentary History* of the principal arguments made in Parliament in favor of moderating the peace settlement to be made with France to end the Seven Years' War, a contrast was made as to the policy proper for England and that for a country like Holland. The economic value of the British conquests of French colonies in America was great. Nevertheless it was to be remembered:

> . . . that the value of our conquests thereby ought not to be estimated by the present produce, but by their probable increase. Neither ought the value of any country to be solely tried on its commercial advantages; that extent of territory and a number of subjects, are matters of as much consideration to a state attentive to the sources of real grandeur, as the mere advantages of traffic; that such ideas are rather suitable to a limited and petty commonwealth, like Holland, than to a great, powerful, and warlike nation. That on these principles, having made very large demands in North America, it was necessary to relax in other parts.[56]

---

tracted debate, refused to make the practice illegal. Cf.: *Parliamentary History* (Cobbett, ed.), XII, 7–26 (for 1741); [Corbyn Morris], *Essay towards Illustrating the Science of Insurance, particularly whether it be Nationally Advantageous to Insure Ships of our Enemies*, London, 1747; Admiral H. W. Richmond, *The Navy in the War of 1739–48*, Cambridge, England, 1920, III, 248–250; C. Ernest Fayle, "The Deflection of Strategy by Commerce in the Eighteenth Century," and "Economic Pressure in the War of 1739–48," *Journal of the Royal United Service Institution*, LXVIII (1923), 281–294, 434–446; Charles Wright and C. Ernest Fayle, *A History of Lloyds*, London, 1928, pp. 80 ff.

[54] Cited by F. M. Powicke, "The Economic Motive in Politics," *Economic History Review* XVI (1946), 91.

[55] A. Jal, *Abraham du Quesne et la Marine de son Temps*, Paris, 1873, I, 470.

[56] *Parliamentary History of England*, XV (1813), 1271–1272 (for December 9, 1762). For similar views as to the propriety of a country like Holland confining her foreign policy to commercial matters and to defense, without attempting to participate otherwise in *Haute Politique*, see the instructions prepared in 1771 by the French foreign office for the French Ambassador to Holland, *Recueil*

There was general agreement that in France economic considerations played a lesser role in foreign policy than in England and Holland. In part, this was to be explained by the lesser importance even economically of foreign trade to France and by the lesser role of French merchants in French politics. George Lyttelton, an English observer at the Soissons Congress of 1729, where the question of the maintenance of the alliance with England was at issue, reported to his father:

> Affairs are now almost at a crisis, and there is great reason to expect they will take a happy turn. Mr. Walpole has a surprizing influence over the cardinal [Cardinal Fleury, in charge of French foreign policy]; so that, whether peace or war ensue, we may depend upon our ally. In truth, it is the interest of the French court to be faithful to their engagements, though it may not entirely be the nation's. Emulation of trade might incline the people to wish the bond that ties them to us were broke; but the mercantile interest has at no time been much considered by this court. . . . The supposition, that present advantage is the basis and end of state engagements, and that they are only to be measured by that rule, is the foundation of all our suspicions against the firmness of our French ally. But the maxim is not just. Much is given to future hopes, much obtained by future fears; and security is, upon many occasions, sought preferably to gain.[57]

Frenchmen in the period occasionally professed readiness to yield to Britain predominance in maritime trade if Britain would give France a free hand on the Continent,[58] but it would be a mistake to conclude that this reflected a readiness to concentrate on political objectives alone. Even on the Continent there were

---

des Instructions Données aux Ambassadeurs et Ministres de France, XXII, Paris, 1924, 308.

For comments of the Anglophile Prince of Orange in the course of his attempts to keep Holland neutral during the War of the American Revolution, which proved unsuccessful because of both pressure from France and the financial ambitions of the commercial classes in Holland, see Archives ou Correspondance Inédite de la Maison d'Orange-Nassau, 5th Series, F.J.L. Kramer, ed., Leyde, 1910, I, 607 ff., 618, 635 ff., 677 ff., et passim.

[57] The Works of George Lord Lyttelton, G. E. Ayscough, ed., 3rd ed., London, 1776, III, 243–44.

[58] An instance in point is in a despatch by Louis XIV to his ambassador in London, 1668: "Si les Anglais voulaient se contenter d'etre les plus grands marchands de l'Europe, et me laisser pour mon partage ce que je pourrais conquérir dans une juste guerre, rien ne serait si aisé que de nous accommoder ensemble." Cited by C.-G. Picavet, La Diplomatie Française au Temps de Louis XIV, Paris, 1930, p. 171.

About a century later, in 1772, George III of England, alarmed by the coalition of Austria, Prussia, and Russia to partition Poland, expressed sympathy for the idea of an alliance between Britain and France despite their traditional enmity: "Commerce the foundation of a marine can never flourish in an absolute monarchy; therefore that branch of grandeur ought to be left to England whilst the great army kept by France gives her a natural preeimence on the Continent." (Sir John Fortescue, ed., The Correspondence of King George the Third, London, 1927, II, 428–429.)

economic prizes to be won, though less glittering ones than those naval power could win overseas.

Historians, moreover, may have been too ready to find sharp differences in kind between the role of economic considerations in the making of foreign policy in England and France, respectively, in the age of mercantilism. The differences, though probably substantial, seem in the matters here relevant to have been differences in degree rather than in kind. In particular, the extent of the influence which commercial interests in France could in one way or another exercise on policy as been seriously underestimated by many historians, and both in theory and in practice absolutist government was not as absolute in power nor as noncommercial in motivation as the school textbooks have taught us. French records have been misleading in this regard because the older generation of historians were not interested in economic issues and tended to leave out of their compilations of documents matter of a markedly economic character, and French historians seem for some time to have been moving toward a reconsideration of the role of economic factors in the formulation of foreign policy under the Ancien Régime.[59]

There may have been monarchs who recognized no moral obligation to serve their people's interests, and there were no doubt ministers of state who had no loyalties except to their careers and perhaps to their royal masters. Frederick the Great is said to have declared, with brutal frankness, that "Je regarde les hommes comme une horde de cerfs dans le parc d'un grand seigneur et qui n'ont d'autre fonction que de peupler et de remplir l'enclos," and there is little in the King's voluminous writings which makes this incredible.[60] Some monarchs were, to modern taste, childish in the weight they gave to the routine symbols of prestige

---

[59] For representative contemporary evidence in support of these points, see: *Mémoires de Louis XIV*, Jean Longnon, ed., Paris, 1927, p. 73; a proclamation of Louis XIV reprinted in P. M. Bondois, "Colbert et l'industrie de la dentelle," *Mémoires et Documents pour Servir à l'Histoire du Commerce et de l'Industrie en France, VI* (1921), 263; Vauban, "Description Géographique de l'Election de Vézeley" [1696], in A. de Boislisle, *Mémoires des Intendants sur l'État des Généralités*, Paris, 1881, I, 738–49; G. Lacour-Gayet, *L'Éducation Politique de Louis XIV*, 2nd ed., Paris, 1923, pp. 341 ff. For reconsiderations of the traditional views by modern historians, see A. Jal, *Abraham du Quesne et la Marine de son Temps*, Paris, 1883, II, 352–53; P. Muret (a book review), *Revue d'Histoire Moderne et Contemporaine, IV* (1902–3), 39–41; J. Hitier, "La Doctrine de l'Absolutisme," *Annales de l'Université de Grenoble, XV* (1903), 106–113, 121–31; Charles Normand, *La Bourgeoisie Française au XVIIᵉ Siècle, 1604–1661*, Paris, 1908, pp. 195, 279–287; Henri Hauser, *La Pensée et l'Action Èconomiques du Cardinal de Richelieu*, Paris, 1944, pp. 185 ff.; Philip Dur, "The Right of Taxation in the Political Theory of the French Religious Wars," *Journal of Modern History*, XVII (December 1945), 289–303.

[60] Frederick the Great did recognize, however, at least in principle and in his better moments, that the economic well-being of his people should be one of the major objectives of a monarch. See his "Essai sur les Formes de Gouvernement et sur les Devoirs des Souverains," of which he had printed a few copies only in 1777, *Oeuvres*, IX (1848), 195–210.

and protocol.[61] The personal idiosyncrasies of rulers and, above all, dynastic ambitions, exerted their influence on the course of events. Occasionally religious differences made the course of diplomacy run a little less smoothly by injecting an ideological factor into the range of matters out of which disputes could arise or by which they could be sharpened. But it seems clear that predominantly diplomacy was centered on the governed by considerations of power and plenty throughout the period and for all of Europe, and that religious considerations were more often invoked for propaganda purposes than genuinely operative in fashioning foreign policy. Even the cardinals, who in some degree monopolized the diplomatic profession on the Continent, granted that religious considerations must not be permitted to get in the way of vital national interests, and even genuine missionary enterprises could get seriously entangled with the pursuit of commercial privileges. When Louis XIII in 1626 sent an emissary to Persia with the primary purpose of promoting the Catholic religion, he instructed him at the same time to seek special privileges for French trade as compensation for the diplomatic difficulties with the English and the Dutch which would result from a French attempt to catholicize Persia. ''Sa majesté pensait qu'on ne pouvait éviter cet inconvénient qu'en se rendant maître du commerce du pays, lequel, outre le gain des âmes, qui est celui que sa majesté recherchait, offrirait encore à son royaume de notable avantages.''[62]

[61] To a letter from Louis XIII in 1629 proposing closer commercial relations, Czar Michel Federowitz of Russia replied favorably, but complained about the manner in which he had been addressed: ''Mais nous ne savons à quoi attribuer que notre nom, nos titres et nos qualités aient été oubliés à la lettre que vous nous avez écrit. Tous les potentats de la terre . . . écrivant à notre grande puissance, mettent notre nom sur les lettres et n'oublient aucun des titres et des qualités que nous possédons. Nous ne pouvons approuver votre coutume de vouloir être notre ami, et de nous dénier et ôter les titres que le Dieu tout-puissant nous a donnés et que nous possédons si justement. Que sí, à l'avenir, vous désirez vivre en bonne amitié et parfaite correspondance avec notre grande puissance, en sorte que nos royales personnes et nos empires joints ensemble donnent de la terreur à tout l'univers, il faudra que vous commandiez qu'aux lettres que vous nous récrirez à l'avenir toute la dignité de nostre grande puissance, notre nom, nos titres et nos qualités soient écrits comme elles sont en cette lettre que nous vous envoyons de notre part. Nous vous ferons la semblable en écrivant tous vos titres et toutes vos qualités dans les lettres que nous vous manderons, étant le propre des aims d'augmenter plutôt réciproquement leurs titres et qualités que de les diminuer on retrancher.'' *Recueil des Instructions*, VIII (1890), 29.

[62] G. deR. de Flassan, *Histoire Générale et Raisonnée de la Diplomatie Française*, 2nd ed., Paris, 1811, II, 395–6.

In 1713 Charles XII of Sweden wrote to Queen Anne demanding that England, in conformity with her treaty obligations, give him assistance in regaining his territories in the Germanic Empire. ''It was not possible,'' he said, ''that Anne could allow her mind to be influenced by the sordid interests of trade; the protectress of the Protestant religion could not fail to support the Protestant power of the north,'' as against Russia. But Russia at the time was seeking admittance into the Grand Alliance against Louis XIV, and England, alarmed at the ambitions of both monarchs, made no choice. See Mrs. D'Arcy Collyer, ''Notes on the Diplomatic Correspondence between England and Russia in the

The role of the religious factor in Cromwell's foreign policy has been much debated. The literature of historical debate on this question is voluminous, but it is not apparent to the layman that any progress toward a definitive decision has been made, unless it is that Cromwell was a complex personality on whom economic, religious, and power considerations all had their influence, but in varying degrees and combinations at different times. George L. Beer quotes Firth as saying about Cromwell that: "Looked at from one point of view, he seemed as practical as a commercial traveller; from another, a Puritan Don Quixote," and gives as his own verdict that "It was 'the commercial traveller' who acted, and the 'Puritan Don Quixote' who dreamt and spoke."[63] Other historians have given other interpretations.[64]

I have unfortunately not been able to find an orthodox neo-Marxian study dealing with these issues for this period. If there were one such, and if it followed the standard pattern, it would argue that "in the last analysis" the end of foreign policy had been not power, and not power and plenty, but plenty alone, and plenty for the privileged classes only, and it would charge that members of these classes would always be there in every major diplomatic episode, pulling the strings of foreign policy-making for their own special benefit. Writing a few years ago in criticism of this theory as applied to more recent times, I ventured the

First Half of the Eighteenth Century," *Transactions of the Royal Historical Society*, New Series, XIV (1900), 146 ff.

[63] Cromwell's Policy in its Economic Aspects," *Political Science Quarterly*, XVII (March 1902), 46–47.

[64] Cf. John Morley, *Oliver Cromwell*, New York, 1902, p. 434; Guernsey Jones, *The Diplomatic Relations between Cromwell and Charles X. Gustavus of Sweden*, Lincoln, Neb., 1897, pp. 34–35; Frank Strong, "The Causes of Cromwell's West Indian Expedition," *American Historical Review*, IV (January 1899), 245; M. P. Ashley, *Financial and Commercial Policy under the Cromwellian Protectorate*, Oxford, 1934; [Slingsby Bethel], *The World's Mistake in Oliver Cromwell* [1668], in *The Harleian Miscellany*, London, 1810, VII, 356–57.

I have not been able to find any systematic or comprehensive study of the role of the religious factor in power politics. The following references are a fair sample of the material bearing on this which I have come across: Leon Geley, *Fancan et la Politique de Richelieu de 1617 à 1627*, Paris, 1884, pp. 264–290; "Discours sur ce qui peut sembler estre plus expedient, & à moyenner au sujet des guerres entre l'Empereur & le Palatin," [1621], in *Recueil de Quelques Discours Politiques*, no place given, 1632, pp. 314 ff; C. C. Eckhardt, *The Papacy and World Affairs as Reflected in the Secularization of Politics*, Chicago, 1937, p. 89; S. Rojdestvensky and Inna Lubimenko, *Contribution à l'Histoire des Relations Commerciales Franco-Russes aut XVIIIᵉ Siècle*, Paris, 1929, p. 4; *Mèmoires de Noailles*, Paris 1777, I, 126; Cheruel, "Le Baron Charles D'Avaugour Ambassadeur de France en Suède, 1654–1657," *Revue d'Histoire Diplomatique*, III (1889), 529; [Jean Rousset de Missy], *The History of Cardinal Alberoni*, London, 1719, p. 105; W. E. Lingelbach, "The Doctrine and Practice of Intervention in Europe," *Annals of the American Academy*, XVI (July 1900), 17, note; "Les Principes Généraux de la Guerre," *Oeuvres de Frédéric le Grand*, XXVIII (Berlin, 1856), 50; C.-G. Picavet, *La Diplomatie Française au Temps de Louis XIV*, Paris, 1930, pp. 8, 160–166; Georges Pagès, *La Monarchie d'Ancien Régime en France*, Paris, 1928, pp. 67 ff.

following comment: "While I suspect that Marx himself would not have hesitated to resort to the 'scandal' theory of imperialism and war when convenient for propaganda purposes, I am sure that he would basically have despised it for its vulgar or unscientific character."[65] I was "righter" than I deserved to be.

Karl Marx studied the British diplomacy of this period, even making use of the unpublished records in the British Foreign Office, and discussed the role played by commercial objectives in British foreign policy. The ruling oligarchy needed political allies at home, and found them in some section or other of the *haute bourgeoisie*.

> As to their *foreign policy*, they wanted to give it the appearance at least of being altogether regulated by the mercantile interest, an appearance the more easily to be produced, as the exclusive interest of one or the other small fraction of that class would, of course, be always identified with this or that Ministerial measure. The interested fraction then raised the commerce and navigation cry, which the nation stupidly re-echoed.

Eighteenth century practice thus "developed on the Cabinet, at least, the *onus* of inventing *mercantile pretexts*, however futile, for their measures of foreign policy." Writing in the 1850's, Marx found that procedure had changed. Palmerston did not not bother to find commercial pretexts for his foreign policy measures.

> In our own epoch, British ministers have thrown this burden on foreign nations, leaving to the French, the Germans, etc., the irksome task of discovering the *secret* and *hidden* mercantile springs of their actions. Lord Palmerston, for instance, takes a step apparently the most damaging to the material interests of Great Britain. Up starts a State philosopher, on the other side of the Atlantic, or of the Channel, or in the heart of Germany, who puts his head to the rack to dig out the mysteries of the mercantile Machiavelism of "perfide Albion," of which Palmerston is supposed the unscrupulous and unflinching executor.[66]

Marx, in rejecting the economic explanation of British friendship for Russia, fell back upon an explanation of both a sentimental pro-Russianism in high circles in Britain and an unjustified fear of Russian power. It is a paradox that the father of Marxism should have sponsored a doctrine which now sounds so non-Marx-

---

[65] "International Relations between State-Controlled National Economies," *American Economic Review Supplement*, XXXIV (March 1944), 324.

[66] Karl Marx, *Secret Diplomatic History of the Eighteenth Century*, Eleanor Marx Aveling, ed., London, 1899, pp. 55–56. The italics are in the original.

ian. I cannot believe, however, that the appeals to economic considerations which played so prominent a part in eighteenth-century British discussions of Anglo-Russian relations were all pretext, and I can find little evidence which makes it credible that friendly sentiment towards foreigners played a significant role in the foreign policy of England in the eighteenth century. Leaving sentiment aside, England's foreign and European foreign policy in general, was governed by joint and harmonized considerations of power and economics. That the economics at least was generally misguided, and that it served to poison international relations, is another matter which, thought not relevant *here*, is highly relevant now.

5

BENTHAM AND J. S. MILL: THE
UTILITARIAN BACKGROUND

THE ONE-HUNDREDTH ANNIVERSARY of the publication of J. S. Mill's *Principles of Political Economy* falls in the year 1948, and the American Economic Association in the programming of its meetings takes advantage of anniversaries of births, deaths, and dates of publication to remind its members that our discipline has a past. This is a proper occasion, therefore, for a paper on J. S. Mill. The inclusion of Bentham in the scope of my paper is of my own contriving, but perhaps I can technically legitimatize it by appeal to the fact that British learned circles have been celebrating during 1948 the two-hundredth anniversary of Bentham's birth. There is no intellectual difficulty, however, in associating Bentham with Mill. The intellectual history of Mill is in large part a history, first, of faithful discipleship, then of rebellion from, and finally of substantial return, to the Benthamite set of doctrines.

The general lines of Bentham's thought were wholly of the eighteenth century, as I could demonstrate if there were time. Of English intellectuals who have had great influence, Bentham was perhaps the least original in his stock of general ideas, but clearly the most original in finding means and devices for putting his philosophy to practical use. To the nineteenth century Bentham was important as a carrier of eighteenth century thought and, still more, as a translator of this thought into a program of social reform. It was the seventeenth century which was the Age of Genius. The philosophers of the eighteenth century were, nonetheless, fertile in ideas. They were, however, almost completely devoid of zeal for the application of these ideas to change of institutions, or even of zeal in generating ideas which would call for change in existing institutions.

We economists like to think of Adam Smith as an exception in this regard, but he was so only to a moderate extent. The one social issue on which Adam Smith was a zealot was the issue of freedom of trade *versus* mercantilism. But Smith had little confidence in the ability of ideas to move worlds. It is often overlooked

Reprinted from the *American Economic Review* 39 (March 1949): 360–82.

that it was with reference to internal as well as to international free trade that Adam Smith made his famous statement that "To expect, indeed, that the freedom of trade should ever be entirely restored in Great Britain, is as absurd as to expect that an Oceana or Utopia should ever be established in it," and this although when he wrote, by obsolescence rather than by deliberate repeal, the restrictions on internal freedom of trade had already become largely inoperative. There is no evidence that Smith was more optimistic about the prospects for international than for domestic free trade, or that, beyond writing his book and preparing a few memoranda for the government when called upon, he ever felt moved to do anything, and especially to resort to anything rude or, in the eighteenth-century meaning of the term, to "enthusiasm," to obtain acceptance and execution of his reforming ideas.

The eighteenth century, in Britain if not in France, and before the American and the French Revolutions if not after, was the age of social complacency, political, economic, moral, of satisfaction with the *status quo* at least to the extent of belief that the costs of substantial change would exceed the benefits of removal or moderation of whatever evils were recognized to prevail. British eighteenth-century government was oligarchic, corrupt, inefficient, though it was generally not tyrannical in intent and usually too lax, too inert, too decentralized, and too sceptical to be seriously tyrannical in effect. Until the end of the century there was no major figure who even mildly suggested the need for major political reform. Whether the economic condition of the masses of the people was improving or deteriorating, and whatever its trend, whether it was desperately bad or moderately good as compared to later standards, I frankly have no idea. We may rest assured, however, that it was not idyllic, if only because it never is.

Nevertheless, there was not until the very last moments of the century either a single major political debate which turned on the economic conditions of the poor or a single major writer who had important suggestions as to how to improve them, with the sole exception of Adam Smith's plea for freedom of trade. It was even a common doctrine of the century that the poor should never be relieved of their poverty above the level of a bare subsistence plus perhaps a few crumbs of cake, and it was at least the quasi-official doctrine of the Church of England that the poverty of the poor—and the prosperity of the bishops—were in accordance with the Divine Will.

Bentham and the Benthamites, on the other hand, were never complacent about the condition of the people of England. They were "Radical Reformers," and they worked hard at their reforms: by working out detailed blueprints for them; by propaganda, agitation, intrigue, conspiracy; and, if truth be told, by encouragement to revolutionary movements up to—but not beyond—the point where resort to physical force would be the next step. Bentham, moreover, was a successful social reformer, more successful perhaps than anyone else in history except Karl Marx—I have in mind here only the realization and not the merits of programs of change—if he is given credit for those changes which came after his death as the result largely of the efforts of his disciples.

The list of reforms in England which derive largely from Bentham is a truly impressive one, and I present it here only in part: fundamental law reform in many of its branches; prison reform; adult popular suffrage, including woman suffrage; free trade; reform in colonial government; legalization of trade unions; general education at public expense; free speech and free press; the secret ballot; a civil service appointed and promoted on merit; repeal of the usury laws; general registration of titles to property; reform of local government; a safety code for merchant shipping; sanitary reform and preventive medicine at public expense; systematic collection of statistics; free justice for the poor. Bentham was the first person to propose birth-control as a measure of economic reform, and this *before* Malthus had published his first *Essay on the Principle of Population.*[1] The Ministry of Health which he proposed would be made responsible not only for general sanitation and routine public health work, but also for smoke prevention, local health-museums, and the policing of the medical profession to prevent their formation of monopolies.

Related to the conditions of the time when these reforms were proposed, Bentham's program was comprehensive, radical, and progressive without being visionary. The modern "democratic socialist" would find it wanting, since Bentham did not approve of tampering with the system of private property except through inheritance taxation and insisted on "compensation" where reform measures would involve violation of "reasonable expectations." He apparently never formulated any concrete proposals for social security on an insurance basis, but he approved in principle of government-administered and government-subsidized insurance against every conceivable type of social hazard for which individual prudence could not make adequate provision. It was too early for proposals to stabilize employment through monetary or fiscal measures, although Bentham did explore the possibility of increasing real investment and production through the "forced frugality" induced by the issue of paper money.[2] Pronounced indi-

---

[1] See J. Bentham, "Situation and Relief of the Poor," *Annals of Agriculture*, Vol. XXIX (1797), pp. 422–23 (p. 31, in the separate pamphlet version). See also Norman E. Hines, "Jeremy Bentham and the Genesis of English Neo-Malthusianism," *Economic History* (Suppl. of *The Economic Journal*), Vol. III (1936), pp. 267–76

[2] Bentham's treatment of this still remains in large part in manuscript. Extracts from these unpublished manuscripts and comments by Ricardo on them have recently been published by Edmund

vidualist though he was, his specific program of reforms in both the content and the processes of legislation, in governmental organization, and in public administration, made him a major source of inspiration for the Fabian socialists as well as for the laissez-faire liberals.

To belief in political democracy Bentham came only slowly, and only as their failure to adopt his proposals eroded his faith in the good intentions of the British aristocratic politicians. The Benthamite case for political democracy was first elaborately expounded by James Mill in his famous essay on Government first published in 1820. It turned out to be an embarrassment for Bentham and his other disciples because by the scholastic formalism of its argument and the extreme lengths to which it carried Bentham's doctrine it was seriously vulnerable to rebuttal and, even worse, to ridicule. Starting out from the proposition that the sole proper purpose of government is to promote the greatest happiness of mankind, James Mill proceeded by purely *a priori* analysis, without any reference to history or to contemporary fact, from the premise that legislators served *only* their "sinister interests"—a stock Benthamite term for the self-interest of rulers or a ruling class—to the conclusion that good government was therefore obtainable only by making it, through popular suffrage and frequent elections, the self-interest of the elected to serve the interests of the electors.

Bentham, writing in the 1780s, had conceded that if at any time legislators "have suffered the nation to be preyed upon by swarms of idle pensioners, or useless place-men, it has rather been from negligence and imbecility, than from any settled plan for oppressing and plundering of the people," but in 1814 he appended a note withdrawing the concession. "So thought Anno 1780 and 1790.—Not so Anno 1814.—J. Bentham."[3] By that time he had adopted the doctrine of "Sinister Interests." But James Mill carried the doctrine further than was necessary to meet Bentham's requirements and probably further than Bentham's belief in it. As Tawney has remarked: "To [James Mill] the State is not a band of brothers, but a mutual detective society: the principal advantage of popular government is that there are more detectives, and therefore, presumably, fewer thieves."[4] Bentham always, but James Mill rarely, if ever, conceded that men, even legislators, could not only be influenced by the praise and blame of other men, but could even display some measure of pure benevolence. As Barker has commented: ". . . while all—or nearly all—of the theorems of Mill's article may be found in Bentham, they have undergone a change. The egoism is more

---

Silberner, "Un Manuscrit Inédit de David Ricardo sur le Problème Monétaire," *Revue d'Histoire Économique et Sociale*, Vol. XXV (1940), 195–259, and were then also already in page proof in Piero Sraffa's long-forthcoming edition of Ricardo's works.

[3] Bentham, "Principles of Morals and Legisiation," *Works* (Edinburgh, 1838–1843), I. 5.

[4] R. H. Tawney, preface to *Life and Struggles of William Lovett*, new ed. (New York, 1920), p. xxi.

egoistic; the negativism is more negative,"[5] and it may be added the *a priori* analysis more "high *priori.*" In the seventeenth century Harrington had denied that Hobbes could work the miracle of "making you a king by geometry." Macaulay was now to deny that the Benthamites could depose an aristocracy by geometry.

Macaulay, a young man anxiously seeking fame by his fluent and facile pen, found the opportunity in James Mill's essay on Government. Reviewing in 1829, in the magisterial *Edinburgh Review,* a reprint of this essay of James Mill, Macaulay raked it high and low, primarily on the basis of its use, without benefit of historical induction or of reference to contemporary facts, of the *a priori* or, in the language of the time and earlier, the geometrical method, but also on the more concrete ground that the proposition that legislators *always* and *invariably* act in terms of their selfish interests was preposterous whatever the method by which it was attempted to establish it.[6]

The Benthamites were shaken by the attack, and J. S. Mill most so, as we shall see later. But Macaulay himself, without withdrawing anything of what he had written, soon thereafter made his peace with James Mill and from then on was an exponent of political democracy on the basis of a line of argument which Paxton in his *Civil Polity* had already presented in 1703, and which should have been the original and was to become the standard line of the Benthamites, namely, that only by democratic voting could there be an adequate guarantee that legislators would *always* or predominantly serve the general interest, without denial that they might sometimes do so even in the absence of democracy.

I come now to deal more systematically with the most difficult and the most controverted aspect of Benthamism, namely, its psychological and ethical justifications for utilitarianism as legislative policy.

Bentham's main concern with ethics was with the ethics which should be followed by moral leaders, not with the ethics of the ordinary man, not with private morals, except as they were data to be operated on by the elite. "The science," he said, "whose foundations we have explored can appeal only to lofty minds with whom the public welfare has become a passion."[7] And by them, Bentham held, its lessons should be pressed on legislators, whether *their* minds were lofty ones or not. As Bentham acknowledged,[8] he sometimes overlooked this, and

---

[5] Sir Ernest Barker, in the preface of his edition of James Mill, *Essay on Government* (Cambridge, England, 1937), p. xv.

[6] See the preface, pp. ix–xi and pp. 160 ff. of *The Miscellaneous Writings and Speeches of Lord Macaulay*, Popular Edition (London, 1891).

[7] *Theory of Legislation*, C. M. Atkinson, ed. (London, 1914), II. 337.

[8] *Cf.* for example, the preface, first added to the 1823 edition, of his *Introduction to the Principles*

wrote as if what he had to say was directed at private morals, and critics have made much of this oversight without treating it merely as a lapse from his fundamental purposes. It was Benthamism interpreted as a system of private ethics, didactic as well as descriptive, that has aroused the most violent and the most emotional antagonism. Even as private ethics, however, Benthamism has seemed so vulnerable a target to *odium theologicum* and *odium ethicum* only because the private ethics of the critics permitted them to attack Bentham's words without taking pains to ascertain what the thoughts were which these words were intended to communicate.

Bentham starts from the standard eighteenth-century proposition, common to theologians and to sceptical philosophers alike, that man operates "under the governance of two sovereign masters, pain and pleasure." Happiness is a net sum or aggregate of individually experienced pleasures and pains.[9] Man, he claims, acts only in response to his "interests," by which he usually, and fundamentally, means whatever men are interested in, but, unfortunately, frequently allows to mean what men regard as in their self-interest. Men normally are interested to some extent in the happiness of others than themselves, and in exceptional cases are capable of "universal benevolence," or a dominating concern with the happiness of mankind at large, but generally, if they are left to themselves, there will be serious discrepancy between the actual behavior of individuals and the behavior which would conduce to "the greatest happiness of the greatest number." It is the function of legislation to coerce or bribe individuals to make their behavior coincide with that required by the greatest-happiness principle, and of education and moral leaders to mould men's desires so that they spontaneously associate the happiness of others with their own happiness.

Bentham nowhere attempts or asserts the possibility of a positive demonstration that greatest happiness, whether as hedonism or as eudaemonism, is the proper moral objective for the common man, the moral leader, or the legislator, and his only argument in support of the greatest-happiness principle is the negative one that the rival principles proposed by other ethical systems are either resolvable upon scrutiny to verbal variants of the utility principle, or are sheer *ipse dixitism,* or are meaningless patterns of words.

"Pleasure" and "happiness" were to Bentham widely inclusive terms, involving not only the pleasures of the senses but also those of the heart and the mind. Pleasures, moreover, which in their "simple" or primary form, genetically

---

of *Morals and Legislation,* where he says that "an introduction to a plan of a penal code" would have been a title better indicating the nature of its contents.

[9] *Cf.* "Gamaliel Smith" [=Jeremy Bentham], *Not Paul, but Jesus* (London, 1823), p. 394: "happiness, to be anything, must be composed of pleasures: and, be the man who he may, of what it is that gives pleasure to him, he alone can be judge."

speaking, were pleasures of self could by "association of ideas" become associated with the pleasures of others. Man, by living in society, by education, and by acts of parliament, could be made good. The eighteenth-century utilitarians may have traded, as a German philosopher has put it, "in the small wares of usefulness (*Nutzlichkeitskrämerei*)." Or it may be that to accept the pursuit of pleasure as a proper end of man is "swinish doctrine," if it be proper to assume that man pursues swinish pleasures. But a utilitarian does not have to be a Philistine. If in Bentham's exposition of his psychology there was often undue stress on the selfish sentiments, this fault—which was much more evident in James Mill than in Bentham—was the result of lack of imagination and of feeling, or of faulty observation—itself the consequence of these lacks—rather than any inherent incompatibility of broader views with the logic of his system. One important manifestation of this—systematic on the part of James Mill but only occasional and incidental on the part of Bentham—was the assumption that even when one's own pleasure had through association of ideas become involved in the pleasure of other persons, the affectionate sentiments toward others still contained an element of conscious reference back to one's own pleasures. This, by implication at least, was a proclamation of the universal prevalence of psychological hedonism.[10]

The eighteenth century is often termed the "Age of Reason," and it is correctly so termed if by the phrase is meant that it was the age in which philosophers held that the credibility of all things should be tested by reason. But from the point of view of its prevailing psychological doctrines, it could more properly be called the "Age of the Passions" because of its stress on the emotions and the instincts, the affections and aversions, and its playing down of the role of reason in the behavior of the ordinary man. David Hume was writing in the spirit of his times when he declared that: "Reason is and ought only to be the slave of the passions, and can never pretend to any other office than to serve and obey them." The normal role of reason was that of an obedient servant of the passions, a passive agent for the comparison of their relative intensities and for the justification of the choices made between them. "So convenient a thing," said Benjamin Franklin, in his *Autobiography*, "it is to be a reasonable creature, since it enables one to find or make a reason for everything one has a mind to do."

For the moral philosopher and the properly conditioned legislator, however, Bentham assigned more important roles to reason, first, that of moulding the passions of individuals so that they would contribute more to the augmentation

---

[10] In notes to his edition of James Mill, *Analysis of the Phenomena of the Human Mind* (London, 1869), J. S. Mill, without fully admitting that his father had held this doctrine, points out passages which could be interpreted as implying it. See II. 217, note; II. 233 ff., note; II. 286 ff. note, etc.

of general happiness, and second, that of providing a technique for the comparison of passions of individuals with a view to making a socially oriented choice between them where choice had to be or could be made. It was for this social purpose, and not for the routine behavior of routine individuals, that Bentham endeavored to construct what he at different times labelled as a "moral thermometer," a "moral arithmetic," a "felicific calculus."

Much amusement has been derived from Bentham's attempt to develop a technique by which the quantities of pleasure and pain could be measured by the legislator or the benevolent philosopher. Wesley Mitchell's well-known essay on "Bentham's Felicific Calculus,"[11] is the fullest and the least unsympathetic account I am acquainted with of Bentham's position on this question. Mitchell points out the excessive degree of hedonism attributed by Bentham to mankind, and comments penetratingly on Bentham's attempt to find a common denominator through money for the pleasures of different persons. Mitchell says that in fact Bentham used the calculus not as an instrument of calculation, but as a basis of ordinal classification. "It pointed out to him what elements should be considered in a given situation, and among these elements *seriatim* he was often able to make comparisons in terms of greater and less." I think this is a somewhat misleading description of Bentham's method. The "classification" was not *seriatim*, was not in terms of higher and lower, but merely of pro and con, of pleasure and pain, and was wholly preliminary to rather than part of the calculus. The "calculus" as he actually used it was merely a metal comparison of the comparative weights of the pros and cons, a technique which neither calls for fancy labels nor is properly conducive either to merriment or to measurement.

Bentham did not invent the concept or the terminology of "moral arithmetic." Play with the idea of measuring the unmeasurable and resort to the language of measurement where it was silly to attempt to apply it goes back to at least the seventeenth century, when the prestige of geometry and later of algebra tended to trap all philosophers with scientific pretensions into casting their analysis into pseudo-mathematical form. Mandeville, as early as 1730, laughed at physicians who studied mathematics because it was fashionable, and cited one who had advised that for certain diseases "the doses of the medicines are to be as the Squares of the Constitutions."[12] Thomas Reid, in his *Essay on Quantity* of 1748, questioned the possibility of reducing to measurement such things as sensations, beauty, pleasure, and the affections and appetites of the mind, even though they "are capable of more and less," and he warned that to apply mathematical lan-

---

[11] Reprinted in W. C. Mitchell, *The Backward Art of Spending Money* (New York, 1937), pp. 177–202.

[12] Bernard Mandeville, M.D., *A Treatise of the Hypochondriack and Hysterick Diseases*, 2nd ed. (London, 1730), p. 184. Compare the history of "Lullism."

guage to non-measurable things is "to make a show of mathematical reasoning, without advancing one step in real knowledge."[13]

Bentham never went far afield for the sources of his ideas, and I suspect that Benjamin Franklin was his source, direct or indirect, for this idea of classification by "bipartition" plus "measurement" of the relative weight of the two classes. Franklin a few years earlier, in 1772, had been expounding it in private correspondence with Joseph Priestley and Richard Price—with all three of whom Bentham had personal contacts—in very much the same terms as Bentham was later to use, and under the similar, and already old, label of "moral or prudential algebra."[14]

None of Bentham's immediate disciples showed any interest in this aspect of Bentham's thought, and it was not until Jevons drew attention to it and made it the basis of his subjective theory of economic value that it had any influence, for good or bad. I like to think, more so probably than Wesley Mitchell would have appreciated, that Bentham's felicific calculus was merely one more manifestation of the inferiority complex which practitioners of the social "sciences" had in the eighteenth century, and have reacquired in the twentieth, towards mathematics, towards the exact sciences, and towards quantification as one of the higher virtues. Since with the application of "political arithmetic" to "moral arithmetic" we now all accept without protest the derivation of measured "propensities" from correlations between psychologically and otherwise promiscuous statistical aggregates compiled catch-as-catch-can on anything up to global scale, our readiness to laugh at Bentham's modest and wholly platonic gestures in this direction excites my propensity for amazement.

There remains one question, specially important for economics, where the influence of Bentham on J. S. Mill is obvious, the question of laissez-faire, or the economic role of government. Élie Halévy, in his great but tendentious work on the Benthamites,[15] has made much of the existence in Bentham's system of a conflict between his juristic and his economic doctrines. According to Halévy, Bentham in his juristic theory makes it the primary function of government to create an *artificial* harmony between the interests of individuals and the public interest, whereas in his economic theory he reaches laissez-faire conclusions on the basis of an implied natural or spontaneous harmony of interests. This has become a stereotype of present-day comments on Bentham, and although there may be exceptions to the natural law which proclaims that stereotypes in the field

[13] *The Works of Thomas Reid*, Sir William Hamilton, ed., 3rd ed. (Edinburgh, 1852), p. 717.

[14] *The Monthly Repository*, Vol. XII (1817), p. 13, and *Proceedings of the Massachusetts Historical Society*, 2nd ser., Vol. XVII (1903), p. 264.

[15] *La Formation du Radicalisme Philosophique*, 3 vols. (Paris, 1901–1904). There is an inferior edition in English in one volume.

of the history of ideas provide a light which blinds rather than guides, this is not one of them.

Bentham did interpret the function of government, under the influence largely of Helvétius, as that of creating, through the application of rewards and punishments, an approach to harmony between the interests of individuals and the social interests. He did prescribe limits for the field for governmental intervention in economic matters, but these limits were not, as we shall see, very narrow ones, and in any case were not so narrow as to give scope for a doctrine of natural harmony of interests, in the sense of a harmony preordained or inherent in the nature of man living in a society unregulated by government. Of explicit formulation by Bentham of a doctrine of natural harmony I can find not the slightest trace in his writings, and such a doctrine would be in basic conflict not only with his juristic theories but with his whole cosmological outlook. Faith in natural harmony always stems from either faith in the continuous intervention of a beneficent Author of Nature or faith in the workings of a natural evolutionary process, and the Benthamites rejected the former and had not yet heard of the latter.

It has been common since Adam Smith's day to take for granted *in economics* the role of the state with reference to the protection of legal property rights and the enforcement of contracts, leaving it to juristic inquiry to explore the problems of theory and of practice in this field. Such was also the procedure of Bentham, and in his juristic writings he keeps very much in mind that "passion . . . from the excesses of which, by reason of its strength, constancy, and universality, society has most to apprehend; I mean that which corresponds to the motive of pecuniary interest."[16] Here he deals with the problem of "repression" of harmful economic activity by means of civil and penal law. If Bentham believed that there was a natural harmony of private and public interests in the economic field, it was one, therefore, which would prevail only after the magistrate and the constable had performed their duties.[17]

But Bentham does not advocate anything like "anarchy plus the constable." His most general proposition of a laissez-faire character is as follows:

> With the view of causing an increase to take place in the mass of national wealth, or with a view to increase of the means either of subsistence or enjoyment, without some special reasons, the general rule is, that nothing ought to be done or attempted by government. The motto, or watchword of government, on these occasions, ought to be—*Be Quiet.*[18]

[16] "Introduction to the Principles of Morals and Legislation," *Works*, Vol. I, pp. 90–91.

[17] Bentham deals briefly with the relations between political economy and law in "A General View of a Complete Code of Laws," *Works*, Vol. III, pp. 203–4.

[18] "Manual of Political Economy," *Works*, Vol. III, p. 33. All subsequent citations of Bentham are from the "Manual."

This may sound like a sweeping enough support of laissez-faire, if, as is common though rarely desirable practice in such matters, it be read carelessly and out of its context. There are important qualifications, explicit or implied, within this apparently emphatic text. First, the text deals with "encouragement" and not with "repression" of economic activity. As I have already pointed out, Bentham deals with the problem of repression of harmful economic activity as a problem in law and not in economics. Second, the general rule of doing nothing positive is applicable only if there is no special reason to the contrary. A rule is not equivalent for him to a principle, nor a "motto" to a dogma.

Bentham presents three grounds for the general rule against governmental activity of a positive kind in the economic field: (1) in this field, individuals know their own interest better than government can; (2) individuals operate more ardently and more skillfully in pursuit of their own interests than government can or will operate on their behalf; (3) governmental intervention means coercion, either directly or indirectly through taxation, and coercion involves "pain" and therefore is an evil.

Bentham is ready to approve of any departure from the general rule, however, if a case can be made for such departure on utility grounds. "Indiscriminate generalizations" are an error, he says, and "In laying down general rules, [even] fortuitous and transient cases ought not to be forgotten." And he lives up to his doctrine as, for instance, when he says that "what ought not to be done with the intention of supporting an unprofitable branch of trade, may yet be proper for preventing the ruin of the workmen employed in such business," or, when opposing in general any restrictions on the introduction of labor-saving machinery, he approves, however, of transitory aid to workmen injured economically by such introduction.

Bentham does not, moreover, limit his exceptions from the non-intervention rule to fortuitous and transient cases, but presents an elaborate analysis of the circumstances under which government should not ("non-agenda") and those under which it should ("agenda") intervene. The argument may, to some tastes, be weighted too heavily on the side of *non-agenda*, but it is free from any dogma except the utilitarian one with which it is supposed by Halévy to clash.

Whether government should intervene, says Bentham, should depend on the extent of the power, intelligence, and inclination, and therefore the spontaneous initiative, possessed by the public, and this will vary as between countries. "In Russia, under Peter the Great, the list of *sponte acta* being a blank, that of *agenda* was proportionally abundant." Government has special responsibilities for providing security against food shortages as well as military security. He approves of government aid in the construction of roads, canals, iron railways, of public hospitals for the sick, hurt and helpless, of public establishments for the "occasional maintenance and employment of able-bodied poor," and, as we have seen, of public health activities on a scale still unknown. He was an ardent advocate of general education at public expense and he urged the extension of governmental registration services to make fraud more hazardous—and also of the systematic collection of economic statistics, but with a proviso which I suspect saps his concession of most of its virtue for modern statisticians, namely, that "no institution should be set on foot for the furnishing any such articles, without a previous indication of the benefit derivable from such knowledge, and a conviction that it will pay for the expense."

Whatever its merits or defects, this treatment of the economic role of government is not in manner or substance doctrinaire, is not in any detail, as far as I can see, inconsistent with his general "principle of utility," and does not have in it, explicitly or implicitly, and trace of a doctrine of natural harmony of interests. It is to be borne in mind, moreover, that the best Bentham hopes for after all that can be done artificially to harmonize private interests with the public interest will still be far from perfect harmony. This has, indeed, been made the basis from another point of view of attack by moral philosophers of other faiths against utilitarianism: it is taken to task for failing to build a bridge between individual and general happiness. But this would be a valid criticism only if either it had professed to have succeeded in doing so and failed, or if it were a proper demand of *any* moral philosophy that it should provide a *practicable* scheme of perfect harmony of interests. Bentham did not completely bridge the gulf between private interests and the general interest, but neither did he deny the existence of such a gulf, and he did propose two ways, education and government, by which the gulf could be somewhat narrowed—with religion, though grudgingly, accepted as a useful part of education in so far as it educates for virtue. Does anyone know of a third way?

I turn now to John Stuart Mill. His famous *Autobiography*—revealing, but not as much so as he no doubt intended—made generally known the extraordinary intellectual régime to which he had been subjected as a boy by his father, and the precocity which resulted from it. In 1822, at the age of sixteen, he was engaging the redoubtable Robert Torrens in battle in the pages of an important newspaper about the theory of (economic) value. Before he was twenty he had edited Bentham's five-volumed work on the *Rationale of Evidence*, had published at least seven major articles in important periodicals on economic, political, and legal matters, had pointed out with great assurance and even less reverence the literary, political, economic, philosophical, and ethical shortcomings of the august *Edinburgh Review*, and had been arrested for distributing birth-control pamphlets.

In this first stage of his career, drilled to a rigid adherence to the Benthamite canon, J. S. Mill was a zealous exponent of Bentham's and of his father's moral and political doctrines and of Ricardo's economics. In 1826, however, when still in his twentieth year, he underwent a mental crisis, which continued intermittently for several years and which brought him sieges of mental depression, as well as an intellectual conversion which he was later, in his *Autobiography*, to describe as akin to a religious "conviction of sin," the sin being in effect Benthamism.

It is conceivable that J. S. Mill's main trouble was primarily due to overwork, but his own explanation was that the sudden realization that the Benthamite doctrines left the nobler human feelings too much out of account and did not offer a sufficiently full prospect for human happiness had proved more than he could take. During these and subsequent years, he manifested the characteristic which was to remain prominent in all the rest of his career, his susceptibility to influence from widely diverse ideas or, as he was later to put it in his *Autobiography*, his "great readiness and eagerness to learn from everybody, and to make room in my opinions for every new acquisition by adjusting the old and the new to one another." New winds of doctrine were impinging on his mind, which was then as open as a prairie: Wordsworth's nature-poetry, with its reverence for beauty and its revelation—for a Benthamite—that there were other fruitful sources of impressions than those provided by syllogisms; the reading of one of Comte's early works and personal associations with Saint-Simonians, which brought him into contact with the new historical approach to social thought; Macaulay's refutation in the *Edinburgh Review* of his father's *a priori* demonstration of the superiority of democracy to aristocratic government; the conservative political views and the more-or-less orthodox religious views of his friends John Sterling and Frederick Maurice; the feudalistic and pre-fascistic doctrines being expounded with fiery moral passion by Carlyle; and so forth. From all of them he borrowed something, although never as much as he then supposed, and for the most part not for keeps.

For a time, while his dour and magerful father still lived, the younger Mill did not break openly with the Benthamites, but his personal relations with the school became strained—more so, in fact, than he was ever to be aware of. Bentham, however, died in 1832 and James Mill in 1836, and freed from the restraint of their disapproval and evident disappointment, J. S. Mill began to explore the new ground on which he not too firmly stood by the hazardous procedure of putting his thoughts in print for the public to read.

The break was sharpest in the field of private ethics, where Bentham's and James Mill's interest had been least. In his economics, J. S. Mill remained faithful to the Ricardian doctrines as he understood them—and, to some extent, improved upon them in the process of interpreting them. In any case, the Ricardian economics was not wholly acceptable to Bentham, nor Bentham's economics at all acceptable to Ricarado. In the fields of politics and of law, J. S. Mill proclaimed some major departures in his thinking from the views of Bentham, but he never specified what they were. I think that, apart from some wavering as to the virtues of political democracy and some approaches to the benevolent Toryism of Coleridge, Wordsworth, Sterling, and Maurice, these were mainly methodological, loss of faith in the adequacy of the "geometrical" method in politics, rather than substantive.[19] With his father's writings he never, it seems to me, dealt with complete frankness, and he reserved for Bentham blows which could more justly have been directed against James Mill. The harshness and vehemence of the attack on Bentham was no doubt a subconscious manifestation of the urge he was under to free himself from what he had come to feel was an intellectual straitjacket, but it had been his father rather than Bentham who had placed it on him.

The attacks on Benthamism began in 1833, while his father was still living but after Bentham had died, with critical "Remarks on Bentham's Philosophy" included, under cover of anonymity, as an appendix to Bulwer-Lytton's *England and the English*. In 1838, or two years after his father's death, he published in the *London and Westminster Review* his famous full-dress article on Bentham, again anonymous, but with the authorship inevitably known at once to friends and foes. In 1840, he published in the same *Review* an article on Coleridge, which, by its sympathetic treatment of the latter's ethical and political views, was indirectly a criticism of Benthamism.

Meanwhile, in 1835, in a review in the *London and Westminster* of a book by Adam Sedgwick which criticized utilitarian ethics as expounded by Paley, he had defended the principle of utility when properly expounded, but without mentioning any names had remarked that for a full exposition of it additional materials were needed beyond those already to be found in the writings of philosophers.

In these articles Mill was clearly endeavoring to salvage, or at least shrinking from abandoning, a utilitarian system of ethics while rejecting such features of Bentham's system as he could no longer tolerate. There was high praise, therefore, for Bentham as well as sharp blame. His main criticism of Bentham related to his treatment of private morals and of psychology, and especially the stress Bentham put on the role played in human behavior by calculation of gain or loss.

[19] For his attempt to substitute, under Saint-Simonian influence, a philosophy-of-history approach, see his series of essays on ''The Spirit of the Age,'' originally published anonymously in the *Examiner* in 1831, and reprinted in 1942 by the University of Chicago Press, with a characteristically learned and penetrating introduction by F. A. Hayek.

He objected also that Bentham, by shifting from a technical (or broad) meaning of terms—and especially of the term "interest"—to a popular (or narrow) meaning, often slid into an account of human behavior which pictured it as inherently selfish. He explained this—unkindly—in terms of Bentham's personality. Bentham, said Mill, intellectually recognized the possibility of generous action, of benevolence, but "the incompleteness of his own mind as a representative of universal human nature" led him to regard genuine benevolence as rare and therefore unimportant in real life.

> In many of the most natural and strongest feelings of human nature he had no sympathy; from many of its graver experiences he was altogether cut off; and the faculty by which one mind understands a mind different from itself, and throws itself into the feelings of that other mind, was denied him by his deficiency of Imagination.[20]

There was a basis for Mill's criticisms. That Bentham frequently fell into language which pictured human behavior as if it consisted almost solely of action based on calculations of personal gain and that his imagination was deficient with respect to the possible range of human emotions is beyond dispute. But Mill goes further in his criticism at some points than the texts he cites, or their context, justify, and in doing so disregards peculiarities of the Benthamite terminology which at other times, when his attitude had changed, he was to invoke against misinterpretations of Bentham at other hands. I can here deal with only one of these misinterpretations. Mill points out that if in Bentham's *Table of the Springs of Action* we find such words as "Conscience," "Principle," "Moral Rectitude," "Moral Duty," which in the mouths of others represent recognition of such a thing as conscience as a thing distinct from philanthropy, affection, or self-interest in this world or the next, it is as synonymous for "love of reputation," and that the word "self-respect" appears not at all either here or in any of Bentham's writings.[21] The critics of Bentham who have since made the same criticism and cited his *Table of the Springs of Action* as evidence are beyond enumeration.

There is only too much ground for criticism of Bentham for not using words quite as other men do, provided that deviation on his part from the common use of terms is not taken as reliable evidence of deviation from the common run of thought on the questions with which these words are usually associated. But Mill, who should have known better, makes use here of this kind of argument against

---

[20] "Bentham," reprinted in J. S. Mill, *Dissertations and Discussions*, 3rd ed., L. 1875, I. 353.
[21] *Ibid*. I. 359.

the one person of all who by his discussions of the logic of language had made himself least vulnerable to it. Moreover, Bentham in his writings does use "conscience" and "duty" very much as other men do, and if he did not use "self-respect," his stock of synonyms was adequate to fill the void.

The *Table of the Springs of Action*, however, itself provides a more direct, though only a partial, answer to Mill's criticism. The psychology of Hartley and of James Mill from which Bentham started distinguished between "simple" pleasures, and "complex" or "compound" pleasures derived from the "simple" ones genetically by the processes of "association of ideas." Benevolence, generosity, duty, justice, conscience, and so forth would be "compound" pleasures. But Bentham expressly says of the *Table*—which is sufficiently formidable as it stands—that: "The pleasures and pains here brought to view are, every one of them, *simple* and *elementary*."[22] He does cite a few "Compound Pleasures," as illustrative of one broad category of such excluded from the table. One of these, "Love of Justice," has as one of its components "Sympathy for the community at large, in respect of the interest which it has in the maintenance of justice." Mill was later to emphasize love of justice as one of the major virtues. His present refusal to be satisfied with Bentham's recognition of it as one of the "Springs of Action" was perhaps a not too captious suspicion that the words added to it by Bentham made of it a less admirable virtue than if Bentham had written merely "Love of Justice (Period)." But it was common ground among the Benthamites, including J. S. Mill, that the tone and moral significance of "compound pleasures" could be radically different from the tone and original significance of their component elements, the "simple pleasures" from which they had been compounded.

By the time Mill was working on his *Principles of Political Economy*, he had swung back a large part though not all of the way to Bentham's political theory and moral philosophy. What was left of his revolt was confined mostly to a continued insistence on recognition of the complete range of human feelings and a consequent endeavor to avoid exaggerating the role of rationalistic hedonism in human behavior.

William Whewell, an anti-utilitarian professor of moral philosophy at Cambridge University where an even narrower type of utilitarianism with hell-fire trimmings—"theological utilitarianism," it was later to be labeled—had until his advent reigned unchallenged for over a century, in 1838, on the appearance of Mill's article on Bentham, had in private correspondence with a friend welcomed Mill's recantation, but complained—with some justice—of its manner:

[22] *Works*, I. 207.

It is certainly very encouraging to see on all sides strong tendencies to a reform of the prevalent system of morals. The article [by Mill] in the *London Review* is an indication of this, and appears to me to be in many important points right, and at any rate right in the vigorous rejection of Bentham's doctrines and keen criticism of his character. But I confess I do not look with much respect upon a body of writers, who, after habitually showering the most bitter abuse on those who oppose Bentham's principles, come round to the side of their opponents, without a single word of apology, and with an air of imperturbable complacency, as if they had been right before and after the change. Nor do I see any security in their present creed, against a change of equal magnitude hereafter.[23]

This was real prescience on Whewell's part. In 1843, in conversation about the surviving disciples of Bentham, Mill made the remark which "though smilingly uttered . . . was not at all a jest" that as for himself: "And I am Peter, who denied his Master."[24] In 1852 Mill was to write a critical review of Whewell's *Lectures on the History of Moral Philosophy in England*, published in the same year. Conceding very little error in the Benthamite doctrine, Mill rejected vehemently Whewell's objections to utilitarian ethics in general and to Bentham in particular, even when they were very similar indeed to his own criticism of Bentham in 1838.

The final stage in Mill's presentation of his ethical views was in 1863, when his essays on Utilitarianism appeared. In form, these still represented an adherence to the doctrine, but so modified by the admission without obvious absorption of foreign elements that they have been the despair of its friends and the delight of its critics ever since. Acts were to be morally appraised solely in terms of their consequences for happiness—a strictly Benthamite proposition. *All* consequences, however, were to be taken into account, including the effects on the character of the agent—an early doctrine of Mill's, which he derived from Coleridge and which he regarded as contrary to Bentham's views, mistakenly, I think. Happiness was conceived broadly enough to cover every type of wish or aspiration man could experience. Mill—unwisely, I think—went a step further than Bentham ever ventured by offering a "proof" that happiness was the proper criterion of virtue: namely, that competent judges accepted it as such, a type of proof which eighteenth century critics of the "moral sense" school of ethics had exposed to ridicule for its circularity.

Mill now attempted also to incorporate into utilitarianism a novel element for it and one which many moral philosophers hold to be incompatible with it,

[23] Mrs. Stair Douglas, *Life of William Whewell* (London, 1881), pp. 270–71.
[24] David Masson, "Memories of London in the 'Forties'," *Blackwood's*, Vol. CLXXXIII (1908), p. 553.

namely, the recognition of non-homogeneity of pleasures and consequently the existence of qualitative differences of a hierarchial nature, as well as quantitative differences, between pleasures:

> It is quite compatible with the principle of utility to recognize the fact, that some *kinds* of pleasure are more desirable and more valuable than others. It would be absurd that while, in estimating all other things, quality is considered as well as quantity, the estimation of pleasures should be supposed to depend on quantity alone.[25]

The test of quality as between two pleasures was the preference "by those who are competently acquainted with both" of the one above the other despite the fact that the other represented a much greater quantity of pleasure.[26]

I venture to suggest: (1) that the problem as Mill presents it, that is, within the limits of utilitarianism, is a spurious one; (2) that what he proffers as a solution is even more spurious; and (3) that Bentham and his predecessors to some extent and modern economists using utility theory to a larger extent, have provided a technique which, while it does not solve any fundamental moral problem, suffices to show that a dichotomy and possible clash between ratings of values on the basis of quality and their rating on the basis of quantity is not one of the fundamental moral problems.

Pleasures—or desires—are of course not homogeneous with respect to every conceivable quality they may possess—any more than are any other objects of human attention except abstract numbers. Comparison is—or should be—always with respect to specified qualities of objects, and if there is possibility of and proper occasion for measurement the measurement is also with reference to these specified qualities.

Mill confuses the issue by attempting at the same time to give predominant importance to the ordering of *classes* of pleasures on a higher-lower scale and to leave room for legitimate preference in particular cases of a pleasure of a lower order over one of a higher. This is the famous and ancient false dilemma of the water-*versus*-diamonds problem in economics, extended to the whole field of values. Whatever may be the case for didactic purposes, for actual behavior—including "moral" behavior—the issues arise in the form of necessary choices

---

[25] J. S. Mill, *Utilitarianism*, 3rd ed. (London, 1867), pp. 11-12.

[26] *Ibid.*, p. 12. In an undated manuscript "On Social Freedom," found in Mill's house at Avignon after his death, and published, among other places, in *Living Age*, 7th ser., Vol. XXXVI (1907), pp. 323–36, there is a stronger statement of the higher-lower thesis with the order of rank made a pure matter of "feeling," not subject to demonstration or to argument—a complete swing back to the eighteenth century "moral sense" school.

between units and not between classes of objects. Bentham's famous dictum "Quantum of pleasure being equal, pushpin [a children's game] is as good as poetry" would meet all the proper requirements of the utilitarian principle if re-stated somewhat as follows: "Desire being equal at the margin of choice, a marginal unit of pushpin is as good as a marginal unit of poetry." The utilitarian but didactic moralist would still be free to insist that since in fact experienced choosers don't plump for even a first unit of pushpin until they are gorged with poetry, *in that sense* poetry as a class is higher on the scale of values than pushpin as a class.

I come now at long last to Mill's *Principles of Political Economy*. He wrote this two-volume book in less than two years, and when he began it he expected it to take only a few months to write. For at least ten years prior to this, he had not given much attention to economics. It was designed to do for Mill's time what Adam Smith had done for his, and to present what was known of the "Principles of Political Economy" as a science, together with their applications to concrete problems and, in the words of its title page, "some of their Applications to Social Philosophy." By the "science" of political economy Mill meant a body of deductive analysis, resting on psychological premises derived from introspection and observation of one's neighbors, and even with respect to these premises abstracting from all aspects of human behavior except those most intimately and most generally associated with the business of buying and selling. When Malthus, in 1824, objected that the "new school" of Ricardians had "altered the theories of Adam Smith upon pure speculation," Mill had replied: "it would, indeed, have been somewhat surprising if they had altered them on any other ground."[27] Later, as the result of Comtean influence and of his investigations in logical method, Mill was more receptive in principle to the possibilities of historical induction. But it is clear that he never assigned to it the right to an independent role in the "science" of political economy. Writing in 1835 with respect to the historical form of the inductive method, he had said:

> History is not the foundation, but the verification, of the social science; it corroborates, and often suggests, political truths, but cannot prove them. The proof of them is drawn from the laws of human nature; ascertained through the study of ourselves by reflection, and of mankind by actual intercourse with them. . . . The usefulness of history depends upon its being kept in the second place.[28]

[27] In a review of the article by Malthus in the *Quarterly Review*, Vol. 30, January 1824, criticizing McCulloch's "Political Economy" article in the *Supplement* to the fourth edition of the *Encyclopedia Britannica, Westminster Review*, Vol. III (1825), p. 213.

[28] "Professor Sedgwick's Discourse on the Studies of the University of Cambridge," *Dissertations and Discussions*, Vol. I, pp. 112–13.

This was, of course, standard methodological doctrine, and to a large extent practice, in English social thought since Hobbes. Inquiry was to be pursued by means of deductive reasoning resting on psychological premises obtained empirically, but chiefly through introspection—which, it should always be remembered, was universally regarded in the past, whatever may be the fashion today, as an "empirical" technique of investigation, and sharply distinguished from intuition, or "innate ideas." But in J. S. Mill, as methodological doctrine, it has less significance than for most of his predecessors, since he confines it to the "scientific" part of Political Economy, stresses the importance of "applications" which can proceed by a wider range of logical methods, gives repeatedly at least platonic warnings that any abstraction from reality must be allowed for before the results of such analysis are made the basis for pronouncements on policy, and rejects it for every other established branch of social thought.

Of his earlier rebellion against the psychology of Bentham and of his father, the most important residue for his economics was probably his repeated emphasis on the importance of custom as a rival to the competitive principle, especially in connection with land-tenure and the relations of landlord and tenant. Here he showed the influence of Richard Jones, one of the pioneer advocates of resort to systematic induction in economics. But this presented J. S. Mill with somewhat of a methodological dilemma, which he never succeeded in resolving. "It is unphilosophical," he wrote, "to construct a science out of a few of the agencies by which the phenomena are determined, and leave the rest to the routine of practice or the sagacity of conjecture."[29] On the other hand, "only through the principle of competition has political economy any pretension to the character of a science,"[30] a proposition which F. Y. Edgeworth was later in effect to repeat, when he wrote that if monopoly should prevail over a large part of the economic order:

> Among those who would suffer by the new regime there would be [included] . . . the abstract economists, who would be deprived of their occupation, the investigation of the conditions which determine value. There would survive only the empirical school, flourishing in a chaos congenial to their mentality.[31]

We seem, however, to have found another alternative, that of becoming amateur lawyers.

Mill thus had no technique for dealing systematically with the analysis of economic process where competition was encroached upon either by custom or by

[29] *A System of Logic*, 3rd ed., Vol. II, p. 472.
[30] *Principles of Political Economy*, Bk. II, Chap. IV, "Of Competition and Custom."
[31] "The Pure Theory of Monopoly," [1897], *Papers Relating to Political Economy* (London, 1925), Vol. I, pp. 138–39.

monopoly, and when he did mention custom—or monopoly—he left it to the reader to estimate its importance and to make the necessary corrections in the conclusions he had reached on the basis of abstractions from these complicating factors. For himself, he assumed the responsibility only for that "uncertain and slippery intermediate region," between "ultimate aims" and "the immediately useful and practically attainable."[32] Logicians and physical scientists have the right, I suppose, to jeer at Mill's failure to extricate himself from this plight. For those among us, however, upon whom the redeeming grace has not as yet been bestowed of that special ideology which takes the form of faith in the capacity of statistical method to perform logical miracles, humility is prescribed, since we are all in the same fix.

The *Principles* thus has no single methodological character. As is the case with the *Wealth of Nations* of Adam Smith, some portions are predominantly abstract and *a priori*; in others, there is a substantial measure of factual data and of inference from history. Its wide range of subject matter; the success with which the lucidity of its style and the nobility of its outlook on life divert attention from its lack of logical rigor; the patent honesty and open mindedness with which controversial issues are treated; these and other qualities made it probably the longest-lived textbook our discipline has ever had or ever will have. It was the text used in the first college course in economics I took, over sixty years after its first publication. Francis Walker's *Political Economy* was also assigned to us, and I think we showed good judgment when we labeled the course, as students will, "Milk and Water." Writing in 1832, Mill had presented a forceful case in defense of ambiguity in language, on the ground that it was for many persons the price which would have to be paid if important ideas which by their richness and variety of content it is difficult to make clear were not to be sacrificed on the altar of logical clarity.[33] The *Principles*, I think, demonstrate that for Mill himself this was good doctrine; it would have been an inferior book, much less rich in content—and much smaller in size—if Mill had thrown out all that was ambiguous and lacking in strict logical consistency.

What most struck his contemporaries in the contents of the *Principles* was the sympathetic manner in which Mill dealt with proposals for radical change along socialist lines in the economic structure of society. The sympathy was in large degree platonic, for in no major concrete instance did Mill actually commit himself to the desirability of a specific drastic change. Mill aspired after the millennium, but he found abundant reason why it was not and should not be wished to be imminent. He looked forward, mostly on ethical and humanitarian grounds,

[32] *Autobiography* (London, 1873), p. 189.
[33] Review of G. C. Lewis, *Use and Abuse of Political Terms*, *Tait's Edinburgh Magazine*, Vol. I (1832), pp. 164ff.

to substantial socialization of the institution of property at some time in the vague future. Meanwhile, however, he warned against any weakening of the institutions of private property, free competition, and the rule of the market. This combination of hard-headed rules and utopian aspirations was just exactly the doctrine that Victorians of goodwill yearned for, and it made a large contribution to the popular success of the book.

Mill's handling of the problem of laissez-faire was a case in point. Except for the difference in tone and feeling, the fuller expression of lofty ideals and impracticable aspirations, it was substantially similar in method of analysis and nature of conclusions to Bentham's treatment. Like Bentham, and like all the other major classical economists except perhaps Senior—who was not a Benthamite— J. S. Mill gave only a very qualified adherence to laissez-faire. It was for him only a rule of expediency, always subordinate to the principle of utility, and never a dogma. The dogmatic exponents of laissez-faire of the time were the Manchester School, and Mill—like Torrens before him and Cairnes, Jevons, Sidgwick, Marshall, Edgeworth and others after him—denied repeatedly, and forcefully almost to the point of blasphemy, that the Cobdenites had either authority or logic to support them when they invoked the "Laws of Political Economy" to stop government from coming to the relief of distress.

It is, fortunately, not part of my assignment to appraise the technical economics of Mill's *Principles*. What I have tried to do is to show the intellectual relations between two men important in the history of our discipline. From these two men several generations of British and American—and above all Canadian— economists, and to some extent also "liberal" continental economists, derived in large part the psychological, ethical, political, and methodological presuppositions upon which they built their economic analysis. With the ebbing of liberalism in the profession, the importance of knowing what its intellectual foundations were has become chiefly historical, and to those under fifty the historical is not obviously important. But for those *over* fifty, a comment of Tawney's is relevant. "It is a wise philosopher," he writes, the flatterer really meaning "economist," "who knows the source of his own premises."[34] I would go even further. It is an unusually alert economist who knows what his premises are, regardless of their source. For those over fifty study of Bentham and of Mill can do something to remedy both of these lacks. Beyond this remark, I make no attempt to draw any moral from what I have said. But I believe that in exercising this unaccustomed measure of self-restraint I am conforming to the "Principle of Utility" if broadly enough interpreted.

[34] Introduction to Raymond W. Firth, *Primitive Economics of the New Zealand Maori* (New York, 1929).

6

INTRODUCTION TO BERNARD MANDEVILLE, *A LETTER TO DION* (1732)

THE *Letter to Dion*, Mandeville's last publication, was, in form, a reply to Bishop Berkeley's *Alciphron: or, the Minute Philosopher*. In *Alciphron*, a series of dialogues directed against "free thinkers" in general, Dion is the presiding host and Alciphron and Lysicles are the expositors of objectionable doctrines. Mandeville's *Fable of the Bees* is attacked in the Second Dialogue, where Lysicles expounds some Mandevillian views but is theologically an atheist, politically a revolutionary, and socially a leveller. In the *Letter to Dion*, however, Mandeville assumes that Berkeley is charging him with all of these views, and accuses Berkeley of unfairness and misrepresentation.

Neither *Alciphron* nor the *Letter to Dion* caused much of a stir. The *Letter* never had a second edition,[1] and is now exceedingly scarce. The significance of the *Letter* would be minor if it were confined to its rôle in the exchange between Berkeley and Mandeville.[2] Berkeley had more sinners in mind than Mandeville, and Mandeville more critics than Berkeley. Berkeley, however, more than any other critic seems to have gotten under Mandeville's skin, perhaps because Berkeley alone made effective use against him of his own weapons of satire and ridicule.[3]

Reprinted from Bernard Mandeville, *A Letter to Dion* (1732), Berkeley, Calif., University of California, William Andrews Clark Memorial Library, 1953. Augustan Reprint Society publication 41, 1953, pp. 1–15.

[1] In its only foreign language translation, the *Letter*, somewhat abbreviated, is appended to the German translation of the *Fable of the Bees* by Otto Bobertag, *Mandevilles Bienenfabel*, Munich, 1914, pp. 349–398.

[2] Berkeley again criticized Mandeville in *A Discourse Addressed to Magistrates*, [1736], *Works*, A. C. Fraser ed., Oxford, 1871, III. 424.

[3] *A Vindication of the Reverend D—B—y*, London, 1734, applies to *Alciphron* the comment of Shaftesbury that reverend authors who resort to dialogue form may "perhaps, find means to laugh gentlemen into their religion, who have unfortunately been laughed out of it." See Alfred Owen Aldridge, "Shaftesbury and the Deist Manifesto," *Transactions of the American Philosophical Society*, New Series, XLI (1951), Part 2, p. 358.

Berkeley came to closest grips with the *Fable of the Bees* when he rejected Mandeville's grim picture of human nature, and when he met Mandeville's eulogy of luxury by the argument that expenditures on luxuries were no better support of employment than equivalent spending on charity to the poor or than the more lasting life which would result from avoidance of luxury.[4]

Of the few contemporary notices of the *Letter to Dion*, the most important was by John, Lord Hervey. Hervey charged both Berkeley and Mandeville with unfairness, but aimed most of his criticism at Berkeley. He claimed that *Alciphron* displayed the weaknesses of argument in dialogue form, that it tended either to state the opponent's case so strongly that it became difficult afterwards to refute it or so weakly that it was not worth answering. He found fault with Berkeley for denying that Mandeville had told a great many disagreeable truths—presumably about human nature and its mode of operation in society—and with Mandeville for having told them in public. He held, I believe rightly, that Mandeville, in associating vice with prosperity, deliberately blurred the distinction between vice as an incidental consequence of prosperity and vice as its cause: vice, said Hervey, "is the *child* of Prosperity, but not the *Parent*; and . . . the Vices which *grow* upon a flourishing People, are not the Means by which they became so."[5]

T. E. Jessop, in his introduction to his edition of *Alciphron*, characterizes Berkeley's account of the argument of the *Fable of the Bees* as "not unfair," and says: "I can see no reason for whitewashing Mandeville. The content and manner of his writing invite retort rather than argument. Berkeley gives both, in the most sparkling of his dialogues. Mandeville wrote a feeble reply, *A Letter to Dion*."[6] F. B. Kaye, on the other hand, says of the exchange between Berkeley and Mandeville that "men like . . . Berkeley, who may be termed the religious-minded . . . in their anguish, threw logic to the winds, and criticized him [i.e., Mandeville] for the most inconsistent reasons."[7]

Objective appraisal of the outcome of the debate between Berkeley and Mandeville would presumably lead to a verdict somewhere between those rendered, with appropriate loyalty to their authors, by their respective editors. It is mainly

---

[4] Francis Hutcheson, a fellow-townsman of Berkeley, had previously made these points against Mandeville's treatment of luxury in letters to the *Dublin Journal* in 1726 (reprinted in Hutcheson, *Reflections upon Laughter, and Remarks upon the Fable of the Bees*, Glasgow, 1750, pp. 61–63, and in James Arbuckle, *Hibernicus' Letters*, London, 1729, Letter 46). In the *Fable of the Bees*, Mandeville concedes that gifts to charity would support employment as much as would equivalent expenditures on luxuries, but argues that in practice the gifts would not be made.

[5] Lord Hervey, *Some Remarks on the Minute Philosopher*, London, 1732, pp. 22–23, 42–50.

[6] *Alciphron, or the Minute Philosopher*, T. E. Jessop, ed., in *The Works of George Berkeley, Bishop of Cloyne*. Edited by A. A. Luce and T. E. Jessop. London, etc., III. (1950), 9–10.

[7] In his edition of the *Fable of the Bees*, Oxford, 1924, II. 415–416. All subsequent references to the *Fable of the Bees* will be to this edition.

for other reasons, however, that the *Letter to Dion* is still of interest. There is first its literary merit. More important, the *Letter* presents in more emphatic and sharper form than elsewhere two essential elements of Mandeville's system of thought, the advocacy, real or pretended, of unqualified rigorism in morals, and the stress on the role of the State, of the "skilful Politician," in evoking a flourishing society out of the operations of a community of selfish rogues and sinners. The remainder of this introduction will be confined to comments on these two aspects of Mandeville's doctrine. Since the publication in 1924 of F. B. Kaye's magnificent edition of the *Fable of the Bees*, no one can deal seriously with Mandeville's thought without heavy reliance on it, even when, as is the case here, there is disagreement with Kaye's interpretation of Mandeville's position.

It was Mandeville's central thesis, expressed by the motto, "Private Vices, Publick Benefits," of the *Fable of the Bees*, that the attainment of temporal prosperity has both as prerequisite and as inevitable consequence types of human behavior which fail to meet the requirements of Christian morality and therefore are "vices." He confined "the Name of Virtue to every Performance, by which Man, contrary to the impulse of Nature, should endeavour the Benefit of others, or the Conquest of his own Passions out of a Rational Ambition of Being good."[8] If "out of a Rational Ambition of being good" be understood to mean out of "charity" in its theological sense of conscious love of God, this definition of virtue is in strict conformity to Augustinian rigorism as expounded from the sixteenth century on by Calvinists and, in the Catholic Church, by Baius, Jansenius, the Jansenists, and others. Mandeville professes also the extreme rigorist doctrine that whatever is not a virtue is vice: in Augustinian terms, *aut caritas aut cupiditas*. Man must therefore choose between temporal prosperity and virtue, and Mandeville insists, especially in the *Letter to Dion*, that on his part the choice is always of virtue:

> . . . the Kingdom of Christ is not of this World, and . . . the last-named is the very Thing a true Christian ought to renounce. (p. 18)[9]

> "Tho' I have shewn the Way to Worldly Greatness, I have, without Hesitation, preferr'd the Road that leads to Virtue." (p. 31)

Kaye concedes: that Mandeville's rigorism "was merely verbal and superficial, and that he would much regret it if the world were run according to rigoristic morality;" that "emotionally" and "practically, if not always theoretically," Mandeville chooses the "utilitarian" side of the dilemma between virtue and

---

[8] *Fable of the Bees*, I. 48–49.
[9] All page references placed in the main text of this introduction are to the *Letter to Dion*.

prosperity; and that "Mandeville's philosophy, indeed, forms a complete whole without the extraneous rigorism."[10] Kaye nevertheless insists that Mandeville's rigorism was sincere, and that it is necessary so to accept it to understand him. It seems to me, on the contrary, that if Mandeville's rigorism were sincere, the whole satirical structure of his argument, its provocative tone, its obvious fun-making gusto, would be incomprehensible, and there would be manifest inconsistency between his satirical purposes and his procedures as a writer.

Kaye argues that rigorism was not so unusual as of itself to justify doubt as to its genuineness in the case of Mandeville; rigorism was "a contemporary point of view both popular and respected, a view-point not yet extinct." To show that rigorism was "the respectable orthodox position for both Catholics and Protestants," Kaye cites as rigorists, in addition to Bayle, St. Augustine, Luther, Calvin, Daniel Dyke (the author of *Mystery of Selfe-Deceiving*, 1642), Thomas Fuller (1608-1661), William Law, and three Continental moralists, Esprit and Pascal, Janesenists, and J. F. Bernard, a French Calvinist.[11]

Christian rigorism by Mandeville's time had had a long history. From and including St. Augustine on, it had undergone many types of doctrinal dilution and moderation even on the part of some of its most ardent exponents. In Mandeville, and in Kaye, it is presented only in its barest and starkest form. Kaye, however, required by his thesis to show that Mandeville's doctrine was "in accord with a great body of contemporary theory,"[12] while accepting it as "the code of rigorism" treats it as if it were identical with any moral system calling for any measure of self-discipline or associated with any type of religious-mindedness.[13] He also identifies it with rationalism in ethics as such, as if any ratio-

[10] *Fable of the Bees*, II. 411, I, ixi, I, lvi.

[11] *Ibid*. I. li, I. lv, I. cxxi.

[12] *Ibid*. I. cxxiv, note.

[13] For example, Kaye cites from Blewitt, a critic of Mandeville, this passage: "nothing can make a Man honest or virtuous but a Regard to *some* religious or moral Principles" and characterizes it as "precisely the rigorist position from which Mandeville was arguing when he asserted that our so-called virtues were really vices, because not based *only* on this regard to principle." (*Ibid*. II. 411. The italics in both cases are mine.) The passage from Blewitt is not, of itself, manifestly rigoristic, while the position attributed to Mandeville is rigorism at its most extreme.

As further evidence of the prevalence of rigorism, Kaye cites from Thomas Fuller the following passage: "corrupt nature (which without thy restraining grace will have a Vent.)" *Ibid*. I. cxxi, note. But in Calvinist theology "restraining grace," which was not a "purifying" grace, operated to make some men who were not purged of sin lead a serviceable social life. (See John Calvin, *Institutes of the Christian Religion*, Bk. II, Ch. III, pp. I. 315–316 of the "Seventh American Edition," Philadelphia, n.d.) As I understand it, the rôle of "restraining grace" in Calvinist doctrine is similar to that of "honnêteté" in Jansenist doctrine, referred to *infra*. The rascals whom Mandeville finds useful to society are not to be identified either with those endowed with the "restraining grace" of the Calvinists or with the "honnêtes hommes" of the Jansenists.

For other instances of disregard by Kaye of the variations in substance and degree of the rigorism of genuine rigorists, see *ibid*. II. 403–406, II. 415–416.

nalistic ethics, merely because it calls for some measure of discipline of the passions by "reason," is *ipso facto* "rigorist."[14]

Mandeville was presumably directing his satire primarily at contemporary Englishmen, not at men who had been dead for generations nor at participants in Continental theological controversies without real counterpart in England, at least since the Restoration. If this is accepted, then of the men cited by Kaye to show the orthodoxy and the contemporaneity of rigorism only William Law has any relevance. But Law was an avowed "enthusiast," and in the England of Mandeville's time this was almost as heretical as to be an avowed sceptic. Calvinism in its origins had been unquestionably—though not unqualifiedly—rigoristic. By Mandeville's time, however, avowed Calvinism was almost extinct in England; even in Geneva, in Scotland, in Holland, its rigorism had been much softened by the spread of Arminianism and by a variety of procedures of theological accommodation or mediation between the life of grace and the life of this sinful world. On the Continent, Jansenists were still expounding a severe rigorism. But Jansenist rigorism was not "orthodox." Though not as extreme as Mandeville's rigorism, it had repeatedly been condemned by Catholic authorities as "*rigorisme outré.*"[15]

To take seriously Mandeville's rigorism, the narrowness with which he defines "virtue," the broadness with which he defines "vice," his failure to recognize any intermediate ground between "virtue" and outright "vice," or any shades or degrees of either, the positiveness with which he assigns to eternal damnation all who depart in any degree from "virtue" as he defines it, is therefore to accept Mandeville as a genuine exponent of a rigorism too austere and too grim not only for the ordinary run of orthodox Anglicans or Catholics of his time but even for St. Augustine (at times), for the Calvinists, and for the Jansenists.

Kaye justifiably puts great stress on the extent of Mandeville's indebtedness to Pierre Bayle. There is not the space here to elaborate, but it could be shown, I believe, that Mandeville was also indebted greatly, both indirectly through Bayle and directly, to the Jansenist, Pierre Nicole, and that Mandeville's rigorism was a gross distortion of, while Bayle's was essentially faithful to, Nicole's system.[16] Nicole insisted that "true virtue" in the rigorist sense was necessary for salva-

---

[14] See especially F. B. Kaye, "The Influence of Bernard Mandeville," *Studies in Philology*, XIX (1922), 90–102.

[15] Cf. Denzinger-Bannwart, *Enchiridion Symbolorum*. (See index of any edition under "Baius," "Fénelon," "Iansen," "Iansenistae," "Quesnell.")

[16] The most pertinent writings of Nicole for present purposes were his essays, "De la grandeur," "De la charité & de l'amour-propre," and "Sur l'évangile de carême," which in the edition of his works published by Guillaume Desprez, Paris, 1755–1768, under the title *Essais de morale*, are to be found in volumes II, III, and XI.

tion, but at the same time expounded the usefulness for society of behavior which theologically was "sinful." But it was the "sinful" behavior of *honnêtes hommes*, of citizens conforming to the prevalent moral standards of their class, not of rogues and rascals, which Nicole conceded to be socially useful.[17] Mandeville, on the other hand, not only lumped the respectable citizens with the rogues and rascals, but it was the usefulness for society of the vices of the rogues and rascals more than—and rather than—those of honest and respectable citizens which he emphasized. In the flourishing hive, prior to its reform, there were:

> . . . Sharpers, Parasites, Pimps, Players,
> Pick-pockets, Coiners, Quacks, South-sayers,
>
> ·   ·   ·   ·   ·   ·   ·   ·   ·   ·   ·   ·   ·   ·
>
> These were call'd Knaves, but bar the Name,
> The grave Industrious were the same.[18]

The moral reform which brought disaster to the "Grumbling Hive" consisted merely in abandonment of roguery and adoption of the standards of the *honnête homme*.[19]

The contrast between his general argument and that of Nicole or Bayle throws light on the role which Mandeville's professed rigorism played in the execution of his satirical purposes. It not only supports the view of all his contemporaries that Mandeville's rigorism was a sham, but also the view that he was not averse to having its insincerity be generally detected, provided only that it should not be subject to clear and unambiguous demonstration. By lumping together the "vices" of the knave and the honest man, Mandeville could without serious risk of civil or ecclesiastical penalties make rigorism of any degree seem ridiculous and thus provide abundant amusement for himself and for like-minded readers; he could then proceed to undermine all the really important systems of morality of his time by applying more exacting standards than they could meet. Against a naturalistic and sentimental system, like Shaftesbury's, he could argue that it rested on an appraisal of human nature too optimistic to be realistic. Against

---

[17] For a similar distinction by Bayle between honnêtes hommes who are not of the elect and the outright rascals, see Pierre Bayle, *Dictionaire historique et critique*, 5th ed., Amsterdam, 1740, "Éclaircissement sur les obscenitez," IV. 649.

[18] *Fable of the Bees*, I. 19.

[19] In the French versions of 1740 and 1750, the title, *The Fable of the Bees: or, Private Vices, Publick Benefits*, is translated as *La fable des abeilles ou les fripons devenus honnestes gens*.

For the "honnête homme" in 17th and 18th century usage as intermediate between a knave and a saint, see M. Magendie, *La politesse mondaine et les théories de l'honnêteté en France*, Paris. n.d. (ca. 1925), and William Empson, *The Structure of Complex Words*, London, 1951, ch. 9, "Honest Man."

current Anglican systems of morality, if they retained elements of older rigoristic doctrine he could level the charge of hypocrisy, and if they were latitudinarian in their tendencies he could object that they were expounding an "easy Christianity" inconsistent with Holy Writ and with tradition.

Mandeville clearly did not like clergymen, especially hypocritical ones, and there still existed sufficient pulpit rigorism to provide him with an adequate target for satire and a substantial number of readers who would detect and approve the satire. As Fielding's Squire Western said to Parson Supple when the latter reproved him for some misdeed: "At'nt in pulpit now? when art a got up there I never mind what dost say; but I won't be priest-ridden, nor taught how to behave myself by thee." Only if it is read as a satire on rigorist sermons can there be full appreciation of the cleverness of the "parable of small beer" which Mandeville, with obvious contentment with his craftsmanship, reproduces in the *Letter to Dion* (pp. 25–29) from the *Fable of the Bees*. Here the standard rigorist proposition that there is sin both in the lust and in the act of satisfying it is applied to drink, where the thirst and its quenching are both treated as vicious.[20]

Mandeville, as Kaye interprets him, resembles the "*Jansénistes du Salon*" who prided themselves on the fashionable rigor of their doctrine but insisted on the practical impossibility of living up to it in the absence of efficacious grace. In my interpretation, Mandeville was both intellectually and temperamentally a "libertine" patently putting on the mask of rigorism in order to be able at the same time to attack the exponents of austere theological morality from their rear while making a frontal attack on less exacting and more humanistic systems of morality. The phenomenon was not a common one, but it was not unique. Bourdaloue, the great seventeenth-century Jesuit preacher, not very long before had called attention to libertines in France who masqueraded in rigorist clothes in order to deepen the cleavages among the members of the Church: "D'où il arrive assez souvent, par l'assemblage le plus bizarre et le plus monstrueux, qu'un homme qui ne croit pas en Dieu, se porte pour défenseur du pouvoir invincible de la grâce, et devient à toute outrance le panégyriste de la plus étroite morale."[21]

The *Letter to Dion* has bearing also on another phase of Mandeville's doctrine which is almost universally misinterpreted. Many scholars, including economists who should know better, regard Mandeville as a pioneer expounder of laissez-

---

[20] Kaye in a note to this parable, *Fable of the Bees*, I. 238, cites as relevant, *1 Cor. x. 31*; "Whether therefore ye eat, or drink, or whatsoever ye do, do all to the Glory of God." Even more relevant, I believe, is *Deut. xxix. 19*, where in the King James version, the sinner boasts: "I shall have peace, though I walk in the imagination of mine heart, to add drunkenness to thirst."

[21] "Pensées diverses sur la foi, et sur les vices opposés,"*Oeuvres de Bourdaloue*, Paris, 1840, III. 362–363.

faire individualism in the economic field and as such as an anticipator of Adam Smith. Kaye accepts this interpretation without argument.

The evidence provided by the *Fable of the Bees* in support of such an interpretation is confined to these facts: Mandeville stressed the importance of self-interest, of individual desires and ambitions, as the driving force of socially useful economic activity; he held that a better allocation of labor among different occupations would result, at least in England, if left to individual determination than if regulated or guided; he rejected some types of sumptuary legislation.

All of this, however, though required for laissez-faire doctrine, was also consistent with mercantilism, at least of the English type. The later exponents of laissez-faire did not invent the "economic man" who pursued only his own interest, but inherited him from the mercantilists and from the doctrine of original sin. English analysis of social process had in this sense always been "individualistic," and in this sense both mercantilism and the wisely-prevalent theological utilitarianism were at least as individualistic as later laissez-faire economics. Englishmen, moreover, had long been jealous of governmental power, and at the height of English mercantilism they insisted upon limits to appropriate governmental intervention. It is not safe, therefore, to label anyone before Adam Smith as an exponent of laissez-faire merely on the ground that he would exempt a few specified types of economic activity from interference by government. It would be misleading also to apply to eighteenth-century writers modern ideas as to the dividing line between "interventionists" and exponents of "liberalism" or of "laissez-faire." As compared to modern totalitarianism, or even to modern "central economic planning," or to "Keynesianism," the English mercantilism of the late seventeenth and the eighteenth century was essentially libertarian. It is only as compared to Adam Smith, or to the English classical and the Continental "liberal" schools of economics of the nineteenth century, that it was interventionist.

Adam Smith is regarded as an exponent of laissez-faire because he laid it down as a general principle (subject in practice to numerous and fairly important specific exceptions) that the activities of government should be limited to the enforcement of justice, to defense, and to public works of a kind inherently unsuitable for private enterprise. He based this doctrine partly on natural rights grounds, partly on the belief that there was a pervasive natural and self-operating harmony, providentially established, between individual interest and the interests of the community, partly on the empirical ground that government was generally inefficient, improvident, and unintelligent.

There is nothing of such doctrine in Mandeville; there is abundant evidence in his writings that Mandeville was a convinced adherent of the prevailing mercantilism of his time. Most English mercantilists disapproved of some or all kinds of sumptuary regulations on the same grounds as Mandeville disapproved of some of them, namely, the existence of more suitable ways of accomplishing their objectives or the mistaken character of their objectives. Mandeville's objection to charity schools on the ground that they would alter for the worse the supplies of labor for different occupations was based on his belief that England, unlike some other countries, already had more tradesmen and skilled artisans than it needed. Mandeville, in contrast to Adam Smith, put great and repeated stress on the importance of the rôle of government in producing a strong and prosperous society, through detailed and systematic regulation of economic activity.

It is a common misinterpretation of Mandeville in this respect to read his motto, "Private Vices, Publick Benefits," as a laissez-faire motto, postulating the natural or spontaneous harmony between individual interests and the public good. The motto as it appeared on title pages of the *Fable of the Bees* was elliptical. In his text, Mandeville repeatedly stated that it was by "the skillful Management of the clever Politician" that private vices could be made to serve the public good, thus ridding the formula of any implication of laissez-faire.

This is made clear beyond reasonable doubt by the *Letter to Dion*. Berkeley, in *Alciphron*, had made Lysicles say: "Leave nature at full freedom to work her own way, and all will be well." Mandeville, taking this as directed against himself, disavows it vigorously, and cites the stress he had put on "laws and governments" in the *Fable of the Bees*. (pp. 3–4; see also 55). He repeats from the *Fable of the Bees* his explanation that when he used as a subtitle the "Private Vices, Publick Benefits" motto, "I understood by it, that Private Vices, by the dexterous Management of a skilful Politician, might be turned into Publick Benefits." (pp. 36–37). Later he refers to the role of the "skilful Management" of the "Legislator" (p. 42), and to "the Wisdom of the Politician, by whose skilful Management the Private Vices of the Worst of Men are made to turn to a Publick Benefit." (p. 45). "They are silly People," he says, "who imagine, that the Good of the Whole is consistent with the Good of every Individual." (p. 49).

A recent work[22] provides indirectly unintentional support to my denial that Mandeville was an exponent of laissez-faire. In this work we are told that "The most famous exponent of what Halévy calls the natural identity of interests is Bernard Mandeville" and that "What Mandeville did for the principle of the natural identity of interests Helvétius did for that of their artificial identity," that is, "that the chief utility of governments consists in their ability to force men to act in their own best interests when they feel disinclined to do so." It so happens, however, that Helvétius as an apostle of state intervention was not only not de-

---

[22] John Plamenatz, *The English Utilitarians*, Oxford and New York, 1949, pp. 48–49.

parting from Mandeville but was echoing him even as to language. Helvétius said that motives of personal temporal interest sufficed for the formation of a good society, provided they were "maniés avec adresse par un législateur habile."[23]

Here also there is a close link between Mandeville, Bayle, and the Jansenists, especially Nicole and Domat. All of them adopted a Hobbesian view of human nature. All of them followed Hobbes in believing that the discipline imposed by positive law and enforced by government was essential if a prosperous and flourishing society was to be derived from communities of individuals vigorously pursuing their self-regarding interest. Mandeville's originality was in pretending that in the interest of true morality he preferred that the individual pursuit of prosperity be abandoned even at the cost of social disaster.

[23] Helvétius, *De l'esprit*, Discours II. Ch. XXIV. In the French version of the *Fable of the Bees*, the phrasing is almost identical: See *La fable des abeilles*, Paris, 1750, e.g. II. 261; "ménagés avec dexterité par d'habiles politiques." When the Sorbonne, in 1759, condemned *De l'esprit*, it cited the *Fable of the Bees* as among the works which could have inspired it. (F. Grégoire, *Bernard De Mandeville et "La Fable des Abeilles,"* Nancy, 1947, p. 206.)

Kaye, in his "The Influence of Bernard Mandeville" (*loc. cit.*, p. 102), says that *De l'esprit* "is in many ways simply a French paraphrase of the *Fable*." In his edition of the *Fable of the Bees*, however, he says, "I think we may conclude no more than that Helvétius had probably read the *Fable*." (*Fable of the Bees*, I. CXLV. Note.) Kaye systematically fails to notice the significance of Mandeville's emphasis on the rôle of the "skilful Politician."

[EDITOR'S NOTE: The following pages were part of Viner's original manuscript on Mandeville, but were deleted prior to publication to economize on space. Viner edited the final manuscript to cover their absence, although these pages appear to fit best on page 180, paragraph 3 of this volume where he writes that "There is not the space here to elaborate, but it could be shown, I believe, that Mandeville was also indebted greatly . . . to the Jansenist, Pierre Nicole. . . ." The first of the deleted pages starts with the last word of a sentence from a previous page and contains this footnote reference: "Mandeville refers to Nicole several times in *Free Thoughts on the Religion, the Church, and National Happiness*, 2nd ed., London, 1729, pp. 68, 78, 81. My belief in Mandeville's direct indebtedness to Nicole is based more, however, on the fact that the material which Nicole, Bayle, and Mandeville all use in common is systematically and elaborately presented by Nicole, whereas it is to be found in Bayle's writings only in incidental and scattered passages."]

On one point, however, which is crucial for present purposes, Bayle, with the possible exception of his treatment of foreign policy,[1] follows Jansenists doctrine accurately, even if perhaps not sincerely, whereas Mandeville gives it a perverse distortion out of which derives the special characteristic of the *Fable of the Bees*, its systematic refusal to distinguish between the vice of the rascal and the "vice" of the *honnête homme*.[2] It will suffice, therefore, to treat the resemblances and differences between the rigorism of Nicole and that of Mandeville, without further reference to Bayle. Since there has been scanty recognition of the relationships between Mandeville's and Nicole's doctrines, they deserve, I believe, the space here given to their exposition.[3]

[1] In dealing with the compatibility of a rigorist code of behavior with the requirements of successful *foreign* as distinguished from *domestic* national policy, Bayle's approach was perhaps closer to that later to be followed by Mandeville than to Nicole's.

[2] As an illustration of the distinction which Bayle, like the Jansenists, makes between the *honnêtes hommes* who are not of the elect and the outright rascals, see Pierre Bayle, *Dictionaire historique et critique*, 5th ed., Amsterdam 1740, "Eclaircissement sur les obscenitez," IV. §iv, p. 649.

[3] Kaye makes a number of minor references to Nicole as one of many anticipators of Mandeville with respect to the possibility of the transmutation of "vice" into "virtue." See especially, *Fable of the Bees*, I, 2.) Kaye does not refer at all to the fact that whereas the "vices" which Nicole finds useful for society are the "vices" of *honnêtes hommes*, not of rascals, Mandeville lumps together the "vices" of the rascal and those of the good citizen as equally "vicious" and equally useful and denies or questions, which the Jansenists did not do, the usefulness of such virtues of the good citizen as frugality, sobriety, and charitableness to the poor.

A parallelism on one point between the *Fable of the Bees* ("Remark P") and Nicole is noted by

For Nicole, and for the Jansenists in general, conduct is truly or "spiritually" virtuous only if done from love of God. Behavior engaged in from love of self ("amour-propre"), or from love of God's creatures without reference to God, may be "humanly virtuous," may be materially or objectively good, but it is theologically sinful nevertheless.[4] Full or "spiritual" virtue, however, can be attained only by the elect, those who have received or are destined to receive efficacious grace, probably a minor fraction even of the pious Christians. The bulk of the professors of Christianity and all heretics and pagans will at their practical best operate on the basis of the prevailing standards of morality, those of the *honnêtes hommes* according to their class and occupation.

This is not good enough for salvation, but it is good enough to create peaceful and flourishing societies. Through the operation of enlightened self-interest ("amour-propre éclairé") when subject to the external restraints of good laws and government, there results a pattern of social behavior in communities of sinners and even of pagans in which everything is externally beyond criticism. Although all of this behavior rests internally on cupidity, or sin in the sight of God, such societies not only manifest all the outward marks of "charity" but are externally as well ordered, as civil, as peaceful, as just, as honest, and as productive of ease, as would be a republic of saints.

In one essay Nicole goes even further. He warns against preaching such exacting doctrine with respect to economic affairs as would, if carried out, bring ruin to commerce. Such rigorism, he says, would operate as an obstacle to moral reform, by giving occasion for the charge that its expounders were laying down rules of conduct which would call for the abandonment of all kinds of occupations, including even those most necessary for the conservation of states.[5]

That society and government could be so organized as to lead the bulk of mankind to salvation, Nicole, with the rest of the Jansenists, would have regarded

F. Grégoire, *Bernard De Mandeville et la "fable des abeilles,"* Nancy, 1947, p. 163. Gilbert Chinard says of Nicole, and of *Les Lois civiles* of Domat, a friend and disciple of Nicole, "En plus d'un sens, ils annoncent Bernard Mandeville, l'amer moraliste qui . . . entreprit . . . de peindre 'l'homme considéré dans l'état de simple nature et dans l'ignorance du vrai Dieu' et de montrer dans l'intérêt personnel 'bien compris' la source même des vertus sociales et de la prospérité économique." *En lisant Pascal*, Lille, 1948, pp. 115–116. Aside from bare citations in commentaries on Mandeville, of Mandeville's explicit references to Nicole, I know of no other instances of recognition of intellectual relationship between them.

[4] The most pertinent material for our purposes is in Nicole's *Essais de morale*, first published 1671 to 1678, but there is also relevant material scattered through his other writings. In the edition of Nicole's works available to me, that of Paris, 1765–82, published by Guillaume Desprez, the title changes, but *Essais de morale* is used to cover much more material than was originally published under that title. *Essais de morale* will here be used as title for all the volumes. The application of his views to social problems is to be found especially in the essays, "De la charité & de l'amour-propre," III. 134–193 and "De la grandeur," Ch. VI, II. 172–181. "Sur l' évangile du Jeudi-Saint," in *Essais de morale*, XI. 296–310, is also important.

[5] *Essais de morale*, "Si c'est usure que de vendre plus cher à crédit," VI, §xx, pp. 136–137.

as heretical doctrine.[6] That men who served society honestly and well should nevertheless be doomed to eternal damnation, Nicole conceded was difficult doctrine, not "conforme aux pensées humaines." The difficulty, however, was in the doctrine itself, which rested on divine revelation, and therefore must be accepted, and not in its expression.[7]

There are obvious and genuine resemblances between the doctrine of Nicole, as here expounded, and that of Mandeville. There are also, however, some important differences.

Nicole accepted the incompatibility of his rigorism with the successful conduct of the world's affairs, but he wrote primarily for a religious-minded élite, and without either hope or desire that the affairs of the world should be widely abandoned by persons in search of salvation. Since it was in accordance with the ultimate purposes of God that civil society, though comprised mostly of sinful men, should nevertheless live in peace and prosperity, it was incumbent on the mass of men to conform, as a minimum, to the customary standards of good behavior, to obey the civil laws, and to be at least *honnêtes hommes* when they could not, or would not, rise above these standards. The *honnêtes hommes*, though they fell short of true virtue, were only half-sinners, "demi-pêcheurs."

The Jansenist morality was, in effect, a three-level one. The most exacting code was directed to the putatively or potentially elect. For the mass of good citizens, adherence to the customary standards of "honnêteté," of "human virtue," was nearly all that in practice could generally be expected. If regulated by good government and good laws, it sufficed to serve the temporal purposes of this world, and differed from the behavior of the truly righteous solely or mainly in its internal motivation. In his *Traité des lois*, Jean Domat, a fellow-Jansenist and colleague of Nicole's, systematically expounded the principles of natural and positive law, including incidentally, mercantilist principles of economic regulation, which could make a prosperous society out of a community of *honnêtes hommes*.

[6] See Charles Droulers, *La cité de Pascal*, Paris, 1928, pp. 40–41.
[7] See Nicole to Quesnel, *Essais de morale*, VIII[2], letter XLI, p. 211.

7

"FASHION" IN ECONOMIC THOUGHT

UNLIKE, NO DOUBT, the speakers who have preceded me, and unlike also, no doubt, the ones who are to follow, I do not know what "Fashion" means in this context in the minds of those who framed the program! It is not to me a term of art. There is in economics a certain body of literature on the economics of "fashion" with reference to ladies' garments, and so on. It is a respectable field and one undoubtedly of some importance, but I do not know anything about it. It probably is a field that people really interested in fashion in other senses might find of interest. For my present purposes, I will treat "fashion" as meaning: first, a widely prevalent procedure which endures, however, for only a limited period of time; second—and here I don't think I am using it in at all the same sense as the preceding speaker—as a procedure which is questionable, even on the basis of what was known or could easily have been discovered in its own period of prevalences; and third, a procedure that is followed voluntarily, and often unconsciously, by its practitioners, rather than followed in submission to authority— what I have in mind by this third limitation is that a military uniform is not a reflection of fashion, but rather a submission to powerful authority.

With fashion so defined, the history of economics as a discipline is to quite a large extent a history of fashion in economic thinking. In economics, fashion can have regional boundaries. Economic thought was probably at its most universalistic in the late middle ages when the scholastics engaged in it for a special purpose, a moral and theological purpose, in order to appraise current economic behavior in terms of the moral and theological teachings of the church. The scholastics were universal, not national. They moved around, and got their education, internationally. They used, for scholarly purposes, a single language. I do not think that one could fruitfully distinguish the economic thinking of western from eastern scholastics, or northern from southern, or of French from Belgian or Italian scholastics. But for almost any later period, while one will always be able to find resemblances between countries, in the patterns of economic thinking one

Reprinted from the Association of Princeton Graduate Alumni, *Report of the 6th Conference*, June 19–20, 1957, pp. 42–54, 55–56, 58–59.

will also almost always be able to find, if one looks hard enough, significant differences which conform to different circumstances of some kind with respect to countries or regions.

Mercantilism was common in a sense in the 16th to 18th centuries to all of western Europe. Nevertheless, there were some important national differences. The maritime countries distributed their emphases, defined their economic goals, somewhat differently from the land-based countries. The French were in between, say, Prussia, on the one hand, and on the other hand England or Holland, as being less land-based than Prussia and less oriented to foreign commerce than England and Holland. American economic thought for at least two centuries followed very closely English, and I should add, importantly, Scottish thought. But from the very start, apparently from early in the 17th century, there began to appear characteristic American differences. American economics remained religion-oriented for I believe a full century after English economics had been practically completely secularized, and that means up to shortly before World War I, whereas English economics had been pretty fully secularized by the end of the 18th or early in the 19th century. The Americans in the 19th century followed the English in developing both an economic theory and a social gospel of laissez faire, of non-interventionism by government. "Laissez faire" as a term has not got a stable and precise meaning. A man who would today be regarded as an exponent of laissez faire would in 1830 in England or in this country have been regarded as an exponent of state-interventionism, or of the welfare state, or whatnot. Nevertheless, a basic bias against activity of government in the economic sphere was a common doctrine of English and American economics. But the Americans subjected their laissez faire doctrine to an important exception. Predominantly, American economics was protectionist in commercial policy, whereas the English found the greatest scope for reform through laissez faire, for reform through retreat from government activity, in the field of foreign trade, in the adoption of free trade. There was a pessimistic undertone, though often exaggerated by modern commentators, in the English Classical economists in their forecasts for the future, whereas in the United States there was almost unlimited optimism as to the future destiny and the future prosperity of the American people, and this showed itself in a partial rejection by early 19th century American economists of certain phases of the Malthusian population doctrines and of the Malthusian-Ricardian rent doctrines which were key elements in the English classical system of economic thought.

So much for the possibility of national differences in fashions of economic thought. There may also be contending fashions of thought within a country—rival and inconsistent fashions prevailing at the same time within a country, although I think my fellow economists would call them "schools" rather than "fashions." In England, for instance, during the period of the origination, development, and substantial dominance of the classical, laissez faire, "liberal" thinking, there was also a substantial body of thought that has not been very much studied by economists—although it is studied by others—which conflicted with and was hostile to the classical doctrine, namely, the romantic school, with Wordsworth, Southey, Coleridge, and later Carlyle and Ruskin, as leaders. Toward the end of the 19th century, there developed a split in England, following a similar split on the continent, between what could be called an abstract analytical school and a historical non-theoretical school. The split was a clean one. Roughly, the so-called professors of "economics" in the English Universities were in the classical tradition, while the Professors of Economic History were hostile to the classical tradition. The ones in the classical tradition were liberals in politics, while the others tended to be protectionist, to be pronouncedly nationalist, and also to be possibly more orthodox or more traditional in their religious thought. The neo-classical school was intellectually much more important, with much more influence over student body and writers than the historical school.

The fashions that dominate the thought of economists may be with respect either to the objectives or the methods of their analysis. Modern economists, starting perhaps as far back as 1830, have explicitly debated among themselves as to whether economics should be *wertfrei*, or non-normative, like the natural sciences; that is, purely descriptive, seeking only to discover causal relationships, without appraising the desirability or the beauty or anything else but the truth of what they find, or, instead, whether economics should be directly and immediately a tool both for the selection of worthwhile social objectives and for the selection of means whereby they can be attained. That debate still goes on. I suspect it is going to go on forever. It is largely an unreal debate—the most pronounced exponents of the *wertfrei* or non-normative economists, not universally but, I think, fairly typically, and the ones most obviously bound emotionally to a particular ideology which dominates their thinking, and which has its origin not in basically economic analysis but in a special set of social values. It is possible that some of those who preach a non-normative economics do so because they know, or fear, that a normative economics would pick up the prevailing norms, which they do not like. If so, then what really concerns them is not that economics should not be harnessed to causes, but that it should not be made a servant of what they regard as evil causes.

In my ignorance, I conceive of bridge-building as intellectually a many-layer activity: first, pure mathematics, and then applied mathematics, and then pure physics and after that possibly an applied physics, and then comes the engineering proper, and beyond that business analysis or statesmanship which puts dollar figures on the input items and output returns involved in a particular bridge and makes the final decision as to whether the bridge should be built. No one man or discipline has to work on all these levels.

Theoretically, economics might have evolved in the same way, and it may be a better way than the one economics has in fact followed. But it is no longer a real possibility. As individuals, economists will consciously or unconsciously make different combinations of levels to work on. At times we will *as economists* support "causes"; at other times we will confine ourselves to exploring causal relationships.

So also with methods of analysis. There has been, since the scientific revolution of the 17th century, an economics borrowing techniques from outside itself. There is a constant dialectic between the empirical and rationalistic approaches. It has never been settled except on the basis of changing intellectual fashions. At certain times one approach is dominant, at other times another, and unless you believe that one is demonstrably the "right" approach to the exclusion of the other, "fashion" must be appealed to explain the temporary dominance of either approach. There have been times when the profession has been historical-minded, and has sought for genetic or evolutionary explanations of current phenomena. There have been other times when economists have succeeded in being as ahistorical as an educated man can perhaps possibly be, and have given no hint that they know that there has been historical change in social institutions, and that social processes—and social values—are in some degree at least relative to time and place. Then also, there is constant debate within our circles as between the appropriate scope of what mathematical economists call, on the one hand, the mathematical approach, and on the other hand, the "literary" approach, thus flattering those of us who are neither mathematicians nor literary. Within the mathematical approach I see, as an outsider, signs of what I could call changing fashions in terms of my definition, where at one time the whole trend of the brighter young men is enthusiastically in the direction of an algebraic approach, at other times enthusiastically in the direction of a geometrical approach.

There is also the question of the quantitative, or statistical, versus the non-quantitative approach. As far back as the 17th century there were already over-enthusiastic exponents of premature quantification and almost immediately there were critics saying that not all things can be subjected or should be subjected to measurement; that if you confine yourself to quantities, you are leaving out a lot that matters and that is important, and so on. That issue also will never be settled, I think.

Then also, with respect to abstract, analytical economics, there are fashions in the form of the models used; economists have great concern about the contours of their models; some like to work with rather complex ones, others content themselves with very simple models and even make simplicity a dominant objective. Sometimes this turns on conflict as to the degree and character of abstraction which is legitimate. I take for granted that we all agree that in all thinking some degree of abstraction is absolutely necessary—we can't take account of everything simultaneously. But some pursue, apparently, the maximum degree of abstraction, and some show no concern as to the particular pattern of their abstraction. They say, "let us start from these assumptions," without thinking it important to argue why these assumptions and not some alternative set should be used. There even occurs, in current economic literature, the proposition that lack of realism of assumptions does not, of itself, detract from their relevance, including, I take it, relevance to matters that are of concern to non-economists.

It may be that the dispute here has some affiliations with the discussions with respect to the field of poetry, of literature, of ballet, of the legitimacy of "art for art's sake," as distinguished from art for some other purpose, such as giving pleasure, or improving morals, or supporting religious faith. Julian Huxley, when he was director of the Regent Park Zoo, told the story that a nice lady visiting the zoo, fascinated by the hippopotamus, asked the keeper whether it was a male or a female, and received the reply: "Lady, I should think that that would be a question that would be of interest only to another hippopotamus." The same thing, I fear, speaking from inside the profession, can be said of a good deal of modern economic theorizing.

Economics, of course, is a stepchild of other disciplines; the direct line of descent is from the moral theology of the late middle ages through the deistic moral philosophy of the 18th century, to the secularized utilitarian ethics of the 19th century. Economics still carries the stamp of its origins. These origins also were "fashions," and they may have had a longer life within economics than outside it.

So also with social policy attitudes, and objectives, used by economists as a tool of persuasion or of propaganda, and served by economics. As a servant to specific social objectives, economics tries to find techniques whereby the appropriate economic means can be selected for the attainment of given social ends. Here also the objectives have not been discovered, or initiated, by economists; they have been taken from the "outside world." Now the outside world is a complex thing. Economics sometimes takes its social objectives from what you may call the "ruling classes" and at other times from a rebellious section of the outside world, some non-ruling class or group that wishes a changed world.

Let me give you a historical example. I have a great deal of respect for a good

deal of the economic analysis of the scholastics. But it was so tied to other purposes than mere discovery of truth for its own sake, that most economists give
the credit for the foundation of economics as a somewhat autonomous and near-
"scientific" discipline with intellectual standards and achievements of its own to
the French Physiocrats of the 18th century. But the Physiocrats were exponents
of what they called "enlightened despotism," partially at least derived from
Hobbesian doctrine. The French have always understood Hobbes more accurately
than the English or the Americans. He was an exponent, not of tyranny, but of a
monopoly, preferably monarchical, of political power. But he wanted a monopoly of political power largely in order to make sure that this power should not be
exercised. He wanted all possibility of force to be concentrated in one hand, or
one set of hands, in order that other sets of hands should not be able to use force;
but he wanted parsimony in the exercise of power by the sovereign. That helps
to explain why some moderns find the origin of laissez faire and liberalism in
Hobbes, while others find in his doctrine the origins of Nazism, Fascism, and the
all-powerful monolithic state. By Hobbes, I think, practical liberalism and unlimited state power were both advocated without logical conflict. But you have to
distinguish between the unlimited possession of power and the restrained exercise
of it to understand what Hobbes was driving at. Enlightened despotism was a sort
of a fashion in 18th century Western Europe; it was not confined to the Bourbons
in France, but Frederick the Great of Prussia, Catherine of Russia, Joseph of
Austria, all held it as doctrine and to some extent practiced it, and there were
other German princelings who were undoubtedly aiming to be enlightened des-
pots, to use a monopoly of political power for the welfare of their community,
with "welfare" fairly liberally and widely interpreted. This fashion of enlightened despotism certainly influenced the conclusions of the Physiocrats and of
other 18th century continental economists.

There was also the intellectual "fashion" manifesting itself, among other
ways, in the Augustinian tradition of the preponderant and ineradicable evil in
man, which economics took over in large part and has in large part retained, and
starting from which they built the concept of the *homo economicus*, the economic
man, who in his economic transactions gives weight to nothing but his own self-
interest. There developed out of this tradition a self-interest psychology and
ethics called in the 18th century by its opponents the "selfish" philosophy, and
economics has continued largely to build on that, making it an important element
in its basic set of underlying assumptions, but using it in two radically divergent
ways.

The first economic "school," that later was known as "mercantilism," which
was dominant from the 16th to the 18th century, while it conceded that self-

interest was an essential motive to economic activity, maintained that if left un-regulated it would often lead to action which would be in conflict with the com-mon interest. The state, therefore, must guide and restrain and channel private economic activity, through legal and administrative rewards and punishments, so as to make the activities of individuals seeking their private gain serve the na-tional interest. The State, therefore, had all-important economic functions.

In the 18th century there developed in France another school, the Physiocrats, who believed that like the order of nature the social order was providentially designed so that left to itself it would serve well the common interest. They sup-ported this belief by appeal to analogy between the social order and the physical order of nature, as well as by pointing out many ways in which men seeking to serve only their private interests were at the same time contributing to the public good. At about the same time, but as far as is known independently, Adam Smith in Scotland was developing almost identical economic doctrine. Human behav-ior, he believed, was a compound of both pursuit of self-interest and response to social "sentiments," but with respect, at least, to activity in the economic mar-ket-place it was the self-regarding motives which in the main governed men's actions. Government was needed to enforce justice, to provide public works of a kind unsuitable for private enterprise, and to maintain national security. Beyond this, men should be left to their own devices, without government intervention, in the economic sphere. If government went beyond these limits, it would detract from, rather than support, the prosperity of the commonwealth. Stemming from Adam Smith and the Physiocrats, there evolved the "classical school" of eco-nomics which dominated economic thought in the English-speaking countries in the 19th century and was an important aspect, from the point of view of social policy, was its advocacy of "laissez faire," or the restriction of government ac-tivity in the economic sphere to a minimum.

These doctrines I regard, for present purposes, as "fashions" since they were widely held as demonstrable or obvious truths although it was not then, nor is it now, possible to demonstrate their validity by rational argument.

Economics has in large part borrowed its fashions from outside its own bound-aries, but it has also demonstrated its capacity to generate fashions, at least for economics, from within its own resources. This last, however, has been true only to what seems to me to be a quite limited extent. Economics is not sufficiently an autonomous discipline to be able to go far in its own way with respect to goals, to objectives, or to methods of analysis. With respect to objectives, economics is not sufficiently an autonomous discipline: it is too much dominated by public opinion, by government, or by affiliations with ruling or dissatisfied classes, to select them strictly on its own. With respect to methods of analysis, it is unavoidably too much subsidiary to, step-child of, the basic disciplines which are concerned with the fashioning and the standards of manipulation of the tools of thought to be expected to do much to develop instruments or analytical methods of its own beyond a modest amount of adaptation of standard methods to its special needs and interests.

Economics may nevertheless have intellectual fashions which at a particular time do not have their counterpart in other disciplines, as the result of a cultural lag which results in certain modes of thought surviving within economics that have died long ago, perhaps deservedly, perhaps not, in the other fields from which economics had originally borrowed them. Until recent years, and possibly even today, some of the terminology of economics, and some of its operational thinking, rests on psychological hedonism, which most modern psychologists tell us was always wrong, was always seriously wrong. It may also have been an intellectual lag that at least in some countries a large portion of the economics profession remained pretty solidly laissez faire after the rest of the world, including its sister social disciplines like political science and sociology, had long abandoned it. I would suppose, also, that if free trade still has any life, almost the last vestiges of it that survive need to be sought among the professional economists: everywhere else it's dead. I cannot appropriately say that it is deservedly dead, since I am myself one of the last surviving free-traders, but I do know that I cannot appeal to the general intellectual climate of my time in support of my belief in free trade, but must seek other ways of justifying it.

Economics has usually kept pretty much in harmony with its period. It has been said of economics that it never had a good press. That may have been due to the manner of its exposition, because the substance of its doctrine has generally been such as to have entitled it to a good press in at least some important quarters. It has probably followed public opinion, or important sectors of public opinion, much more than it has led it.

So far, I have treated fashions as facts. The question suggests itself—how do intellectual fashions originate? Obviously a great teacher may start it, or it may represent conformity to an external pressure, meaning an external fashion. Or conceivably, as with the role of psychological hedonism in modern economics, it may be merely an inherited habit or, perhaps, to use a less neutral term, a rut— a disciplinary rut. With respect to the "business cycle," it is easy to see why there should be tendencies toward cyclical patterns in the economic behavior of Jones, or of wheat growers, or of the United States Steel Corporation. It is also easy to see why such tendencies should be transmitted to some extent from person to person, or industry to industry, or country to country. But what is *not* easy to see, at least for me, is why these tendencies should periodically synchronize to produce one overall cycle in a community, or a country, or the world, instead of off-setting and neutralizing each other.

Similarly with intellectual fashions. What is it that creates enough synchronization in the attitudes, the beliefs, the goals, the intellectual habits, of men so as to produce a fairly common pattern of thought for large bodies of them? I don't know. But the fashions in economics are easiest to explain when they are obviously reflections of external fashions that impinge upon them, just as it is easy to explain a cycle in United States Steel Corporation activities, or in the volume of American bank deposits, when it is fairly clearly the result of an over-all cycle in the American economy. But that merely changes the locus of the mystery instead of resolving it.

Economics, as I have tried to indicate, has important intellectual links with other disciplines, and it also has important value links, links as to goals and objectives, with important social groups, which may or may not be the ruling groups. English and American economists have on the whole been very urban-oriented, rather than agrarian, and the mark of their urban orientation is to be seen in their selection of problems to be attacked and their methods of reaching conclusions. But autonomous, internally-generated fashions in economics are harder to explain. Why the stress by economists on history at one time and complete disregard of it at other times, including times when the rest of the world tended to be historical-minded, or to be becoming historical-minded? Why the fashion in American economics from say 1910 to 1930, to seek the answer to economic questions in psychology, in technical psychology—and also, why its demise? Did economists really learn that they were up a blind alley, or did the fashion expire merely because some other and more appealing fashion came along? Why the care about the social relevance of their assumptions that economic theorists often used to show in the past, and the almost total disregard of relevance of many of them today? Or to end up with an attempt, a weak one, I fear, to find a link with the preceding paper, why the great concern which our brightest and most promising younger economists show today for the aesthetic side of economics, for the formal rigor and elegance of their models, apparently at whatever cost in terms of relevance, realism, significance, except as economics is pursued as a form of art.

[EDITOR'S NOTE: Viner responded to two queries at the end of his talk. The first question concerned the reception of the ideas of economists, such as Thorstein Veblen, who are critical of the existing social order. The second, from Oscar Morgenstern, was the suggestion that progress in economics is unsteady precisely because its problems are largely posed by the outside world, which quickly moves from one problem to another.]

DR. VINER:—I did make a reference to uniformity in pattern of writing because of external coercions, by which I meant a regimenting state, or church, so that things are taught as one is told to teach them. Out of fear, too, you may get uniformity. I do think that fear is operating in this country to an extent, but I think to a moderate extent, as a restraint on freedom to teach and to print. But most economists are men enough so that they would take their chances on telling the truth even though they thought this would involve some kind of risk. But in the case of Veblen, given his doctrines, and given the atmosphere of the time, the risks were more real for him than for any economist today unless he were an outright communist. He developed a style of double-talk—of Aesopian language—long before the communists did, and therefore you must read between the lines completely to understand Veblen. I knew him in his later years, and I think that by that time this language had become second nature to him. He would no longer talk ordinary English, he would not make a positive statement, where his beliefs were concerned. He would say "It has been charged that I believe that." But it was or had become more a matter of fun or of habit than of fear. He used it as a mode of rhetoric or of dialectic—he was an artist in English, whether you like his style or not. I think he sought ways of phrasing it that should be out of the routine. One of his favorite words was "stereotype," and I think the one thing you cannot say about Veblen's English is that it is stereotyped.

DR. VINER:—There has at times been recurrence of old fashions in economics. Mercantilism for instance, has come to life again, in the past 20 years or so. It is now again a respectable doctrine in the profession, after having been read out as nonsense or error, and even as evil doctrine. A question one could ask is how does one distinguish a "fashion" from a valid step in the progress, in the evolution, of knowledge? I tried to give an answer of sorts when I said that a "fashion" doesn't last indefinitely, is rejected in time, and also that even in its own time its validity is questionable on the basis of what is already knowable. But a fashion may be a whole complex, of which some elements may be new and valid discoveries which will survive or be revived. On the other hand, what if a discipline is, or seems to be, unstable in the sense that it frequently changes its methods and findings, or at any time has no or little generally-accepted matter?

In a country where they have, say, only five economists, they have to be stable and to conform to common standards of what is sound. They have a function to perform, and they can't perform it if they go off chasing wild geese, each on his own. But a country like the United States, rich enough to have thousands of economists, can afford to have these economists experimenting in methods and approaches all over the lot. It would be very presumptuous certainly for an economist to suggest that these movements, even if undesirable, should be restrained or suppressed. I am sure we gain more out of the freedom which the economists have to go off on their own than we would gain if uniform doctrine were prescribed by some authority, and who it could be I cannot even imagine. We don't want the state, certainly, to assume this role. We have no ''academy.'' I would not want university departments to try to influence mature, or even immature, economists as to what they should think. Fashions bring good as well as bad, they bring product as well as waste. They at least bring variety. If it were not for conflicts of fashion, or the lingering on of old fashions when new ones were winning a place for themselves, economic controversy among economists would be much less interesting, much less exciting, perhaps even much less rewarding. For these and perhaps also other reasons, I don't regard the prevalence of fashion in economics as one of the major problems of the universe. I suspect the same thing is true of many neighboring disciplines.

8

THE INTELLECTUAL HISTORY OF
LAISSEZ FAIRE

WHAT I PROPOSE to do in this lecture is to discuss the logical or rhetorical nature of the arguments by means of which exponents of laissez faire or of marked movement in its direction have attempted to win converts to their cause. My lecture will be focused not on the inherent merits or defects of laissez faire as social doctrine, but on the logical character of the case that its adherents have presented in support of it. My examination will be critical in large part, and in one major respect will not be judiciously balanced, since I would in many instances be even more critical of the arguments with which laissez faire has been attacked, but will not similarly examine these arguments. It does not add much, however, to the inherent strength of a doctrine that some deplorably bad arguments have been used against it.

It is really not the laissez faire doctrine as such, but the art of persuasion as used in social thought, which it is the purpose of this lecture to explore. I have chosen the history of the advocacy of laissez faire doctrine as the particular field in which to observe the art of persuasion at work, partly because it is a field with which I have some familiarity, and partly because the doctrine has legal and political and ethical aspects as well as economic ones, so that it is a subject of discourse more appropriate to the present occasion than would be a lecture on a narrowly technical economic issue. If in my wandering outside the boundaries of economics, I mishandle legal, political, or ethical concepts, I beg of the experts present to temper their judgments of my misdeeds in the light of the innocence of my intentions.

I will carefully avoid using the term laissez faire to mean what only unscrupulous or ignorant opponents of it and never its exponents make it mean, namely, philosophical anarchism, or opposition to any governmental power or activity whatsoever. I will in general use the term to mean what the pioneer systematic exponents of it, the Physiocrats and Adam Smith, argued for, namely, the limi-

The second Henry Simons Lecture given at the University of Chicago Law School, November 18, 1959. Reprinted from the *Journal of Law and Economics* 3 (October 1960): 45–69.

tation of governmental activity to the enforcement of peace and of "justice" in the restricted sense of "commutative justice," to defense against foreign enemies, and to public works regarded as essential and as impossible or highly improbable of establishment by private enterprise or, for special reasons, unsuitable to be left to private operation. Both the Physiocrats and Adam Smith gave some sanction to the limited expansion of governmental activity beyond these limits. Following their example, I will not deny the laissez faire label to any writer who in general accepts the limitations I have enumerated to governmental activity, even if he occasionally, incidentally, and inconsistently relaxes these limitations slightly to permit either of a restricted list of minor exceptions or of temporary suspension of the laissez faire code in case of emergency or abnormal conditions, such as war, famine, or earthquake.

No social doctrine has a meaningful historical life except with reference, explicit or implicit, to an existent or conceivable alternative or array of alternatives. It is a useful simplification as a first approximation to regard the alternatives to laissez faire as lying along a straight line measuring degrees of governmental intervention in the field of economic activity. Looking in one direction, this straight line represents Herbert Spencer's road to "The Coming Slavery," or Friedrich Hayek's "Road to Serfdom." It is only since the eighteenth century "Enlightenment" that slavery and serfdom have been regarded as pejorative terms. Those well-disposed towards laissez faire should therefore perhaps use in preference such terms as "Road to Tyranny" or "Road to Totalitarianism," labels which as far as I know no one would ever have chosen for highways on which he wished mankind to travel. Looking in the other direction, however, this highway also represents the Road to Anarchy. In any case, along this road are many conceivable stopping-places, and no one may be interested in either of its terminal points. Route 1, a great national highway which connects Boston, New York, Philadelphia, Baltimore, and Washington, begins at Fort Kent in Maine and ends at a sand-dune at the southern tip of Florida. Except on the arbitrary assumption that travel on this road, in either direction, is totally without benefit of brakes, the terminal points of our metaphorical road are often assigned an extravagant degree of practical significance in discourse in this field. Until quite recent years, actual and vital discussion in the public forum has turned mainly on the comparative merits as resting-places along our highway of points not greatly distant from each other, or perhaps more accurately, as between no movement at all and a limited amount of movement, sometimes in both directions simultaneously, from the existing resting-place. Before World War I the issue in debate was never, as far as I can see, between laissez faire and totalitarianism, or between the welfare state and philosophical anarchism. As I will be dealing mostly with pre-1914 facts or ideas, I will spend no time on St. George-and-the-dragon types of argument.

The historical debates in this field before the Bolshevik Revolution also were to but slight extent in form and to even less extent in substance debates about "freedom" in a general or universal sense. If the debate did use the terminology of "freedom," it was likely in form and even more likely in substance to be debate about particular "freedoms" or "liberties," often recognized to be rival to, or only distantly related, if at all, to other particular "freedoms," or to be debates about desirable degrees of a particular freedom, about "true" freedom versus "false" freedom, or about "freedom" versus "license." Great men have differed, moreover, as to whether submission to an authority by voluntary consent, revocable or irrevocable, is a mark of freedom, or a mark of servitude, as to whether a man enslaved by force becomes truly a free man if he disciplines himself into, or has been brainwashed into, not wanting the things, including freedom from slavery, which his status as a slave makes inaccessible to him. If stone walls do not a prison make, nor iron bars a cage, "freedom" becomes a much less important concept historically than the historians have usually taken for granted. This is true also in the economic field if the important freedom here is freedom of choice, but absence of power in the sense of economic resources, or of acquired knowledge and skills, or of the appropriate complexion, makes subjective exercise of that freedom of choice little more than indulgence in wishful daydreaming. Freedom defined, as it often has been, as the power to do what it is right to desire to do, with some external authority, often claiming to be speaking for God, deciding what it is right to desire to do, also seems to me an intellectually uninteresting variety of freedom, although I would not for a moment deny that thousands of men have willingly died for that kind of freedom.

On the relation of freedom to act to power to act, the only kind of power to act which a sampling of the voluminous literature on freedom as an abstract or general concept persuades me it is usually safe to ignore is the kind of power to act which would be fairly represented by such acts as jumping over the moon or moving mountains by exhortation or hanging up one's cloak on a moonbeam. Even here, however, caution is needed lest we attribute the existent limitations on the power of a particular man to act which have a social origin to Providence or to the laws of physical or human nature. I will return to this later. In any case, not only does the history of discussion about "economic freedom" offer abundant evidence in support of St. Thomas Aquinas' dictum that "When reason argues about particular cases, it needs not only universal but also particular principles,"[1] but it provides some warrant for going farther, and maintaining that

---

[1] Summa Theologica. I.II. q. 58.a.5.

universal principles that are meaningful and serviceable to some good purpose can be derived, if at all, only from such particular principles as can be formulated in the attempt to deal wisely with particular cases.

As a general and systematically expounded doctrine, the doctrine of laissez faire made its first appearance in the eighteenth century. As is always the case for complex doctrines, however, it made use of ideas and maxims inherited from earlier times. Combining them with some new ideas, it constructed, from the old and the new, a doctrine which was without a close previous counterpart. To point out some elements of earlier thought which were to be embodied in the eighteenth-century laissez faire doctrine will be my next task.

The economies of ancient Greece and Rome rested on a foundation of slavery, and, by the leading philosophers at least, the merchants were regarded with suspicion as to their morals and with aristocratic contempt as to their role and status in the good society. In this setting, an ethical doctrine of individual freedom in the economic sphere, whether for merchants or for manual laborers, would have had infertile ground to grow up in, and neither Greek nor Roman philosophers were sufficiently interested in such lowly matters as production and the market to apply their wits to the formulation of an economic case for or against economic freedom. Early Christian thought held temporal matters as of only trivial and transitory significance, regarded commercial activity as almost inevitably motivated by avarice and permeated by cheating and exploitation, and insisted that the only truly valuable freedom in temporal matters was the subjective freedom which could be won by the suppression of desire for temporal goods not unqualifiedly necessary for survival. The slave who had disciplined his passions was declared authoritatively to be in all that really mattered freer than his master who eagerly pursued worldly goods.

A few ideas from classical times, however, were later to be rediscovered and developed to constitute elements in a full-fledged laissez faire doctrine. The defense of private property as against communism presented by Aristotle, and taken over by several of the early Christian Fathers, included the proposition that private property alone imbued men with the incentives necessary for care in the preservation of scarce assets and for industrious application to producing useful goods. Aristotle's description of man as a political or social animal was to be made the keystone later of the case for laissez faire on the basis of a natural harmony of interests between individual and community. The beginnings of a doctrine of the providential ordering of nature included the proposition, later to be used to give a religious flavor to the argument for free trade in international commerce, that Providence had assigned different climates and resources to different peoples, in order that they should be mutually dependent on each other for subsistence, and thus, through the medium of commerce, should join in the universal brotherhood of man. The maxim of Horace, "You may drive nature out with a pitchfork, but it will always return," and other Roman maxims about the necessity of "following nature," were later to be repeatedly invoked to support the proposition that governments could not succeed in directing particular economic activities counter to the restraints set by physical nature and the instincts and drives of human nature. More to the point, though perhaps intended only as descriptions of the status of an elite rather than as general social norms, were the four freedoms which the priests of Apollo at Delphi around 200 B.C. formulated as constituting the difference between freedom and slavery: protected legal status in society; freedom from arbitrary seizure or arrest—or *habeas corpus*, if you like; freedom of choice of economic occupation; right of unrestricted movement from place to place.[2]

The "rule of law rather than of men" doctrine which was later to be held to be an essential safeguard of economic and other freedoms was presented in a qualified and ambiguous version by Aristotle:

> . . . laws, when good, should be supreme; and . . . the magistrate or magistrates should regulate those matters only on which the laws are unable to speak with precision owing to the difficulty of any general principle embracing all particulars.[3]

It was later to be pointed out, and still later to be forgotten, that against the gain of legal certainty and of protection against tyrants afforded by "the rule of law" was to be set the loss of equity and of adaptation of rules to the peculiarities of particular cases.

It was a commonplace among the Romans that the most corrupt republics had the greatest number of laws. I suspect that this was sometimes not meant as advocacy of a minimum of law, but as an expression of a preference for "court law" and for common law over statutes, which were by the Romans resorted to comparatively infrequently, to deal either with emergencies or with situations requiring uniform applications of measured penalties, or measured uniformity in some other respect.

From the time of classical Greece on, there was prevalent the doctrine that government was as "natural" as the family or as society. Cicero held that government grew or evolved by as "natural" a process as did customs or mores, and later this was to develop into the doctrine that the growth of government made

---

[2] See Westermann, Between Slavery and Freedom, 50 Am. Hist. Rev. 216 (1945).

[3] Politics, iii. 11. 19; 1282b ff. 125 (Jowett, tr., Oxford, 1908).

little more demand on genius and over-all design than did the growth of language. The counter-doctrine that government was a necessary evil, arising out of the fall of man and original sin, and having as its sole reason for existence the disciplining of sinful man, seems to have entered the mainstream of western thought with the advent of Christianity. "Law," said St. Paul, "is not made for a righteous man, but for the lawless and unruly, for the ungodly and sinners. . . ."[4] St. Augustine struck a similar note, and the Augustinian phase of the Christian tradition kept emphasizing this idea, which is prominent in Jansenism and also, as a reply to anarchistic ideas, in Luther and Calvin. In seventeenth and eighteenth century England, the idea in secularized form was repeatedly presented as an argument for narrowly restricting the range of activity of government. John Locke, David Hume, Adam Smith, all made some use of the argument, but its most famous statement was by Thomas Paine, in *Common Sense* (1776):

> [Natural] Society is produced by our wants, and government by our wickedness; the former promotes our happiness positively by uniting our affections, the latter negatively by restraining our vices. The one encourages intercourse, the other creates distinctions. This first is a patron, the last a punisher.
>
> Society in every state is a blessing, but government, even in its best state, is but a necessary evil. . . . Government, like dress, is the badge of lost innocence.[5]

Modern Catholic critics of what they term "capitalistic individualism" and "economic liberalism" have charged the spread of Roman law teaching throughout Europe from the thirteenth century on with facilitating their rise by undermining Church and canon law influence in favor of civil power and secular law, and thus replacing the moral influence of the Church by the individualistic spirit of the Roman law. They claim that there was for centuries an open and sharp conflict between the Church and the Roman lawyers, with the ultimate victory of the latter preparing the way for the disastrous dominance of laissez faire and of the undisciplined capitalist spirit.[6] Other scholars have claimed that the extent of the hostility of the Church to Roman law has been exaggerated and that what friction there was resulted in the main from other causes, political rather than doctrinal.[7]

[4] I Timothy, 1:9.

[5] I The Writings of Thomas Paine 69 (Conway, ed., New York, 1894).

[6] See, for example, C. de Monléon, L'Eglise et le Droit Romain (Paris, 1887); G. Ardant, Papes et Paysans 40–41 (Paris, 1891); J. Jannsen, II History of the German People at the Close of the Middle Ages 169 ff. (translated from the original German) (London, 1896). *Cf.* P. Vinogradoff, Roman Law in Medieval Europe 142 ff. (2d ed., Oxford, 1929).

[7] See Digard, La Papauté et l'Etude du Droit Romain au XIIIᵉ Siècle, 51 Bibliothèque de l'Ecole des Chartres (1890); Fournier, L'Englise et le Droit Romain au XIIIᵉ Siècle, 14 Nouvelle Revue Historique de Droit Francais et Etranger 80–119 (1890), with useful bibliography.

It would not be fair to compare for their level of edification, as has been done, a treatise on Roman law, with its strict attention to practicality and working-rules for adjudication of property rights, to medieval *Summa*, with its disorderly mixture of legal rule, ethical precept and counsel, and spiritual exhortation. It may be true that there was in Roman law an individualistic spirit and a degree of recognition of individual "rights" which influenced Continental lawyers in a direction favorable to the reception of an approach to the laissez faire doctrine. But the great Roman law codes concentrated on private law, and the issues involving the relations of citizens and government arose mainly in the fields of public and administrative law. A major precept of private law always is "to render to every man his own," and much of the content of the Roman law of property and of sales consisted of rules framed, apparently admirably, on the basis of convenience rather than on abstract principle, for determining the validity of claims of individuals *on other individuals*. The claims of government against individuals were a matter of public law. A large area, moreover, even of private law was left uncovered by specific rules, and was governed by so-called principles of "good faith" or of equity, which meant in practice the discretion of the magistrate, guided by his interpretation of the prevailing moral code.[8]

In criticisms of Roman law on the ground that it gives unduly free reign to economic individualism, two specific charges are repeatedly made: that it defines individual property rights in too absolute a manner and that in the law of sales it follows the doctrine of *caveat emptor*. It has been asserted by modern experts, however, that the first charge rests on a definition of property rights which is mistranslated and cannot be found in any Roman law text; that the second charge is based on a term which is not meaningful in Latin, and is also not to be found in any Roman law text; and that both charges misinterpret the spirit of Roman law.

With respect to property law, the phrase *jus utendi et abutendi*, on which the charge is made to rest, has never been found in a classic Roman law text. In any case, instead of being translated, as it usually is, as "the right to use and abuse," it apparently should be translated as "the right to use and to use up in consumption," which takes the sting out of it.[9] In the Middle Ages there was cited as a maxim of Roman law: "It is expedient for the commonwealth that a man should not use his own property badly."[10]

[8] *Cf.* C. P. Sherman, II Roman Law in the Modern World 149 ff. (Boston, 1917); F. Schulz, Principles of Roman Law 30, 150 ff. (Oxford, 1936); Levy, West Roman Vulgar Law: The Law of Property, 29 Memoirs of the American Philosophical Society, *passim* (1951).

[9] See D. L. Douie, The Nature and the Effect of the Heresy of the Fraticelli 203 (Manchester, 1932) for insistence by a medieval cleric that this latter was the correct translation. See also V. Brants, L'Economie Politique au Moyen-Age 61–62 (Louvain, 1895), for the origin of the phrase.

[10] B. Tierney, Medieval Poor Law 38 (Berkeley, 1959).

In the Roman law of sales, the dominant principle was that "a bargain was a bargain," but only subject to complete absence of fraud or deception, to reasonable disclosure of defects of merchandise by the vendor, enforced by strict rules of warranty, and to good morals in general.[11] The great Roman law codes cited the dictum that the law tolerates a certain amount of "over-reaching" in the higgling of the market. This did not mean, however, sanction of fraud, and modern experts have ascribed more rigor in some respects to the Roman law of sales than to the corresponding provisions in English or American common law as applied in our times.

What seems to be true is that by its precision and its systematic and practical character the Roman law provided valuable foundations for the development of a body of commercial law under which private enterprise could successfully operate. Beyond this, it does not seem likely that the "free market" of modern capitalism has any important indebtedness to Roman law.

Medieval moral theology appears to have laid down only a few points of doctrine which have close bearing on the issue of laissez faire. The primary concern of the scholastics in their treatment of economic matters was to keep economic behavior, and especially the intentions and objectives of the merchant, within the limits of moral principle, as defined by Revelation and by the law of nature. Aside from the issue of usury, where dogma was rigorous and was to prove excessively specific and inelastic for permanence, the scholastics condemned no specified objective behavior, no concrete acts as such, in the economic field, unless they found in them clear evidence or a strong presumption of a violation of commutative justice. Aside once more from the issue of usury, the scholastics and canonists generally exercised great care not to lay down precepts which would interfere unnecessarily with the pursuit by individuals of legitimate economic gain. On the other hand, they showed no interest in freedom in the abstract, or in particular freedoms, except as the freedom was from a tyrant forcing evil practices on or dealing unjustly with his subjects or was from burdensome legislation not directed toward the "common good." They condemned no existing social institution, not even either slavery or feudal serfdom. They always dealt respectfully with government as such, except perhaps when it engaged in tampering with the coinage, and insisted that unquestioning obedience to official authority, except where divine law would thereby be violated, was a religious and moral obligation. On concrete economic issues, they accepted official decisions as presumptively correct or wise, and in any case as lying outside the realm of criticism by ordinary individuals. St. Thomas Aquinas, like other theologians

---

[11] *Cf.* Levy, Natural Law in Roman Thought, Pontificum Institutum Utriusque Juris, 15 Studia Et Documenta Historiae Et Juris 21 (Rome, 1949); M. Radin, The Lawful Pursuit of Gain 30 ff., 52 ff., 137 ff. (Cambridge, Mass., 1931).

before and after him, rejected the doctrine that government was in any way unnatural, was a necessary evil, and had become necessary only with the fall of
man. Leadership and rule would have been necessary, Aquinas stated, in an
earthly Paradise, even if Adam had not sinned, as it was necessary among the
angels.[12]

On at least two points, however, the scholastic doctrine provided material
which nineteenth-century Catholic writers with laissez faire tendencies were to
make use of in building up a case against state interventionism in the economic
field.

The medieval moral theologians were united in holding that an essential part
of the merit in charity to the poor was in its being voluntary. Almsgiving from
one's superfluity was urgent precept, not counsel, but how much to give was a
matter of private conscience. For this reason, there was considerable opposition
within the Church to tithes. For this and other reasons, there was strong opposition to provision of poor relief under state supervision and from tax revenues.
After the Reformation, the Elizabethan poor laws making it compulsory for English local authorities to relieve the poor out of special taxes levied for that purpose were criticized by a long succession of Catholic writers as constituting an
illegitimate encroachment of the state into an area which should be left to private
initiative and to the Church. In the nineteenth century, this objection to poor relief
under state auspices was by many Catholic writers made part of a wider case
against attempts to deal with the problem of poverty through state action, as com-
promising with socialism.[13]

More important for present purposes was the medieval doctrine of the "just
price" and, though to a lesser degree, of the "just wage." The scholastics maintained that it was a violation of commutative justice to sell at a higher price or to
buy at a lower price than the "just price," which they explained as the price
according to "common estimation." Until recently, this has been commonly interpreted as meaning the fixing of prices by civil authorities or by wise men, in
the interests of justice and as a restraint on the avarice of merchants, and as demonstrating that the medieval Church was hostile to the free market. Modern scholarship, however, has conclusively demonstrated that, except for a few nominal-
ists, the standard late-medieval meaning of "common estimation" was market
price under free competition, and that some of the scholastics even used the term
equivalent to "common estimation in or by the market." That they meant by the
"market" a competitive market, operating under normal circumstances, they

[12] Summa Theologica, I. q. 96. a. 4.

[13] See G. Ratzinger, Geschichte der kirklichen Armenpflege 447 ff., 556 ff. (Freiburg im Bres-
gau, 1884); F.M.L. Naville, De la Charité Légale (Paris, 1836); Abbé A. Delaporte, Le Problème
Economique et la Doctrine Catholique 422 (Paris, 1867).

made sufficiently clear by their uniform condemnation of all monopolies, and by the exceptions they made for appeal to official or non-market determination of prices when abnormal conditions, such as famine or siege, or unusual absence of business skills or lack of bargaining power, made particular individuals unable to cope adequately with market processes.[14] To interpret the scholastics, however, as enthusiasts for the free market either because of zeal for economic "freedom," or because of recognition of the merits of competition as an organizer and regulator of economic activity in general, would be to misinterpret them in the opposite direction. As far as is apparent from their texts, their acceptance of the desirability of competition rested solely on belief in its efficacy in protecting individuals from exploitation as sellers or as buyers.

From the sixteenth century on, there began to appear briefs on behalf of greater freedom of business from government interference, including defense of practices charged with being monopolistic. In the sixteenth century, defense of rugged individualism even when it had a monopolistic taint appeared paradoxically enough in Protestant apologetics for Old Testament morality, in connection with discussions of the account in Genesis of Joseph's successful venture in grain speculation. The defense sometimes took the form of justifying Joseph's operations on the ground that they were not for private profit but were carried out in the public name and for the public good. John Calvin used this argument, but he carried his defense further so that it should cover Joseph's transactions even if he had acted on his own behalf as a profit-seeking merchant. In the first place Joseph did not have a complete monopoly, since others were free to store grain if they wished. Secondly, if others out of free choice sold at a low price in time of plenty what they could have held for a time of scarcity, the losses they thus incurred were just punishment for their negligence, presumably in mastering the technique of business forecasting. Calvin did not meet squarely the issue that Joseph, enjoying divine guidance, had kept his inside knowledge to himself, instead of broadcasting it and thus adding to the probability that enough grain would be stored in the fat years to enable the Egyptians to withstand with less suffering the lean years, but he ended his defense of Joseph's conduct with the comment that divine guidance sometimes excuses actions otherwise reprehensible.[15]

[14] On this issue, see the various writings of J. Höffner, especially Wirtschaftsethik und Monopole im fünfzehnten und sechszehnten Jahrhundert (Jena, 1941), and "Statistik und Dynamik in der scholastischen Wirtschaftsethik," Arbeitsgemeinschaft für Forschung des Landes Nordrhein-Westfalen Geisteswissenschaften, Heft 38 (Cologne, 1955). See also: A. Sandoz, La Notion de Juste Prix, 45 Revue Thomiste 291 ff. (1939); de Roover, Joseph A. Schumpeter and Scholastic Economics, 10 Kyklos 134 ff. (1957). For material which seems to me to point to a similar interpretation of the scholastic doctrine of the "just wage," see L'Abbé Manuel Rocha, Travail et Salaire à Travers la Scolastique (Paris, 1933).

[15] See A. Williams, The Common Expositor. An Account of the Commentaries on Genesis 1527–1633, 225 ff. (Chapel Hill, 1948).

It was in England that a stock of ideas and values from which a general doctrine of laissez faire could be constructed with the aid of some ingenuity in selection and synthesis was soonest and most abundantly available. Many modern scholars, mistaking scattered and discrete ideas as constituting a general theory, have found essentially laissez faire doctrine prevalent in England long before Adam Smith. The language of "freedom" was popular in England from really ancient times. There was constant appeal to "freedoms," or "liberties," or "immunities," or "franchises," or "properties," or "rights," all of these being substantially synonymous terms and none of these being synonymous with "freedom" in the singular. There was Magna Carta and all that. There was as early as 1040 the message which a rebellious lot sent to King Hardecanute when his agents roughly demanded payment of taxes for which there was no precedent: "We are freemen born and freemen by nurture; we will obey no ruler who treats us unjustly; we are dedicated either to liberty or to death."[16] Even when specific "liberties" were being argued for, the most ardent advocates explained that what was in issue was "liberty within the law," and not an absolute liberty to do as one pleased, which would be "license," that was in issue. "Liberty within the law" meant liberty from the exercise of authority by an unqualified agency, or without "due process of law"; it did not mean liberty from interventionist legislation; it often meant submission without complaint to a severe but accepted agency of coercion where even a mild exercise of authority by a disliked agency would be furiously rejected. Of the notion of adding specific liberties to each other so as to obtain a maximum amount of liberty in general, I can find no clear trace before Adam Smith. Of the notion that "freedom" is indivisible, I can find no clear trace until the twentieth century,[17] and then I cannot fathom its meaning.

It has been held that the English common law was a great and good friend of economic freedom. The common law lawyer inevitably has a professional jealousy of any forms of law-making other than through court decisions resting their claims to validity on earlier court decisions. In the Stuart period, law was not only being promulgated without the customary sanction of Parliament, solely by royal prerogative, but new courts had been established by monarchial act which decided cases without express appeal either to statutes or to past court decisions. It was in this period that Sir Edward Coke appealed to the common law as a traditional barrier to the interference by government with the economic and other "freedoms" of the individual. It seems now to be generally agreed, however,

---

[16] The incident is reported in William of Malmesbury, Gesta Regium Anglorum, [1125], but I have misplaced my source for the Latin text of this anticipation of Patrick Henry.

[17] Compare, however, 77 Edinburgh Rev. 224 (1843): "Be assured that freedom of trade, freedom of thought, freedom of speech, and freedom of action, are but modifications of one great fundamental truth, and that all must be maintained or all risked; they stand or fall together."

that Coke, in his righteous indignation against usurpation of power by the king, distorted and misinterpreted the past common-law tradition to make it seem more strongly favorable to what we would now call economic liberalism than it was in fact.[18]

Even to Coke, moreover, the "liberty" of the common law was a much narrower, a much more specific and limited obstacle to any species of government interference with private economic activity, than would be the "liberty" or "freedom" of full-fledged laissez faire doctrine. It was a maxim of Coke himself that "the common law will rather suffer a private injury than a public inconvenience," and evidence is lacking that common-law lawyers were less adept or less willing than bureaucrats or legislators to discover public inconvenience or "public policy" reasons for not protecting a private right. In a 1607 common law case, where a candlemaker was indicted for causing a nuisance by the odor of his process, the court held that "Le utility del chose excusera le noisomeness del stink,"[19] but it could equally well have decided otherwise.[20]

Material for building up a case for laissez faire exists even in the writings of the mercantilists, despite the fact that what we now call "mercantilism" consisted primarily of a body of doctrine expounding and of practice employing ways and means whereby government could make private interest, when subjected to taxes, import and export duties and prohibitions, subsidies, and other regulatory and coercive measures, operate to augment national wealth and national power.

Few if any mercantilists had an undiscriminating, unmotivated, and unlimited passion for state intervention in all its conceivable forms, degrees, and applications. Most mercantilists had some particular freedoms which they cherished either for themselves or for their fellow-citizens. Even mercantilists were aware that there were limits to the capacity and wisdom of government; that attempts of government to interfere where individuals had interests to which they were intensely devoted were liable to result in breakdown; that, as compared with direct controls, indirect controls often were more efficient, aroused less resistance, involved the public in less inconvenience. Horace Walpole was a routine moderate mercantilist, but it was with genuine amusement that he related how his "aunt, Mrs. Kerwood, reading one day in the papers that a distiller had been burnt by

[18] See Wagner, Coke and the Rise of Economic Liberalism, 2 Econ. Hist. Rev. 30–44 (1935–36); Letwin, The English Common Law concerning Monopolies, 21 U. Ch. L. Rev. 355–56 (1954). But see, per contra, Pound, The development of American Law and its Deviation from English Law, 67 Law Q. Rev. 58 (1951).

[19] Sir James Fitzjames Stephen, A General View of the Criminal Law of England 106 (London, 1890).

[20] See the comment on this case in R. Burn, II The Justice of the Peace, and Parish Officer 482 (7th ed. 1762).

the head of the still flying off, said she wondered that they did not make an Act of Parliament against the heads of stills flying off.'' On specific issues, the moderate mercantilist could often sound like a moderate exponent of laissez faire, and mercantilists would not dispute the general principle that the state should not interfere except where the public interest or the common good would best be served by interference. Even between extreme mercantilists and extreme advocates of laissez faire the difference in avowed general principle might consist only in that the mercantilist would stress the duty of intervention unless, by exception, good reason existed for leaving things alone, while the laissez faire doctrinaire would insist that the government should leave things alone unless by exception special reasons existed why it should intervene. It is thus not difficult, by judicious selection of passages from the literature of English mercantilism, to make out a plausible case for its ''liberal'' character. The only questions that remain are what we are to do about the passages, by far more numerous, which have a contrary tenor, and how we are to explain the three centuries of statute books stuffed with legislation of a nature to set Adam Smith's teeth violently on edge. It does not seem possible, on the basis of any reasonable definitions, to find any trend in England away from ''interventionism'' and toward laissez faire, in doctrine or in legislation, between, say, 1660 and decades after the publication of the *Wealth of Nations* in 1776. In the field of public administration, of enforcement of interventionist legislation, the period was marked by slackness, by an approach to administrative nihilism. But the slackness had no doctrinal basis. It was commonly deplored, not lauded.

The mercantilists adhered to the ancient psychological doctrine that man was a ''selfish,'' or at least a ''self-regarding'' animal; they followed the unanimous opinion of their predecessors that out of individual selfishness, unless regulated and disciplined by a superior authority, there could not come a good society; they accepted without scrutiny the proposition that for individuals (though not for governments or princes) the predominant self-regarding interests were economic in character; they accepted man's selfish nature as a fact, without special interest in appraising it in moral or religious terms; they saw in an active and interfering government the only force strong enough to harness all of this selfish energy to a desirable social, that is, national, set of objectives.

I turn now to an English author, Thomas Hobbes, who is occasionally cited as one of the sources of English laissez faire doctrine, but is more often cited as an early exponent of the totalitarian state. It is not too difficult to explain how Hobbes came to be for some the archetype of the totalitarian and for others a pioneer exponent of liberal doctrine. Hobbes was an exponent of centralization of coercive power, of its monopolization by the sovereign. That is why he is regarded by many as an exponent of totalitarianism. But, like the later Physiocrats, who were greatly influenced by him, he wanted power centralized in order to minimize its use, in order that no one except the sovereign should be in a position to exercise coercion over individuals. The sovereign should exercise the power under his command only for legitimate purposes and to the minimum degree consistent with the realization of such purposes. In all his many writings there is very little advocacy of any use by the sovereign of his power except for national defense and to assemble, and so-to-speak to put under lock-and-key so that it would not be used, any segments of coercive power which might otherwise be available for use by Church, by private armies, by particular groups, or by over-rugged individuals. According to Hobbes, man living in a state of nature would be constantly engaged in a war of all against all, and government was necessary if man's wolfish instincts were not to govern his behavior. It seems clear, however, that Hobbes would have conceded, if asked, that man, once he is living in civil society, displays and, with safety to himself and benefit to his community, exercises a wide array of social and cooperative instincts which in the state of nature would be fatal to his survival. In any case, Hobbes put less stress than did the mercantilists generally on the strictly economic character of man's objectives in civil society. ''The business of the World,'' he stated, ''consisteth in nothing else but a perpetual contention for Honor, Riches, and Authority.'' In a well-policed state such contention could presumably proceed without undermining civil order and with beneficial effect on the community's general well-being. Beyond its policing function, the state need not be an active or meddling or planning state. It is not absurd, therefore, to interpret Hobbes as primarily an exponent of a state powerful enough to assure and protect individual freedom. His political and ethical doctrines, and his intolerance of any sharing of power with the Church, however, made his views exceedingly unpopular in the England of his time. In France, the wide acceptance of Gallicanism with respect to the relations of Church and State, and of monarchical absolutism and centralization in the political field, made for a more receptive attitude towards Hobbesian doctrine.

In England the most important intellectual developments which finally prepared the ground for the formulation of an economic doctrine of laissez faire consisted of contributions by moral philosophers and theologians whose major objective often was to rebut Hobbes, even though on strictly economic matters Hobbes was probably less state-interventionist than many of those who opposed him on ecclesiastical and moral issues. The major ethical doctrines developed to rebut Hobbes were in the eighteenth century distinguished as the ''selfish'' and the ''sentimental'' schools. Both of these schools provided ingredients for the laissez faire doctrine even in its mature nineteenth-century form.

The ''selfish school'' consisted predominantly of a long succession of Cambridge University moral philosophers, to whose doctrine there was given in the nineteenth century the appropriate-enough label of "theological utilitarianism." To serve their purpose of demonstrating a vital social function for the belief in immortality and in future rewards and punishments, or in other words for orthodox religion, they attacked Hobbes's stress on the adequacy of the state—or of the policeman—as a moralizer of society. On the other hand, to rebut the optimistic account of human nature given by the sentimental school, which seemed to make unnecessary either a strong police force or powerful religious sanctions, they retained and even accentuated the pessimistic appraisal of human nature when left to its own devices presented by the Augustinian tradition within religion and by Hobbes and the libertines outside it. The connection with laissez faire of this school is a tenuous one—by stressing the theological sanctions for good social behavior and the limited scope and efficacy of governmental sanctions, they directed attention away from, though without expressly denying, the need for extensive social discipline applied by government.

The "sentimental school" had much greater importance for laissez faire doctrine. It was launched in the seventeenth century, as a reply to Hobbes, by theologians of deist tendencies and by laymen of even more doubtful religious orthodoxy, of whom Lord Shaftesbury was most prominent. The essence of their doctrine for present purposes was the stress on the social sentiments, on the nonrationalistic social instincts and affections of men, which led them to serve their fellowmen out of sympathy and fellow-feelings. Francis Hutcheson, the teacher of Adam Smith at Glasgow, was a member of this school, and the "moral sentiments" of Adam Smith's *Theory of Moral Sentiments* were essentially variants of the sympathy, the benevolence, and "the moral sense" which were the key elements in the social philosophy of Shaftesbury and of Hutcheson.

It is necessary to mention one other line of doctrine formulated in rebuttal of Hobbes, the doctrine of Bishop Richard Cumberland, which influenced both the Physiocrats and Adam Smith. Cumberland argued that the social order was so constituted that there was essential harmony between rational self-interest and the common good, and that even in the absence of government, or of hope for future rewards and fear of future punishment, rational men would constitute a good society—though not as good a society as if religious and political sanctions for good social behavior were also operative. It needs to be noted that while the sentimental school relied on instincts for good social behavior, Cumberland put his emphasis on the double rationality: of men and of good social behavior.

The Physiocrats arrived at their laissez faire doctrine by way of a curious blend of the myth of a beneficent physical order of nature, of Hobbesism, of Cumberland's and Cartesian rationalism, and of some fresh and important economic analysis of the coordinating, harmonizing, and organizing function of free competition. There was a providential harmonious and self-operating *physical* order of nature, which, under appropriate social organization and sound intellectual perception, could be matched in its providential character, in its automatism, and in its beneficence, in the *social* order of nature. Through proper education this would become "evident" (in a special sense of the word) to all men; by *reasonable* men what was the "evident" course of behavior to follow in the social interest would be seen also to be the proper course of behavior in their own individual interest. It was the role of economists to perceive and to expound, to government and to the public, this "evident" truth. It was the role of government, through its Hobbesian monopoly of power, its "legal despotism," to bring about, with the help of the economists, the general acceptance of the "evident" doctrine, and to suppress inconsistent or hostile action on the part of ignorant or malicious individuals, of monopoly groups, and of unfriendly foreign countries. Beyond this, the normal operation of free competition would suffice, without further state intervention, to produce in the social order that harmony, mutual cooperation, and efficiency "evident" in the physical order of nature. It can be argued that, aside from their economics, for which their indebtedness was to earlier French writers, notably Boisguillebert and Cantillon—who was really Irish—and from their doctrine of "evidence," which derived, with distortions, from Descartes, the heaviest indebtedness of the Physiocrats was to Hobbes and Cumberland.

In Adam Smith's system of laissez faire, the functions assigned to government were substantially identical with those assigned by the Physiocrats: maintenance of inter-individual justice; defense; and essential "public works," including education as such, of a kind which private initiative would not or could not undertake, or which for special reasons, such as their monopolistic character, it would not be safe to leave in private hands. For Adam Smith, laissez faire in the economic sphere found its intellectual basis in terms of a comprehensive system of social thought which drew eclectically from a wide variety of earlier sources, but added discussion of freedom or "natural liberty" understood in a general or universal sense to discussion in the traditional way of particular "freedoms" or "liberties." For the social system as a whole, excluding its market aspects, the beneficial outcome of laissez faire, according to Smith, results from the social instincts imbedded in human nature, as well as from the "moral sentiments": sympathy for others, the desire for social approval, the dictates of conscience, and, to a minor extent, benevolence toward others. In the economic marketplace, as described in the *Wealth of Nations*, the beneficial outcome of laissez faire is ascribed to other factors than instincts and social sentiments, except as the simple rules of commutative justice are voluntarily obeyed. Within the family, in relations with one's friends and one's immediate neighbors, in one's operations as a patriotic citizen of one's country, the instincts, the social sentiments, conscience, the desire for public approval, sympathy, benevolence, patriotism, suffice to produce a good society. In the market, however, one is dealing as with strangers; to use later terminology, the market is "anonymous," is ruled by the "cash nexus." The social sentiments, therefore, are not aroused into action, and man behaves in response to calculating, rational self-interest. Fortunately, however, the nature of economic process is such, it involves such a high degree of harmony of interests between the individuals participating in it, that government, provided only that it enforces the rules of justice, need do little else to assure a flourishing economy.

It is not clear that Adam Smith believed that laissez faire would carry the wealth of a nation to some kind of theoretically-conceivable maximum. What is clear is that, subject to a vague and in part logically inconsistent list of qualifications, he believed that economic society left to its autonomous operation would produce a higher level of economic welfare than would accrue if government, inefficient, ignorant, and profligate as in practice it was, should try to direct or regulate or operate it. It is clear, moreover, that for Adam Smith laissez faire, beyond its material benefits, had ethical or moral value in that it left to the individual unimpaired that "natural system of liberty" to which he had a natural right. It is quite probable, therefore, that Adam Smith would have rejected an extensive program of state regulation of economic enterprise even if he had believed that the wealth of nations could thereby be augmented.

The post-Smithian English doctrine of laissez faire as expounded by the English classical economists, while heavily indebted to the Physiocrats and to Adam Smith, did have some original ingredients. The classical economists thoroughly secularized the doctrine, and dispensed with appeal to the "invisible hand" to bolster up the argument that man acting in the pursuit of his own interests would at the same time best serve the community interest. In the second place, here following Adam Smith but deviating from Cumberland and the Physiocrats, they attributed the socially beneficial behavior of individuals not to a rationalistic perception by these individuals that the common good was also their own private good, but to an inherent quality in competitive economic behavior which made the common good an incidental and not deliberately sought by-product of the pursuit by the individual of his own particular good. Thirdly, as an analytical device, instead of relying on the real man psychologically speaking such as they observed him to be in fact, they invented a construct, the economists' "economic man," who, as an abstraction, corresponded closely to Adam Smith's whole man or real man as he was when operating in the market-place. But the classical school did not present the "economic man" as more than a somewhat distant approximation to the real man even as he behaved in the market-place. They accepted this as a useful abstraction, in the belief that it was sufficiently close to reality to provide a substantially correct over-all account of the behavior of the competitive market under laissez faire. In principle, however, they were always, and in practice they were sometimes, prepared to qualify their analysis whenever it was observed that the behavior of the real man was substantially different from that of the "economic man."

With the later Manchester School and with that most facile and most superficial of the expounders of laissez faire, the Frenchman Bastiat, as with the early academic exponents of laissez faire in the United States, the "invisible hand" returned as a substitute for genuine economic analysis in the explanation of the natural harmony between private and public good. For Richard Cobden, "Free trade was the international law of God" and presumably domestic laissez faire was the domestic law of God. In principle, however, if by no means universally in practice, later exposition of laissez faire by economists was made contingently to rest on the presumed behavior of an "economic man" coldly calculating, rational, alert, well-informed. But they recognized this "economic man" to be an analytic construct differing in some unspecified degree in the psychology attributed to him from the real flesh-and-blood and heart-and-incomplete-mind types that were alone visible in the real world. They all consequently acknowledged at one time or another that the issue as to the desirable degree or kind of state intervention could not be satisfactorily resolved logically by abstract argument alone, based on the workings of a system of free competition in a society composed of "economic men." Judgment, wisdom, knowledge, even upon occasion charity, needed also to be called upon. This might justifiably lead in particular instances, transient or lasting, to major exceptions being properly made to the principle of non-intervention. This was true particularly of the later classical and neo-classical economists. They all expressly and vehemently disassociated themselves from the Manchester School and from those other fanatic exponents of laissez faire who proclaimed with much assurance and sometimes with the appearance of complacency that it was impossible for the state to assume any general and positive responsibility for the relief of even major distress without ultimately accentuating that distress.

A detailed listing of the concessions and qualifications ceded by writers who were or who later were regarded as leading expositors of the doctrine of laissez faire would constitute a lengthy and impressive document. But these exceptions and qualifications were rarely, if ever, integrated with the laissez faire part of their doctrine in such a way as to disclose the principles by which the proper time and form and degree of departure from laissez faire could be judiciously determined, or by which the cases where departure was indicated could be differentiated from those which fell unquestionably within the scope of laissez faire. Bentham, perhaps, came closest of all to formulating on a reasoned and consistent basis the considerations which should decide, to use his terms, the ''Agenda'' and the ''Non-Agenda'' for government, but later Fabian socialists as well as later economic liberals were to derive their doctrinal inspiration from him.

To quote a second time a dictum of St. Thomas Aquinas which impresses me as having direct and weighty bearing on the intellectual history of laissez faire: ''When reason argues about particular cases, it needs not only universal but also particular principles.'' Except for playful intellectual exercise, or as a first stage of a first approximation in a sustained logical argument, universal principles seem to me to have no useful role in argument, and particular cases or restricted classes of cases to comprise almost everything that is worth arguing about—or dying for. And information, wisdom, judgment, measurement-of-a-kind of things not scientifically measurable, compassion for the weaker segments of mankind, always—or nearly always—need to be permitted to corrupt the logical rigor of abstract argument if the final result is to be reasonably applicable to particular cases, and if in a democratic society it is to find wide and lasting acceptance. Good abstract argument is an essential tool for the organization of knowledge and for bringing values to bear on public issues. But the rhetoric of abstract argument has no built-in devices to guard against neglect or oversight of relevant major values, and abstract argument is a tool for processing information, not a substitute for it.

The good citizen will—or should be—passionately devoted at any moment to a number of general principles, often recently acquired, often part of an ancient intellectual inheritance, often largely contradictory among themselves. In practice, he will unconsciously compromise them, or choose between them in the light of the emphasis being given them in the current flow of rhetoric to which he is being subjected. The effective crusader for good causes will in any campaign of persuasion deliberately or by temperament or in ignorance select for emphasis as supreme above all others at least in the existent circumstances a single general principle, or a small number of presumptively harmonious general principles, and will leave to those hostile to his cause the search for intellectual or practical flaws in his argument. There is a third kind of rhetoric which also has logical and practical claims to merit and to utility, whose task it is to explore the conflicts between principles, to search out the importance of degree, relation, and proportion, to discover for particular values their appropriate place in the process of persuasion.

To me this last kind of rhetoric seems a most appropriate one for the academic scholar and providing moral and material support for those who attempt to use it seems the most valuable service a great university can render to the process of reaching worthy decisions on questions of social policy.

It is permitted to the crusader to argue for the desirability of laissez faire, as a routine application of some general principle, such as that liberty is desirable and laissez faire is an important form of liberty. The rhetorician in my third category, however, does not permit himself to forget that there is a great variety of species and degrees of liberty, interrelated in complex and changing patterns of mutual dependence, of mutual reinforcement, of rivalry, of conflict, and that particular species of liberty can have widely-different significance for individuals differing in their psychological make-up and in their material circumstances. Even if liberty in some general sense were the one supreme and absolute good for all men, it would still remain necessary—and often difficult—to seek light on whether the establishment or retention or restoration of a particular liberty added to or subtracted from the system of liberties as a whole. Particular liberties may clash, moreover, not only with other liberties, but with other values than liberty, as, for example, individual or national security, prosperity, internal peace and order, equity. The tragic element in decision-making arises often, not from the conflict of good with evil, but from the conflict of true values with each other.

A "general principle" always beloved of those content with the status quo is that since major social institutions evolve slowly through time, without benefit of over-all design by geniuses, there is a strong presumption that at any given time existing institutions of ancient origin must have wisdom and merit in them. This is another of those general principles whose axiomatic character is not obvious to me, but whatever its validity, it has weight only as an argument against rapid social change, or against certain procedures for bringing change about. Governmental interventionism has also, until recently, and with a nineteenth century interlude of retrocession, evolved slowly. The bearing of all this on laissez faire seems to be only that movement away from laissez faire or movement towards laissez faire should be cautious and piece-meal. Cournot, a distinguished nineteenth-century economist and philosopher, held that the limits of state intervention must be set piecemeal, by trial and error, in the light of circumstances, of established customs, of ruling ideas, and cannot be dealt with as within the realm of scientific determination. I would be prepared to buy this as a persuasive "general principle." He proceeded, however, to argue that there were excellent reasons why, in the conflict between freedom and regulation, freedom should in the last resort be the winner. For just as each freedom leads to other freedoms, so each governmental regulation leads to other regulations, with this difference, that there is only one method of letting things alone, whereas there are an infinite number of ways of interfering, all more or less arbitrary.[21]

I am puzzzled as to what weight should be given to this ingenious argument against state-interference. Testing its cogency by applying it to other situations where the issue lies between acting and not acting, I find, for instance, that there is only one way of not eating whereas there is an infinity of ways of eating, all of them more or less arbitrary.

For economists laissez faire is most persuasive when it is presented as an argument for the free market. If the market is a competitive one, it is an impersonal—more-or-less—social institution performing a great organizing service with respect to allocation of resources to production, determination of prices, distribution of the current products of industry. There is no theoretical basis that I know of whereby, without introducing assumptions counter to fact, it can be demonstrated that the resultant allocation of resources, price structure, or distribution of current income is an ideal or "optimum" one. But what can be persuasively argued—perhaps even "proved" in the sense in which David Hume and John Stuart Mill used that word, as meaning an argument so persuasive that any reasonable man will accept it and act according to it until a better argument or fuller information comes along—is that random interferences with the working of a competitive market will make it a less efficient organizer of economic activity. A fortiori, stupid or malicious or clumsy interference by legislature or bureaucrats will impair its working. The total suppression of the free market would, I am sure, for any modern country, including Soviet Russia, mean an approximation to total chaos, but no one of consequence has apparently ever proposed it seriously.

This still leaves open, however, a large area suitable for reasoned debate even about the market. Can anything like a general rule in the service of economic efficiency, or of an ethical ideal, or of "freedom" in general, be laid down against selective tampering with the free-market process by a government well intentioned and reasonably intelligent? Tampering of a kind continuously goes on in the courts or legislatures of all countries in the interest of commutative justice: to take care, for instance, even in cases of free contract between two individuals, of the interests of the young, of the especially ignorant, of those caught in emergency situations not forseeable at the time of the contract, and of particular individuals not parties to the contract, but affected by them.

Bentham, in his general exposition, held that to interfere with a free contract in a free market in the supposed interest of the parties, where there was no recognized adverse impact on particular non-participants in the contract, would be

---

[21] A. A. Cournot, Considérations sur la Marche des Idées 87 (F. Meurte, ed.; Paris, no date).

to make the absurd assumptions that a government or an official can know better than a man knows what that man wants, and can know better than that man knows what are the most efficient means for him of satisfying his wants. I can only say that I fail to see the axiomatic nature of either of these propositions, and that a plausible case can be made for a substantial mass of legislation and of court-law which takes for granted that reasonably definable sets of circumstances do arise under which an authority can know better than an individual both what that individual wants, if more than a moment is taken into account, and how that individual can most efficiently satisfy his want.

The classical exponents of laissez faire always qualified their enthusiasm for the free market by the condition that it should be a competitive market. Adam Smith, for instance, intensely disliked monopoly in all its forms. He regarded merchants as perpetual seekers of monopoly power. Also, because he thought that in all but routine activities they would inevitably be inefficient, he disliked all large-scale privately owned companies. Adam Smith believed that the merchants of his time, large-scale and small-scale, were in constant conspiracy to establish monopoly control over prices, and that their conspiracies were often successful.

In one field of commerce, however, the internal corn trade, where opinion in general was most disposed to share his belief in the prevalence and the evil of a monopolizing tendency, Smith displayed a marked scepticism. It was here, he said, of all trades that monopoly is least possible of organization, because of the great size of the industry, the great number of dealers, and their general geographical dispersion. He also clearly believed that rural landlords and farmers were of all economic groups least disposed to seek monopoly profits, and that therefore their cooperation could not be obtained by would-be organizers of a corn-trade monopoly.

The English classical school all followed Adam Smith in their dislike of monopoly. They extended, however, to almost the whole range of industry and trade Smith's argument *re* the corn-trade that the size of the task, the number of persons involved, and their dispersion over space, made the establishment of an enduring monopoly a practical impossibility. They applied this reasoning also to the question of the possibility of raising wages through the formation of trade unions. The general position of the post-Smithian classical school in this respect is accurately and compactly stated in the following quotation from David Buchanan:

> It is well known that no body of traders ever can frame an effectual combination against the public, as all such engagements are broken by the partial interests of the individuals concerned. No trader will keep up his prices for the profit of others;

he will always sell when it suits his own convenience; and upon this principle accordingly is founded all that rivalship of trade.[22]

The later verdict that this was substantially erroneous reasoning seems valid to me. Even in the corn-trade the high transportation costs of the period made a regional monopoly much less difficult to establish, at least temporarily, than Adam Smith supposed. Adam Smith and his followers argued excessively from the tacit assumption that a monopoly which was temporary only or which was not "perfect" in the modern sense could not yield appreciable monopoly revenue. In any case, we now know that, apparently without exception, every English industry of Adam Smith's time whose history has been studied was riddled with price-rings or equivalent arrangements, often only on a regional basis but sometimes on a national basis. There is no a priori reason for assuming that these were predominantly or universally of negligible effect, and the fact that their practice was so widespread provides an empirical presumption that they brought to their practitioners in some significant degree the realization of their price-raising objectives.

To this scepticism of the English classical school about the possibility of monopoly must undoubtedly be attributed in significant part the absence of any anti-monopoly legislation in nineteenth-century England. On the other hand, it was the continued fear of monopoly when the scale of enterprise was large which was responsible for the withholding of general statutory sanction for the incorporation of limited-liability joint-stock companies without limitation as to scale of operations until after the middle of the nineteenth century, and the classical economists of the time were divided as to the wisdom of this repeal of the ancient restrictions on "big business." It is quite clear that the general public was confused by the combination in the doctrine of the classical school of a pronounced condemnation in principle of monopoly and a refusal to recognize its existence in fact; a confusion well expressed by a cartoon of the time which showed one of the marchers in a street-demonstration carrying a banner reading: "No Monopoly!" and another carrying a banner reading: "No Competition!"

In any case, monopoly is so prevalent in the markets of the western world today that discussion of the merits of the free competitive market as if that were what we were living with or were at all likely to have the good fortune to live with in the future seem to me academic in the only pejorative sense of that adjective.

Modern advocates of an approach to laissez faire recognize that whatever rationale it has rests on the assumption that economic society under laissez faire

---

[22] In a note in his edition of A. Smith, I Wealth of Nations 100 (Edinburgh, 1814).

would be, or could be made to be, substantially competitive. Towards the monopolistic aspects of modern society they take various attitudes. Some look upon them as serious obstacles to economic welfare, and would have an otherwise laissez faire state vigorously suppress all important manifestations of monopoly that are not for special reasons to be accepted. Others maintain that government itself is, directly or indirectly, the major support of monopoly and that in a laissez faire economy monopoly, with minor exceptions, would not be able either to establish or to maintain itself in the absence of government support. Others while expressing in principle hostility to monopoly deny its practical importance and contend that in the main moderate elements of monopoly can be tolerated without serious loss, or even with benefit, in a predominantly competitive, laissez faire economy; like the competitive "economic man," the monopolistic firm, without intending it, is, as if guided by an invisible hand, serving the public interest.

I would not dispute that even a monopoly-ridden market would be preferable to any economic system trying to operate without any kind of a market. But given the prevalence or the danger of substantial intrusion of monopoly into the market, the logic of the laissez faire defense of the market against state-intervention collapses and there is called for instead, by its very logic, state-supression or state-regulation of monopoly practices, which one may wish to call, as Henry Simons called it, an instance of "positive laissez faire" or, as I prefer, as an instance of deliberate departure from laissez faire.

The free-market phase of the laissez faire doctrine is only one phase of that doctrine and is most relevant to the issues of commutative justice, of just relations in economic transactions between pairs of individuals. There is also the area of distributive justice, of the intervention of state-authority directly or indirectly with the intention of changing an existing pattern of distribution of this world's goods. When economists discuss the workings of a free competitive market, they agree that the existing pattern of distribution of wealth, of income, and of individual knowledge, capacities, and skills, affects the price-structure. They presumably agree also that the price-structure of today affects the income-structure of tomorrow. It is not appropriate, therefore, in a final appraisal from either an ethical or an economic-efficiency point of view of the mode of operation of an economic system, to consider the operations of the market on the assumption that the existing pattern of income distribution is the consequence of a dispensation of Providence. It is not reasonable to treat an existing income distribution, for the purpose of analyzing the market, as if it just "happened," as if it were as independent of influence by the market and as incapable of influence on the market, through the effect of aggregate human exercises of will and economic power, as the Rocky Mountains or storms and earthquakes are free from human control.

Even the impact of storms on mankind, moreover, is affected by the pattern of distribution of income.

> The rain it raineth on the just
> And also on the unjust fella;
> But chiefly on the just, because
> The unjust steals the just's umbrella.

FERGUSON BOWEN

It is not necessary, nor helpful, to my argument to introduce any suspicion that "stealing" plays a significant economic role in a modern society. But the decline of laissez faire in England, and the growth there of systematic state-interference not only with the economy as a whole, but with the free market, came largely as the result of dissatisfaction with the prevailing distribution-of-income pattern. Sir Winston Churchill, writing when a young man about the breakdown of the hold of laissez faire on English public opinion, which he dated as occurring in the decade of the 1880's, commented that with it came to a close "the long dominion of the middle classes," and "the almost equal reign of liberalism."

> The great victories had been won. All sorts of lumbering tyrannies had been top-pled over. Authority was everywhere broken. Slaves were free. Conscience was free. Trade was free. But hunger and squalor and cold were also free and the people demanded something more than liberty. . . . How to fill the void was the riddle that split the liberal party.[23]

No modern people will have zeal for the free market unless it operates in a setting of "distributive justice" with which they are tolerably content. There is, however, a great deal to be said, much of the best of which has been said on this Chicago campus, for so devising any measures aiming at distributive justice as to minimize their interference with free-market processes, and for making such interference as has general objectives operate indirectly, rather than by direct controls, on market transactions. But a laissez faire program which confined its efforts to preserving or restoring a free market, even a competitive market, while remaining silent on or opposing any proposals for adopting new or retaining old measures in the area of distributive justice, would seem to me glaringly unreal-istic with respect to its chances of political success, and highly questionable also with respect to more exalted criteria of merit. It was the combination, in the nineteenth-century English laissez faire program, of hostility to measures aiming

---

[23] W. S. Churchill, Lord Randolph Churchill 268–269 (New York, 1906).

at distributive justice and a hands-off attitude to the market which resulted in England getting a "welfare state" with what is to my very private taste an excess of "distributive justice" and a deficiency of free competitive market. A prettier Utopia to me would be a society with as completely free and competitive a market as was attainable in the setting of a welfare state in which mass poverty had been eliminated, the business cycle tamed, and opportunity made as equal as was consistent with the survival of private property, the family, and biological differences, as between men, in capacities and motivations. Such a Utopia would be nearer to the modern "welfare state" than to laissez faire. It would nevertheless be a Utopia in which many attractive freedoms could flourish and prosper side-by-side with other ingredients of the good life not consistent with laissez faire. I would not make a plea for it, however, by appeal to "general principles," nor would I make any claim that any others are bound by logical considerations to accept it as their own Utopia.

9

THE ECONOMIST IN HISTORY

I FEEL IT PRUDENT to begin by explaining the title of my paper. It is not, except
indirectly, a paper on the history of economic thought, although I must confess
that several times in the past I have been guilty of smuggling some history of
thought into our Association's meetings, and may possibly do so again here. Nor
is my paper an account of the influence the economist and his ideas have had on
the actual course of history. Keynes may have been right when he said that "the
ideas of economists and political philosophers . . . are the chief rulers of the
world; . . . it is ideas, not vested interests, which are powerful for good or evil."
The techniques, however, by which it is discovered what are the ruling causes in
history fall outside the limits of my acquaintance, let alone my capacity to use
them effectively. If I may judge by the most conspicuous attempts to demonstrate
the dominance of ideas over passions and affections and interests, the techniques
involve more dependence on imagination and conjecture than on crude fact la-
boriously collected. I am also impressed by the extent to which vested interests
and going institutions seem to have the power to generate ideas congruent with
themselves. Napoleon in his student days read the *Wealth of Nations*. It has been
suggested that this is why he later supported sound money, severe economy in
public expenditures, and other economic virtues more cherished by Adam Smith
than practiced by statesmen. But Napoleon also read economic treatises which
opposed these particular virtues. Late in life, moreover, he claimed that he had
always believed that if an empire were made of granite the ideas of economists,
if listened to, would suffice to reduce it to dust. Even the sector of the world
which is reported to have been most influenced by the ideas of economists—the
realm of business—seems to have been in the past little disposed to listen to
economists, even to those whom it hired or subsidized. If it did absorb ideas from
the economists, it must have done so mainly by some process of osmosis not
involving deliberate reading or listening. As recently as the late 1920's a leading
businessman, important in political and international affairs as well as in busi-

The Richard T. Ely Lecture delivered before the American Economic Association, December 28,
1962. Reprinted from the *American Economic Review* 53 (May 1963): 1–22.

ness, was reported to have said that of economics he read not at all, as it was "critical, opinionated matter," and that he preferred to form his own opinions from the facts because he felt that "there is always great danger of having your mind all cluttered up with other folk's opinions." This is certainly a real hazard inherent in wide reading, and one that I may not have sufficiently surmounted myself.

If it is not the history of economic thought, nor the history of the causal influence of economists and their ideas on the course of social history which is the subject of my paper, what then can it be? I had considered giving my paper the title: "Why has economics always had a bad press?" This would have described with adequate accuracy the intent of the paper; I had misgivings, however, as to my capacity to make the content of the paper justify this title, and I had in mind the sad fate that befell the author of a book, published in the 1850's, with too revelatory a title: "Comets considered as Volcanoes, and the Cause of their Velocity and other Phenomena thereby explained." A reviewer, Augustus de Morgan, disposed of the book in one sentence: "The title explains the book better than the book explains the title." I have therefore chosen a title which promises nothing in particular. What I try to do in the paper, however, is to sketch the image which economists and their intellectual goings-on have presented over the years to the vision of the lay public, including in the latter the members of other learned disciplines. With internal controversies within the ranks of the economic profession, I am concerned in this paper only so far as there was an outside public which was interested in these controversies and even participated in them.

Since general recognition of economics as a distinguishable discipline or art and of economists as specialized practitioners of it came only late in history, I find little ancient material that is relevant to my topic. I will begin, therefore, with the mercantilists.

It has become somewhat of a fashion to deny that there ever existed a body of doctrine sufficiently distinct and sufficiently self-consistent to justify attaching to it an "ism" label such as "mercantilism." I acknowledge that most abstract terms ending in "ism," including, for instance, capitalism, socialism, liberalism, individualism, conservatism, puritanism, Americanism, inevitably accumulate about them a haze of uncertainty and imprecision. But that is the characteristic of most abstract terms when they acquire mental associations with concrete things or with groups of things which are not in all relevant respects absolutely homogeneous. One can of course attempt to make do with words which have narrowly restricted connotation, but only at the cost of a verbosity aesthetically intolerable both to lecturer and audience and extravagantly consumptive of time. That mercantilism as a term designating a distinguishable body of doctrines and governmental practices is more vulnerable to the charge of imprecision than the general run of terms used by social scientists for such purposes I cannot see. If there is lack of coherence in the doctrine subsumed under the term, the fault, assuming it to be a fault, should be charged against the mercantilists and not against the term. Incoherence is itself a legitimate abstract label for a regrettably pervasive intellectual phenomenon, and if German scholars have not already invented it, I feel sure that they would welcome *Incoherentismus* as an addition to their vocabulary. It is sometimes the same economic historians who object to the term "mercantilism" as empty of content in the absence of a matching body of doctrine who insist that the body of doctrine and of practices to which the label has been applied had in its prime a degree of suitability approaching the miraculous to the contemporary needs of mankind and far exceeding the claims made, as far as I have observed, for any other body of doctrine and practices recognized to be of purely terrestrial origin.

I feel free, therefore, to deal with mercantilism as if it once existed. I will nevertheless say little about it because it had one characteristic which reduces its relevance for the central theme of my paper. It was essentially not a scholar's doctrine, but a folk-doctrine, and I know of no scholar of even third-rate rank who made any contribution to it except that of lopping off one or more of its more obviously diseased branches. As a folk-doctrine it had in the days of its prime no organized opposition, although a variety of vested interests were always pulling at it to make it serve a special group or pecking at it to win a special freedom from its impact. In England, at least, it was not until mercantilism as a body of practices was entering into a coma from internal causes that there began to emerge any systematic and general attack on it as doctrine, with David Hume and Adam Smith as the sole prominent leaders of the attack; and it was not until the English classical school of the nineteenth century made its surviving relics a major target that mercantilism in England also had to endure in increasing measure a partially bad press. It was not until long after the repeal of the Corn Laws that it had a predominantly hostile press, and by that time it was a corpse that was being reviled in the justified fear that there was under way a conspiracy to revive it. I need not, therefore, for present purposes, spend any further time on mercantilism in its days of English glory.

The physiocrats had many of the characteristics of a sect and were so regarded by many of their contemporaries. They had a "master," Quesnay, whose texts they tended to treat as having something of the oracular about them. Although on several issues they never reached unanimity, if one considers how many writers made contributions to the literature of the school and how voluminous their writings were, the degree of unanimity they did attain was remarkable even for a sect.

How wide the following of the physiocrats among the general public was it is hard to say, but the evidence is abundant that they won many disciples and obtained a selective acceptance of their ideas from many others. Among their disciples was a scattering of writers of some prominence in most of the countries of Europe, as well as a few ruling princes. but they also had many critics. All their major doctrines, their general doctrine of laissez faire, their exposition of competition as basically a means of organizing mutual co-operation on a voluntary basis instead of as a field of exercise for egoism, their doctrine of free trade as being useful chiefly as a means of maintaining a "good price" for the products of agriculture, their doctrine of the "sterility" of all nonagricultural activity, their doctrine of "legal despotism" based on the Hobbesian paradox that the most practicable way of assuring the essential freedoms to the people was to establish a complete monopoly of power to an enlightened monarch to be sparingly exercised by him—all of these doctrines underwent severe criticism from many quarters. Among the critics were writers notable in the general intellectual history of France (for example, Linguet, Mably, and Voltaire) and writers of stature in the history of economic thought (for example, Graslin, Forbonnais, and the Abbé Galiani). Voltaire exercised his satiric brilliance on their paradoxical doctrine that since in the last analysis all taxes fell on land rent, with additional costs and inconveniences in the process of shifting from the initial taxpayer to the landlord, they should, in the interest of the landlord himself, be concentrated into a single tax on land rent. Voltaire satirized this in his *L'Homme aux quarante écus*, where a rich banker who is tax exempt makes sport of the poor peasant who pays taxes for both of them. The physiocrats at times fell back on their doctrine of "evidence," or irresistible truth, in expounding what seemed to them to be axiomatic, and they used it also to explain why an absolute monarch, if advised by physiocrats who were ready to display to him the full range of the available irresistible evidence, could be depended on to be a benevolent despot. Galiani disposed in two sentences of the whole doctrine of irresistible evidence, as applied by the physiocrats in support of their assertion that if France removed all restrictions on the export of grain all Europe would follow its example: "It has appeared evident to the economists that the evidence of their evidence would render evident to all nations the evident advantage of free exportation of grain and that all nations would adopt it. Not a single nation has done so." All France laughed with Galiani as it had laughed with Voltaire before. The most damaging satire is that which makes even the victims laugh. From that fate the physiocrats were rendered immune by their constitutional lack of a sense of humor. They were not amused, and they recruited a battalion of disciples to reply. The solemnly serious tone of the replies brought only additional peals of laughter. It seems always to have been true that the only effective rejoinder to clever satire which hits a target at a vulnerable spot is comparably clever countersatire, but it is not characteristic of sects to recruit wits to their ranks, or long to retain any of them that might have blundered their way in.

The single-tax proposals of the physiocrats and their opposition to the feudal privileges of the great landlords turned the aristocracy against them. Their free-trade views antagonized the manufacturers and the privileged merchants. On the two occasions on which restrictions on the export of grain were removed under physiocratic counsel, bad harvests and local famines followed, and this intensified the hostility of the humanitarians to them. Much of the advice of the physiocrats seems to me to have been sound advice for times less politically unstable. Their valuable and lasting contributions to economic analysis as distinguished from policy are on the record. But as has often been the way of economists, the physiocrats too often stepped on the toes of the powerful at wrong times to have been politically successful. To this failure their bad press made a sizable contribution.

From this point on, I will concentrate on the developments in England and will digress to other countries chiefly to point out contrasts with and parallelisms to English experience.

In 1776, Adam Smith published the *Wealth of Nations*. Its subsequent great influence on ideas and even on the course of policy, abroad as well as in England, few would deny. Its influence was slow in becoming manifest, however. The next twenty-five years were perhaps the leanest period in the history of at least English economic thought from the 1690's to the present day. There was not in this period a single general critique of the *Wealth of Nations* in England of any consequence because of the prominence of its author or the quality of its content. In Scotland the record was only a little better. Of all of Smith's students at Glasgow, I can identify only John Millar as a scholar who made any contribution of consequence to economics either as thinker or as expositor. Adam Smith, however, set the pattern of approach and launched the central ideas for a wide range of issues which were after 1800 to be emphasized by the classical school, most notably in the areas of value and distribution theory and of taxation and above all of laissez faire in general and free trade in particular.

I turn now to the reception of the English classical school as a whole at the hands of the English public. Much of this reception was hostile, even bitterly hostile. Only a few noneconomists praised the school. It nevertheless gradually converted at least the ruling segments of the English population. Part of this conversion can be explained as the consequence of a decline in relative numbers of the most hostile groups as well as a decline of their influence and of their control over publication media. Many of the converts, moreover, were more fully converted in their minds than in their hearts, and adopted classical doctrine with qualms of conscience. In many respects, also, the economists in the classical tradition modified or abandoned some of the classical tenets. The difference, for instance, between the general tone of James Mill's and Alfred Marshall's handling of the economic gospel was greater than that between Marshall and the most sentimental opponent of the rigor and austerity of the classical school in its early days. James Mill, however, was so extremely rigid, austere, pontifical, narrow, belligerent, as to be almost a caricature of the classical school in its less endearing aspects, while Marshall, on the other hand, shrank from participation in open controversy, was so irenic as upon occasion to praise to the skies an economist, notably Schmoller, with whom he had almost nothing in common, strove constantly to blur rather than to sharpen the differences between contending schools and doctrines, and by persistent practice became the great virtuoso in economics of the art of comfortably maintaining a sitting posture between two stools without visible recourse to any substitute means of support. This, I need not tell you, was, however, one of the lesser of his long list of achievements. In any case, when I speak of the English classical school, please keep in mind, even when I fail to do so, its fairly steady progress, from, say, James Mill's approach to problems, to the moderate, the balanced, the disciplined eclecticism and flexibility of that part of present-day economics which still remains substantially respectful of the original classical school, although it has been charged with substituting flabbiness for bigotry. Also, with the compulsions to brevity to which external forces hopefully expect me to submit, I will refrain from bringing to your attention the range of internal dissension, the departures from rigidity of doctrine, the concessions to critics, to be found even within the ranks of the original members of the classical school.

For a school charged with being excessively abstract and removed from reality, it is noteworthy how little there was in the conclusions and the wide range of policy recommendations of the classical school which was not highly relevant to current practical issues, beliefs, convictions, and vested interests. It was only in its choice of premises and in its mode of reaching its conclusions that the school was vulnerable to the charge of undue and arbitrary abstraction. Outside theology, no lay public is normally concerned with the manner in which intellectuals reach their conclusions unless it objects strongly to the conclusions. But almost every one of the major conclusions and the concrete policy recommendations of the classical school touched on the sensitive nerves, ideological or financial, of some important sectors of the population, especially the substantially-allied group of the agrarian landlords and the Church of England as well as the sentimental humanitarians of both conservative and radical species: Laissez faire, free trade, radical reform or abolition of the poor laws, currency reform—on which the school had diverse views—the treatment of rent as unearned income subtracted from the product of labor and capital, the opposition to tithes, taxation reform, the condemnation of extravagance and high-level corruption in government finance, the condemnation of legal monopolies such as the East India Company, the condemnation of the class-restricted electoral suffrage, and so on. From Adam Smith to Lord Sherbrooke in the 1870's, the opposition of one sector of classical economics to withdrawal of religion and higher education from the market test of their proper scope was especially provocative to Anglicans and intellectuals.

The incorporation into the classical economics of Malthusian population theory contributed especially heavily to the dislike of and hostility to the school in important quarters. First, there was the proposition that there was a tendency for population to increase at a rate faster than was consistent with increase or even maintenance of the existing level of living of the working classes. This proposition was held to be one of the premises contrary to fact on which the classical school built its doctrines and its acceptance by the school was interpreted as a gratuitous reflection on the working of providence: "either man has been made too prolific, or the earth too sterile." Second, there was the proposition that to counteract this tendency, the pressure on the poor to exercise prudence in breeding children should be strengthened by withholding from them relief of any kind except in very extreme circumstances, and even then under conditions so burdensome and unpleasant that the poor would have every possible incentive to keep from having more children than they could provide for by their own industry and thrift. This was objected to both as harsh and unfeeling, and as neglecting the fact that a minimum level of comfort and ease was a prerequisite for a large portion of the poor if instead of giving way to demoralizing despair they were to adopt a prudent and self-disciplined pattern of life. The third proposition, as presented by Malthus himself, was that the best available way to keep population in check was deferment of marriage. Malthus, of course, held that such deferment should, morally speaking, be accompanied by chastity prior to marriage. He frankly admitted, however, that by many men this would not be achieved, but claimed that the sexual promiscuity that would accompany deferred marriage was a lesser evil than the misery and consequent vice which early marriages and the consequent unrestricted growth of population would be likely to result in. Bentham and the two Mills, although with less frankness, chose birth control as the remedy. Malthus opposed this, both as morally inacceptable and because he thought that if the sexual instinct could easily be satisfied without involving procreation there would not be population enough. Like their modern successors almost without exception, most of the critics failed to read Malthus carefully enough. They generally failed to see that the classical economists differed in their choice of remedies between two alternative modes of "prudential restraint," birth control within marriage, and deferred marriage with its inevitably attendant sexual promiscuity, although all of them rejected "moral restraint" as impracticable though ideal. However sincere the horrified rejection by the critics of either birth control within marriage or sexual promiscuity outside marriage, their horror at the spectacle of such proposals being presented for public discussion seems to have been completely genuine.

The nature and range of the hostility to the classical school will perhaps be made clearer if I cite a few specific examples of indignation made vocal. The utilitarianism on which the classical economists rested consisted essentially of the propositions that the merit of an act was to be appraised in terms of its consequences, and that "good" consequences were those that served the actor well without injuring others, while for the legislator the sole criterion for judgment of legislation and institutions should be their consequences for the community in general. To the critics this was an ethics of "expediency," of "calculation," instead of one of subjection to the mandates of conscience or of revealed or long-established or self-evident moral rules. Edmund Burke had in his *Reflections on the French Revolution*, in 1790, already exclaimed: "The age of chivalry is gone. That of sophisters [that is, theorists], economists and calculators has succeeded; and the glory of Europe is extinguished for ever." In the same spirit, Lucy Aikin, the biographer, wrote, in 1830: "There is a pseudo science called political economy which dries up the hearts and imaginations of most who meddle with it . . . [it is] a grovelling thing; and . . . a lofty philosophy would act, I believe, as a counterpoise of great value." And Coleridge: "It is this accursed practice of ever considering *only* what seems *expedient* for the occasion, disjoined from all principle or enlarged systems of action, of never listening to the true and unerring impulses of our better nature, which has led the colder-hearted men to the study of political economy." And Carlyle: "Of all the quacks that ever quacked, political economists are the loudest. Instead of telling us what is meant by one's country, by what causes men are happy, moral, religious, or the contrary, they tell us how flannel jackets are exchanged for pork hams, and speak much of the land last taken into cultivation." "May Heaven in its mercy," prayed the Earl of Stanhope in 1826, "preserve us from all the professors of that pretended science, who are more to be dreaded than the Plagues of Egypt." M. T. Sadler, factory reformer and anti-Malthusian, in 1831 called the economists "the pests of society and the persecutors of the poor." I spare you the equally harsh words with which our intellectual ancestors were greeted by Wordsworth and Southey, later by Thomas Arnold and his son, Matthew Arnold, by Charles Dickens, and Charles Kingsley, by John Ruskin, by Benjamin Jowett, and by many others. All of these were persons of considerable eminence, and even if some of them were, to my mind, given to hysteria at times, or were sentimentalists, romantics, of diverse species, it is surely of some significance that they should have reacted in this way even if it is debatable what that significance was, although as I grow older I become increasingly sensitive to the possibility that there are times when sentimentalism and even hysteria may temporarily be socially useful even though always intellectually reprehensible.

Unsentimental politicians did find in the classical economics much that they could usefully adapt to their purposes, and especially, the removal of the remaining inheritance of obsolete and class-biased restraints on individual initiative. But even then there was complaint of the lack of agreement among the economists, the variability of their positions from year to year, and their lack of realism. Lord John Russell, in 1821, at an early stage of his political career, opened an essay on political economy, with these rather innocent defects of economics in mind, with the sentence, "Political economy is an awful thing." At about the same time Daniel Webster in the United States wrote in a letter that "I give up what is called the 'science of political economy.' . . . If I were to pick out with one hand all the mere truisms, and with the other all the doubtful propositions, little would be left."

The criticism of the classical school was made to turn largely on their methodology, on the way in which they appeared to reach their conclusions and the logical form in which they presented them to the public for acceptance. Were it not for the widespread dislike for the conclusions of the classical economists it would be hard to explain why so much critical interest was shown in their methodology. Some of their more astute and sophisticated critics apparently saw that their methodology was more vulnerable to attack than their conclusions and that by attacking the methodology they could lessen the appeal of the conclusions without opening themselves as much to charges of self-interested partisanship. It is not true of course that a correct conclusion cannot be reached from faulty premises or from faulty manipulation of undisputed premises. But that is the way for a prudent man to bet, and the critics made the most of this principle in their effort to discredit the conclusions and recommendations of the classical economists. Following the lead of the critics, I will concentrate on the character of the premises used by the classical economists, on what led them to make the particular choice of premises to use, and on what the critics had to say about the quality of this choice. Pure theorists tend to concentrate on what the methodological sophisticates call immanent criticism, or the appraisal of the logical rigor and the elegance with which an economist moves from his premises, whatever they may be, to his conclusions. The critics had some objections to make against the classical economics even in this area, but to engage in immanent criticism effectively one must accept at least provisionally one's opponent's premises, and one must be at least as skillful an abstract theorist as he is. For the most part the critics were unwilling to grant even provisionally the validity of the classical school premises, and were unwilling to undergo the effort needed or were lacking in the capacity to acquire sufficient skill to be able to engage in battle with the classical economists on the field of abstract theory, especially as such battle would have to be fought on ground which the classical economists had chosen. The critics therefore relied mainly on transcendental criticism, although most of them would no doubt have been surprised to learn that they were engaged in so esoteric an activity.

The classical economists worked in the main from categorical premises, treated as axiomatic, or as derived from introspection, or from their own general observation of the external world, or from their impression of recorded historical experience. With a few notable exceptions—for example, Ricardo in the field of money, Malthus in his demographic work—they did not check inductively for validity. They also much exaggerated the extent to which serviceable and genuine axioms are available.

The classical economists conceded that theirs was a "hypothetical" science, increasingly so through the years in response to the weight of criticism. They differed, however, as to what they meant by this. They increasingly conceded that they operated on two levels, the level of "science," and the level of "art," or application, and it was often only the latter which they admitted to be "hypothetical," because the necessary validity of its conclusions was dependent on their conformity to unexplored facts, or on the absence of "disturbing factors," or on their consistency with noneconomic norms or values which the statesman must take into consideration but from which they had abstracted in their analysis. The critics maintained, however, that even the "science" or pure theory sector of the classical economics was "hypothetical" since its premises were not genuinely categorical, but were "iffy" or "speculative" or doubtful, or counter to known fact, or insofar as they were normative in character were arbitrary dogma, were "ipsedixitism," which there was no obligation on anyone's part to accept, and which they believed they had valid grounds to reject outright. They further objected that to be able to distinguish, as the classical economists took for granted that they could do, between fundamental causes and disturbing causes, or between permanent and stable causes and occasional and unstable causes, called for a degree of factual information which one could not come by without a degree of systematic effort which the classical economists made no claim to have engaged in, and that the economists wrongly took for granted that because a factor is a "disturbing" one, or less powerful or less stable than the principal ones, it is *ipso facto* permissible to give no consideration to it in policy making.

The critics still further objected, with special reference to the readiness of the classical economists, from a "higher compassion," to tolerate present misery in the interest of the improvement of the condition of the poor in the distant future, that they were giving too little weight to short-run considerations when these differed from long-run ones. The critics insisted that as a moral principle, as well as because of the uncertainties of life, to say nothing of those of economic analysis, it was wrong to put strong reins on compassion for suffering in the here and now.

This is too favorable an account of the quality of the methodological criticism directed against the classical school by its English critics before, say, 1850. It omits the criticisms made on foolish methodological grounds. It undervalues the contribution which good judgment resting on general information can make to the formulation of a usable set of premises even for policy guidance. It presents the criticisms in my terms, which are more sophisticated, or so I hope, than the naïve gropings of many of the critics. But I believe I can document each one of these criticisms as having been made or implied or approximated by at least one critic, and Whewell in particular stated a number of them with clarity and precision. To the best of my knowledge and judgment, they are all legitimate in principle. They are open to rebuttal only by inductive refutation or by demonstration or judgment that they are properly counsels of perfection and cannot be fully lived up to in practice. If due consideration is given to this, the critics were no doubt often guilty of gross exaggeration of the extent to which the classical school violated them. In the course of the controversy the classical school conceded the validity of much of the criticism in principle. In their best methodological statements they incorporated portions of it. But they made no reply to some of it, and too rarely supplied inductive refutation or made any confession of past or continuing sin in their methodological practice. Of their laissez faire recommendations, Arnold Toynbee, the elder, wrote in 1884: "The bitter argument between economists and human beings has ended in the conversion of the economists." This is not exactly how I would word it, but it correctly reports how much of the world saw it.

Later developments in the controversy over method, although closely watched by members of other disciplines, were of little interest to the more general public. There were now fewer extremists inside or outside the profession than earlier, and, as I have already said, a substantial amount of moderation of doctrine on both sides occurred to make possible, if not a happy marriage, a greater willingness to live in neighborliness without pretensions on either side that they could by themselves adequately cover the whole ground of abstract theory, of systematic induction, of application of theory, and of formulation of social policy, and emerge with definitive answers to all the legitimate questions. To Plato's question, "Granted that there are means of reasoning from premises to conclusions, who has the privilege of choosing the premises?" the correct answer, I presume, is that anyone has this privilege who wishes to exercise it, but that everyone else has the privilege of deciding for himself what significance to attach to the conclusions, and that somewhere there lies the responsibility, through the choice of the appropriate premises, to see to it that judgment, information, and perhaps even faith, hope, and charity, wield their due influence on the nature of economic thought. If a professional group regards itself as having a message to deliver to others than its own members and makes any public claims in that respect, it thereby gives others the right to scrutinize the methods whereby that message was discovered, including the principles, or possibly prejudices, followed in choosing premises. The critics, early and late, of the classical school, and of its neoclassical successors, centered their attack on the classical school premises. They continue to do so. Cunningham in 1891 remarked that in their choice of premises "it is not always easy to tell when a professor of the dismal science is making a joke" and I suspect that Cunningham meant that if the professor was not joking, then he was making a fool of himself. More recently a distinguished economic historian, Postan, complained that "the economists, like the theoretical sociologists of old, only more so, tried to solve the largest possible problems from the least possible knowledge." I have no disposition to concede that the economic historians, or for that matter any other social disciplines, have solved their methodological problems even as well as have the neoclassical economists. In my opinion none has in this respect been reasonably successful, none has given sufficient mental effort to the task, and the chances of real progress in this respect would be maximized if they and we and expert methodologists were to attack the problem together.

The classical economists, as I have already mentioned, met the criticism that their premises were too narrow to lead to usable conclusions by drawing a distinction between the "science" and the "art" of economics, and claiming that the criticism was relevant, if at all, for the latter, but was irrelevant for the "scientific" or "pure" aspect of the economist's operation. Senior, with "pure" economics in mind, said that "political economy is not greedy of facts; it is independent of facts," but he also said that on practical problems political economy has not a syllable of advice to give. What in essence Senior was saying was that it was possible to make honest fictions out of what previously, although without benefit of tradition or revelation, had been treated as authoritative dogma. Walter Bagehot, not always given to using kind words in his references to classical economics and its expounders, even remarked once that "no real Englishman in his secret soul was ever sorry for the death of a political economist; he is much more likely to be sorry for his life." On one occasion, however, he came to the rescue of the economists, on the same line as that taken by Senior, by claiming that they no longer presumed to be both scientists and practitioners of an associated art: "Modern economists know their own limitations; they would no more undertake to prescribe for the real world, than a man in green spectacles would undertake to describe the colors of a landscape." Except for the small but important and esteemed group of economists who today live a completely happy life devoted to dalliance with elegant models of comely shape but without vital organs, how many present-day economists are there for whom Bagehot's statement is even approximately true?

With the growth in numbers of the economists from, say, the 1880's on, and the emergence of a variety of kinds of economists, so that no layman needed to be at a loss in finding some school of economics which provided him with professional justification for whatever policies he was attached to, methodological controversy has now largely ceased to be one between economists and the outside public and has become almost wholly a private dispute within our professional ranks, except that our sister disciplines continue to take pleasure in demonstrating that the motes in our eyes are of larger dimensions than the beams in their own. I will therefore confine my further remarks on the methodological issue, except for a later digression on statistics, to the so-called *Methodenstreit*, in the 1880's and later between the economic historians and the economic theorists. My fellow theorists tell me that the theorists won a definitive victory in this battle when Carl Menger, in the 1880's, demolished Gustav Schmoller. I cannot agree. I believe that the battle was mostly a sham one, and that while Schmoller certainly carried off no laurels, the ones that have ever since been bestowed on Menger for his victory in this battle are tinsel ones.

Schmoller denied to economic theory, at least in its then shape, any usefulness. He claimed that the task for the economist, at least for another twenty years or so, was to accumulate historical data, after which would come a stage when the accumulations of factual data, having then presumably reached the critical size, would reveal, to the economist contemplating them, the pattern of the historical and other laws which express the causal relations between social phenomena.

Menger succeeded in exposing to ridicule the notions that disciplined thought could proceed without any recourse to abstraction, and that the mechanical accumulation of data, historical or contemporaneous, could in some spontaneous way contribute to understanding without the aid of selection, classification, and analysis of these facts under the guidance of some kind of theoretical, that is, abstract, reasoning. But Schmoller was not a worth-while target for methodological attack. His own practice was superior to his doctrine; even his close associates regarded his doctrine as too extreme. I have not been able to find any economic historian whose practice was nearly as vulnerable as Schmoller's doctrine. Menger, in his repeated attacks on Schmoller, admittedly made under great provocation, "thrice routed his feeble foe, and thrice slew the slain."

The real challenge which Menger should have faced was not that of justifying in principle recourse to abstraction by economists, but of justifying the particular extent and manner in which he and his fellow theorists practiced it. As justification for the economic theorist's practice, Menger appealed to the theoretical chemist who mentally separates water into pure hydrogen and pure oxygen. Schmoller pointed out that the laboratory chemist was there to take up where the speculative chemist left off. He could have replied also that the speculative chemist had himself taken off from a body of well-authenticated fact, and that between even the laboratory chemist and final application of the analysis there were the pilot plant, and the artificial controls against disturbing factors in the commercial-scale plant itself, which had been installed with the aid of scientific experiment and of trial and error by experts. To Schmoller's reference to the chemical laboratory, Menger replied that Schmoller misunderstood the role of abstraction in economics, which consisted not in random abstraction, but in the separation of the "essential" from the "accidental" causes. Elsewhere he spoke of economic theory as concentrating on the "ruling" causes and of "causes" as distinguished from "conditions." It seems to me that this begs most of the important questions because the real issue here turns on how at the pure-theory stage one can distinguish an "essential" from an "accidental" cause, a "ruling" from a non-ruling cause, a "cause" from a "condition." It is at least a plausible conjecture that successful achievement of these results requires, among other things, a methodical pursuit of factual knowledge with the aid of tools of art whose use calls for special skills with which the pure theorist as such is not endowed by nature and which he must either borrow from other disciplines or acquire by painful effort.

A major one of these tools is, of course, statistical method, and it is one of the major glories of our profession that it has made important contributions to its progress to its present magnificent status. Its first stage, political arithmetic, in the seventeenth century, had William Petty, an economist, as one of its founders.

In the eighteenth century came moral arithmetic, whose link with political arithmetic is not that it makes use of statistical method, but that it also was concerned with measurement of a kind and made use of mathematics of a kind. Francis Hutcheson, Adam Smith's teacher, made an unsuccessful attempt to apply it to psychological entities, but abandoned it when it met with ridicule. Bentham tried to develop a "felicific calculus" by means of it. Much later, Jevons built on Bentham, for the first time, to develop utility theory. Early in the seventeenth century in England there had been a wave of intellectual enthusiasm for measurement, although without any immediate product outside the natural sciences in actual measurement, as far as I know. The term "pantometry" was then coined to signify belief in the possibility of and zeal for extending measurement to all phenomena. The term did not take hold, but it would have fitted very well the fad for measurement in the form of counting, or of statistics as consisting of the computation of aggregates and averages, which in the 1820's on spread like a contagion over Europe and the United States and led to the foundation of a large number of statistical societies. With most of these developments economists in the Smithian tradition had relatively little to do until the advent of Edgeworth and Bowley. Adam Smith had declared in the *Wealth of Nations* that "he had no great faith in political arithmetic" and although some of the classical economists made use of statistical data, they did not discuss statistics as science or art. Since there was, however, some participation by economists in the early statistical societies, and since the compiling of data in statistical form occurred largely in the area of economic data and of closely associated demographic data, a critical outside public which found in the operations of the statistician food both for indignation and for laughter tended to lump statisticians and economists together as a common group of counters and of calculators to be scolded or laughed at as a unit. This was not the first nor the last time that economists have been charged with guilt by association, but one expert on the period has remarked that the only change he could see as the result of the shift of interest from theoretical polemics to statistical fact gathering was a progress "from Humbug to Humdrum." The efforts at quantification were pioneer efforts, pursued with simple and unsophisticated tools, and often premature, and those who were engaged in these efforts were in many cases simple amateurs facing better-educated and more philosophical-minded critics. To indicate the character of the criticism, I will give some specific examples, although I must acknowledge that I have made my selection from the large body of available material partly with a view to its possible entertainment value.

Jonathan Swift, Daniel Defoe, Bernard Mandeville—a formidable team of satirists indeed—had already in the eighteenth century taken their swipes at political arithmetic, for the unreliability of its results and the presumed unmeasurability of some of the data it measured. They discovered early that a fool can be a bigger fool with the aid of mathematics than without. Edmund Burke later, in perfect dead-pan, presented an exercise in political arithmetic, in which he proves that there had been seventy-five times as many persons killed as a result of wars as there were persons alive at the time of writing. He guesses almost at random the number of dead in various wars, adds up these guesses by means of erroneous arithmetic, and then multiplies this sum by 1,000 to allow for possible error. This may be carrying parody of honest and pioneering effort a little too far. But it has been more than matched by a statement made in 1948 by a distinguished Princeton atomic scientist: "The present experiments indicate that the negative mesons are absorbed by atomic nuclei only one billionth as rapidly as calculated by the theoretical physicists. This would be a major error even for an economist."

Later, the travels of the nineteenth-century statisticians and economists to different congresses and annual meetings were a special irritant to some. Section F of the British Association for the Promotion of Science, first called the Statistics Section and later the Economic Science and Statistics Section, was in this respect a popular target. The annual meetings of the Association were held in a different town each year, and they even met in Montreal one year. There was always much publicity and much crowding, but Section F tended to outdraw the other sections both in numbers in the audience and in press publicity, perhaps because the intellectual level of the lectures was closer to that of the general public than when the topic was in the field of astronomy or of physics. In the criticism of the peripatetic character of the meetings, I am not aware that the objection was raised that it was an impious anticipation of the millennium, for Daniel (XII.4) had promised as one of the millennial blessings that: "Many shall [then] go to and fro, and knowledge shall be increased." But a Dean of York protested at his bishop's acting as chairman at one of the Association's meetings, as it was a gathering of "peripatetic philosophers," of no benefit to science and injurious to religion. Charles Dickens published a parody on the meetings of Section F, entitled, "Full Report of the First Meeting of the Mudfog Association for the Advancement of Everything, Section C . . . Statistics," which included an account of a census of the nursery rhyme books read by London children, of an enumeration of the number of chairs in a Yorkshire town which revealed that there were not enough chairs to give every one a seat simultaneously, and of a careful compilation of the extent to which members of Parliament from a particular section of England evaded the property qualifications for such membership, which showed that both the total and the average amount of such qualifying property held by these members equaled £O.s.O.d.O.

Punch, in its first year, 1841, instituted as an annual feature a report of the annual meetings of the London (later Royal) Statistical Society, which satirized the promiscuity, the triviality, and the futility of the statistical compilations presented at these meetings, but unfortunately with a humor heavier than lead. Perhaps in the fear that the widespread ridicule of the Section F meetings would injure the dignity of the other sections, perhaps because, as the statisticians insinuated, the scientists were slightly jealous of the superior drawing power of Section F, but with the stated ground being that the meetings of Section F did not approximate a scientific character closely enough to warrant having a place on the British Association's program, the Association, in 1877, considered abolishing Section F, but after some negotiations with the statisticians abandoned the idea. Section F, I understand, continues to flourish, without any question now being raised about its scientific credentials.

In France, also, there was apparently readiness in some quarters to have fun at the expense of the statisticians. At the Fiftieth Jubilee meeting, in 1885, of the Royal Statistical Society, A. De Foville, a delegate from the corresponding French Society, read a paper on "Statistics and Its Enemies," which I would have been happy, if time permitted, to quote *in extenso*. De Foville gives an account of a character, an illustrious statistician, in a novel by Goudinet (*Panache*), who finds that in his *Département* there were 17¾ married men per square kilometer but only 16½ married women and points to the need, therefore, to marry 1½ men to 2¾ women per square kilometer if things are to be brought into balance. De Foville reports also on another statistician, a character in a novel by Louis Reybaud (*Jerôme Paturot*), who tries to recruit a retired hosier to the profession. The latter hesitates because of his lack of confidence in his ability to carry out statistical computations. The statistician replies: "It's but a bagatelle, my friend. . . . All that is necessary is a little bit of self-confidence. For instance, you announce: 'There have been harvested in Spain 3,500,300,000 and a half sheaves of wheat. Take note of that *half*, it is essential; it is the touchstone of a meticulous calculation. That *half* will capture the respect of your audience.' 'Look,' they will say, 'what exactitude. These experts count to a fraction.' . . . With your half a sheaf of wheat, you have won more convinced hearers than with your three billion."

One's eyebrows rise at the lightness with which De Foville treated his discipline at what presumably was a very solemn occasion. I tremble slightly at the idea of the consequences of a comparable performance at an annual meeting of our own Association. De Foville, moreover, did not stop here. Such stories, he said, do not bother statisticians. "Instead of recognizing himself in these caricatures each of us has available the resource of seeing in them the portrait of his colleagues, and why not then laugh more heartily than anyone else?'' And as if all this were not more than enough, he ended his talk with the comment: ''I add that it may even be possible for us to draw some useful lessons from this banter.'' All things considered, perhaps it was fortunate that De Foville delivered his talk in French.

I should mention two more criticisms of statistics that were occasionally made. The early statisticians regarded their operations as a substitute for, or at least an improvement on, the economic theory approach to the study of economic problems. But Whewell, who criticized classical theory as unduly abstract and as making excessive claims for its conclusions, was not himself antitheoretical in principle or in practice, and at an early stage in the history of statistical societies he urged them to recruit theoretical-minded men and to avoid confining their activities to mere fact gathering and counting. Second, underlying some of the objections to statistics was the fear that the growth in its popularity would lead to an inappropriate application to phenomena for which they had no true relevance of the language if not the substance of measurement and of mathematics. There could not then be foreseen the development of statistics itself into a theoretical discipline and the discovery of ways of making useful servants to economic theory in general not only of statistical theory and of the classical types of mathematics, but also of non-quantitative mathematics, and eventually, perhaps, even of nonmathematical mathematics. What now seems criticisms resting merely on bigotry, or ignorance, or professional jealousy, could then, therefore, have been criticism somewhat justified in the circumstances of the time.

Coleridge's objection, with reference to geometry, of the application of time-concepts and space-concepts to mental phenomena for which he thought they were meaningless, is a case in point.

''There are,'' said Coleridge, ''Acts and forms of Being as alien and heterogeneous to *Time*, as our Thoughts, Affections and Passions are to Space. For example, what should we think of one who said that his Love of his Wife was North West by West of his Passion for Roast Beef?'' For Coleridge as a poet, the finding of similarities between things seemingly totally incomparable with each other and the invention of modes of speech indicating these similarities was a standard trick of the trade. We may imagine, therefore, that it was the treatment as similars of love and roast beef, or perhaps the treatment of love in terms of so prosaic a thing as geometry, which Coleridge found objectionable, rather than the use of geometrical ways of comparing things on the same level of prosaicness. I doubt whether Coleridge would have objected, if he had come across it, to Bobby Burns's assertion that ''love is like a red, red rose.'' Coleridge, in any case, could not have foreseen the development of welfare-indifference-curve technique, for which the comparison in geometrical terms, not only for individuals but for communities as a whole, of, say, a pound of roast beef and an hour of felicitous leisure spent with one's love, where these were alternatives, would be accepted by the expert as neither insuperable nor unintelligible.

I will conclude with some comments on the occasional endeavors made by economists in the nineteenth century and since to increase their effectiveness as guides to the public by organizing themselves into groups or societies which should speak to outsiders with an approach to a single voice. In England, the Political Economy Club of London was founded with the promotion of free trade as one of its objectives, although it deliberately maintained a small membership, kept its meetings private, and almost at once discovered that inside and outside its meetings its members would display no disposition to attain a uniform view on anything. The Manchester School was a frankly partisan group. No economist of any distinction, as far as I know, was among its members, and a number of the leading economists disavowed any connection with it and its extreme laissez faire dogmas. In the great battle in the first decade of the twentieth century over ''Tariff Reform'' the British economists divided publicly and sharply into two groups, and each issued manifestoes to the public, with the prominent theorists on the free-trade side, and a mixture of economic historians and others on the wrong side. I am not aware of any other moves towards the organization of economists on partisan lines in the history of the economics profession in England.

In France, the liberal, free-trade economists throughout most of the nineteenth century had their separate organization and publications and much of the time controlled some of the major teaching posts in Paris. The Liberals, as commonly in Catholic countries, were anti-clerical, while the church authorities and those writing under its discipline were anti-individualistic in principle and also anti-laissez-faire. Catholic moral theologians, moreover, then as now, opposed the separation of economics from ethics and religion. Except for a few recent instances in the United States, I know of no works in ''pure economics'' written under official Catholic auspices, and these American instances present the ''pure'' theory only on a contingent basis, subject before application to policy to correction for any possible lack of conformance to Catholic ethical and religious doctrine. What this means is that ''liberal'' or laissez faire economic doctrine has always had a predominantly bad press in Catholic circles, and that ''Catholic economics'' has throughout the world been presented to the public in a substantially uniform pattern as far as ethical presuppositions and social-policy recommendations are concerned.

In Germany, there was a tendency for ''economic'' organizations, including those in which academic economists participated heavily, to have a unified doctrine with respect to social policies, and some of these associations were affiliated with political parties. With the Prussian military successes after 1860 and the political unification of Germany in 1871, opinion on the part of the economists moved with public opinion in general. The free-trade and liberal organizations shrank in numbers and influence, and the academic economists became increasingly adherents of the nationalist, expansionist, and antidemocratic doctrines dominant in the German ruling classes—a development for which I see no parallel in the economics profession in other countries.

In 1872 was founded, under the sponsorship, among others, of Gustav Schmoller and Adolph Wagner, of the *Verein für Sozialpolitik*, which almost at once became by far the most influential organization of economists in the world. It had its internal divisions with respect to policy, but throughout most of its history it strove to attain a common policy, and for many years it was substantially unified in support of an "ethical" or anti-laissez-faire program of social legislation, of "socialism of the (academic) chair," of protectionism, and of expansionist nationalism. Later in its history it came closer to being a "scientific" or eclectic organization and at the advent of the Nazi regime it had among its membership adherents of almost every school of economic doctrine and almost every political party except outright Marxian socialism. A few of its prominent members embraced Nazism, and Nazi intellectuals discovered in Adolph Wagner, with some but not gross exaggeration, an anticipator of Nazi doctrine with respect to authoritarianism, racialism, militarism, expansionism, and state socialism, and paid due reverence to his memory. The *Verein*, unwilling to submit unconditionally to the stringent terms which the Nazi regime made a condition of its continued existence, in December, 1936, liquidated itself.

Because German economists generally found themselves predominantly in harmony with the reigning political tendencies and their organizations were affiliated with powerful political parties, they never seem to have stood out, as did to a large extent the English classical school and the French liberal economists, as either an isolated intellectual group or a group belonging to a political and social minority. There was no shortage in Germany of public criticism by one more-or-less organized group of economists of another such group, but I have not been able to find any trace of a German literature of protest against economics as such or economists as such.

Americans who went to Germany for their graduate training were prominent among the founders of our Association, and some of these undoubtedly looked upon the *Verein für Sozialpolitik* with its ethical, welfare state, and anti-laissez-faire approach to economics as, in these respects at least, a suitable model for the Economic Association. This led to internal struggle within the Association and to some reluctance to accept membership on the part of a few economists who were strongly in the English classical school tradition. Before long, however, as in the *Verein* itself in Germany, and as in England, doctrinal divisions became less sharp among us, and the Association became what it is today: a professional organization of economists with its sole objectives those of promoting the interests of the profession and the discipline, with no desire of and no machinery for committing the Association to any particular social program or economic doctrine. So may it continue.

I have not said anything about the attitude of the American public to the economics profession. We have had our days of bad press in the past. One cause was our free-trade predilections which did not please some powerful sectors of the population. That many economists should be free-traders was, of course, a provocation to right-thinking men in the days before World War I. Theodore Roosevelt wrote to Henry Cabot Lodge in 1895: "... thank God I am not a free-trader. In this country pernicious indulgence in the doctrine of free-trade seems inevitably to produce fatty degeneration of the moral fibre." Until I read this letter, I had always wondered what was wrong with my moral fiber. Now I know. American business organizations and businessmen trustees and regents of colleges and universities, who in the past have at times acted as if they had played hookey in their school days from the classes on civics, have at times made life somewhat miserable, momentarily at least, for worthy members of our profession, including several of our founding members who were laissez faire with respect to foreign trade, but not laissez faire with respect to trusts, monopolies, the trade-union movement, and pauperism. Some of our views on monetary policy and on progressive taxation have also at times failed to endear us in these circles. The addiction of some of us to that mystery of iniquity, aggravated Keynesianism, has attracted the painful attentions of a group of the more solid-headed alumni of Harvard. It was held against some of the early American economists that they opposed slavery, and against some others that they were not opposed to slavery, moral principle then, as always, and perhaps more so in this country than in others, varying with geography.

"On the whole," however—or, with reliance rather on promiscuous averaging than on promiscuous aggregating, I should perhaps say "on the average"—the American economist has been dealt with fairly by the American public. It has laughed at us at times, because we do not always speak with a single voice and because despite many years of sad experience to the contrary some of us persist in operating as if we can forecast. But these are appropriate objects for moderate laughter. In England, in France, and in other countries in the nineteenth century organized religion mildly chastised certain schools of economics, but in our nineteenth-century America much of the teaching of economics was in the hands of the clergymen, and whether it was laissez faire, or antislavery, or free trade that was in issue, or later, the American version of socialism of the chair and the pulpit, religion and economics each pursued the good life, largely side by side, and sometimes hand in hand. So may it continue.

"And here shall be an end."

10

ADAM SMITH

ADAM SMITH (1723–1790) was born in Kirkcaldy, Fifeshire, a fisheries and mining town near Edinburgh. He was the son, by a second marriage, of Adam Smith, comptroller of the customs at Kirkcaldy, who died early in 1723; his mother, Margaret Douglas, was the daughter of a substantial landowner in Fifeshire. Smith lived with his mother whenever he was in Scotland until her death in 1784; he was her only child, and he remained a bachelor until his death.

Smith received his elementary schooling in Kirkcaldy and entered the University of Glasgow in 1737, graduating with an M.A. in 1740. He then went to Oxford University as a Snell fellow at Balliol College, where he stayed until 1746. Beyond the fact that at Glasgow he was a student of Francis Hutcheson, almost nothing is reliably known about his intellectual experiences either at Glasgow or at Oxford. From 1746 to 1748 he lived with his mother in Kirkcaldy, presumably continuing his studies and awaiting an opening for a career in some remunerative post. Between 1748 and 1751, under the sponsorship of some of the leading intellectuals of Edinburgh, he gave several successful series of public lectures, on rhetoric and belles-lettres, on jurisprudence, and perhaps on other subjects. On the strength of the reputation gained by these lectures, he was elected in 1751 to the professorship of logic at the University of Glasgow. When the chair of moral philosophy became vacant later in the same year, he was elected to that superior post, which he occupied until 1763. In 1759 he published his first book, *The Theory of Moral Sentiments*.

Early in 1764 Smith went to France as tutor of the young duke of Buccleuch, stepson and ward of Charles Townshend. Smith remained in France from early in 1764 until late in 1766, most of the time in Toulouse but for some months in Paris, where he saw a good deal of the leading physiocrats and *philosophes*. He also visited Geneva, where he made the acquaintance of Voltaire. After his return to England in 1766, he was until early in 1767 an adviser to Charles Townshend, then chancellor of the exchequer and working on his fatal plan for taxing the

Reprinted from *The International Encyclopedia of the Social Sciences*, ed. David L. Sills, Vol. 14 (New York: Macmillan and the Free Press, 1968), pp. 322–29.

American colonies; Smith's contribution to this plan, if any, is unknown. Endowed with a generous pension for life from the duke of Buccleuch, Smith returned in 1767 to Kirkcaldy, where he remained until early in 1773, working on *The Wealth of Nations*. From 1773 until early in 1776 he was again in London, completing the book but also advising the government occasionally on economic matters. On March 9, 1776, *The Wealth of Nations* was finally published, and soon thereafter Smith returned once more to Kirkcaldy. Early in 1778, he was appointed a commissioner of customs for Scotland and also a commissioner of the salt duties. These were not sinecure posts, as has often been alleged, but required his presence in Edinburgh for the greater part of each week throughout the year. For the rest of his life, he held these posts and lived in Edinburgh, where he died on July 17, 1790.

Overview of Writings

The Theory of Moral Sentiments and *The Wealth of Nations* were the only full-length books that Smith wrote; however, he kept revising both of them for successive editions, and the additions in the sixth edition of *The Theory of Moral Sentiments*, which was published only a few weeks before his death, were substantial in extent and importance. He contributed three essays to periodicals in 1755 and 1761, and a collection of essays on literary and philosophical subjects was first published posthumously in 1795 ("Essays on Philosophical Subjects" 1963). In 1896 Edwin Cannan edited and published a recently found student's report of Smith's economic lectures as given in 1763 at the University of Glasgow (*Lectures on Justice . . .* 1964). In 1963 John M. Lothian edited and published a student's report on Smith's lectures on rhetoric and belles-lettres at Glasgow in 1762/1763 (*Lectures on Rhetoric . . .* 1963), which he had shortly before purchased at an auction sale in Scotland. W. S. Howell, in an as yet unpublished manuscript, describes these lectures as "an important and original revolutionary document in an important revolution in the history of rhetorical theory," the "revolution" consisting of the substitution for the old rhetoric stemming from Aristotle and Cicero of a new rhetoric based on the new learning of Bacon, Descartes, Locke, and others. At the same auction Lothian also purchased a student's report of Smith's economic lectures at Glasgow. This report, which is now in the possession of the University of Glasgow, is substantially fuller and also, it has been stated, superior in quality to that published by Cannan in 1896. Smith is said to have lectured also at the University of Glasgow on natural theology. Shortly before his death he supervised the burning of almost all of his manuscripts, some 16 folio volumes.

Smith clearly had a wide range of interests. The evidence available suggests that he reached his basic methodological and philosophical principles early in his career and that his destruction of manuscripts before his death was probably motivated much more by dissatisfaction with their form or with their incomplete state than by any fundamental change in his views.

Almost everything Smith wrote, in its methodological implications if not in its concrete subject matter, has some relevance for social thought, but it is expedient here to concentrate on the two books he published during his lifetime. Many writers, including the present author at an early stage of his study of Smith, have found these two works in some measure basically inconsistent. But in much of his writing Smith worked from what he called systems and what today would be called models. He was aware that "systems" are incomplete in the factors they take into account. Had he been able to complete his total system, he would probably have demonstrated that the apparent inconsistencies were often not real ones, but were merely the consequences of deliberate shifts from one partial model to another.

In a letter of November 1, 1785, to a French correspondent, Smith wrote that he had ". . . two other great works upon the anvil; the one is a sort of Philosophical History of all the different branches of Literature, of Philosophy, Poetry and Eloquence; the other is a sort of theory and History of Law and Government. . . . But the indolence of old age, tho' I struggle violently against it, I feel coming fast upon me, and whether I shall ever be able to finish either is extremely uncertain" ([1785] 1896, p. 166). The manuscripts of these two "great works" presumably were among those destroyed shortly before his death.

"THE THEORY OF MORAL SENTIMENTS"

The first thing to note about *The Theory of Moral Sentiments* is its title. It is a "theory" or "system," that is, it consciously and deliberately employs some measure of patterned abstraction and thus does not profess to account for all the relevant facts of the real world. Its primary concern is only with that part of human psychology which is involved in the interrelationships of men living in communities—the "moral sentiments," that is, the passions, propensities, affections, feelings, whether of approbation or of disapproval, aroused by these interrelationships. These sentiments are intermediate, in degree of reflection or "reason" involved, between the basic instincts that man shares with the animals and the calculation or ratiocination of sophisticated man as a reasoning being. When and how and in what degree these sentiments operate Smith discovered through observation of his neighbors, and presumably also, although he apparently never explicitly said so, through disciplined introspection exercised on the assumption that men are substantially alike in their subrational psychology.

To show how the sentiments operate to socialize the individual, to fashion him into a disciplined member of a harmonious social group, Smith introduced into his model the concept of "spectators," distinguishing two main species. There is, first, the spectator external to yourself, the "real" spectator, who, by manifesting in some manner his sentiment of approval or disapproval of your behavior, exercises an influence on you. There is, second, the internal spectator, yourself, operating on two distinct levels: first, your imagination of what the reaction of a hypothetical external spectator would be to your actual or contemplated behavior; second, your own moral judgment, the judgment by your own conscience, by "the man within your breast," by the "impartial spectator." This whole complex mechanism of psychological response by men to their neighbors' feelings of approval or disapproval, which Smith called sympathy, he regarded as the major factor in creating and maintaining a socialized community. It involves, according to Smith, not only the desire to win the praise or approval of others but also the desire to be praiseworthy; when the two desires are in conflict, conscience decrees that the latter shall prevail.

Commentators have objected that Smith here described a circular process, operating through sympathy like a set of "mirrors," and that he failed to explain adequately either what behavior is approved and what is disapproved or the origin or genesis of the social passions. Yet, at least by implication, Smith did offer such an explanation. He emphatically rejected human reason as the source of these sentiments. Also by implication he denied that there is a natural evolutionary process in which groups with a pattern of sentiments that is predominantly useful survive, whereas those groups with a pattern of antisocial sentiments perish. Smith maintained that man is endowed by God with his moral sentiments and that these sentiments bind men to each other because the deity so made them in its concern for the happiness of mankind. Smith ridiculed those who attributed to man's wisdom what is really the wisdom of God, or of nature. Here Smith was, of course, invoking "final causes," or "the invisible hand."

It is hard for some people today to believe that Smith's optimistic deism was completely sincere, and they tend to attribute his exposition of it to prudential considerations or to concessions to a mode of speech called for by the standards of propriety of the time. But in the "enlightened" Scottish circles of Smith's time optimistic deism, sincerely held, was practically universal. Although orthodox Calvinists rejected its optimistic aspect as not religious enough and David Hume rejected it as calling for too much religious faith, aside from Hume, no one among Smith's teachers, colleagues, friends, or followers is identifiable as a critic of optimistic deism.

There may be genuine difficulty in reconciling Smith's deistic interpretation of the origin of the moral sentiments with other aspects of his social thought, including some of his specifically economic thought. Smith attributed to providence the original endowment of mankind with a set of moral sentiments conducive to the happiness of mankind. But unless he also assumed that providence intervenes constantly or intermittently to make appropriate adjustments in these sentiments as the physical or human environment changes through time (for which belief there is no evidence in anything he wrote), Smith would seem to have been postulating a static social psychology, at least on the subrational level, in what he himself admitted to be in many relevant respects a constantly changing and evolving world. Smith did recognize the impact of the variability of custom and fashion on the mode of operation of the moral sentiments, but, in spite of this variability, he specifically recognized only one major historical affront to the system of moral sentiments—the prevalence of infant exposure in the later period of ancient Greek civilization. He disposed of this exception as a temporary aberration, outweighed by the many outstanding virtues of Greek civilization at the time. Nowhere did he attempt to explain how antisocial passions and aberrations in conflict with the "Author of Nature's" design came into existence. But in keeping with the notion then held by some scientists that there is in nature a self-equilibrating mechanism by which aberrations are prevented from prevailing, a notion having some analogy to the modern scientific notion of "homeostasis," Smith held that there is an inherent tendency in the moral sentiments to overcome such aberrations.

Smith's treatment of "justice" in *The Theory of Moral Sentiments* is especially important for a proper interpretation of *The Wealth of Nations*. Smith always used the word to mean substantially what Aristotle and the Schoolmen meant by "commutative justice." Justice is a negative virtue; it consists of refraining from injury to another person and from taking or withholding from another what belongs to him. It is thus distinct from benevolence, friendship, or charity. Smith considered justice, so understood, to be the necessary foundation of a viable society. It is a moral sentiment and thus finds voluntary or natural expression. The natural or spontaneous sentiment of justice is not, however, strong enough in ordinary men to meet the needs of society. Consequently, men have been endowed with the propensity to formulate rules of justice on the basis of their experience and reason, and they accept these rules for themselves and press them upon others. But even this is inadequate for the needs of society, and therefore government is established, its chief function being the coercive enforcement of justice on the individual members of the community through law and the magistrates.

The moral sentiments operate at different levels of intensity according to the nature and the strength of the external stimuli impinging upon men. Smith's discussion here closely parallels Hume's discussion in *A Treatise of Human Nature* (1739–1740, book 2, part 2, especially sec. 4) and elsewhere: in describing the way in which the strength of the "passions" between individuals varies with the closeness of their relationship with respect to duration, space, kinship, nationality, occupation, rank, and so forth, Hume repeatedly used the term "distance" metaphorically to signify any factors separating individuals from each other, a usage that goes back at least to Aristotle and Thomas Aquinas. Although Smith stressed distance in its primary spatial sense as an important factor in weakening the intensity of the moral sentiments—"To what purpose should we trouble ourselves about the world in the moon? All men, even those at the greatest distance, are not doubt entitled to our good wishes, and our good wishes we naturally give them. But if, notwithstanding, they should be unfortunate, to give ourselves any anxiety upon that account seems to be no part of our duty" ([1759] 1966, p. 197)—he also used the same idea, if not the actual term "distance," for the absence not only of spatial proximity but also of membership in the same family, village, town, province, country, circle of friends, guild or company, church, social class, or some other psychologically unifying bond. In similar manner he took it for granted that the participants in a large number of the transactions which occur in the market are (in the metaphorical sense) at an extreme distance from each other; they are, in relation to each other, anonymous, or strangers, so that there is limited occasion for any moral sentiments other than justice to come into operation.

In *The Theory of Moral Sentiments*, Smith minimized the contribution that even the highly successful pursuit of wealth or of higher social status makes to the happiness of an individual. Both in this work and in *The Wealth of Nations* Smith treated increase in *aggregate* wealth as a highly worthy objective for a country, but apparently in only one passage in either work is increase in *per capita* wealth or income expressly mentioned as a reason for the advantage of an increase in aggregate wealth. Smith attached little importance to an increase above a quite modest level of *per capita* income, but he attributed great value to the increase of population that an increase in aggregate wealth fosters and supports. With his optimistic view of the amount of happiness ordinarily enjoyed even by the poor, Smith believed that growth of population is ordinarily conducive to growth in the aggregate amount of human happiness. He also found value in increase of aggregate wealth because it makes possible an increase in handsome buildings and great avenues in the towns, the "magnificence" so extolled by the writers of classical antiquity and of the Renaissance, but he treated these as public rather than individual riches. Smith also included as an advantage of growth of aggregate wealth the progress of aesthetic and intellectual culture and of "civilization" in general, which he associated with communal enrichment.

"THE WEALTH OF NATIONS"

The Wealth of Nations is of great importance for three main reasons. First, it presents an impressive collection of economic data, gathered together by Smith from wide reading in publications from the time of the ancient Greeks and Romans to his own time and from acute observation of Britian and France in his own time. Smith used this material to illustrate and support his analysis of contemporary economic process, to provide a factual basis for his frequent ventures into the philosophy or theory of economic development, and at times to digress into narrative history presented without any clear relationship to his theoretical endeavors. *The Wealth of Nations* was heavily drawn on as a reliable source book for factual data by several generations of writers on economic matters, especially, of course, in the English-speaking countries. It is still useful for this purpose.

Second, it was the most comprehensive and ambitious attempt up to Smith's time to present in comprehensive, and at the same time coordinated, fashion the nature of economic process in a predominantly "individualistic," or "competitive," or "market," or "capitalistic" society, to use modern adjectives. For a long time it largely determined the selection of issues and the initial analytical approach of economists in many countries, even when in their treatment of *The Wealth of Nations* they were much more critics than disciples.

Third, it was an evaluating and crusading book, which sharply criticized existing society and government and argued strongly for changes in national policy, especially in relation to the extent and nature of government intervention in economic matters—domestic, colonial, and international. Not immediately, but within a generation, it became a powerful influence on writers on economic policy. Later still, both directly and indirectly through those influenced by it, it became a significant factor in determining the course of national policy not only in Britain but in other countries as well. This is much more than any other economic work has ever achieved; and Smith probably has had much more influence than any other economist.

Economic Development

Smith was deeply interested in the history, the causes, and the natural and artificial limitations of what we now commonly call "economic development" and what he referred to as "progress," "improvement," "progress of improvement," and "progress of opulence." His treatment of economic development is scattered throughout almost the whole work. He put most stress on the following factors as favorable to economic development: abundance of natural resources; technological progress as promoted by extension of division of labor; freedom of private enterprise from its own propensity to monopolistic organization; freedom from such hurtful artificial institutions as primogeniture; and freedom from official policies and practices that act as brakes on individual initiative or misdirect it. The basic source of economic progress, however, he found in the striving of individuals to improve their economic status or their rank in society—". . . the desire of bettering our condition, a desire which . . . comes with us from the womb, and never leaves us till we go into the grave" ([1776] 1950, p. 323). He did not believe that this desire does or should operate without restraint. It is disciplined by the sentiment of justice and by governmental enforcement of justice. It has to compete, beneficially or otherwise, with "the passion for present enjoyment," which acts as a restraint on accumulation; with indolence; with the occasional "liberality" of employers to their workmen and of landlords to their tenants; and with "the pride of man [which] makes him love to domineer," so that a plantation owner may prefer the service of slaves to that of freemen even where the latter would be more profitable. All of these are factors that are present in a different degree in different orders of society and in different circumstances. Smith, moreover, saw the desire for individual enrichment and the desire to preserve or improve one's social status as occasionally coming into conflict, as, for instance, when one's rank calls for profuse expenditure but the preservation or augmentation of one's estate calls for frugality.

Smith placed great emphasis on the division of labor as a requisite of economic development; he also stressed the interrelations of the division of labor with technology and with commerce. He found a subrational or nonutilitarian origin for the resort to specialization (although not for its intensification) in a "propensity to truck and barter" innate in mankind. Here, following certain predecessors, he identified three contributions that the division of labor makes to productivity: by permitting indefinite repetition of simple tasks, it promotes dexterity; it eliminates the loss of working time involved in changing from one task to another; it facilitates invention of machinery, both by the artisans on the job and by outside observers. Smith stated that extension of the division of labor makes more capital necessary and therefore makes frugality and accumulation economic virtues. He always minimized the differences of innate ability or aptitude between different persons and thus gave little or no weight to the advantage claimed for specialization by a continuous chain of writers from ancient Greece on—that it makes possible the assignment of workers to those tasks for which they have the greatest aptitude. Smith pointed out that the division of labor is limited by the extent of the market and that growth of population both constitutes an extension of the market and is made possible by the increase of aggregate production that results from an extension of the division of labor. Growth of population, growth of aggregate wealth and income and extension of the division of labor are thus explained as mutually dependent and mutually supporting factors.

Smith recognized, under the influence of Rousseau, that the division of labor has a drawback from a humanitarian point of view: the worker as a person tends to be degraded by the monotony of his work and the enlistment of only a narrow range of his mental faculties. Smith though, however, that this predicament could be remedied by education. This is one of the reasons that Smith accepted as a desirable function of government the financing, at public expense, of elementary education for the children of the poor. Smith's discussion was cited by Karl Marx in his presentation of the thesis that a degradation or "alienation" of labor is a consequence of division of labor; but Marx was unaware of the prior treatment of the subject by Rousseau to which Smith was indebted.

Smith's belief that the tendency to aggregate improvement is "natural," i.e., essentially the product of man's basic psychology, may have been a factor contributing to his skepticism about the possibility that government may make major positive contributions to economic development. While he charged government in general with operating as a brake on economic progress, Smith nevertheless remained an optimist. In man's zeal to better his condition, the "wisdom of nature" had provided a counterforce to mistaken government policies and practices that was sufficiently powerful to make possible, in most cases, a thriving and prospering economy.

Smith's Eclecticism

It is a common error to interpret *The Wealth of Nations* as an unqualified eulogy of private enterprise and the businessman. It was only private enterprise operating in a fully competitive manner that Smith praised. He depicted businessmen in general as having a constant propensity to organize themselves into groups capable of exercising "monopoly" power, groups to which he undiscriminatingly attributed the capacity and, by implication, the will to exact the highest price at which any sales can be made. He also charged businessmen with major responsibility for persuading or pressing government to establish special privileges and legal monopolies for favored groups. Where monopoly is unavoidable, he preferred government to private operation. He had only deep and violently phrased scorn for the morals of businessmen organized in groups either to operate as monopolists or to obtain special privileges from government. *The Wealth of Nations* does lavish praise on the businessman, but only when he is on his good behavior.

Smith's main merits as an "analytical" or "scientific" theorist, to use modern eulogistic terms for "pure" economic theory, lie in his eclectic spirit. While deliberately resorting to abstraction, he very much doubted that abstraction could provide either understanding of the real world or, by itself, safe guidance for the legislator or statesman. On specific points of economic analysis some predecessors did better than Smith, and he failed to absorb fully some of the genuinely valuable analytical contributions of Hume, the physiocrats, and Turgot. If "analytical" as a eulogistic term is to be interpreted strictly in terms of degree of rigor, internal consistency, and close analogy to abstract mathematical operations, Schumpeter's verdict that "the *Wealth of Nations* does not contain a single *analytic* idea, principle, or method that was entirely new in 1776" (Schumpeter 1954, p. 184) is difficult to challenge, and not merely because valuable ideas that are "entirely new" are hard to spot in any area of intellectual endeavor.

In both his major works Smith repeatedly amended his system, bringing into his discussion some hitherto neglected variable, some fresh observation of fact, some new objective. He has been rightly charged by critics with resorting profusely to such qualifications as "perhaps," "generally," and "in most cases," with the consequence that his models are not tight or rigorous. It is arguable, however, by those who, if forced to choose, prefer realism, or at least the pursuit of it, to rigor and elegance of analysis, that both of his major works are on the whole made better by the qualifications he sprinkled in their pages and that he would have made them still better, although still untidier, if he had used even more qualifying adjectives or phrases. He would at least have made it harder for later critics to use short quotations, out of context or stripped of their qualifications, to show his inability to avoid flagrant self-contradiction.

The question of the relation of relative labor input to exchange value is one instance where Smith appears repeatedly to have shifted from one belief to another; however, it may be that actually he was only shifting from one abstraction to another, while decorating his exposition (in a manner common then and not unknown now) with traditional maxims exalting the role of labor—maxims whose familiarity alone made them seem to carry logical or empirical weight.

Smith can be quoted in support of all of the following propositions: that labor is the sole "source" of market value; that labor is the sole regulator of exchange value; that labor has, among the elements entering into production, a peculiar and perhaps even an exclusive value-creating power; that the relative values of different commodities are, or should be, proportional to their labor-time costs or to their wage costs; that all incomes are extracted from the product of labor. For some economists any one of these propositions suffices to label its exponent a "labor theory of value" theorist. It seems safer, nevertheless, not to attribute to Smith much more than the belief that in commercial or capitalist economies relative labor-time costs per unit of product have a large part in the determination of the exchange values of different commodities, and relative wage-costs even more.

Economic Policy

The separation of normative from non-normative, or policy, economics was a late development in the history of economics, and even today it is hard to fully execute this separation because many of the standard terms used in economic analysis carry with them an almost automatic normative or evaluative implication: for example, "productive," "utility," "value," "equilibrium." Prior to Smith's time it was rare for any writer to attempt to distinguish between, on the one hand, the study of economics in the purely "scientific" sense of the pursuit of understanding for its own sake, and, on the other hand, the use of economic analysis as an instrument for the formulation or evaluation of national economic policy. (Richard Cantillon was one of the few who did make this distinction.)

When Smith wrote *The Wealth of Nations* the term "political economy" was already in wide use. It was used with some ambiguity, but predominantly with emphasis on "political," indicating reference to national policy. The term "economics" was rarely used by itself except in its original Greek meaning of household management. When Smith chose as the title of his book *An Inquiry Into the Nature and Causes of the Wealth of Nations* instead of something like "Principles of Political Economy," it may be surmised that he did so because he thought of his book as including both an objective study of processes and causes, such as would be the subject matter of a treatise on physics or physiology, and a discussion of "political economy" proper, or an evaluative or hortatory treatment of governmental economic policy. Smith used the term "political economy" a dozen or so times, and every time, except perhaps once, he meant the economic policy of a nation. Since Smith generally took a dim view of the benefits to be derived from national economic policy, political economy must for him have been nearly synonymous with "economic poison."

Smith, of course, was not an exponent of philosophical anarchism, which apparently had nowhere been systematically expounded before William Godwin's *Enquiry Concerning Political Justice* (1793). If Smith had adopted the term "laissez-faire" as an appropriate label for his own policy views, he undoubtedly would not have interpreted it literally as a condemnation of all government interference with the activities of private individuals. He was as emphatic as he could be on the vital need for government enforcement of justice, and there is evidence in *The Wealth of Nations* that he would have included in this function not only the formulation of rules of justice and the provision of machinery for the punishment of their infraction, but also the prevention of certain infractions by such enactments as standardization of weights and measures, requirements that commodities offered for sale be so stamped as to indicate their quality, and the establishment of building standards that would hinder individuals from subjecting others to the risk of fire or to other hazards to their property or their personal safety. Smith assigned to government the care of the defense of the community against foreign aggression or internal disorder and the levy of taxes to finance these activities. He also conceded to government the provision of those services needed by the community which could not practically be entrusted to private enterprise, because of the scale on which they had to be carried out or for other special reasons. On at least two issues—a "standing" or professional army versus a militia and the autonomy of the East India Company—Smith expressed a strong preference for governmental control in addition to or instead of private management. In general, where monopoly was unavoidable, he much preferred that it be under public rather than private control.

Nevertheless, it is as an exponent of free enterprise; free trade; noninterference of government in the individual's choice of occupation, residence, or investment; freedom for the individual to make his economic decisions of all kinds in response to the price movements of free and fully competitive markets—in short, of "economic liberalism" or "laissez-faire," as these terms were used in the nineteenth century—that Smith made his chief mark on the history of economics and on the economic and social history of the Western world.

These economic freedoms were to Smith "natural rights," essential constituents of the dignity of man. He also valued them from a utilitarian point of view, as giving maximum scope for incentives to industry and to efficiency. In the international sphere he saw in them the most solid factors working to bring peace between nations. Modern economists find Smith's arguments oversimplified and perhaps also too emotional and one-sided. But many of them still acknowledge a strong influence of his writings on their system of values and gladly continue to do homage to his name.

REFERENCES

WORKS BY SMITH

(1759) 1966 *The Theory of Moral Sentiments*. New York: Kelley.

(1776) 1950 *An Inquiry Into the Nature and Causes of the Wealth of Nations*. Edited by Edwin Cannan. London: Methuen. A two-volume paperback edition was published in 1963 by Irwin.

(1785) 1896 [Letter to the Duc de la Rochefoucauld.] *Economic Journal* 6:165–166.

Essays on Philosophical Subjects. Volume 5, pages 49–399 in Adam Smith, *The Works of Adam Smith*. Aalen (Netherlands): Zeller, 1963.

Lectures on Justice, Police, Revenue and Arms, Delivered in the University of Glasgow . . . Reported by a Student in 1763. Edited by Edwin Cannan. New York: Kelley, 1964. The Cannan edition was first published in 1896.

Lectures on Rhetoric and Belles Lettres, Delivered in the University of Glasgow . . . Reported by a Student in 1762–63. Edited by John M. Lothian. London and New York: Nelson, 1963.

The Works of Adam Smith. 5 vols. Aalen (Netherlands): Zeller, 1963.

SUPPLEMENTARY BIBLIOGRAPHY

Adam Smith, 1776–1926: Lectures. 1928 Univ. of Chicago Press. Contains lectures by John Maurice Clark and others to commemorate the sesquicentennial of the publication of *The Wealth of Nations*.

Bittermann, Henry J. 1940 Adam Smith's Empiricism and the Law of Nature. *Journal of Political Economy* 48:487–520, 703–734.

Bonar, James (1894) 1932 *A Catalogue of the Library of Adam Smith*. 2d ed. London: Macmillan.

Godwin, William (1793) 1946 *Enquiry Concerning Political Justice and Its Influence on Morals and Happiness*. 3d ed., rev. 3 vols. Univ. of Toronto Press.

Harvard University, Graduate School of Business Administration, Baker Library, Kress Library of Business and Economics 1939 *The Vanderblue Memorial Collection of Smithiana*. Boston, Mass.: The Library.

Hume, David (1739–1740) 1958 *A Treatise of Human Nature*. Edited by L. A. Selby-Bigge. Oxford: Clarendon. Reprinted from the original edition and edited with an analytical index.

Macfie, A. L. 1959 Adam Smith's *Moral Sentiments* as Foundation for His *Wealth of Nations*. *Oxford Economic Papers* New Series 11:209–228.

Macfie, A. L. 1961 Adam Smith's *Theory of Moral Sentiments*. *Scottish Journal of Political Economy* 8:12–27.

Rae, John (1895) 1965 *Life of Adam Smith*. With an introduction and guide by Jacob Viner. New York: Kelley.

Rosenberg, Nathan 1965 Adam Smith on the Division of Labour: Two Views or One? *Economica* New Series 32:127–139.

Schumpeter, Joseph A. (1954) 1960 *History of Economic Analysis*. Edited by E. B. Schumpeter. New York: Oxford Univ. Press.

Scott, William R. 1937 *Adam Smith as Student and Professor*. Glasgow: Jackson.

Spengler, Joseph J. 1959 Adam Smith's Theory of Economic Growth. *Southern Economic Journal* 25:397–415; 26:1–12.

11

MERCANTILIST THOUGHT

"MERCANTILISM" IS THE LABEL commonly given today to the doctrine and practices of nation-states in the period roughly from the fifteenth to the eighteenth centuries with respect to the nature and the appropriate regulation of international economic relations. In this doctrine great emphasis is put on the importance of maintaining an excess of exports of goods and services over imports as the sole means whereby a country without gold or silver mines can obtain a continuous net inflow of the precious metals, regarded as essential to national wealth and strength. In the eighteenth century the elder Mirabeau and Adam Smith applied to this doctrine the terms "mercantile system" and "commercial system" to emphasize its contrast with the doctrine of the physiocrats, which minimized the importance of foreign trade and put its emphasis instead on the importance of agricultural production. In the 1860s German writers introduced the term *Merkantilismus*; corresponding terms, such as "mercantilism" in English, thereafter gradually became standard in all the languages of the Western world. The term is sometimes objected to because it is often used in a pejorative sense, or because it is held, justly, that although often so used, it inadequately represents the varied content of the economic thought of some four centuries. Similar objections can, of course, be made against most general abstract terms ending in "ism," but it does not seem possible to do without them and it does seem possible to use them with disciplined restraint. In this article an attempt is made to limit the application of the term to the special and dominant aspects of thought and practice with respect to international economic relations during the fifteenth to eighteenth centuries.

THE DOCTRINE

The essentials of the doctrine can be summarized in terms of five propositions or attitudes: (1) policy should be framed and executed in strictly nationalistic

Reprinted from *The International Encyclopedia of the Social Sciences*, ed. David L. Sills, Vol. 4 (New York: Macmillan and the Free Press, 1968), pp. 435–43.

terms, that is, national advantage alone is to be given weight; (2) in appraising any relevant element of national policy or of foreign trade, great weight is always to be put on its effect, direct or indirect, on the national stock of the precious metals; (3) in the absence of domestic gold or silver mines, a primary national goal should be the attainment of as large an excess of exports over imports as is practicable, as the sole means whereby the national stock of the precious metals can be augmented; (4) a balance of trade "in favor" of one's country is to be sought through direct promotion by the authorities of exports and restriction of imports or by other measures which will operate indirectly in these directions; (5) economic foreign policy and political foreign policy are to be pursued with constant attention to both plenty and "power" (including security under this latter term) as coordinate and generally mutually supporting national objectives, each capable of being used as a means to the attainment of the other.

This constituted the solid core of mercantilist doctrine, from which there was little dissent before the 1750s by writers on economic matters, but it left room for extensive debate within the ranks of adherents of the doctrine. There could be major differences in the reasoning presented for adherence to the respective propositions here listed, and there could be sharp differences of opinion as to the choice of means by which the accepted objectives could best be pursued.

Mercantilism was essentially a folk doctrine, evolved in the light of the prevailing historical circumstances and values by simple inference from the apparent facts. It was a doctrine of practical men not given to subtle economic analysis, which was in fact sparsely available in the age of mercantilism. The philosophers before the 1750s, the theologians, and the universities neither challenged it nor made any important contributions to it. It was not an area in which disciplined scholarship showed any deep interest.

DIFFERENCES WITHIN THE DOCTRINE

The most striking difference of doctrine within the ranks of the mercantilists turned on why the indefinite accumulation of the precious metals should be regarded as an important national objective. The terms "wealth," "treasure," and "riches" were used with considerable ambiguity, sometimes in a broad sense to cover stocks of valuable goods of any kind which could command a price, but more often in a narrow sense to signify only the precious metals. The narrow usage was occasionally extended to commodities (other than the precious metals) which had great durability and high value per unit of bulk, such as precious stones and even tin and copper. The emphasis with respect to enrichment, to economic improvement, was never in terms of the level of consumption, and when it was in terms of the level of production or output, it was usually with reference to the contribution such production could make, directly or indirectly, to the acquisition and retention of "wealth" or "riches" or "treasure" in the narrow sense. It was on *accumulation* that the emphasis was put, and there was a widespread assumption, tacit or explicit, on the part of the mercantilist writers of the period that accumulation over long stretches of time could be achieved only or predominantly by the piling up of stocks of durable and high-value-per-unit commodities, especially of the precious metals. Often the only link with consumption as an economic objective was the recognition of their ready convertibility through exchange into essential consumers' goods as a reason why a limited number of specified durable goods were to be regarded as pre-eminently constituting items of national "wealth" or "riches."

The emphasis on the "store-of-wealth" function of the precious metals competed, however, with the emphasis of other mercantilist writers on the "circulation" function of the precious metals in their role as money, an emphasis which led to hostility to the use of the precious metals as hoards or in plate and jewelry. These writers believed that production and employment varied in physical volume in close proportion with the variations in the amount of money in circulation. They thus overlooked or denied that the main consequence of an increase in the amount of money might be a general rise of prices; they perhaps were taking for granted that there normally existed large amounts of unemployed labor and natural resources. At least for the later mercantilists emphasis tended to shift from the store-of-wealth to the circulation function of the precious metals. But when paper money was introduced, it became more difficult to reconcile emphasis on circulation with continuing stress on the importance of the precious metals and on a favorable balance of trade as the means of acquiring them.

One method used was to deny the advantages of paper money, or to support limitations on the issue of paper money which would prevent it from acting as a stimulus to the export and a deterrent to the import of the precious metals. But as long as the emphasis continued to be on the circulation function of the precious metals, the absence of any obvious answer to the question why paper money could not perform this function adequately and more cheaply tended to lead either to a return to the older emphasis on the store-of-wealth function of the precious metals or to the substitution—for stress on the monetary and balance-of-trade aspects of mercantilism—either of protectionist ideas resting in large part on non-mercantilist arguments or a new receptivity toward free trade ideas.

An additional and widely expounded ground for emphasis on the desirability of indefinite national accumulation of the precious metals was based on the observation that the rate of interest and the availability of credit varied with the quantity of money, the former in the inverse direction and the latter in the same direction. It was argued that cheapness and abundance of credit would promote enterprise, employment, and production and would increase the ability to compete in foreign trade by lowering the interest element in the costs of production of domestic goods. Before the 1750s no one appears expressly to have pointed out that a given increase in the national stock of money, to the extent that it caused a rise in the price level, would either leave the rate of interest unchanged or cause it to rise rather than to fall and would leave unchanged the real availability of credit, as distinguished from its amount measured in monetary terms. With the advent of paper money, moreover, it was no longer necessary to have a net inflow of precious metals from abroad in order to have an increase in the national stock of money.

Writers who saw an inflow of the precious metals as increasing the rate of employment of human and other productive resources presumably perceived that this would result in increased consumption on the part of the owners of these resources. There was also widespread—but by no means universal—acceptance of the general desirability of an increase in the population and the number of potential workers and no doubt a recognition that such an increase would involve increased consumption. But the emphasis on increased production was made to rest much more on the contribution it could make to a favorable balance of trade, on the support it could give to an increase in population, and on its role in alleviating the moral and other evils of involuntary unemployment, of vagrancy, and of pauperism than on an acceptance in principle of the desirability of a higher level of per capita consumption for the general public. "Luxury" expenditures, for example, on the part of the working classes were almost universally deprecated, and even for the well-off were much more often disapproved than approved, except as they were believed to be necessary means to the employment of otherwise idle resources or to the maintenance of appropriate status and dignity for the upper classes. Increase in production was sought primarily for the contribution it could make to the accumulation of wealth in the form of durable, valuable commodities, at least if one judges by what the writers of the period expressly said.

IMPLEMENTATION

In the early stages of mercantilism it was often the practice to seek the general objectives by more or less direct and particular regulation of the details of individual commercial transactions involving trade with foreigners. Thus, in England there was for a time regulation by the Royal Exchanger of foreign exchange trans-actions and by other official agencies of transactions in commodity markets, so as to make sure that *each* individual transaction should as far as possible make a net contribution to the national stock of the precious metals. Later commentators on mercantilism labeled such practices as "bullionism" or "balance-of-(individ-ual)-bargain system." It was believed that attention should be given not only to the aggregate balance of trade but also the separate balances in the trade with particular countries or in particular sectors of commercial activity. There was considerable suspicion, for instance, that the trade with the East Indies was for all of Europe a "losing" trade involving a chronic drain of the precious metals to the East. Thomas Mun first formulated a persuasive defense of the English trade with the East Indies even if it did involve, in its first effect, a net drain from England of the precious metals. This drain, he claimed, was not an ultimate one, since by re-export at higher prices of its imports of Indian commodities, England more than regained the precious metals which had initially been sent to India. Mercantilist literature, however, long continued to support discrimination be-tween countries in the regulation of imports according to the usual state of the trade balances with such countries, or as an incident to tariff bargaining, or as an instrument of power politics.

The mercantilists gave priority status with respect to eligibility for export to goods with a high labor content in relation to their value. Export of manufactures was favored over export of agricultural products ready for consumption; exports of raw materials such as raw wool, or minerals, was regarded as injurious or wasteful. The export of machines and tools and the emigration of skilled workers were regarded as specially injurious. Underlying these positions were the beliefs that labor was in such abundant supply that it was permissible to treat it as nearly equivalent nationally to a free good, and that restriction of export of raw materials or of machines would not substantially diminish their domestic rate of production and would result in their retention for domestic processing or use. Such restric-tions would thus work to make the balance of trade favorable and to increase domestic employment.

The general mercantilist position was that imports of goods and services were in principle desirable only if (*a*) they were essentials which could not be pro-duced, at whatever cost, at home, or (*b*) they were raw materials which could not be produced at home in the needed quantities except by the withdrawal of scarce resources from the production for domestic use or for export of goods with a higher labor content in proportion to their value, or (*c*) they needed to be imported as a *quid pro quo* for other countries' allowing their nationals to import from the country in question. The implicit mercantilist ideal was zero import, and export only in exchange for the precious metals. In France, Colbert and others gave this ideal express formulation in replying to objections raised by Frenchmen that the severity of French import restrictions would result in other countries' prohibiting entry of French products. Colbert claims that France alone had the potentiality to produce at home the whole range of commodities essential to national prosperity, whereas none of its neighbors could dispense with France's commodities.

A variant of mercantilist doctrine, expounded mostly but not exclusively by English writers, substituted for a favorable balance of trade in terms of monetary values a "balance of labor" in terms of the relative labor content of the exports and the imports—with an aggregate excess of the labor content in the exports over that in the imports treated as "favorable." This has been regarded by some modern commentators as a "refinement" or improvement of the balance of trade doctrine. It would, however, be easily possible for a given trade situation highly unfavorable by trade balance criterion to be highly favorable by the balance of labor criterion, and vice versa. Under the balance of labor criterion, moreover, the fewer units of import commodities obtained on the average per unit of export commodity, other things being equal, the more "favorable" would be the balance of labor.

Political Objectives

Mercantilism had political as well as strictly economic objectives in view. The *minimum* objectives were an even balance of trade and an even balance of power. But as large an excess of exports over imports as possible was an aspiration of all countries, and the great powers sought more than an even balance of power. They sought enough superiority of power to "give the law" to other countries, to enable conquest of adjoining territory or overseas colonies, or to defeat their enemies in war. It was general doctrine that strength was necessary as a means of protecting wealth and of augmenting it, while wealth was a strategic resource, necessary to produce strength and to support its exercise. With wealth one could finance and equip armies and navies, hire foreign mercenaries, bribe potential enemies, and subsidize allies. Power could be exercised to acquire colonies, to win access to new markets and to shut foreigners out of one's own markets, and to monopolize trade routes, high-seas fisheries, and the slave trade with Africa. "Power" was clearly and obviously a relative matter; what mattered was the ratio of power, not the terms of the ratio. It was also true of power that geography had great importance in determining what comparisons were relevant; landlocked countries had little occasion to concern themselves with their power relative to a distant maritime power, and being a neighbor to a strong country could mean being under constant threat. It was also a distinctive feature of political relations that comparisons of strength were relevant not only between pairs of countries but also between groups of actual or potential allies. The emphasis on international comparisons, on ratios, which was highly relevant in the political sphere in a world of power politics, whether the power was expected to serve national aggression or national security, was often carried over to the economic sphere, where it had little relevance. It could and did lead to gross confusion about the nature and significance of national wealth and national economic well-being.

When great emphasis was placed, in the economic sphere, as it logically was in the sphere of power rivalries, on an inherent conflict of interests, this had grave consequences both for economic policy and for international politics. If it was relative status that solely or mainly mattered, economic damage to a rival country could logically be treated as equivalent to economic benefit to one's own country, and famine abroad, to bountiful harvests at home. Such reasoning abounds in the mercantilist literature, and it was moral or sentimental revulsion against it more than superior economic analysis which brought much of the late eighteenth-century Enlightenment to the support of free trade ideas. Even among writers who were primarily interested in economic matters, the mercantilist "jealousy of trade" fostered, as overcompensation, an exaggerated belief in the harmony and mutuality of economic interests between countries.

The doctrine that low real wages (per hour of per day or per piece) were in the national interest was widely prevalent in England in the seventeenth and eighteenth centuries and has sometimes been labeled by modern writers as "the mercantilist labor doctrine." Many English writers did expound this doctrine, with favorable balance of trade considerations obviously in mind. But a substantial number of writers denied the proposition on which the doctrine was based, namely, that English laborers, once their minimum needs were taken care of, preferred idleness to more (or superior) commodities, or, as one eighteenth-century writer phrased it, that for workers in general "the luxury of indolence tends always to swamp the luxury of goods." Or, if they accepted the proposition as true to fact and regarded voluntary idleness as an evil, they proposed, on humanitarian and other grounds, the search for remedies less oppressive for the poor than low rates of real wages. It seems difficult to find on the Continent any trace of a special affinity between mercantilist thought in general and the low-wage doctrine, perhaps because it was generally impossible for the poor there to attain a basic minimum of subsistence without working to nearly the limits of their endurance, perhaps because in Catholic countries the frequency of religious holidays when work was prohibited satisfied their cravings for rest, leisure, and time-consuming dissipation.

DISTINCTIVE ASPECTS OF MERCANTILISM

Mercantilism was a doctrine of extensive state regulation of economic activity in the interest of the national economy. It took for granted that man was inherently self-regarding and would pursue his own interests without concern about the consequences of such behavior for the interests of the community. It accepted as axiomatic that if individuals were in their economic behavior left free from tight regulation, the consequences for the community would be disastrous. But this had been practically universal doctrine from classical antiquity on, and therefore did not distinguish mercantilist from pre-mercantilist thought.

Substantially new in mercantilist thought, however, was its systematic adjustment to the concentration of power and the monopolization of loyalty by nation-states, which in their relations with other states followed a "Machiavellian" or amoral code, and were more extensive in area of jurisdiction than the earlier city-states and feudal barons but less extensive than the empires of classical antiquity and than the universal Catholic church of the Middle Ages. Also substantially new in mercantilism were its greater concern with economic matters as one phase of the then prevalent secularization of thought and practice, the change in the specific character of the economic objectives of the political authorities, and the new administrative patterns of regulation of communal life. These new features were the product of the growth of commerce and of the changes in political organization associated with the breakdown of the Holy Roman Empire and of feudalism and the absorption of the hitherto substantially autonomous city-states by the new nation-states. Mercantilism was a doctrine of state intervention in economic life, but of state interventionism of a special pattern and with some special objectives. It was thus in sharp contrast with the later laissez-faire doctrine. It was also, however, in sharp contrast with some present-day systems of state interventionism, such as socialism, Russian communism, and the welfare state, for in principle at least these do not have the accumulation of the precious metals, favorable balances of trade, and national limits to moral obligations as central and ultimate objectives.

DIFFERENCES IN PRACTICE

Agreement on the general mercantilist objectives left abundant room for major differences both among periods and among countries in the choice of methods used in pursuing these objectives and in the degree of vigor of their pursuit. Practice was conditioned by limitations of administrative capacity; pressure of conflicting national objectives; domestic resistance arising out of regional, class, and occupational special interests; military weakness; and the idiosyncrasies, the apathy or enthusiasm, and the dynastic loyalties of monarchs.

The techniques adopted could be monetary ones, involving control of exchange markets and of the movement of the precious metals across national boundaries. They could take the form of regulation of individual commercial transactions; of regulation by general tariffs, prohibitions, or quantitative restrictions; or of subsidies to exports or to exporting or import-competing industries. The governments could themselves set up and operate factories producing for export or replacing imports; they could set up and operate companies engaged in foreign trade; they could grant monopoly privileges to privately owned chartered companies to produce and sell specified products in the domestic market, to engage in foreign trade on the basis of special privileges, and to administer overseas colonies. Governments could encourage immigration, restrict emigration, or promote early marriages in the belief that growth of population would serve the general mercantilist objectives. Wages and interest rates could be subjected to legal maxima in the belief that this would improve the national competitive position in foreign trade. Wars could be embarked upon for mercantilist reasons. On all of these matters, while ultimate objectives could be static within countries and uniform as between countries, the selection of means to serve these objectives could differ between countries and could undergo constant change through time within countries because of change of circumstances and of opinions.

Mercantilism in practice always in some measure fell short of what doctrine called for. Perhaps the most important deviations of practice from doctrine were those resulting from the fiscal necessities of government. All governments in the age of mercantilism found it difficult to finance their general activities. To adhere to mercantilist objectives without regard to fiscal considerations would often involve the exemption of important categories of exports from customs duties, the substitution of outright prohibition of specific exports and imports for customs duties—with a consequent loss of revenues—or the grant of subsidies to favored industries, shipping, fisheries, or colonies, all of these being measures which would involve an increase of government expenditures or decrease of government revenues.

Restraints on importation carried beyond some uncertain point could lead foreign countries injured thereby to adopt retaliatory or defensive measures, with the possible result that the gross contribution to a "favorable" balance of trade made by the import restrictions might even in the short run be more than offset by the adverse effect on exports.

Most mercantilist measures involved a burden on some occupational or regional sectors of the population. Such sectors, without challenging the general objectives of mercantilism, would commonly resort to all the forms of pressure and persuasion available to them to obtain a relaxation of the measures or a revision of them which would shift the burdens elsewhere. Thus, in England the graziers would press for a relaxation of the restrictions on the export of raw wool, and the independent merchants would protest vigorously against the special privileges granted to the trading companies. Even where absolute monarchy prevailed, governments found it necessary to make concessions to such dissenting groups.

Every measure restrictive of trade established a possibility of private profit from its evasion or violation, and no country was able to prevent extensive violation of the regulatory measures by smugglers, tax evaders, merchants operating illegally in restricted trades ("interlopers"), and bribed enforcement agents. Public resistance to particular restrictive measures and to the personnel endeavoring to enforce them, and lax administration at the top levels often led to apathy in enforcement. When Adam Smith, in 1778, entered into his duties as a commissioner of customs, he was astonished to find, expert though he already was, how much of his own personal effects consisted of articles of foreign manufacture which it was illegal not only to import but also to possess, and he warned a friend that the latter's wife, upon investigation, would probably find that she was even a worse offender.

In Britain in particular, although there was general approval in principle of mercantilism, there was almost equally general dislike of the administrative institutions and practices essential to its effective execution. The British public was jealous of the exercise of power by the executive branch of the national government, of administration conducted by the central authorities in London instead of locally, and of agents of the central government with powers of inspection and arrest. Legislation was more centralized than in most countries, but enforcement was highly decentralized and was largely left to unpaid local magistrates with considerable autonomy and to suits brought on their own initiative by interested parties or by voluntary informers who were remunerated from the monetary penalties imposed by the magistrates as a result of such suits. The higher the customs duties and the more burdensome the regulations and prohibitions, the greater was the incentive to evade or violate them, so that in many cases difficulty of enforcement led to restraint in the severity of legislation or to partial or complete abandonment of serious attempt at enforcement. It seems quite plausible, therefore, that at least in England mercantilist measures were in practice not nearly as severe a restraint on foreign trade in the eighteenth century as were, say, the transportation costs of the time or than are the ordinary tariffs of present-day protectionism.

While there was a substantial unity of doctrine throughout the Western world with respect to the proper objectives of commercial policy, the differences between countries in political organization, administrative structure, and geographical circumstances led to very substantial differences in the intensity with which, and the selection of devices whereby, they pursued these objectves. In the smaller Germanic states, for instance, mercantilism was little more than a vague general doctrine. The major interests of German intellectuals relating to economic and political matters, as represented by the contents of cameralist writings and university courses, were directed to the principles of management of the absolute rulers' finances, of organization and conduct of professionalized public administration, and of management of official property, including mints, mines, forests, and an occasional factory. In France, although public administration was on the whole centralized to an extent without parallel in England, taxation (including customs duties), property law, and guild regulations were largely under autonomous local administration following traditional and regionally diverse patterns and principles.

The Decline of Mercantilism

Criticism of the prevalent methods of pursuing mercantilist objectives was always fairly common in countries where some free discussion was tolerated. Much of this criticism, however, whatever its analytical merit, was special pleading by spokesmen for a political faction, an industry, a region, a particular port or town, or a particular privileged company.

In the 1750s there first began to appear comprehensive criticism of the basic principles of mercantilism by persons of stature with no visible private axes to grind. One major source of criticism was from exponents of an essentially new gospel of individualism which extolled the merits, on ethical and political as well as on economic grounds, of freedom of the individual from detailed regulation by the state. Here important voices were those of Adam Smith in Britain and of the marquis d'Argenson, the physiocrats, and Turgot in France. Important also was the widespread revulsion among intellectuals against the past record of almost continuous war and preparation for war, for which mercantilism was largely blamed. It was, in fact, much more the pacific and cosmopolitan views of the *philosophes* and the Illuminati on the Continent and of men like David Hume and Adam Smith in Britain than the more strictly economic argument of these and other writers which first put mercantilism seriously on the defensive among intellectuals.

In the early years of the nineteenth century the English classical school of economists rejected mercantilism on the basis of economic analysis, of which a part was substantially original with them. The school claimed that trade conducted under individual initiative and free from official regulation was inherently of mutual profit both to the individuals directly involved and to the community as a whole, and they applied this to domestic and international trade alike. Here they had had since the 1750s a number of important predecessors. They added, however, an analytical justification of this position which was essentially new, the principle that allocation of resources to production in accordance with comparative costs would maximize aggregate output and that the operations of individuals acting in their own interest in a free and competitive market would conform with this principle. They did not deny that this was subject to the qualification that producers knew both what their relevant costs were and what were the prices at which their products could be sold. But they claimed, as an obvious proposition, that businessmen were better informed on these matters than government could be. From this reasoning, they proceeded to the policy conclusion that the determination of what commodities and in what quantities a country could export and import to its greatest advantage should be left to the outcome of the decisions of individual businessmen operating to maximize their own incomes. This was a sharp break with mercantilism's insistence on the necessity of regulation of economic behavior and its ranking of the desirability of export and import of particular commodities according to whether they were manufactures or agricultural products or raw materials and according to their labor content. To the classical school these were more or less arbitrary classifications, whose correspondence, if any, in practice with classification according to the comparative cost principle would be fortuitous.

The classical school also rejected the mercantilist stress on the balance of trade and on the national supply of the precious metals. They claimed that in the absence of government regulation an international automatic equilibrating mechanism would bring each country the amount of specie appropriate to its needs and circumstances and would prevent trade balances from getting into serious disorder. Here they had predecessors in the eighteenth century, most notably, perhaps, Isaac Gervaise and David Hume.

It is to be noted that neither the mercantilists nor the classical school distinguished clearly and systematically between short-run and long-run effects, and that insofar as one can judge from the historical context and the implications of their writing, the mercantilists were as a rule thinking in terms of short-run effects and the classical school in terms of long-run effects. Appraisal by economists of the comparative analytical merits of the mercantilists and their classical school critics should therefore give careful consideration to the distinction between short-run and long-run analysis, if they regard this, as does the writer, as a crucial distinction.

The classical school doctrine with respect to international trade became dominant for a while in England and obtained a wide degree of qualified acceptance elsewhere. There followed in England over half a century of approximately complete free trade, and elsewhere it led to a substantial liberalization of foreign trade policy. The restrictions on foreign trade which continued to be imposed were supported on grounds which were largely nonmercantilist in character; they were often designed, in fact, to protect agriculture rather than manufactures. Survival into the present of mercantilist doctrine and practice is by no means rare. There are, however, important differences between mercantilist doctrine and the doctrines by which present-day state regulation of foreign trade are mainly supported, and major differences also in the respective patterns and techniques of regulation. As far as scholars are concerned, support of mercantilism as it operated in its prime, based on express acceptance of its objectives, its doctrine, and the appropriateness of its practices to its doctrine, seems today to be confined to a minority, mostly economic historians. The analytical grounds on which mercantilism has been supported or criticized are in both cases sometimes of very disputable merit. Where policy is concerned, final appraisal, here, as generally in the social sciences, needs to deal expressly, as it often fails to do, with political, ethical, and socioeconomic values, as well as with the abstract logic of relations between actual and supposed matters of fact. It needs to call, therefore, on the resources of all the major social disciplines.

REFERENCES

PRIMARY SOURCES

Colbert, Jean Baptiste 1861–1873 *Lettres, instructions et mémoires de Colbert*. Edited by Pierre Clément. 7 vols. Paris: Imprimerie Impériale. A general errata list and an analytical table by Pierre de Brotonne were published in 1882.

Forbonnais, François Vérnon D. de 1754 *Éléments du commerce*. 2 vols. Paris: Briasson.

Friedrich II, der Grosse, King of Prussia *Oeuvres de Frédéric le Grand*. 31 vols. Berlin: Imprimerie Royale, 1846–1857. See especially Volume 9, part 2, pages 212–240, "Exposé du gouvernement prussien" and "Essai sur les formes de gouvernement et sur les devoirs des souverains."

McCulloch, John R. (editor) (1856) 1954 *Early English Tracts on Commerce*. Cambridge Univ. Press. A photo-offset reprint of the 1856 edition was published by the Political Economy Club as *A Select Collection of Early English Tracts on Commerce, From the Originals of Mun, Roberts, North and Others*.

[Melon, Jean F.] (1734) 1739 *A Political Essay Upon Commerce*. Dublin: Woodward & Cox. First published in French.

Steuart Denham, James (1767) 1805 *The Works, Political, Metaphisical, and Chronological, of the Late Sir James Stewart of Coltness, Bart*. Volumes 1–4: An Inquiry Into the Principles of Political Oeconomy: Being an Essay on the Science of Domestic Policy in Free Nations. London: Cadell & Davies.

Uztariz, Gerónimo de (1742) 1751 *The Theory and Practice of Commerce and Maritime Affairs*. London: Rivington. First published in Spanish.

SECONDARY SOURCES

Buck, Philip W. (1942) 1964 *The Politics of Mercantilism*. New York: Octagon.

Cole, Charles W. 1931 *French Mercantilist Doctrines Before Colbert*. New York: Smith.

Cole, Charles W. (1939) 1964 *Colbert and a Century of French Mercantilism*. Hamden, Conn.: Shoe String Press.

Cole, Charles W. (1943) 1965 *French Mercantilism: 1683–1700*. New York: Octagon.

Heckscher, Eli F. (1931) 1955 *Mercantilism*. Rev. ed. 2 vols. London: Allen & Unwin; New York: Macmillan. First published in Swedish.

Johnson, Edgar A. J. 1937 *Predecessors of Adam Smith: The Growth of British Economic Thought*. Englewood Cliffs, N.J.: Prentice-Hall.

Schmoller, Gustav von (1884) 1931 *The Mercantile System and Its Historical Significance: Illustrated Chiefly From Prussian history*. New York: Smith. A translation of a chapter from Schmoller's *Studien über die wirtschaftliche Politik Friedrichs des Grossen*.

Schumpeter, Joseph A. (1954) 1960 *History of Economic Analysis*. Edited by E. B. Schumpeter. New York: Oxford Univ. Press.

Suviranta, Bruno 1923 *The Theory of the Balance of Trade in England: A Study in Mercantilism*. Helsinki: Suomalaisen Kirjallisuuden Seura.

Viner, Jacob (1921–1951) 1958 *The Long View and the Short: Studies in Economic Theory and Policy*. Glencoe, Ill.: Free Press. See especially pages 277–305, "Power Versus Plenty as Objectives of Foreign Policy in the Seventeenth and Eighteenth Centuries."

Viner, Jacob 1937 *Studies in the Theory of International Trade*. New York: Harper.

12

MAN'S ECONOMIC STATUS

I HAVE FOUND MYSELF struggling somewhat with the assigned title of my paper. To give me some finite bodies of matter to focus on, I will concentrate on restricted categories of 'man', of 'society', and of material that can justify the 'economic' label. Since neither 1701 nor 1801 have appreciable terminal significance for any problem or issue with my range of knowledge, 1688, the year of the Glorious Revolution, will be my approximate beginning date, and the period after 1776 will be referred to only now and again, not because this later period is unimportant or uninteresting to me, but on the contrary because it differs enough for my purposes from the period that preceded it to justify its being segregated for separate treatment. 'Britain' I will take to mean England. Scotland even after the Union remained largely another country, different substantially in its social thought, its legal system, its political and economic structure, its educational and religious institutions and principles. Ireland was a colony of a peculiar kind, even more distinguishable from England in many respects relevant for my lecture than were Scotland and the American Colonies. If 'versus' means opposed to, I will spend more time on 'Society versus Man' than on 'Man versus Society,' and will even pause to ask 'What is Man?' and attempt a reply in terms of different social categories of man as he was in eighteenth-century England. Aside from these particulars, I will conform strictly to the assigned title of my lecture.

'Man versus Society' or 'Man versus the State' would have served me very well as the title for a lecture on *laissez faire* or on 'economic individualism', in eighteenth-century England, were I not at a loss for supporting data of historical significance prior to the publication, in 1776, of Adam Smith's *Wealth of Nations*. Even Adam Smith did not succeed in making *laissez faire* a live issue for discussion and agitation until the turn of the century, and I am not enough of an economic historian to detect a clear trend in the actual course of events in these respects in either direction as between 'freedom' and 'social control' before the beginning of the nineteenth century. There was of course much talk of 'freedom'

Reprinted from *Man Versus Society in Eighteenth-Century Britain*, ed. James L. Clifford (Cambridge: Cambridge University Press, 1968), pp. 23–53.

or of 'liberty' before and throughout the eighteenth century, but it was not often in the sense of any modern abstract term of wide meaning. Even when the talk was of 'liberty' in the singular as far as phrasing went, it was often of 'liberties' in the plural or of a very specific type of liberty as far as meaning went. It was often quite clear that what its possessor called a liberty was by those who did not possess it but would have liked to enjoy it regarded as a special privilege, and by those who wished no one to possess it was looked on as licence. Abstract terms in '-ism' were not yet current outside the field of theology and indeed I can think of only one instance of the use of an '-ism' term in the period in a work of economic relevance. This was in the title of a 1713 anonymous tract, *Torism and Trade Can Never Agree*, a title whose translation into twentieth-century English would call for some fairly detailed acquaintance with the political issues of that year. In the interest of keeping as close as is practicable to my eighteenth-century sources, I have tried, I believe successfully, to resist the temptation to use in this lecture any '-ism' terminology.

In the England of my period, the miracle was performed of simultaneous tight regulation of foreign trade, wide-ranging though somewhat haphazard intervention by government in domestic economic matters, and limitations of government personnel to a minuscule national and local bureaucracy and government-employed work force except in the field of tax collection. Even such activities as police, fire protection, the conduct of the Mint, the postal service, the construction and maintenance of roads, canals, harbours, lighthouses, education, the provisioning of the army, the operation of jails, the servicing and accounting of the national debt, street-cleaning, garbage disposal, water supply, street-lighting, regulation of domestic industry and trade were in large part or in entirety farmed out or abandoned to private-profit enterprise, to individual charitable initiative, or to the ancient guilds. The government of British India was entrusted to a chartered company operating for profit.

This was in a sense a manifestation of 'man versus the state', of citizenry limiting the scope of direct activity of government. It was especially a manifestation of mistrust by the ruling sector of the public of the English central government as it had operated in the past and, if permitted, would probably operate in the future. There was jealousy of executive power, as contrasted with parliamentary power or with power of the judiciary. Parliament could not itself undertake administrative tasks involving large numbers of employees. Entrusting the executive with such tasks meant entrusting it with large payrolls, which could be used to buy political support, to make placemen out of members of parliament and members of parliament out of placemen, to reward political service rendered to the executive by members of either House and by anyone else. To strength the executive meant to strengthen the role of the Crown as against that of the nobility and the gentry. To avoid this, parliament held the executive to a total bureaucratic force other than military personnel and tax officials of, at the end of the century, barely 2,000 men for the entire central government, inclusive of holders of sine-cure posts. This combination of intervention through legislation with only a skel-eton of bureaucracy to operate the system has in modern times been labelled 'administrative nihilism'. It could be labelled 'indirect government', or 'govern-ment with a minimum of bureaucracy.'[1]

Mistrust of the central government was associated with mistrust of and dislike of the direct exercise of power by its officers. It was not opposition to government on principle. The mistrust did not extend, moreover, to the magistrates, to whom fell many tasks which in other countries were performed by administrative per-sonnel. The agent of the central government whom an ordinary citizen of middle rank was most likely to encounter would be a collector of excise or of customs. A member of the lower classes in a seaport might encounter also a press-gang endeavouring to seize him for service in the Navy. No national government em-ployees were to be seen building roads or canals or water-supply systems, or teaching, or providing police or sanitation services, or giving weather-reporting services to the public. I do not suppose that there is now or ever was particular affection in any country for customs and tax collectors. If it was with these cate-gories of central officialdom that citizens would mainly have contact, mistrust of government and mistrust and dislike of its agents would reinforce each other. Contact with government in action would readily be felt to involve or threaten an invasion of the privacy of the individual by an agency, the state, foreign to him and hostile to him.

In 1733 the Robert Walpole administration was forced by a nation-wide out-burst of protest to withdraw its bill to substitute excise duties on tobacco and wines collected internally at the warehouses of the merchants for the existing customs duties collected at the ports at the time of landing and the associated drawbacks of tax upon such portions of the imports as were re-exported to foreign countries. It was the objective of the bill to provide a remedy for the wholesale frauds associated with both the collection of the import duties and the payment

---

[1] For a rich supply of information bearing on the extent of decentralisation and of surrender to private agencies of governmental functions, see: Frederick Clifford, *A History of Private Bill Legis-lation*, 2 vols. (London, 1885, 1887); E. G. Dowdell, *A Hundred Years of Quarter Sessions. The Government of Middlesex from 1660 to 1760* (Cambridge, 1932); and the series of studies of English local government, beginning in 1906, published by Sidney and Beatrice Webb. See also, for the role of private informers in the detection and prosecution of crime, M. W. Beresford, 'The Common Informer, the Penal Statutes and Economic Regulation', *Economic History Review*, 2nd ser. X (1957), 221–38.

of drawbacks, and involving, the government claimed, serious loss of revenue. The proposal, however, would have required an expansion of the hated corps of excisemen, the inquisitorial visitation of tradesmen's premises, and, according to the opposition, an escape by the executive of dependence on annual vote by parliament with respect to the expenditure of the revenue derived from the proposed excise taxes. The opposition also aroused the public to interpret the proposal as only the first step in an insidious programme to expand indefinitely the scope of the excise tax system, and harped on the fact that persons charged with violations of tax laws faced more arbitrary administrative and legal hazards if the taxes were excises than if they were import duties. It was this last point which Samuel Johnson had in mind when in his *Dictionary* he defined 'excise' as 'a hateful tax levied upon commodities and adjudged not by the common judges of property [that is, the magistrates] but by wretches [i.e. excisemen] hired by those to whom the excise is paid'.[2]

In 1763, public dislike of an excise measure was again to shake the government. In that year the administration, under the leadership of the earl of Bute, had carried through parliament, against strong opposition, an excise tax on cider, probably a more important commodity at the time as an adulterant of wine and thus a means of escape from customs duties on imported wine than as a beverage of its own account. The cider tax authorised entrance by excise officers into homes, to search for and collect tax on home-brewed cider. The old cry was raised that 'an Englishman's house was his castle', although only for the country gentlemen and the substantial farmers was it practicable to make their homes serve also as untaxed cider-mills. But an encroachment on *their* privacy was not a politically viable step. The outcry against the tax forced Bute to resign from office, and the succeeding Rockingham ministry in 1765 repealed the tax.[3]

The preamble of one of the first acts of William and Mary's reign abrogating a hearth-money tax introduced in Charles I's reign explained that the tax was 'not only a great oppression upon the poorer sort, but a badge of slavery upon the whole people; exposing every man's house to be entered into, and searched at pleasure, by persons unknown to him.'[4] A proposal in 1756 in the House of Commons for authorisation of the government to take a census of the number of the people was defeated after a member of the House had attacked the proposal as, among other things, involving an invasion of the people's privacy. 'I did not

---

[2] On Robert Walpole's excise scheme, see: Emanuel Leser, *Ein Accisestreit in England*, in a *Festgabe* for J. C. Bluntschli, Heidelberg, 1879, but also published separately; E. R. Turner, 'The Excise Scheme of 1733', *English Historical Review*, XLII (1927), 34–57. For the general history of controversy in England over excises, see Stephen Dowell, *A History of Taxation and Taxes in England* (New York, 1965), reprint of 2nd ed. (London, 1888).

[3] Stephen Dowell, *op. cit.* IV, 211–12.

[4] Cited by Henry Home, Lord Kames, *Sketches of the History of Man* (Edinburgh, 1774), I, 459.

believe', he exclaimed, 'that there had been any set of men, or indeed, any individual of the human species, so presumptuous and so abandoned, as to make the proposal which we have just heard.'[5] Adam Smith, in *The Wealth of Nations*, condemned income taxes as necessarily involving an unacceptable encroachment on privacy. 'The state of a man's fortune varies from day to day, and without an inquisition more intolerable than any tax, and renewed at least once a year, can only be guessed at.'[6]

What means did the Englishman have of coping with a State he regarded as oppressive or offensive? After 1688, the landowners were in effect the State, through parliament, a long as they kept a bridle on the king and his ministers. Much of the political history of the eighteenth century revolved around the relations of the substantial landowners with the Crown and among themselves in the processes of winning elections, managing parliament, and conducting local political affairs. These landowners were most of the time well able to protect themselves against oppression by the 'State', and there was no other power in a position to oppress or coerce them.

From here on, I will abandon my concern for the landed gentry, and will concentrate on the 'labouring poor', urban and rural, some living on self-employment, but most of them dependent on wages, on public and private charity, or on unrespectable or 'invisible' means of support. The really poor portion of the 'poor' I take to have comprised, with their dependants, at a minimum somewhere between 50 per cent at the beginning and 40 per cent at the end of the century. In this 40–50 per cent would be included, as far as wage labour is concerned, the great bulk of those of whom Adam Smith said: 'Many workmen could not subsist a week, few could subsist a month, and scarce any a year without employment.'[7]

I should warn you, however, that whatever gestures toward quantification I make in this lecture rest mostly on contemporary conjectures. Official statistics were either not gathered or had gross error systematically built into them. Modern presentations of what purport to be statistics of or for the eighteenth century either do not cover the aspects I am concerned with in this lecture, or are too fragmentary or too much the product of promiscuous aggregation to be trusted as representative, or are conjectures expressed in numerical form which owe more to the imagination of their authors than to supporting evidence. Fully as I respect the current zeal for expert quantification of history as a virtue in itself, I regard it, like all other virtues, as competitive with other values, such as, in the present instances, relevance to fact and relevance to questions that non-statisticians care to ask. In this instance, as in many others, I find the judgment or even conjecture

[5] William Cobbett, ed., *The Parliamentary History of England* (London, 1806-20), XIV, 1318–19.

[6] *The Wealth of Nations* [1776], Edwin Cannan, ed. (London, 1925), II, 351–2.

[7] *Ibid*. I, 68.

of a *contemporary* person of presumptive honesty and intelligence often the safest guide available, though rarely a safe guide. It is prudent always to bear in mind that detailed bits of evidence constitute the sole genuine records of high or even moderate reliability that the past bequeaths to us. In any case, from now on my concern will be with a lower segment of the population, substantial in size, constituting those of the urban and rural 'labouring poor' who were poor by inheritance and class status. The poor by accident, the members of families with a tradition of at least moderate prosperity who by misfortune or misconduct had fallen into poverty, were commonly excluded from the category of 'labouring poor'. Of the thinking and the experience of genuine members of the labouring poor we have almost no authentic record. Our knowledge of their feelings and hopes, of their pleasures and pains, of the conditions of their day-to-day life, is based almost completely on the reports of observers, often with personal or ideological axes to grind, and not on the testimony of the poor themselves. Any modern history of 'English thought' in the eighteenth century, we should remember, is almost certain to be solely or mainly, at its most comprehensive, a history of the expressed thought of the upper-half English.

In the vocabulary of the upper half the lower half was often not included, or included in a very qualified sense, in the denotation of the word 'people'. According to Edmund Burke, the natural strength of the kingdom, identified with the 'people', consisted of 'the great peers, the leading landed gentlemen, the opulent merchants and manufacturers, the substantial yeomanry'.[8] A Whig preacher, John Brown, in 1765 defined the 'people' in similar terms: 'the landed gentry, the beneficed country clergy, many of the more considerable merchants and men in trade, the substantial and industrious freeholders or yeomen.'[9] At about the same time, the *Political Register* attacked the problem of definition of 'people' from the other end, specifying those who were to be excluded from the term: 'the illiterate rabble, who have neither capacity for judging of matters of government, nor property to be concerned for.'[10] For the excluded there was no shortage of labels: they were the 'poor', the 'populace', the 'rabble', the 'mob', the 'scum'. To William Petty, they were the 'poor people', constituting, whether wholly or mostly he does not make explicit, 'the vile and brutish part of mankind'.[11] Sometimes they were referred to as 'mere people', as distinguished from those above them in social status and thus more than 'mere'.

[8] *Thoughts on the Cause of the Present Discontents* [1770], *Works*, Bohn ed. (London, 1854), I, 337.

[9] *Thoughts on Civil Liberty* (London, 1765), p. 87.

[10] *Political Register*, J. Almon, ed., II (1768), cited by Simon Maccoby, *English Radicalism, 1762-1785* (London, 1955), p. 84, n. 4.

[11] *Political Arithmetick* (1690), *The Economic Writings of Sir William Petty*, Charles Henry Hull, ed. (Cambridge, 1899), I, 274–5.

It is amusing that in France verbal usage was sometimes the reverse of this: only those who had to resort to physical labour for their living were designated as 'le peuple'. Voltaire especially followed this usage: 'By people I mean the populace that only has its hands to work with. I doubt whether that class of citizens will ever have time or capacity for education.' 'France would be a delightful country if it were not for its taxes and its pedants. As to the people, they will always be stupid and barbarous. They are cattle and what is wanted for them is a yoke, a goad, and fodder.'[12]

The English labouring poor were in England almost completely without the semblance of recognised political power. As employees they could sometimes manage to organise, illegally but with occasional effectiveness, into sketchy anticipations of modern labour unions and strike against or otherwise harass their employers. As individuals they could rebel against their low status in the social order by abandoning steady work and resorting to vagabondage or begging or petty thievery. If sufficiently provoked by events, they could, and frequently did, resort to riot. But only exceptionally did any of them have voting rights of any kind.

The upper classes did not take riots lightly. They attributed to riots a contagious quality, and they were conscious that they could be generated by a wide range of factors which to them were cherished features of the English social structure. Of modern types of police there was scarcely a trace, and once order was disturbed an amateur militia or regular military forces had to be called in on an emergency basis to restore quiet. Benjamin Franklin wrote on the margin of an English pamphlet of 1769: 'I have seen, within a year, riots in the country about corn; riots about elections; riots about workhouses; riots of colliers; riots of weavers; riots of coal-heavers; riots of sawyers; riots of Wilkesites; riots of government [licensed?] chairmen; riots of smugglers, in which customhouse officers and excisemen have been murdered, [and] the King's armed vessels and troops fired at.'[13] In other years he could have seen or read about other occasions for riots, riots against Catholics, of cottagers against enclosures, of farm-labourers against labour-saving machinery, and so on.

Many members of the upper classes were suspicious of the consequences of literacy on the part of the working classes, and many of the working class were illiterate, in fact a majority of them if the ability to write is taken as the test of

[12] Letters of I April 1766, 3 February 1769, *Voltaire's Correspondence*, Theodore Besterman, ed., Geneva, LXI (1961), 3; LXXI (1962), 81.

[13] For the annotation, see *The Writings of Benjamin Franklin*, Albert Henry Smyth, ed. (New York, 1907), X, 239. In a letter to John Ross, 14 May 1768 (*ibid*. V. 132–4), and also in a note on another tract, Franklin made similar remarks. These remarks were responses to British charges that the Americans were using riots as a political weapon against them.

'literacy'. It may be, however, that from the point of view of peace and order there can be either too much literacy or too little, and that literacy restricted to a few of the lower classes is the most dangerous state of all, since a demogogic literate few could capture the minds of the illiterate many by reading to or speaking to them. A Swiss visitor to England reported in 1726, no doubt with at least a trace of exaggeration: 'All Englishmen are great newsmongers. Workmen habitually begin the day by going to coffee-rooms in order to read the latest news. I have often seen shoeblacks and other persons of that class club together to purchase a farthing paper. Nothing is more entertaining than hearing men of this class discussing politics and topics of interest concerning royalty.'[14] An upper-class Englishman might, perhaps, have found the discussion, if he had overheard it, more terrifying than entertaining.

I must now take awkward leave of 'Man versus Society' and the State to turn to society and the State versus the labouring man. There was of course in the class structure of eighteenth-century England a continuous gradation stretching from the dizzy heights of royalty and nobility down to the lowest depths of miserable and hungry and degraded creatures, a gradation known to the theologians and poets of the period as part of that admirable creation of God, the 'great chain of being'. Limitations of time and of knowledge force me to lump together as one group something like half of the links in the human part of the chain, the lower, half, the poverty-in-the-midst-of-plenty half. The lack of data as to the thought of this lower half about their own social condition forces me also to confine myself to the thought of the upper half relating to the other half.

Much of English eighteenth-century upper-class thought about the phenomenon of poverty was of course not peculiar to England or to that century. Influences from the ancient classics, from serviceable elements of the Christian moral tradition, from the Continental Enlightenment, can easily be identified. But the special character of English conditions and traditions and the capacity of the English mind for original or idosyncratic thought did lead to some differences between English ideas with respect to poverty and the ideas prevalent in other countries. Anglicanism, the role in society of the country gentleman, content with the 'Matchless Constitution', the administratively inert and inept government, the pervasive dislike of 'enthusiasm' in all fields, were, in degree and to some extent in kind, aspects of society peculiar to England and operating to give its prevalent doctrines about poverty a distinctive English flavour. There was much that was distinctively English in the English ideas about poverty, and much of what was written in England at the time relating to poverty sounded foreign to foreigners

---

[14] *A Foreign View of England . . . The Letters of Monsieur César de Saussure to his Family* (New York, 1902), p. 162.

and even to Scotsmen. One institution peculiar to England when on a national scale was what was known on the Continent as 'legal charity' or the acceptance by government of legal obligations to relieve on a systematic basis economic distress, the cost to be defrayed by compulsory levies on the propertied classes. I will have occasion later to deal in some detail with this once peculiarly English institution, now of course a nearly universal phenomenon. It gave a special character to all English utterances on voluntary charity, since only in England was there to a significant degree any other kind of charity.

The English Anglican charity sermons provide an invaluable guide to upper-class English thought with respect to the poor. An Anglican clergyman of high status would be a representative member of the upper classes. The charity sermon was periodically addressed to the upper classes at prayer and had as its primary function to persuade the prosperous to continue and, in moderation, to improve on their past record of contributions to charitable purposes. To be successful in achieving its purpose, the charity sermon had to avoid challenging the social philosophy of its audience. To be honest, and to appear so to its audience, the sermon also had to reflect the social philosophy of the preacher. The charity sermons of the great French preachers that I have read were in these respects radically different. The condition of the French poor was probably more desperate than that of the English. Charity in France was not merely a supplement to regularly established and comprehensive legal or official relief, but was the only source of help for the distressed. The issue of life and death of many persons depended on the response made to pleas for charity by the French preachers. The urgency of voluntary giving was therefore greater than in England. The Catholic preacher had less doctrinal sanction for lax preaching. He was also less subject than was an Anglican dignitary to social pressure or pressure from important parishioners to maintain harmony between his utterances and the attitudes of his audience. In consequence, a Bourdaloue, a Massillon, could without hesitation address his most aristocratic audiences as sinners whose salvation was specially in jeopardy and who urgently needed to practice generous and even heroic charity as an afterlife insurance policy.[15]

An English charity sermon was, in contrast, while insistent on the duty of giving, typically abounding in reservations and limitations as to the extent of giving which was religiously or morally obligatory or socially beneficial.[16] It fre-

---

[15] *Les Avocats des Pauvres* (Paris, 1814), is an excellent collection of French charity sermons of the late seventeenth and the eighteenth centuries.

[16] A sermon by Thomas Tenison, archbishop of Canterbury, *Concerning Discretion in Giving Alms* (London, 1681), set the tone for a long line of subsequent sermons advocating or justifying prudent restraint in the giving of aid to the poor. William Law, one of the few outstanding Anglican 'enthusiasts' of the eighteenth century, is the only prominent writer of the century that I have found

quently included expressions of deference to the establishment comfortably seated in the pews and of admonitions specially addressed to the poor standing in the aisles or at the rear concerning their obligations to be industrious, to be frugal, to be humble and respectful to their betters, to be patient in enduring hardship, and to be grateful for benefits received.

Another Anglican eighteenth-century institution was the charity school, on behalf of which special sermons were given annually in London in solicitation of voluntary gifts to support the schools.[17] These charity school sermons were also customary in Ireland, where the charity schools, however, were largely boarding, not day schools, and had as one of their primary objectives the conversion of poor Catholic children to protestantism by drawing them away from their home surroundings. There was in England no publicly financed education to compete with the charity schools. The upper-class judgment as to how much education it was good for the poor, good for the country, and good for the rich that the children of the poor should receive rarely rose above a very elementary level of reading, writing, and arithmetic, and often insisted that the ability to write was a luxury for the children of the rural poor and liable to undermine their willingness to conform to the status providentially assigned to them in the rural pattern of life. Teaching of writing was in many rural charity schools deliberately omitted, lest, in the words of a charity school sermon of 1743 by Bishop Thomas Secker, it 'possibly may turn the minds of children, or of their parents for them, to some other business than husbandry.'[18]

Bernard Mandeville in his *Fable of the Bees* attacked the charity schools on the ground that they were overeducating the children and thus making them unfit for their appropriate function in society, which was to be docile hewers of wood and drawers of water in the service of the national economy.[19] Infidel though he may have been, there is no doubt that on this issue there were many of the faithful who agreed with him, and charity school sermons often included denials of his

who preached unbounded or 'heroic' charity. But disapproval of unlimited or indiscriminate charity was not, as modern scholars sometimes suggest, an innovation of the Protestant Reformation, or of Protestantism, or of the Post-Reformation period.

[17] M. G. Jones, *The Charity School Movement. A Study of Eighteenth Century Puritanism in Action* (Cambridge, 1938), is an informative but mistitled study. The only 'puritanism' involved was 'puritanism' or austerity preached to and for the poor. Annual charity school sermons in London prior to 1729 are conveniently collected in *Twenty-five Sermons Preached at the Anniversary Meetings in . . . London and Westminster* (London, 1729). The sermons of later years are available only as contemporaneously published separate pamphlets or as reprinted in the collected works of the individual authors.

[18] *The Works of Thomas Secker, LL.D., Late Lord Archbishop of Canterbury* (new ed., Edinburgh, 1792), sermon cxxxii, III, 507.

[19] *Fable of the Bees* (1723 and later editions). See F. B. Kaye's edition (Oxford, 1924), entry for 'Charity-Schools' in Kaye's index, II, 459.

charge that the charity schools had these effects on the children. While the sponsors of the charity schools, on grounds of humanity and religion, defended provision of a bare literacy for even the lowest strata of the social structure, they insisted that the teaching was, or should be, carefully kept to a very elementary level, and that religious and moral disciplinary training, suitable to the status in life that the children were providentially destined for, was the primary objective of the schools.[20] The attendance at the schools reached a peak of 60,000 for all of England. Their financing never was easy, and the charity school movement petered out before the end of the century, to be replaced after an interval by the Sunday school, a cheaper substitute, since, as it operated only one day a week, it needed no full-time or professional staff, and did not compete for the time of the children with the workshop or the farm.

I know only of Bishops Butler, Stillingfleet and Shipley and of a few dissenters who in eighteenth-century England explicitly urged a more generous level of education for the children of the poor both on outright religious and humanitarian grounds and to increase upward social mobility.

Shipley delivered in 1777 a charity school sermon which is noteworthy for its explicit and sharp disavowal of the aristocratic bias and the excessive preaching of other-worldliness to the poor in the literature distributed by the charity school movement, including presumably the series of previously published charity school sermons, and for its criticism of the insistence in this literature that 'the sole intention of our religion is to prepare its followers for a better life [i.e. in another world], without any immediate regard to their happiness at present'. 'Prudence in the conduct of life', he claimed, 'is a superior and a master virtue, and should not be debased to superficial and trifling austerities.' It was 'the intention

---

[20] Bishop Secker's statement of the discipline which the schools should impose on the children is more specific and goes into more detail than any of the other charity school sermons I have seen, but except for the sermon of Bishop Shipley I refer to later it seems to me quite in conformity with the spirit of all of these sermons that I have read. As a significant eighteenth-century document, I present a somewhat lengthy extract here from Secker's sermon: '. . . particularly humility should be instilled into them with singular care. They should understsand, that the lowest of those whom their own parents maintain are for that very reason their superiors; and that no education given as an alms can be a ground for thinking highly of themselves. Their usage in all respects should be answerable to such lessons. Cleanliness should be required of them, as far as ever their employments allow it; but no extraordinary provision should be made for it, nor the least affectation of nicety be tolerated in either sex. Their clothes should be no better, if so good, as they may hope to wear all the rest of their lives; no gaiety of colour, no trifling ornaments permitted; nor any distinction between them and other children in which they can possibly be tempted to take pleasure. if they are fed, their food should be of the coarsest sort, and not more than enough. If they are lodged, it should be in a manner that is suitable to every thing else. For, besides that frugality is a most important branch of faithfulness in the management of charities, *it is good that they should bear the yoke in their youth* (Lamentations, iii. 27), be inured to the treatment they must expect to receive; and wrong-judged indulgence is the greatest cruelty that can be exercised towards them.' (Sermon cxxxii, *Works*, III, 505.)

of our creator . . . that all men should concur in procuring that happiness which every man wishes for, and which every man has an equal capacity to acquire and an equal right to expect'.[21]

It was repeatedly claimed in the eighteenth century on behalf of England that 'equality before the law' prevailed there. I know of no grounds for disputing that this claim came closer to realisation in fact in England, and also in Scotland, than in any other important country or region of the world. But the term 'equality before the law' has its due measure of ambiguity.

Richard Savage was a poet, and, although we may regard as somewhat of an exaggeration David Hume's comment that poets are 'liars by profession', I doubt whether anyone in the eighteenth century would have challenged seriously Dryden's statement that it is proper for a poet, when doing honour to his country, to exaggerate its merits somewhat, 'for he is not tied to truth, or fettered by the laws of history'. Savage, therefore, was staying within the customary limits of poetic licence when he claimed on behalf of England:

> Who digs the mine or quarry, digs with glee;
> No slave—His option and his gain are free:
> Him the same laws the same protection yield,
> Who plows the furrow, as who owns the field.[22]

Another poet, James Thomson, freely exercising his poetic licence to pay tribute to 'Liberty' as it prevailed in Britain, dwelt for a moment on what it meant for the poor:

> For Toil, by thee protected, feels no pain,
> The poor man's lot with milk and honey flows,
> And, gilded with thy rays, even death looks gay.[23]

We think of the principle of 'equality before the law' as meaning that all persons who come before the law do so on a basis 'equal' in all relevant respects. The most ardent exponent of equality before the law might hesitate, however, before supporting literally identical treatment of men and women, adults and children, the strong and the weak, the responsible and the idiots. There is in fact

[21] *A Sermon Preached* [*at*] *the Yearly Meeting of the Children Educated in the Charity-Schools in the Cities of London and Westminster* (London, 1777). Also in Jonathan Shipley, *Works* (London, 1792), II, 331ff., where see especially II, 338–9, 350–5.

[22] 'Of Public Spirit in Regard to Public Works' [1736], ll. 45–8, 'Second Version', *The Poetical Works of Richard Savage*, Clarence Tracy, ed. (Cambridge, 1962), p. 226.

[23] 'Liberty' (1735–6), part v, ll. 5–7, *The Complete Poetical Works of James Thomson*, J. L. Robertson, ed. (London, 1908), p. 392. Thomson is here thanking the Goddess of Liberty for her special patronage of Britain.

much in modern law which is widely approved because it deliberately deals more gently with the weak than with the strong.

There were undoubtedly instances in which the impact of English eighteenth-century law was administratively tempered to the shorn lamb, but I have been able to find only one instance of a statute imposing penalties for misconduct where the penalties were graded upward according to the social status of the offender. This was the Profane Oaths Act of 1746, which laid penalties for swearing of one shilling for a day-labourer, common soldier or common seaman, of two shillings for everybody else under the degree of a gentleman, and of five shillings for gentlemen and upwards, including presumably royalty.[24]

Whatever the intent of the framers of legislation, from the time at least of ancient Greece it has been a commonplace, and perhaps therefore true, that, in the words attributed to Anacharsis, 'Laws are merely spider webs, which the birds, being larger, break through with ease, while the flies are caught fast'. In eighteenth-century English law, in any case, the birds and the flies were often not treated alike, and the distinctions made between them by common law, by statutory law, and in the administration of the law, often deliberately and explicitly favoured the birds.

Such was the opinion of Samuel Johnson. 'No scheme of policy', he wrote, 'has, in any country, yet brought the rich and poor on equal terms into courts of judicature. Perhaps experience, improving on experience, may in time effect it.'[25] In Henry Fielding's *Joseph Andrews*, Lady Booby consults the unscrupulous lawyer, Scout, as to the possibility of using the settlement laws to prevent her servant, Joseph Andrews, on whom she had unchaste designs of her own, from marrying his beloved Fanny within the parish. The lawyer replies: 'The laws of this land are not so vulgar to permit a mean fellow [like Andrews] to contend with one of your ladyship's fortune.'[26] Richard Parrott, writing in 1752, criticised the ways in which the laws relating to morals were drawn, leaving the gentlemen exempt. He commented that it was not ordinarily within the power of the magistrates as such to remedy this, but that Henry Fielding, as both a magistrate and a novelist with great influence on the upper classes, was an exception: 'this admired writer has now the sole means of authority over gentlemen, which perhaps no other magistrate in the world ever had; for he is the first who ever joined propriety in active life as a civil officer, with acknowledged superiority as a man of genius.'[27]

[24] 19 Geo. II, c. 21 [1746], *Statutes at Large*, London, X (1811), 216.

[25] *A Journey to the Western Isles of Scotland* [1775], R. W. Chapman, ed. (London, 1924), p. 85.

[26] *Joseph Andrews* (Scholartis Press ed., London, 1929), p. 289.

[27] *Reflections on Various Subjects Relating to Arts and Commerce* (London, 1752), pp. 72–3.

The ferociousness, judged by prevailing present-day standards, of English eighteenth-century criminal law is well known. It was not an eighteenth-century innovation, however, and it was probably exceeded in some other countries. There were eighteenth-century ameliorations, moreover, such as greater resort to the pardoning power, and the refusal of juries to convict because of the severity of the penalties, which operated to make the application of the criminal law less harsh than the letter of the statutes. Modern experts offer different explanations of the revolution in the direction of mildness which occurred in criminal law after the eighteenth century. Much emphasis is put on the defects in the eighteenth-century techniques of prevention and detection of crime and of apprehension of criminals, with the consequence that the respectable classes had great fear of the criminal class and, given the high probability of escape from punishment of any particular offender, were convinced that very severe penalties for those who were caught and convicted were essential if the laws were to have much deterrent effect.

I am here concerned only with the extent to which, in the area of economic offences, the scale of penalties was class structured so as to fall with disproportionate severity on violators of property rights of a kind with which the rich were specially, and even exclusively, concerned, or to fall with disproportionate severity on offences of which the lowest classes were likely to be preponderant or even exclusive perpetrators.

My chief impression in this connection is that so general a lack of apparent system and logic in the criminal law was operative in the eighteenth century that to attribute system and consistency to its biases is, from the point of view of efficiency in government, unduly generous. The criminal law was the product of a disorderly sequence of piecemeal enactments stretching over centuries, unplanned, uncodified, never methodically evaluated as a whole, and administrated with an almost total lack of order and expertise. As a part of the established legal structure of England, entitled as such to respect and even veneration, it was regarded as not properly subject to critical examination, whether for violations of humanity or for inefficiency as instruments of deterrence of crime, or for other kinds of defect. Depending on who does the counting, there were in the eighteenth century from 150 to 250 capital offences, that is crimes for which death was the minimum penalty. By 1850, there were only two. Now, I believe, there is only one, or is it none? Although comparative numbers like these are still repeatedly cited as evidence of the harshness of eighteenth-century penal law, they can be somewhat misleading. As Justice J. F. Stephen, in 1883, pointed out, a single act making larceny in general punishable by death would be more severe than fifty separate acts making fifty specific varieties of larceny so punishable, if there remained some species of larceny not covered by these acts.[28] But we need not worry too much about this fine point, if in the next century *no* species of larceny bore the death penalty. It was, moreover, the apparent lack of rationality as well as the severity of eighteenth-century criminal law which was later to bring about its comprehensive reform. Among the offences subject to the death penalty in the eighteenth century were: stealing from a boat on a navigable river, but not on a canal; stealing from the person to the value of one shilling, from a shop to the value of five shillings, and from a dwelling-house to the value of forty shillings; entering land with intent to kill game or rabbits. Murderous assault, however, was not a capital offence if the victim survived the attack.[29] Data such as these make it entirely plausible that particular penalties manifest clear-cut class bias, but they warn against imputing to the system as a whole any consistent pattern of bias, or any other understandable rationale.

Particular instances of outstanding bias can easily be cited, however, as showing what the century was capable of tolerating. The game laws provide a unique example where it was encroachments on exclusive privileges artificially established by law for the very rich that were capital offences. The trapping or shooting of game was an exclusive privilege of the large landowners. Small landowners and tenants of any scale were not allowed to trap or shoot game on even the land which they owned or occupied. The only justification offered in an eighteenth-century law guide for this aspect of the game laws was that these laws were enacted 'for the recreation and amusement of persons of fortune . . . and to prevent persons of inferior rank from squandering that time which their station of life requireth to be profitably employed.[30] Perhaps, however, the enactors of this legislation had better reasons for it than I have found recorded. Since private efforts to preserve game can be practicable only if they apply to extensive areas of land, only large-scale proprietors would have a definite personal gain from preserving game rather than shooting it as fast as they could. To give exclusive shooting privileges to great proprietors on their neighbour's as well as on their own land and on their own land even when it was occupied by rent-paying tenants may have been the most effective game preservative available. But capital punishment for illegal shooting still seems harsh, especially if, as was notoriously a

---

[28] *History of the Criminal Law of England* (London, 1883), I, 470.

[29] See Charles Reith, *The Police Idea* (London, 1938), p. 10. For the period after 1750 the major authority on most aspects of English criminal law is now the multi-volume work of Leon Radzinowicz, *A History of English Criminal Law and its Administration from 1750*, 3 vols. (London, 1948–56).

[30] Cited by Richard Burn, *The Justice of the Peace* (7th ed., London, 1762), II, 51. On the later history of the game laws, see Chester Kirby, 'English Game Law Reform', *Essays in Modern English History in Honor of William Cortez Abbott* (Cambridge, Mass., 1941), pp. 345–80.

common situation, game birds in their depredations on the growing crops made no exemptions in favour of the crops of small landowners, tenants, and cottagers with a few acres of grain.

The 'benefit of clergy' clause in criminal legislation applying to many types of offences was in effect an indisputable though increasingly imprecise distinction between persons according to their social status. In its twelfth-century origins this phrase signified the right of clergy to be tried for offences in ecclesiastical instead of in civil courts, and it is conceivable that canon law was often more severe than civil law. At that period, few but the clergy were literate. By a centuries-long process the clause evolved into a pattern of substitution for literate offenders, whether they were clerics or not, of other penalties than death if they pleaded benefit of clergy. The eighteenth century inherited this discriminatory practice, but long before the century was over allowed it to obsolesce.[31]

Tampering with the coinage for private profit was from ancient times severely punished because of the conviction that it caused damage to the working of a vital community service and involved the equivalent of stealing of public property. In the early 1690s England was undergoing a major monetary crisis as a consequence of the deterioration of the coinage resulting in part from coin-clipping and other methods of abstracting metal from the coins before passing them on as legal tender. Some years before, capital punishment had been decreed for this offence in substitution for older penalties involving several degrees of mutilation and torture. William Fleetwood, chaplain to the king and later bishop of Ely, in 1694 delivered a sermon against clipping. Fleetwood was one of the many clergymen who compounded his theology with economics and vice versa. Lord Keynes, in 1941, in a letter to Archbishop Temple encouraging him to continue to speak with assurance in public discussion of economic issues, cited Fleetwood as one of a sizeable group of clergymen who in his century were almost alone in developing politico-economic thought.[32] In his sermon Fleetwood expressed regret for the substitution for the penalties imposed for coin-clipping in older times of what he regarded as the unduly mild punishment of death. His sermon is the clearest contemporary expression I have found of the type of reasoning which could then lead men of the most estimable character to accept and approve penalties of the most extreme harshness for what they regarded as major crimes against a country's economic institutions. Here are two relevant passages from his sermon:

> The laws of our country in King Athelstan's time, punished them . . . with the cutting off their right-hand, and fixing them [i.e. their hands] over the place where

---

[31] For the history of 'benefit of clergy', see Stephen, *History of the Criminal Law of England*, vol. I *passim*.

[32] See F. Iremonger, *William Temple Archbishop of Canterbury, His Life and Letters* (London, 1948, pp. 438–9), for the text of Keynes's letter.

they committed the offence. In King Ethelred's days they were to undergo the *treble ordeal*, i.e., to carry a red-hot iron of three pound weight in their hands such a determined space of ground, and if they miscarried there, they were to die. In Henry I's time they were condemned to lose, some their hands, and some their eyes . . . These punishments were after chang'd into the modern executions, and have so continued ever since, altho 'tis probable that punishments of greater pain and constant shame, such as they heretofore were, would secure us better than putting many to a short and easy death . . .

And if there appears but little of Christianity in such sermons [as this one], it will be to such as consider not, how great a part justice and honesty, and fair and righteous dealing, make up of this divine religion, and how great care the doctrines of the Gospel take, not only of men's souls in the world to come, but of the good and welfare of their bodies here.[33]

Imprisonment for debt is the only category of legislation of economic relevance that I have found which from the seventeenth to the nineteenth century gave rise to a continuing and impressive series of protests resting, in part at least, on strictly humanitarian grounds. This series of protests was left substantially unanswered, but some minor changes in the laws in the direction of lesser harshness were made before the end of the eighteenth century.

Humanitarian objection to imprisonment for debt arose from a sense of inappropriateness in degree of the punishment to the offense. It arose also from the failure of the legislation to differentiate between those who were fraudulently delinquent and those who were innocent victims of misfortune. The fact that the jails were managed as private enterprises by licensed jailers operating for private profit and subject to no obligations to feed the prisoners or to maintain prescribed standards of sanitary and other facilities was also subjected to vigorous criticism. The jailers in fact operated what could be called delinquent-debtor hotels, and they depended for their compensation on what they could extort from the inmates or their outside friends for food, quarters, and facilities. Delinquency in debt, it may be important to notice, could happen to members of any social class, and a record of those imprisoned for debt and of their close relatives would include an astounding number of names of authors, artists, poets, clergymen, and others who later attained some degree of eminence. Samuel Johnson, who made some of the most sensible and most constructive criticisms of the laws against debtors published during the century, reported estimates, for a period when the population of England did not exceed 6,000,000, that at any one time 20,000 would be in prison because of debt, of whom about one-fourth would die each year from the hardships of prison life.[34]

---

[33] *A Sermon against Clipping* (London, 1694), pp. 23–4, 28–9.

[34] *The Idler*, no. 22, 16 September 1758 and no. 38, 6 January 1759, reprinted in *The British*

What explanation can be offered for this survival of a practice which in its own time had many critics and few open defenders? The practice did not clearly serve the self-interest of any substantial social group except those creditors who were convinced that the delinquency of debtors was largely wilful and fraudulent or that the indefinite imprisonment of even innocent debtors would coerce their families or friends into liquidating their indebtedness. As in most other areas, legislative ingenuity and good public administration were here woefully lacking, and there had been no real attempt to find procedures whereby the fraudulent debtor could be penalised without treating the innocent debtor in identical manner. There was in the middle and especially the commercial classes a strong feeling that, even without any fraudulent intent, it was sinful to get into debt beyond one's certain ability to repay on schedule. There was among them, as well as among members of other social groups, the belief that the punctual meeting of financial engagements was so vital, so sacred, a part of the code of civilised society, that no considerations of humanity should be permitted to weaken the sanctions which society imposed on those who did not fulfil to the letter the requirements of that code.[35] Harshness of treatment of violators of accepted moral principles, in this as in other fields, was often defended by the theological principle that the obligation of mercy was not applicable for offenders if it involved, directly or indirectly, withholding mercy from their innocent victims, actual or potential. It was a defect of the proposers of reform on humanitarian grounds that they did not adequately apply themselves to formulating alternative procedures which would give promise of preserving and even strengthening pressure for performance of contract without resort to the practice of imprisonment for debt. Progress in this was not to be achieved until the next century.

The English poor laws came close to being a purely English institution without a parallel on a national scale anywhere on the Continent, or, for that matter, in Scotland or Ireland. They required each parish to provide relief in cash or kind to those poor with right of settlement in that parish, and to finance the relief by local 'rates' or taxes based on the rental value of landed property. The poor laws were

---

Essayists (London), XXXIII (1823), 70–3, 122–6. For the efforts of a voluntary agency to alleviate the conditions of those imprisoned for debt, see James Neild, *An Account of the Rise, Progress, and Present State, of the Society for the Discharge and Relief of Persons Imprisoned for Small Debts* (London, 1802). Neild was an officer of this society from 1773 on.

[35] The severity of the treatment of defaulters on debt payment was often as great in ancient Rome, in the Middle Ages, and in post-Reformation Catholic countries as in eighteenth-century England. Cf. Thorsten Sellin's Foreword to Georg Rusche and Otto Kirchheimer, *Punishment and Social Structure* (New York, 1939), p. vi: 'The sanguinary punishments and tortures of old are no evidence of bloodthirstiness or sadism on the part of those who used them. They rather testify to the fact that those who designed them could conceive of no better, that is, more efficient, way of securing protection for the social values which they treasured.'

a post-Reformation institution, and were introduced as a substitute for the alms distributed by the Catholic Church from its landed and other endowments and from the current flow of donations to it by the faithful. The English system was later to be pejoratively labelled 'legal charity' by continental Catholics, and to be characterised by them as morally inferior to a system, consisting exclusively of voluntary individual charity and of more-or-less organised charity administered by the Church, which did not establish legal rights on the part of the beneficiaries or legal obligations on the part of the donors. In Scotland, relief to the poor made obligatory by law was almost universally opposed as presenting obstacles to discrimination between deserving and undeserving poor, and, by making relief in case of distress a safe expectation, undermining the natural incentives for the poor to practice industry, frugality, and other economic virtues. Scottish commentators, with scarcely any exception that I have been able to find before 1840, were uniformly critical of the English system. They found especially objectionable in the English system the necessity of protecting the property owners in the individual parishes from the hazard of unlimited tax burdens by associating, with the obligation on each parish to grant relief to those in need and having legal rights of settlement within that parish, the imposition of an elaborate and harsh code of discipline on even the most industrious and well-behaved of the labouring classes. This code restricted their right of migration from parish to parish, authorised the taking away of young children from the custody of their parents if the latter were on relief, interfered with rights of marriage, and in many other ways abridged basic freedoms of the lower classes. Those who sought escape from the poor-law discipline by resorting to vagrancy or 'going on the road' were subjected to penalties so brutal that a thoroughly unsentimental English authority on the poor laws, Richard Burn, could write in 1764 that 'This part of our history looks like the history of the savages in America. Almost all severities have been exercised against vagrants, except scalping.'[36]

There was little enthusiasm in England itself for the poor laws, and they were supported mostly as partial remedies for evils for which less objectionable remedies were not in sight. In some quarters there was radical opposition to them on principle or because of their unsatisfactory mode of operation. They were of such long standing, however, so deeply entangled with the English wage structure, labour-hiring methods, and lower-class patterns of family formation, that anything more than piecemeal and gradual change would have been a revolutionary step. Major poor-law reform had to wait until the nineteenth century, although throughout the eighteenth century there was a steady flow of suggestions for change in the poor-laws.

[36] *The History of the Poor Laws* (London, 1764), p. 120.

Some of these proposals for change were for more generous treatment of the 'deserving poor', the involuntarily unemployed and the physically handicapped, but almost all of them recommended more severe treatment of the 'undeserving poor'. Some of the proposals advised that the territorial units for assessment of poor rates and for defining the boundaries for legal settlement be extended to include more than a single parish. An ever-present objective was the economic one of making the poor a more productive resource for the national economy, by reducing the number who were voluntarily or involuntarily idle. There were schemes galore for making the poorest of the poor self-supporting by gathering them in workhouses and putting them to work under official supervision, the aged, the young children, the physically or mentally handicapped, the wilfully idle, included. Even without consideration of the desperately low standards, national and local, of public administration in England in the century most of these schemes were visionary in character in their assumption that ways could be found of immediately making the least eligible sections of the population not only self-supporting but producers of a net contribution to the national economy.

The most visionary of such schemes was, if I interpret it correctly, a proposal made by Bishop Berkeley in 1721 that there be raised by act of parliament annually for seven years an amount equal to the average annual yield of the poor rates, the proceeds to be expended on workhouses.[37] Berkeley promised that if prudently managed this 'would for ever free the nation from the care of providing for the poor, and at the same time considerably improve our manufactures. We might by these means rid our streets of beggars; even the children, the maimed, and the blind might be put in a way of doing something for their livelihood.'[38]

In anything like an exhaustive treatment of ideas and practices in eighteenth-century England relating to advocacy of or hostility or indifference to what later generations regarded as 'social reform' I would have to deal extensively with the general field of taxation and at least to mention so peculiarly English a phenomenon as the press-gang as a method of recruiting for the navy, as well as other matters, some of which I am no doubt unaware of. One generalisation I am, however, willing to commit myself to: the politically important sectors of the English population were not *laissez faire* on principle, and accepted as a matter of course a substantial measure of state intervention, provided it used techniques of administration tolerable to them and provided government did not tamper with the prevailing social structure. A present-day eighteenth-century scholar of distinction, Thomas W. Copeland, has heralded as 'probably the most important

---

[37] 'An Essay towards Preventing the Ruin of Great Britain' (1721), in *The Works of George Berkeley*, A. C. Fraser, ed. (Oxford, 1871), vol. III.

[38] *Ibid*. III, 198.

single act of reform achieved in England in the eighteenth century' the Economical Reform Act of 1780, sponsored by Edmund Burke.[39] The Act was in fact in minor scope and of debated and debatable effectiveness, but I nevertheless cannot challenge this appraisal of it. The American and the French Revolutions did serve to widen and deepen the range of political and economic discussion, and to introduce change into the air, although little of this change manifested itself on the ground until after the turn of the century. Of major importance, conducive in a host of subtle ways to social change, was the growth in size of the middle classes relative to the gentry and to the proletariat, but the effects of this growth are in the main not easy to perceive until well after 1800. The French Revolution, in fact, by the fear it engendered in the upper classes of like threat to their own vested interests in England, stimulated reaction rather than either strategic reform or mere continuance of the previously prevailing complacent, moderate, and stagnant conservatism of which Edmund Burke had been the most eloquent exponent.

More significant, I think, than the Economical Reform Act of 1780 as a harbinger of things to come in another generation or two was the astonishing speed with which John Howard, by a one-man effort, persuaded parliament to enact in 1774 a measure of genuine prison reform, requiring government and its agents to accept financial and supervisory responsibility for the payment of jailers, the cleaning of prisons, and the decent care of prisoners. English prisons had been notorious for the unregulated authority their jailers wielded, and for the prevalence in the jails of 'jail-fever', a virulent form of typhus fever not present in continental prisons and attributed by modern authorities to the specially filthy state of the English prisons. It seems clear that credit for this unusually quick success in parliament of a reform proposal was largely due to Howard's care and skill in preparing and presenting his case.[40] This suggests that the history of reform in England in the eighteenth century might have been a great deal more impressive if there had been universities or other institutions where men could have been taught the skills and disciplines needed for effective planning of programmes requiring, for their successful technical application, professional knowledge and administrative imagination. Such training was in some measure already routine in German universities and elsewhere, but it went against the spirit of English government institutions and the incredible torpor of the ancient universities.

[39] *Our Eminent Friend Edmund Burke* (New Haven, 1949), p. 164.

[40] On John Howard's heroic career as prison reformer, see: John Aikin, *A View of the Character and Public Services of the late John Howard, Esq.* (London, 1792); William A. Guy, 'John Howard's True Place in History', *Journal of the Royal Statistical Association*, XXXVIII (1875), 430–7; D. L. Howard, *John Howard; Prison Reformer* (London, 1958).

Systematic search would, I am sure, add somewhat to the meagre list known to me of individual proposals for reform in general and specific reforms in particular and thus qualify, in minor degree, the picture I have given of a dominating complacency with respect to the eighteenth-century *status quo*. In other countries, and in other periods of English history, earlier and later, utopian literature is a good place to look for evidence of the existence of current hopes for social change which it would have been embarrassing or even hazardous publicly to disclose in plain language. In the England of our period, however, such literature was scanty and unrevealing. In the days of the early Stuarts, utopianism was frowned upon by the Church as smacking of the Anabaptistical heresy of dreaming of a perfect state on this earth. In the eighteenth century it would have been frowned upon as smacking of a tendency towards secular 'enthusiasm'. I have found only three utopian items in our period which have much relevance for reformist thought. The anonymous *Free State of Noland* (London, 1696), in which I think I detect a Harringtonian flavour, concentrates on constitutional reform with a moderate equalitarian bias. James Burgh's *Account of . . . the Cessares* (1764), proposes the division of the commons and the wastes among the poor, subject to a moderate annual charge whose proceeds were to be given to those persons who thereby would lose their 'right of commoning', and proposes also that mines should be what we would now call 'nationalised'. Michael Woodhull's *The Equality of Mankind* (1765) was a poem which was anti-monarchical, anti-clerical, and unenthusiastic about the middle class, but it made no specific proposals. Woodhull's sardonic characterisation of the middle class may be of interest:

> Those motley Beings next in order place,
> Whose wavering stations wear a doubtful face,
> Who, dragg'd by Fortune into middle Life,
> That vortex of malevolence and strife,
> Envying the Great, and scoffing at the mean,
> Now swoln with pride, now wasted with chagrin,
> Like Mahomat's unsettled ashes dwell,
> Midway suspended between Heaven and Hell.[41]

I have found in the century only one extreme English radical, Thomas Spence. In 1775 he proposed in a lecture in Newcastle a substantially equalitarian system of land tenure. He later was to attract many followers, and also some official persecution, by his republications of this lecture and by other publications advo-

---

[41] The Equality of Mankind [1765], new ed. (London, 1799), ll. 295–302.

cating agrarian and political radicalism.[42] Henry Brooke, an Irishman who lived at times in England, in 1767 published a novel, *The Fool of Quality*, which contained a medley of mystical and other miscellaneous material, as well as reflections on society which included one of the early manifestations of the influence of Rousseau on British social thought. It is to me a strange book, but in it the author makes one of his characters utter some remarks of a genuinely radical and quite pre-Marxian nature. I cite as an example: 'I look upon the money amassed by the wealthy to have been already extracted from the earnings of the poor, the poor farmer, the poor craftsman, the hard-handed peasant, and the day labourer, whose seven children perhaps subsist on the milk of a couple of cows.'[43]

Jonathan Shipley, who seems to have been the most liberal and least conventional of the Anglican bishops of the time in his references to social issues, in a sermon of 1773 relating to the colonies expressed the hope that a less unequal social structure than the existing one in the homeland might, under different conditions, be established in the colonies: 'May not a method be invented of procuring some tolerable share of the comforts of life to those inferior useful ranks of men to whose industry we are indebted for the whole? Time and discipline may discover some means to correct the extreme inequalities of condition between the rich and the poor, so dangerous to the innocence and the happiness of both.'[44]

Adam Smith, of course, has outstanding claims to being an advocate of social reform, but except for his slashing attack on the settlement laws his major proposals for change were not especially directed at improvement of the relative economic status of the poor. David Williams, a dissenting clergyman, like Jonathan Shipley a friend of Benjamin Franklin, in an undeservedly neglected book, *Lectures on the Universal Principles and Duties of Religion and Morality* (London, 1779), deals at length, in a moderately equalitarian and philosophically anarchistic tone somewhat anticipatory of William Godwin, with the proper economic and ethical relations between the social classes.

I have called your attention to nearly the sum of the English discussions in the century up to the 1770s encountered in my reading which I regard as being clearly social-reformist, expressly or by implication, with respect to the status of the 'labouring poor'. It is, I confess, not a large sum, and better-informed scholars can, I am sure, add to it. I remind you, however, that, to ease my task, I have withheld comment on the post-American-Revolution decades, which are much

[42] Few copies of the 1775 edition of his lecture seem to be extant. The 1793 edition, with a new title, is reprinted in M. Beer, ed., *The Pioneers of Land Reform* (New York, 1920), pp. 5–16. For an account of Thomas Spence, see Olive D. Rudkin, *Thomas Spence and his Connections* (London, 1927).

[43] *The Fool of Quality* [1767], reprint, London, n.d. (*c.* 1925), p. 346.

[44] *Works* (London, 1792), I, 308.

richer in social criticism, and have deliberately excluded from my coverage the works of Scots and Irishmen written in their local surroundings and for local audiences.

Our visual notions of the conditions in which the eighteenth-century English poor lived, especially as far as rural housing is concerned, point more to the picturesque than to the sordid. The eighteenth-century rural cottage, whether as externally observed in its surviving examples or as seen in contemporary prints or paintings, is invariably good to look at, but it is representative of a fraction only of the cottages of the time. The intentionally 'picturesques' cottages were, moreover, built ordinarily on the estates of substantial landlords, and owned, constructed, sited, and designed by them or their agents. We all continued to find them 'picturesque', but their beauty may have been, as in the case of a goodly apple rotten at the core, wholly external, and even this external beauty was created in the service of the landlord, as embellishment to his estate, and to some extent to the disservice of the occupants. It has been said, for instance, that the gables of these cottages used up precious space and their windows often were made never to open. Of the many pictures by the artist, George Morland, which feature the picturesqueness of the English countryside, one, entitled 'Happy Cottagers', shows a pair of sturdy and becomingly dressed adults, three buxom children, a cottage as background, a large tree embracing the house, and an elaborate hanging birdcage at the side of the cottage. The cottage itself is not clearly depicted. It may well represent a one-room shelter for five persons. But the ensemble does make a pretty, if somewhat idealised, picture.[45] Should, however, the fact, if it is a fact, that the one-room cottage had to serve five persons detract from our appreciation of its pleasing exterior? Were the conditions of the poor, moreover, then any better anywhere else? Except for reports by visitors from colonial America, who did find English poverty depressing, and for lack of enthusiasm on the part of visitors from the Continent about the climate and especially about sanitary conditions and the state of public facilities in general in the English towns, most visitors to England appear to have found the condition of the English working classes superior to what they were familiar with in their own countries. English visitors to the Continent, or to Scotland or Ireland, likewise found the conditions of the working classes superior at home to what they were elsewhere.

There has been in our own day, however, all-embracing appreciation often approaching infatuation with what we take to have been the material aspects of

[45] I am relying here mostly on G. E. Fussell, *The English Rural Labourer, His Home, Furniture, Clothing & Food from Tudor to Victorian Times* (London, 1949), ch. V, 'Cottages'. Morland's picture is reproduced on the page opposite p. 65.

English eighteenth-century day-to-day life: church, domestic and public architecture, gardens, interior decorating, paintings, carriages, saddle horses, silver and porcelain, clothing, and so on. It would perhaps contribute to a more balanced picture of the century if we keep in mind that, as in the case of the rural cottages of the poor, the things of beauty and of ease and comfort in the main existed for the service and delectation of the upper classes, and that in the main they were things to be constructed and cleaned and brushed and dusted and repaired by the poor for their superiors rather than to be possessed and enjoyed by themselves. John Chamberlayne, year after year in his year-book, *The State of Great Britain*, had an entry, 'The meanest mechanics and husbandmen want not silver spoons and some silver cups in their houses'.[46] I have often wondered whether we should take his word for those silver spoons and cups. But what of it? Even if they were really only pewter, some of us would still be envious.

I resist deliberately and determinedly, moreover, giving expression to any urge I may be subject to to assert obligations of the eighteenth century to conform to your—or to my—standards of social justice, of freedom, of beauty. Were I to take as seriously all I read in our very literary reviews about the sad cultural predicament we are in to-day as I take the current official reports on the economic condition of our own lower classes up to, say, the 20 per cent line, I should have to conclude that the only ethical superiority that our comfortable classes can claim as compared to eighteenth-century England is that we do have, and even systematically cultivate, a guilty social conscience in relation to the poor. I am not unaware, moreover, that not a few American academic aficionados of the literature of the English Augustan Age find a satisfying substitute for a sense of social guilt in the virtuous weeping of the Augustan literati. They shed their tears very publicly in the cemeteries over tombstones selected at random and in the contemplation of death at large, rather than in the slums as a response to the misery of living poor. But, if there is virtue in tear-shedding, *per se*, why boggle at where they chose to practice it? And was it not a credit to the age that authors could so successfully move their audiences to weep copiously, even if it was only in response to the exhibition of anguish by characters in plays or novels?

I have met few professional students of the English eighteenth century, aside from its theology and its bishops, who were not devoted admirers of not only those aspects of the century with which they were professionally occupied, but of the century as a whole, lock, stock, and barrel. Naturally, therefore, I have premonitions that you have found the enthusiasm expressed in this paper for the English eighteenth century too muted, and my love for it excessively dissembled.

---

[46] See, for example, *Magna Britannia Notitia: Or, The Present State of Great Britain* (London, 1723), p. 189; (1737), p. 177.

If I should nevertheless plead my love for it, it might provoke your saying about me in relation to the eighteenth century what George Eliot made Tom Tulliver say about himself in relation to birds: 'I'm fond of birds—that is, of throwing stones at them.' I would insist, however, that the England of the century we are discussing has always impressed me as a nearly perfect gentleman's utopia. What more can be asked of a commentator on the eighteenth century who claims only to be an aspiring scholar, and who happens to think that a scholar, as distinguished from a gentleman, or from a moraliser, must strive to escape acquiring the habit of appraising a past century in terms of the extent to which it conforms to his own values, preferences, tastes, and moral sentiments? In any case, even the saintly Thomas More's *Utopia* had slaves in it. A guest at a dinner party in Brussels during the French Revolution remarked that he admired the *Ancien Régime* except for its abuses. His émigré hostess exclaimed: 'Les abus! Mais c'est ce qu'il y avait de mieux.' 'The abuses! Why they were its best part!'[47] I do not approve of going quite that far, for in moral matters I am a historical relativist of what is perhaps a peculiar kind. I believe that each century except one's own has a right to its abuses, but that no century has an obligation to condemn, to praise, or to offer apologies for, another century's lapses from perfection.

[47] C. B. A. Behrens, in a review of two books on the French aristocracy under the *Ancien Régime*, *The New York Review of Books*, 6 October 1966, p. 16.

13

SATIRE AND ECONOMICS IN THE AUGUSTAN AGE OF SATIRE

THE INVITATION to contribute to a *Festschrift* in honour of my friend and colleague Louis Landa was very welcome to me. I was somewhat at a loss, however, as to a topic which would both have some relevance to Landa's interests and be within my competence, as an economist, to deal with. Shortly before the receipt of the invitation I participated in a symposium sponsored by Reed College on the Augustan Age of Satire, and in the process of preparing for it I did my first substantial reading of Augustan satirical texts and of what modern littérateurs have said about them. I decided that a reworked version of the lecture I gave at Reed College on some relations between Augustan satire and economics would come closer in relevance of subject-matter to Landa's interests than anything else I could do. That I lack the technical competence to deal in a sophisticated manner with satire as a literary genre I am fully aware. I have persuaded myself, however, that it is better that my topic should be dealt with by an amateur on the literary side than that it should not be dealt with at all. Although my conscience has been calmed, I confess that I would feel much better equipped to deal with my topic if my understanding of the nature of satire were nearly as good as Louis Landa's understanding of the complexities of eighteenth-century English economic thought.

My greatest difficulty in absorbing the professional literature on Augustan satire is in adjusting to the reverential tone with which much of it deals with satire, as if satire were in a realm by itself, above other literary genres; the satirists themselves, by attacking the persons, the classes, and the political, religious, and economic doctrines they abhor, damn these persons and doctrines and become in a way sanctified figures. In both respects, I grant, this attitude conforms with what the satirists regarded as the proper response to their efforts. Pope, for instance, certainly, and Swift probably, sincerely thought of satire, as employed by them, as a 'sacred weapon', used in 'Truth's defence', and 'sole Dread of Folly,

Reprinted from *The Augustan Milieu*, eds. Henry Knight Miller, Eric Rothstein, and G. S. Rousseau (Oxford: Clarendon Press, 1970), pp. 77–101.

Vice, and Insolence![1] Gilbert Highet says of the Augustan satirists that they operated in response to 'the urge to make fun of fools and scoundrels'.[2] I would not dream of questioning this, but I would insist that, like most humans, the satirists did not restrict the use of their aggressive talents to the lashing of rogues and fools. Satire, as far as I can see, has no greater magical power to purify its user, and no more visible tendency to be used only in the service of truth, beauty, and virtue, than poetry in general, or prose in general. I shall, indeed, argue later that an ancient doctrine especially prevalent among the saints, that the use of satire and its associated forms of wit should be left to the sinners, has often operated as a hindrance both to resort to satire by saints and to its effective use as an instrument of persuasion to righteousness.

For the economist *qua* economist what may most matter, and may be all that matters, in a satiric work is its actual influence, direct or indirect, on its audience, regardless of what may have been the intention or the hope of its author. This is fortunate for the economist, for it is generally easier to trace the actual influence of a particular satire than to penetrate the intention of the satirist.

Identification of the 'intention' of the satirist is primarily the task of the professional interpreter of texts. The record shows that in the case of satirical texts performance of the task encounters special difficulties, and often fails to result in a generally accepted resolution of these difficulties, even after centuries of effort. The satirist may have a bundle of intentions, not altogether harmonious, and he may even be unstable in his distribution of emphasis between his various intentions.

A satiric effort may be addressed to a particular audience to please or entertain it, or to arouse or strengthen its support of—or its hostility to—a particular cause or group or individual, or to provoke its audience and cause it discomfort. When Swift or Pope made the 'moneyed interest', or a particular Whig politician, or a particular group of Whigs, or Whiggery in general, the butt of his satire, how can one tell whether his primary objective was the pleasure to be derived from the exercise of his satirical skill, or the giving of pleasure to his Tory audience, or the giving of pain to the Whigs? A Grub-Street satirist, of course, might choose his victim with an eye to finding a paying audience. A satirist might make his audience his target, in the hope of reforming his hearers or readers by making them aware of their shortcomings, as a preacher may use satire to induce in the members of his congregation shame for their misdoings.

An intellectual satirist may satirize an occupation, or discipline, such as natural science, or law, or economics, or moral preaching, either to laugh its prac-

---

[1] 'Epilogue to the Satires, Second Dialogue' (1738), *Works* (London, 1751), iv. 248.
[2] *The Anatomy of Satire* (Princeton, 1962), p. 305.

titioners out of their obnoxious procedures or convictions, or to make it more difficult for them to obtain new followers. It is even conceivable that a satirist may have it as his major objective to hurt his target because of personal enmity, or desire for revenge for some previous affront, or as a phase of political warfare, or simply to find an outlet for his sadistic impulses. Only one thing seems to be exempt, or nearly so, from being satirized, and that is satire itself.

Defoe's *Robinson Crusoe* has been interpreted as a satire on capitalism, perhaps including some self-satire by the author as a complying member of a defective social system. There is no difficulty in principle in recognizing the possibility of deliberate self-satire. In this particular instance, however, I am by no means convinced by the evidence that has been gathered that there is a satirical element in *Robinson Crusoe* directed against capitalism, or against Daniel Defoe as a beneficiary thereof. One ground on which this interpretation seems to rest is that Defoe was trying to show how much an isolated individual could achieve economically without the aid of the economic market, and therefore how exploitative and unproductive was the well-paid machinery of capitalistic society. If this were a correct interpretation of Defoe's intention, he would have blundered as a satirist in giving Robinson Crusoe a rich hoard of capital, in the form of the cargo of the wrecked ship, to draw upon freely. In this important respect Defoe, by putting Crusoe in a situation where some capital goods are to him free goods, differentiated his environment from both that of the happy savage and that of the individual living in a capitalist community, and made Crusoe's situation more akin to that of the religious hermit who lives, in part at least, on the charity of those who toil and save in the market community.

Whatever the intentions of the satirist, to be effective satire requires both skill on the part of the satirist in pursuing his intentions and a not too unfavourable setting for their realization. Some intentions, if they are evident, can operate to make success difficult or unattainable. Some settings are inherently unfavourable for some or for all kinds of satirical intentions, and thus offer a barren field for the successful operation of satire. As an instrument of persuasion to action in a social cause, as a means of changing political attitudes or of helping or hurting a specific occupational or class group, satire thus has some inherent limitations.

Satire is a rhetorical genre which, as compared, say, with open and forthright exhortation, or with straight invective hurled at the enemy, or with positive argument, is peculiarly dependent on a high level of literary or verbal aptitude and sophistication on the part of its audiences, and on their possession in some measure of a sense of humour. It uses some degree of indirection, of paradox, of exaggeration, of distortion, or of disclosure of hitherto unperceived contradictions within established attitudes, as a method of changing the attitudes of its audiences. Some minimum degree of skill on the part of the satirist, together with some minimum degree of intelligence and verbal alertness on the part of the audience, will therefore normally be necessary if attitudes are to be changed upon exposure to the satire, instead of being left unmoved, or even being moved in a direction opposite to that intended by the satirist. Satire is a two-edged weapon; if misunderstood, the wrong edge may cut. If the satirist delivers his effort orally, he can use facial gestures, or modulations of his voice, to help make his intent apparent. If his tongue is at times in his cheek, he can let you see this visually and give you warning. Even then, however, he risks failure of communication if he occasionally shifts his tongue from one cheek to the other. In print, the words have to do the whole work, except for the knowledge or the notions the audience has of the record and the convictions of the author. Satire is thus not a suitable instrument for direct persuasion of a mass audience, and always needs a select audience.

Even for persons of a fair level of sophistication, satire often misfires. One main cause is that the audience it is addressed to fails to perceive when satire is intended, especially when the satirist—notably Jonathan Swift in *The Tale of a Tub*—mixes different modes in the same piece as an exercise in literary virtuosity, or where the audience recognizes that a satirical element is present but is mistaken as to the intended target. In such cases a country-cousin of satire, slanted and invidious invective directed at a frankly designated target, would probably be more effective as persuasion than elaborately wrought satire, and even straight and unshaped invective might do better still. Literary critics sometimes offer us allegedly sure signs of satirical intent, such as giving distorted or ridiculous names to the targets,[3] and this device has certainly been used occasionally by even the most august of the 'Augustan' satirists. I am old enough to be able to remember how effective it was on the modern vaudeville stage. It is still an effective weapon among children. It may well be, therefore, that, if distortion of names is not merely ridiculous but is directed to have some special satirical pertinence, it may be effective also for a higher-level audience. Swift and Pope must have thought so. Later, Dickens was to use this ploy indefatigably, but perhaps not without fatiguing his audience.

It is perhaps when satire is carried to its highest literary levels and is directed to an élite audience that the greatest risks of failure of communication may arise and may lead to the greatest possible amount of doubt, confusion, and misinterpretation. One of the chief literary achievements of the English Augustan Age was to substitute a plain and lucid English prose for the highly decorated and

---

[3] Gilbert Highet (op. cit., p. 275) remarks, 'Distorted or ridiculous names are always a sure sign of satire'.

involuted, but no doubt also magnificent, prose of the previous century. I suspect that one of the literary explanations of the popularity of satire among writers in the Augustan Age was that resort to it enabled them to satisfy in their writing a nostalgia for obscurity, contrivance, impenetrability, while on the surface conforming to the new standards of lucidity and clarity. If they were at first unaware of the risks of failure to communicate that they thus ran, the painful experience which resulted often led them to a second attempt in order to repair the damage.

One writer, noting that 'there seem'd to be much want of a particular note of punctuation to distinguish irony, which is often so delicately couch'd as to escape the notice even of the attentive reader, and betray him into error', published a collection of other authors' poems, punctuated by dots above the ironic passages, as an example of the improvement this simple device would bring to the interpretation of texts.[4] He apparently overlooked the possibility that an author might wish only his circle of like-minded friends, and not the rabble or the enemy, to perceive when he was serious and when waxing ironic or satiric. Swift, in a Preface added in 1710 to *The Tale of a Tub* to explain 'the Authors Intention' (a humiliating thing, I should think, for a satirist to have to do), said that some of the passages most objected to by readers 'are what they call Parodies, where the Author personates the Style and manner of other Writers, whom he has a mind to expose'. In the same year a minor writer, Joseph Trapp, with some overt indication that *The Tale of a Tub* was in his mind, ventured on more dangerous territory than parody, as a satirical device for calling attention to an enemy's flaws, by substituting for parody unaltered replicas of his target's texts. He did this to show that the tract he was attacking 'does not deserve to be answer'd. Or if it does, I will make the Author of it answer himself. . . . I will extract some of his remarkable passages, and lay them in more view before the eyes of the reader.'[5] I suppose this device could be designated 'enforced self-satire'. I have seen it used even in economics textbooks, where an incriminating passage is reproduced from some other book, but with an exclamation mark supplied by the author of the textbook to indicate that he was quoting with satirical intent, and not as a token of approval. Trapp, however, was not really content to rely on this maximum-risk device, which came perilously close to being analogous to a merchant's paying for the printing of his competitor's advertisements. Apart from selecting texts which may seem ridiculous only because they are wrenched from their contexts in an invidious way, Trapp provided tendentious labels for the reproduced texts,

---

[4] Edward Capell, ed., *Prolusions; or, select pieces of antient poetry* (London, 1760), Preface, p. v.

[5] Joseph Trapp, *Most Faults on one Side* (London, 1710), pp. 55–6.

and he inserted, although without deceit, hostile comments into the heart of some of the extracts.

Francis Hare, later to be a bishop, in a satirical tract of 1714 pretended to be dissuading a devout young man of independent mind, in his own spiritual and material interest, from entering the ministry of the Church of England. Hare had been in controversy with the Church hierarchy, in part because of his allegedly Arian views. In this tract he warned prospective clergymen of the pressure and the discriminatory economic treatment to which the lower clergy were subject unless they fully confirmed to the doctrinal views of the hierarchy. In eighteenth-century England this was strong meat. But Hare ended his tract by confessing that he himself regarded what he had written as 'a strange paradox' and 'a very wicked one' if read literally.[6] He presumably was seeking the benefits of satirical licence whilst guarding either his readers or himself or both from the consequences of failure to make clear that his text was not to be interpreted literally. The result for himself was that he was censured by the Lower House of Convocation of the Church of England for treating 'things sacred in a ludicrous and prophane manner'—that is, satirically.

Bishop Joseph Butler, in his *Analogy of Religion, Natural and Revealed, to the Constitution and Course of Nature*, 1736, used as a major argument in defence of revealed religion that the objections made by deists against revealed religion were applicable in like manner to natural theology. To some this seemed a dangerous line of argument, since it seemed to leave open to agnostics the retort that Butler had only demonstrated that Anglicanism and deism were in the same leaking boat. Lord Bolingbroke, as a deist, had been writing in radical manner and with great frankness against revealed religion and the organized ecclesiastical institutions which supported it, although he withheld publication of some of these writings during his lifetime. Edmund Burke, in *A Vindication of Natural Society*, 1756, one of his earliest publications, replied to Bolingbroke by adopting Butler's analogical mode of argument. Unlike Butler, however, Burke wrote satirically. He pretended to be defending 'natural society', or society without government, and to be attacking government. His intent was to demonstrate that the same kind of argument with which Bolingbroke attacked revealed religion could with comparable effectiveness be used to attack government. To show that, in part at least, he was directing his essay against Bolingbroke, and to show also that he was writing satirically, Burke parodied Bolingbroke's style and introduced some patently fantastic argument in derogation of government. It may be that Burke was also parodying Rousseau's primitivism.

---

[6] Francis Hare, *The Difficulties and Discouragements Which attend the Study of the Scriptures in the Way of Private Judgment* (7th edn., London, 1716).

Burke pictured current society under government as permeated by war, by gross social inequality, inefficiency, corruption, and by encroachments on the natural liberty of the individual. In contrast he gave a romantically utopian picture of what society could or would be like in the absence of civil government. To some of Burke's readers, however, the satiric intent of the author in disparaging government in general was not apparent, and the description of government as it operated in the England of the time was not visibly fantastic. To these readers, and to all readers who were in no mood to have the existing political and economic *status quo* undermined even in fantasy, Burke's picture of society under government, including its economic aspects, was made too ugly, too realistic, and too plausible, to represent a successful use of the satirical technique. Within a year Burke brought out a new edition, with an added Preface explaining that his argument for natural society and against government was deliberately 'specious', that is, satirically intended:

> The design was, to show that, without the exertion of any considerable forces, the same engines which were employed [e.g., by Bolingbroke] for the destruction of religion, might be employed with equal success for the subversion of government; and that specious arguments might be used against those things which they, who doubt of everything else, will never permit to be questioned.

Read literally, *The Vindication* was perhaps the most radical social essay published in the century after the time of the Commonwealth. Read literally, it was the first general formulation, at least in England, of the case for philosophical anarchism. It was later to be read as such by William Godwin, and was an influence on him when he was writing his *Political Justice*, the pioneer exposition of sincere English anarchism. *The Vindication* itself was reprinted by American anarchists in 1858 and in 1885. It was respectfully commented on by Rudolf Grossmann, a member of an anarchist sect of communists, in 1907 as a serious plea for 'natural society'. Grossmann interpreted Burke's later Preface to be intended 'as dust for the eyes of the stupid and the great'.[7] An American neo-liberal (or neo-conservative) in 1958 renewed the argument that *The Vindication* was sincere and not basically satirical, and gave some support to the idea that it should be included in the 'individualist camp', 'since there is no sign of enmity to private property as such in this work'.[8]

---

[7] Grossmann wrote under the pseudonym of 'Pierre Ramus'. See Pierre Ramus, *William Godwin, der Theoretiker des kommunistischen Anarchismus* (Leipzig, 1907), pp. 10–11. See also F. E. L. Priestley, ed., William Godwin, *Enquiry concerning Political Justice* (Toronto, 1946), iii. 40, n. 40.

[8] Murray N. Rothbard, 'A Note on Burke's *Vindication*', *JHI* xix (1958), 114–18. See, for a rejoinder, John C. Weston, ibid. 438. See also [John Ward], *Monthly Review* xv (1756), 18–22; and

Another limitation on the effectiveness of satire as an instrument of persuasion was its common, though not necessary, association with humour, and in particular the constant danger that it might lead to laughter. At least from the time of ancient Greece to the eighteenth century laughter was somewhat on the defensive, on religious and on moral grounds. Its condemnation, however, like its occasional praise, was usually subject to reservations, and careful consideration commonly led to an intermediate final verdict as to its respectability. Thus Ecclesiastes 2: 2, 'I said of laughter, it is mad; and of mirth, what doeth it?', but (ibid. 3: 1 and 4) 'For everything there is a season, and a time for every purpose under heaven; . . . a time to weep, and a time to laugh'. Salvian in the fifth century preached: 'Let us laugh, Christians, but in a Christian manner.'[9] As late as the 1740s Edward Young, in his *Night Thoughts*, could write:

> Laughter, tho' never censur'd yet as sin,
> (Pardon a thought that only seems severe)
> Is half-immoral . . . (Night viii).

Shaftesbury early in the century had said in defence of ridicule, and especially of its good-humoured form, raillery, that capacity to withstand it was a good test of truth, and that truth could not be injured by it. This argument continued to be a topic for debate for a large part of the century, and many objected that Shaftesbury was unduly optimistic about the invulnerability of truth to ridicule and held that truth should not be put to this test. Some sensitive souls found repulsive on aesthetic grounds the close association of the sublime and the ridiculous that frequently occurred in satirical works.

Great sectors of the population of eighteenth-century England, for one or the other of these reasons, either must have been unreachable by satire of any subtlety or would not have reacted to it as the satirist intended or hoped. The sense of humour often necessary for the appreciation of satire is certainly not universally distributed by nature. Even if it were, cultural disciplines could suppress it, the disciplines of religious rigorism, of secular puritanism, of some occupational patterns of life, or of an educational system determined to put humour in its place. Where economic issues were involved, and where to achieve the intent of the satirist large numbers of men had to be directly influenced, satirical methods were therefore likely to be inadequate, or even to do more harm than good.

In relation to large groups, satire probably had more service to render as a lash

---

August M. Knoll, *Der soziale Gedanke im modernen Katholizismus* (Vienna, 1932), pp. 41–2, for other instances of literal interpretation of Burke's *Vindication*.

[9] Quoted by Jean Croiset, S.J., *Réflexions sur divers sujets de morale* (new edn., Paris, 1777), i. 137. (The first edition was not later than 1707.)

administered as punishment for sin, or in the service of another smaller group, perhaps chiefly for the latter's entertainment, than as an instrument of persuasion or conversion of the large groups themselves. Moreover, the individual who recognizes that he is being made the target of satire may respond by resentment, where straightforward persuasion might have won him over.

I have found satire contending with satire on anything like an equal basis in only two areas: as an exercise appropriate to the literary arena, where the issues involved were primarily literary; and in the controversies between literary Anglicans and literary deists or freethinkers, where the satirists on each side could be skilled and could hope for sophisticated audiences and vulnerable, because sensitive, targets. This, be it noted, excludes the arena of economic debate, where this kind of sophistication would not ordinarily be present. Satire was thus an upper-class preserve in the main, with the satirists in the free or paid service of their social superiors, if they were not themselves members of a high social group. The upper classes, of course, however they are defined, were not a homogeneous group. They had their internecine quarrels and jealousies, in which satire could play an important role. But I have not succeeded in finding a clear-cut *English* instance in which a satirist, on an economic issue, was attacking a social group clearly higher than the one he belonged to or had been hired to serve. When Swift used satire to attack the *English* government on behalf of *Ireland's* manufactures or trade, he was acting, on principle and not for pay, on behalf of a group which was inferior in power and status to England, and on behalf of a 'national' issue on which he had a substantial sympathetic audience. But when Swift attacked Irish landlords on behalf of the Irish poor, he was attacking the strong on behalf of the weak, and attacking a group higher in some senses than the one he belonged to. But one should always be prepared to accept Swift as an exception to many rules. I shall comment in a moment on a Scottish exception. But were there other exceptions? They can readily be found, no doubt, in France in particular, and in England itself in ages other than the Augustan. It may be that it was only in England, and only in the period 1660 to say 1760, that satire was widely practised and also usually had its darts pointed horizontally or downwards in the social scale, but not upward. This may be worth exploration.

My Scottish exception is John Witherspoon. He was a minister of the Kirk, of the orthodox and ardent Calvinist wing. The Moderates, or the 'enlightened' wing, a minority generally of higher social rank and superior education, and through their property and their connections possessing disproportionate legal control of church 'patronage', could determine in some significant degree who should occupy the pulpits of even ardently orthodox parish kirks. Church of Scotland affairs were the only area left to Scotland under the Union with England where the middling ranks of the people could exercise a vote on things that mattered to them or to Scotland as a whole, and only in the Assemblies of the Church could aspiring youth display its forensic talents before truly national gatherings. In this remnant left to Scotland of representative government, legal rights of membership in the Assembly and of presentation of ministers to the parish kirks which rested on grounds of heredity, of property, and of delegation of authority from London were an alien and oligarchical intrusion that was offensive even to some Scotsmen who, on purely religious grounds or on grounds of social affinity, were more at ease with the Moderates. In the constant tension between the orthodox and 'Popular' party, on the one hand, and the Moderates on the other, the Moderates, as also the few unaffiliated freethinkers, repeatedly subjected the orthodox to satiric jabs and pejorative labels, whose targets were not always expressly disclosed but were never unclear. To the Moderates, the orthodox Calvinists were 'enthusiasts', 'fanatics', addicts of 'superstition'.

As a lone exception among the orthodox Calvinists, John Witherspoon had the combination of capacities necessary to fight the Moderates with their own literary weapons. He was well educated, was skilful with his pen, and was either free from any moral aversion to the use of biting satire or in a righteous cause could keep that aversion under control.

In 1753, while a bitter controversy was under way in the General Assembly of the Church of Scotland between the Moderates and the Popular party, Witherspoon published anonymously, but with the authorship only sufficiently concealed to protect him from prosecution, a bitter tract, *Ecclesiastical Characteristics*, in which the religious beliefs, the personal character, and the patronage practices of the Moderates were subjected to severe satirical treatment. The tract created quite a storm, and Wtiherspoon felt obliged not long after to issue an 'Apology' for it in which he justified his resort to satire in the face of the long-standing tradition hostile to it and defended the severity of its tone. He claimed that 'A satire that does not bite is good for nothing. Hence it necessarily follows, that it is essential to this manner of writing, to provoke and give offence.' He appealed to instances of the use of irony in the Old Testament and to Pascal's attack in the *Provincial Letters* on the doctrinal laxity of the French Jesuit clergy as relevant precedents for his use of satire to expose the character defects of the Moderate clergy.[10] A modern, but clearly not 'Moderate', Scottish Presbyterian comments on *Ecclesiastical Characteristics* as follows:

Its accuracy hit the Moderates in their weak spot—Their sensitiveness to ridicule. It exposed their gentlemanliness as sycophancy [to the powerful and the rich], their

[10] John Witherspoon, *Ecclesiastical Characteristics* (1753), *A Serious Apology for the Ecclesiastical Characteristics* (1763), *Works* (2nd edn., Philadelphia, 1802), iii. 269–313.

culture as paganism, their virtue as self-righteousness . . . satire won more friends for the evangelicals [the modern friendly term for orthodox Scottish Calvinists] than heated denunciation. The orthodox, hitherto armed with archaic weapons, equipped themselves with the modern armaments of their adversaries.[11]

I doubt, however, that Witherspoon had any satirical comrades among the orthodox in Scotland. Their lack of the types of literary skill required for effective satire, and the survival of doubt as to the respectability of satire, seem to have continued indefinitely to bar the appearance of a second Witherspoon. There were among the orthodox some misgivings about Witherspoon's resort to satire even in a good cause: 'As one good soul expressed the doubt: "Alas! would it not have been better to have had recourse to prayer than to satire?" '[12]

Satire had an additional limitation as a tool of persuasion on an economic issue where the intended audience were sober-minded and intellectually scrupulous, and not seeking amusement. Such an audience would look for balanced presentation of pros and cons, for massing of argument and evidence even at the cost of dullness, for the avoidance of exaggeration and patent distortion. This is not the kind of audience nor the kind of rhetoric with which satire can feel at home.

I now venture to relate more concretely to the economic ideas, conditions, and institutions of our period the record of that period's satire, although my knowledge of that record, I regretfully confess, is rather sketchy. It seems clear to me that the satire which survives to later times, or is rediscovered in later times and then made much of by scholars, is mostly of two kinds; that which to later literary taste is aesthetically attractive, and that which to members of specific learned disciplines has important intellectual significance. I shall comment separately on these two categories, but first I have a remark to make on the relations between them. The number of satirists whose *satiric* writings are still studied and praised, both by professional students of literature for the literary effectiveness of their satire, and by philosophers, theologians, economists, political theorists, or other intellectuals, for their contributions to their respective disciplines, seems to be very small. Roaming over the last few centuries and the entire Western world, I can think only of Pierre Bayle, Pascal, Shaftesbury, David Hume, Montesquieu, Voltaire, and Edward Gibbon. Bernard Mandeville would seem to me to be eminently deserving of a place in this list, but for his literary and other admirers it is not his satirical technique that wins their applause. The leading literary student of Mandeville seems indeed to have managed to produce the one undisputedly great work on him without ever using the word 'satire'.

My list is no doubt an inexcusably short one, and even so some may think it

[11] The Revd. A. L. Drummond, 'Witherspoon of Gifford and American Presbyterianism', *Records of the Scottish Church History Society* xiii (Glasgow, 1958), 191.

[12] Varnum Lansing Collins, *President Witherspoon, A Biography* (Princeton, 1925), pp. 38–9.

includes some very questionable names. But if it has any merit, two aspects of the list besides its brevity may be worth mentioning: it includes only British and French writers; and their satire was in each instance largely exercised on controversial issues in the field of religion, or of politics, or, as in the case of Voltaire, of both. This last point suggests to me that one of the reasons for resort to satire in a time when freedom of the press or of speech is far from complete is that it may be safer to wrap one's dangerous thoughts in a satirical shroud than to express them directly and openly. Of the writers I have listed, only one engaged in serious economic discussion in satirical form, and this again was Voltaire. His critique of the Physiocrats was one of the few major satirical achievements in the history of economic thought.

Like other satire, that with economic relevance may be directed against a person or group of persons, a social class, an occupation, a prevalent idea or pattern of behaviour, a learned discipline in its current state, a particular social institution, or the entire institutional structure of existing society.

It can be stated, with little need of qualification, that an outstanding aspect of literate and articulate England for the century from 1660 to 1760 was its contentment with its existing economic institutions and its absence of desire for significant change. As far as institutional reform is concerned, there was minor patching of the system of dealing with the indigent poor, and there was reconstruction of the barriers to foreign trade so as to reduce the weight given to fiscal or revenue considerations and to increase the weight given to mercantilist, or economic and strategic, considerations. Apart from this, nothing much happened in the way of economic-reform legislation or agitation. Although Parliament was incessantly busy legislating, and the volumes of statutes in force were getting fatter and fatter, no single statute can be cited in this entire century as marking an important change in the economic institutions of England, whether by way of destruction, repair, or innovation. What institutional change of consequence was going on was piecemeal, creeping, and largely spontaneous in the sense that it took the form of old legislation falling into obsolescence, and was made possible through parliamentary, judicial, or administrative inertia rather than by formal concerted action. This kind of institutional *status quo* conservatism, as distinct from reactionary conservatism striving to recapture by deliberate and concerted effort a lost Golden Age, or from organized pursuit of institutional innovation, was in matters of economic relevance at least as true of the heroes of Augustan satire as of the articulate public at large.

Once more I have to protect myself by making a qualification over Jonathan Swift. While I know of no important proposal he made for institutional economic change through legislation, it is clear that with respect to the jurisdictional relations of Ireland and England, and with respect to aspects of the Irish economy which only a free Ireland could change, he was an advocate of substantial change. But apart from this the Augustan satirists (as distinguished from the Grub-Street ones, whatever kinds of reform they may have yearned for or advocated) were not advocates of institutional reform by legislation, and, in effect, were not critics of the existing structure of economic and political institutions. They were, nevertheless, social reformers, if to be properly regarded as such it suffices that they were indisputably critics of the morals, intelligence, integrity, manners, marital relations, and religious convictions of the superintendents and janitors of these institutions, above all when the personnel happened to consist of Whigs, or at least of the wrong faction of Whigs.

Devoted to reform of individual morals, the Augustan satirists attacked zealously, and no doubt with just severity, all the Seven Deadly Sins. They also attacked some other sins that were perhaps not mortal, but only venial, that is, not very sinful sins, or only breaches of good manners. They were at times, moreover, systematically respectful of persons, as witness their somewhat automatic tendency to associate Whigs and sinfulness in politics, and dissenters and freethinkers and sinfulness in religious matters. They dwelt with traditional harshness upon the sin of avarice, but they tended to be most alert to its concrete manifestations when it took the form of ungentlemanly pursuit of money by 'moneyed men' and merchants, but not to find worthy of note the gentlemanly pursuit of power, status, or acres. Of a worthy landed family of ancient lineage, belonging to the class whom the Augustan satirists so admired and whom they regarded as alone fit to hold the reins of government, an anonymous contemporary satirist, probably of the Grub-Street variety, remarked: 'They ever let their love light where the land lay.' Again with the exception of Swift, satire seemed to find no appropriate target in avarice manifesting itself in rack-renting and enclosing landlords.

There is a deep and perhaps permanent cleft in social ethics in the economics profession, and in social thought in general, between those who think the reform of society must come through the moral reform of individuals and those who see it as realizable only by concerted community effort reforming social institutions to make possible a great society without necessarily transforming human nature. In between, of course, are a mixed lot of eclectics or pluralists or moderates who think some of both may prove necessary. The Augustan satirists definitely belonged to the first group. On this issue, the satirists seem to have been in complete harmony with the general opinion of the articulate classes of the England of their century; make men better men, and nothing else is required. The situation in France, on the other hand, was strikingly different; social criticism was there largely pointed at institutions rather than individuals.

I have not been able to discover whether in these matters Grub-Street satire had a substantially different set of targets. I can therefore venture no sweeping sociological generalization about the effect of the economic status and class affiliations of satirists on the things they choose to do and the manner in which they choose to do them. John Loftis has successfully demonstrated from an exhaustive study of the texts that as the years went by the authors of stage comedies in the Augustan period treated the manners and morals of the merchants with increasing sympathy. He attributed this to an increased respect for the merchant on the part of both the public and the dramatists, as the merchant rose in status and in affluence.[13] If, however, many of the comedy-writers belonged to Grub Street, and if their more august fellow writers correctly pictured Grub-Street writers as typically poor and mercenary, the simpler hypothesis would be that as soon as merchants came to the theatre in sufficient numbers the dramatists would provide fare which would retain them as customers.

Persons who possessed or acquired wealth without deserving it were often subjected to satirical treatment, as for instance in Gay's *The Beggar's Opera*. This is sometimes interpreted by modern scholars as evidence that the satirists condemned on moral grounds a social system in which wealth was not distributed according to merit. This may be correct, but it does not follow, in the absence of more specific evidence, that the satirists hoped that their satire would lead to some institutional changes in the property system which would help to remove the abuse.

It was a fairly common doctrine of moralists, philosophers, and others that differences in merit between men were somewhat problematic, were not easy to determine in particular cases, and had no clear relation to social or class groupings. To base status on appraisal of merit, it was held, would make adjustment of the social hierarchy a matter of continuous turmoil, since there would never be general consensus as to the relative merit of particular individuals or social groups. But a stable social hierarchy was believed to be essential for political order and authority, and economic inequality was believed to be essential if there were to be incentives to enterprise. Shakespeare said in *Troilus and Cressida*:

> Oh, when degree is shak'd
> Which is the ladder to all high designs,
> The enterprise is sick, . . .
> Take but degree away, untune that string,
> And hark what discord follows. . . .

There is no reason to suppose that Shakespeare thought that 'degree' corresponded to merit, or should be made to do so. A long line of important thinkers,

---

[13] John Loftis, *Comedy and Society from Congreve to Fielding* (Stanford, 1959).

Pascal, Nicole, David Hume, Samuel Johnson, Adam Smith, and no doubt many others, agreed with Shakespeare on the importance of gradation, and of the 'subordination' it involved, and believed also that merit was too uncertain and controversial a basis to provide its foundation. They held, therefore, that factors more objective than merit must serve as the pragmatic criteria of social status, and they agreed that these must be birth and wealth, criteria not difficult to apply. Age was sometimes suggested as an additional criterion for status, one equally easy to apply objectively.

A satirist need therefore wish for no fundamental change in an existing society marked by gross economic inequality unassociated with merit, and yet at the same time with full consistency ridicule individuals who enjoy special advantages solely on account of birth, inherited wealth, or age, especially if these individuals display self-esteem. Reward without merit, taken by itself, could still be legitimately open to ridicule, the satirist could say, even if it could not be systematically eliminated without social disaster.

In the eighteenth century, apologetics for economic inequality flowed in a constant stream from the pulpits, the moral philosophers, and writers on economic matters, but apart from satiric jabs at particularly undeserving examples of privilege without merit very little was said on behalf of greater economic equality as a desirable and practicable goal. Apologists for the existing inequality of status refrained as a rule from claiming that there was corresponding inequality of merit, and on the contrary were often quite prepared to admit that virtue was more widespread among the poor than among the rich. Satire at the expense of the rich, on the stage, or in fiction, or in poetry or essays, could therefore have ample scope despite the fundamental conservatism of the satirist. Henry Fielding, for instance, in his two solemn economic tracts showed himself in full sympathy with the existing social structure, in which merit was not a prerequisite for privilege; in his novels, on the other hand, he freely satirized individuals who enjoyed privilege unassociated with merit.

It may be, as has been claimed, that it is an easy step from ridicule of social inequality not resting on differences in merit to advocacy of the legislative abolition of inequality or its conversion to a system of reward for superior merit. That step, however, was not taken, as far as I know, by any English writer, between 1660 and 1760. I have come across one possible exception, a poem in which ridicule of economic arguments used in defence of inequality is clearly associated with willingness to have the inequality removed by concerted social action. I withhold comment on the aesthetic merits of the poem, and although it seems to me to have an eighteenth-century flavour, it may quite possibly be a late nineteenth-century left-wing fabrication. Whatever its origin, it is social satire at the expense of class inequality, obviously carrying implications of the desirability of fundamental change, and is therefore alien to the general drift of genuine Augustan satire. I have the text, at second or third hand, from an 1890s song-book of the Independent Labour Party, an English Left-wing political organization which was the ancestor of the present British Labour Party.[14]

> Now Dives daily feasted, and was gorgeously arrayed,
> Not at all because he liked it, but because 'twas good for trade;
> That the people might have calico, he clothed himself in silk;
> And surfeited himself with cream, that they might get the milk;
> He fed five hundred servants, that the poor might not lack bread,
> and had his vessels made of gold, that they might get more lead;[15]
> And e'en to show his sympathy with the deserving poor,
> He did not useful work himself, that they might do the more.[16]

Bernard Mandeville was a satirist of the Augustan period who is today commonly interpreted, by both literary experts and economists, as having intentions sharply different from those commonly attributed to him by his contemporaries. I think, nevertheless, that his contemporaries, without important exception, understood what he was after, and that Mandeville had no objection on ethical or religious grounds to the then-existing economic structure of society. He was ready and even anxious to concede that it did not meet traditional moral standards. But he did not genuinely regard this as an important objection. Standard morality, he believed, would if carried into practice bring economic disaster to society, and he had no righteous zeal for economic disaster. What Mandeville was satirizing was not the social structure itself, but the pretence of some of those who flourished under it that they themselves or the structure as a whole operated in harmony with the moral principles they professed. Secondly he attacked these moral principles themselves, and thirdly those who from a sentimental but genuine addiction to these principles advocated even minor changes in existing institutions to bring them nearer to what these principles demanded. What persons he found who did, in fact, advocate this kind of change of institutions I do not know. Mandeville alleged that the charity schools then being established were preparing the way for innovations of this sort, but the sponsors of these schools immediately and earnestly denied that they had any such reformist intentions.

[14] *The Economic Review* viii (1898), 215.

[15] 'Lead' here means pewter. In the late nineteenth century pewter was no longer the cheapest tableware.

[16] In *Speculation; Or, A Defence of Mankind, A Poem* (London, 1780), the lines on pp. 48–9 have a substantial resemblance, in theme and manner, to those quoted above. The poem was published anonymously, but its authorship has been attributed to Christopher Anstey (1724–1805), a Fellow of King's College, Cambridge.

While Mandeville repeatedly asserted his acceptance of the traditional code of ethics in its full rigour, he made every effort to demonstrate the disastrous consequences that would result if it should be generally carried into practice. Mandeville seems to shift back and forth between the role of the rigorous moralist who believes, but is convinced that living according to belief would bring an end to society, and the role of the intellectually honest rogue who regards conventional moral doctrine as a fit subject for laughter, but out of prudence, or to provide more fun for himself and his cronies, or to be more provoking to the professed moralists, whether they be genuine or hypocritical, chooses to do his laughing from behind a satiric veil. If the experts on satire were to analyse Mandeville's satirical procedure, I think they would find that it has some resemblance to the procedure of the young man who insisted on his right of admission in his ordinary street clothes to a masquerade ball restricted to those in costume, on the ground that he was dressed as a man dressed as a woman dressed as a man.

The overwhelmingly conservative tendency of English satire before the nineteenth century is illustrated by the use of the terms 'project' and 'projector'. By early in the seventeenth century it had become predominantly a derogatory term, applied indiscriminately to almost any proposal for innovation, whether in government, religion, industrial and financial procedures, or philanthropy. It carried implications of 'jobs', 'schemes', 'bubbles', 'illegitimate profit', or 'innovations', in presumptuous disregard of the sanctity of established traditions and ways of doing things. Occasionally someone would protest that 'projects' could be good as well as bad, especially when they constituted possibly useful inventions or processes in industry or agriculture. Samuel Johnson was one instance. But apparently almost no one can be cited before Bentham at the end of the eighteenth century who would praise in general terms receptivity to 'projects'. As pejorative terms, 'project' and 'projector' were part of the armoury of satire of the seventeenth and eighteenth centuries, and were frequently resorted to as convenient substitutes for objective argument. The term 'reformer' was in some degree also used pejoratively.

I have not been able to find a corresponding vocabulary available for use in support of proposals for change or for satiric thrusts against resistance to change. It is possible that systematic comparative study of the vocabulary of social satire in England and in France in the eighteenth century would be revealing, as indicating differences in the major targets of such satire in the two countries. I have found some bits of evidence, for instance, that when Continental writers wanted a term equivalent to the English 'project', used pejoratively, they adopted the English word. Some of the satires against 'projects' did have as their targets what we should now regard as frauds or wild schemes. But some of the proposals that were satirized would now be widely regarded as proposals for highly desirable innovations or 'reforms'.

I do not wish to give the impression, however, that I know of a vast English eighteenth-century satirical literature playing an important role in public debate of current economic issues. There may have been such a literature, but it has not come to my attention nor, as far as I know, been confirmed by the bibliographers.

One of the most widely debated and bitterly contested economic issues of the eighteenth century was Robert Walpole's 'Scheme' of 1733 to substitute excise taxes for import duties on wine and tobacco. I have found record of nearly one hundred separate tracts, a majority of them hostile, published in that year with this 'Scheme' as their central topic, and over the years I have examined perhaps thirty of them. In addition there were no doubt many broadsides and articles in periodicals. From the titles of the tracts and from what I know of their contents, it seems to me wholly improbable that satire was an important ingredient in the majority of them. I have found only four tracts, all hostile to the scheme, which were wholly or largely satirical in form.

I will comment on one illustrating some of the minor devices or tricks available in the repertory of an eighteenth-century satirist. The title of the tract is *The Origin and Essence of a General Excise: A Sermon preached on a very Extraordinary Occasion at a noted Chapel in Westminster*. That it was an actual sermon is pretence. It was probably a reply to an actual sermon preached at St. Paul's Cathedral by one of the Whig upper clergy in Walpole's political camp. It bore on its title-page, as the name of the author, Robert Viner, D.D. (or Vyner, or Winer, depending on the edition), in all probability a pseudonym playing on the 'wine' which was the subject of the excise scheme. As the text for the alleged sermon the author gave Luke 2: I : 'And it came to pass, in those days, that a decree went out, that all the world should be taxed.' The satire was unfair, but by the usual standards mild, and it seems to me rather good fun though unlikely to have converted anyone.

The amount of satire I have found in our period which is of economic relevance and which can be plausibly evaluated as having exercised a substantial influence, positive or negative, on the course of legislation is, as I have indicated, quantitatively meagre. Satire, however, need not be directed at men, or at actual proposals for legislation, or at political parties, or at institutions. It may be directed at ideas, and such satire I shall label as intellectual satire. If the ideas are economic ideas, are relevant subject-matter for economic analysis, satire directed at them may be important to economists, and may be important also, indirectly, in affecting the receptiveness of politically significant persons to specific legislative proposals and social trends.

It is part of the history, although often the unrecorded and unanalysed history, of most intellectual disciplines that their procedures, tools, and findings have to face some amount of satirical scrutiny, sometimes from within their own ranks, sometimes from hostile outsiders. When a discipline, any discipline, introduces new tools of analysis, the pioneer sponsors of these tools are liable to be over-enthusiastic as to their potentialities, and to use them clumsily and naïvely. Such was the case with quantification, or statistical procedure, as a tool of analysis in economic thought and in demography. Under the label of 'political arithmetic' it had its critics from its invention in the 1660s to well on in the nineteenth century. Those of its critics who belonged to the literary world were usually men of wider fame than its practitioners among the economists or elsewhere. In our period Swift, Burke, and Defoe are notable as having treated political arithmetic and its exponents satirically. In modern expert opinion some of these criticisms had substantial justification. But the critics were at fault at least in not realizing that the defects they were laughing at were mostly the inevitable shortcomings of a new technique, still in its infant stage but destined to have a great future. In the cases of Swift and Burke the satire, taking the form mainly of parody, was magnificent fun. It may conceivably have done something to stimulate the political arithmeticians to improve on their performance.

I now call attention to another piece of intellectual satire, of even more direct relevance to economic analysis, which was, I think, technically successful from a literary point of view, and which, as far as it went, was sound in terms of economic analysis, but has not, as far as I know, received the attention of either students of Augustan satire or historians of economic thought.

There have always been objections to the introduction of new instruments or new processes in production which enable a given amount of product to be turned out with less expenditure of labour. The oldest basis of objection was religious: man had been sentenced to eat his bread in the sweat of his brow, and to evade this sentence by the use of machines was sinful; to use winnowing machines to winnow corn was impious because man thereby raised an artificial breeze, in defiance of God 'who maketh the wind to blow as He listeth'. In other words, the path to hell was paved with good inventions. Another basic objection rested on the economic argument or belief that labour-saving devices resulted in a reduction in the amount of employment available for the labour force *as a whole*. Finally, there was the objection from, or on behalf of, the particular sector of labour immediately affected that the demand for *its* labour was reduced or eliminated by machinery.

John Arbuthnot, a member of Swift's circle of friends, a wit, a physician, and a good mathematician, published an essay in 1716 entitled *The Humble Petition of the Colliers, Cooks . . . Blacksmiths . . . and Others*, in which he satirized the objections then current against labour-saving devices.[17] A process, he pretended, had been discovered whereby with the aid of burning glasses sunbeams could be substituted for coal in cooking, brewing, smelting ore, and so on. This would be damaging to all whose livelihood depended on the handling, mining, transportation, or use of coal. The petitioners therefore begged that Parliament should either prohibit or tax heavily the substitution of sunbeams for coal. This was good intellectual satire. It decided no issues, but if listened to it forced more profound analysis of the issues involved. A French economist of the middle years of the nineteenth century, Frédéric Bastiat, a man with an exceptionally facile pen, who made up in the lucidity of his prose for what he lacked in profundity of thought, repeated in kind and in manner Arbuthnot's satiric technique for countering the popular objections to labour-saving processes of manufacture. Bastiat in translation, incidentally, had a large and appreciative audience in the United States. It is extremely improbable that Bastiat had ever heard of Arbuthnot, or had been indirectly influenced by him. For students of satirical technique, the incident may, however, be significant as showing that without plagiarism two identical flashes of satirical lightning may, at over a century's interval, hit an identical intellectual target.

Let me sum up briefly what I regard as my main findings as to the relations in England from 1660 to 1760 between satire and the course of English economic thought and economic history.

The century was one of continuous and profound complacency among the English upper classes with respect to the economic structure of the English society. There were conflicts of attitude and policy within these classes, and satire had a role, though a minor one, in the conduct of controversy concerning these conflicts. Manners, individual morals, were freely lashed. But important institutions were left unscarred by satire. The bitter civil strife of earlier decades, involving extensive armed conflict for the last time in English domestic history, became after 1660 an unpleasant memory, which enforced rather than weakened underlying conservative attitudes averse to institutional change and to critical examination of existing institutions. Throughout the period I have been dealing with the great bulk of the people was, for all practical purposes, voiceless. A large portion of it was illiterate, probably a larger portion than in the previous century, when zealous Protestantism was striving to make accessible to every person, as essential to salvation, direct contact with the Word of God as revealed in the Scriptures. Satire itself was a difficult literary technique, requiring literary so-

---

[17] The *Petition* is reprinted in George A. Aitken, *The Life and Works of John Arbuthnot* (Oxford, 1892), pp. 375–8.

phistication on the part of both its creators and its audience, and there was wide-spread aversion to its use, resting on traditional religious and moral considerations. Not one outstanding instance seems to have occurred of a sophisticate using satiric skills in the service of institutional change designed to make England a new Jerusalem, a happy land, for the great mass of the poor.

It would seem an appropriate task for literary critics and social historians to discover why, in ancient times, in the late Middle Ages, in eighteenth-century France, and in nineteenth-century England, but not in the Augustan Age of English satire, there were writers who resorted to the satiric lance as a weapon serviceable in promoting concerted action against the poverty, the misery, and the social degradation, of the depressed masses. In the otherwise rich recent critical and historical literature on English satire I find little emphasis on any of the points I have ventured to make, and no mention of some of them. Unless, as is quite possible, the adequate retort to this charge of neglect of an eminently suitable field for research should be that my acquaintance with the recent literature on English satire is in urgent need of broadening and deepening, there is for the literary experts some work awaiting their attention.

PART III

Review Articles

14

SCHUMPETER'S *HISTORY OF ECONOMIC ANALYSIS*

THE APPEARANCE of Schumpeter's *History of Economic Analysis* constitutes a major event in the history of the *Dogmengeschichte* of our discipline.[1] It is a book large in its physical proportions; its text proper amounts to some 1180 large and closely printed pages, much of it in small type. It covers its subject matter from Ancient Greece to Keynes. It aims to account for every writer who made a significant contribution to the development of economic theory. Greek, classical Latin, mediaeval Latin, Italian, Spanish, Swedish, and Dutch contributions, as well as, of course, German, French, and English literature, are reported on from their original texts. Most important of all, this is a history of theory written on the grand scale by an economist who was an original, a powerful, and a versatile theorist on his own account. Schumpeter, moreover, was interested, deeply interested, in apparently the entire range of matters intellectual, was learned beyond the normal capacities of economists, could exercise with facility and with power the whole range of skills which the economic theorist employs: static analysis, dynamic analysis, historical analysis, mathematical and statistical analysis, partial- and general-equilibrium analysis, and so forth without visible end. He was able to deal familiarly with all ages and with the materials of a wide range of disciplines: physics, psychology, history, sociology, mathematics, philosophy, jurisprudence, and perhaps still others. This is a work written in the polymath manner by perhaps the last of the great polymaths.

This is no doubt an over-ambitious book, and it would not be difficult to assemble from it evidence to support the charge that there runs through it a vein of pretentiousness and of intellectual arrogance towards the common run of economists. The fact remains, nevertheless, that Schumpeter did possess learning and skills manifestly exceeding in range those displayed by any other economist of his or our time, and that in this book he applied these endowments to the enlight-

Reprinted from *The American Economic Review* 44 (December 1954): 894–910.

[1] Joseph A. Schumpeter, *History of Economic Analysis*, edited from manuscript by Elizabeth Boody Schumpeter. (New York, Oxford University Press, 1954.)

enment of his readers with a brilliance and a virtuosity which excite and dazzle even when they fail wholly to persuade. There is, as we shall see, much in this book which is redundant, irrelevant, cryptic, strongly biased, paradoxical, or otherwise unhelpful or even harmful to understanding. When all this is set aside, there still remains enough to constitute, by a wide margin, the most constructive, the most original, the most learned, and the most brilliant contribution to the history of the analytical phases of our discipline which has ever been made.

There is evident only one major limitation to the scope of this history which Schumpeter deliberately adopted. This is a history of "economic analysis," not of economics in general. Social doctrines, practice policies, and the application of economic theory to the solution of practical problems, while repeatedly referred to, are brought into the discussion only to show their relation, or, more often, their lack of relation, to economic analysis.

A history of economic analysis can be written, legitimately, according to any one or any combination of a number of patterns: as a history of concepts and of ideas, the intellectual ingredients of theories; as a history of theories, the constituent elements of systems; as a history of systems; as a history of authors, or of schools or near-schools; as a history of the use of particular tools. Although there is a large measure of validity to his claim that "theorems and not persons are the heroes of [his] story" (p. 384), Schumpeter in fact follows to some extent all of these patterns, and moves from one to another freely as he goes along. There results a considerable amount of overlapping material and of repetition, and a highly complex organization of the book as a whole. For the reader these disadvantages are more than compensated for, however, by the richness of insights and the variety of logical relationships and intellectual filiations which this procedure brings into our range of vision.

Repetition creates opportunity for contradiction and inconsistency, and I have found some, especially with reference to attributions and denials of priorities in discovery. The contradictions, however, are extraordinarily small in total and extraordinarily unimportant, if weighed against the amount of material handled and against the fact that this is a posthumous publication, unfinished, and prepared for publication by his widow, the late Elizabeth Boody Schumpeter, from manuscript which was to some extent still in preliminary and tentative shape at the time of Schumpeter's death.

Schumpeter includes, as "techniques" of economic analysis, economic history, statistics, economic theory, and "economic sociology," the role of economic theory being, apparently, to supply the tools of analysis, and of the other three to provide the content, factual and hypothetical, of the propositions to which the tools can be applied for the purpose of deriving statements of causal relations or interdependencies. He makes adequately clear some of the types of intellectual operations which he regards as outside the field of "economic analysis": mere common-sense or unsophisticated explanations of relations between phenomena (p. 9); nonempirical, "mystical," "metaphysical" propositions (p. 8); "philosophical vision or interpretation of meanings" (p. 422); "factual analysis" and the "immediately practical," presumably when pursued without aid of refined tools (p. 497); "the institutional aspects of economic life" (p. 589); "the attempts of men to apply their reason—and volition—to the task of changing [things]" (pp. 757–58); "the ends themselves, that is to say, the kind of society or culture we want" (p. 1145).

All of these are excluded from the area of study for which he assumes responsibility not on the ground that they are unworthy of study, but as an arbitrary delimitation of his task: "analytic or scientific . . . remember: we do not attach any complimentary meaning to either of these words . . ." (p. 55); "He who writes a history of, say, agricultural technology does not thereby prove that he thinks it more important than the history of religion" (p. 1140). This does not suffice, however, to conceal from us the fairly obvious fact that for Schumpeter it is analytic achievement which above all else entitles an economist to honor and brings intellectual distinction to economics.

It is not made quite clear to what extent "good" economic analysis is dependent on the realism of its assumptions. "Scientific truth" at times seems to include propositions which are factually untrue. On the other hand, "associationist socialism is unscientific because these plans involve assumptions about human behavior and administrative and technological possibilities that cannot stand scientific analysis for a moment" (p. 454). A close investigation might show that Schumpeter unconsciously was less exacting in his demand for realism for authors to whom he was favorably disposed than for authors who rubbed him the wrong way. When defending resort to or acceptance of unrealistic assumptions he appeals to what he regards as appropriate parallels in other fields, especially physics: "It is as important to realize the inevitable discrepancies between theory and fact that must result from [reasoning from unrealistic assumptions in economics] as it is to realize that they do not constitute a valid objection to the former; it is no valid objection to the law of gravitation that my watch that lies on my table does not move toward the center of the earth, though economists who are not professional theorists sometimes argue as if it were" (p. 1031). The problems that may arise for economic analysis because the obstacles to the operation of its theoretical "principles" are more omnipresent and in practice less removable than are tables as obstacles to the operation of the law of gravity are not really explored.

It is a major doctrine of Schumpeter that philosophies, political doctrines, value preferences, psychology, and many other matters, have no contribution to make to economic understanding, which is exclusively the product of acquaintance with facts and of "scientific" analysis. "[David Hume's] economics has nothing whatever to do with either his psychology or his philosophy" (p. 447). The universe of economic analysis and the universe of philosophic discourse "are two different worlds that do not touch anywhere and neither of which can tell us anything about the phenomena . . . in the other without reducing its own arguments to futility" (p. 422, with particular reference to Adam Müller). Beliefs, moral principles, sympathies, preferences, may provide the economic theorists with motivation for finding a logical (and presumably also an illogical) basis for a desired conclusion (p. 383). But economic analysis has nothing to contribute to the choice of ends, which is a wholly subjective affair: "We may, indeed, prefer the world of modern dictatorial socialism to the world of Adam Smith, or vice versa, but any such preference comes within the same category of subjective evaluation as does, to plagiarize Sombart, a man's preference for blondes over brunettes" (p. 40).

Economic theory can serve economic policy, but only by pointing out the appropriate means for attainment of given ends:

> To say that pure theory is of no interest for practice is as unreasonable as to say that pure mechanics is of no interest for building the machines we want. The ends themselves, that is to say, the kind of society or culture we want, we must choose ourselves. No science can do more than indicate the means of attaining whatever it is we want (p. 1145).

This picture of economic analysis as a somewhat ethereal intellectual activity, without roots in values, without entanglements with other social disciplines, without any contribution to make to the rational selection of social ends, represents, I suppose, Schumpeter's subjective ideal. In actual life, means and ends are not so sharply distinguishable, and ends are not frozen and impervious to "analysis." Ends can be means to other ends, and what are means from one point of view are ends from another; economic analysis could in particular cases bring this to light, and merely bringing it to light could result in a modification of ends. Systems of ends, moreover, may be—are perhaps certain to be—complex and incompletely harmonious. Economic analysis, by exposing the source and the character of contradictions in systems of ends, can operate, without need for exhortation, to bring about a revision of an established set of ends, for individuals and for societies. Economic analysis can conceivably show that the means requisite for the attainment of certain ends are not available, or are too costly in some sense, and may thus in effect force a revision of ends. There is no method of influencing ends which falls outside the legitimate scope of economic analysis except the employment of the hortatory method, the appeal to the emotions, and the appeal to authority. To deny any influence to economic analysis is to deny any role to reason in the formation by a sensible man of his system of ends. I cannot quite believe that Schumpeter would have rejected these elementary propositions, but he certainly wrote as if he did.

It could well be inferred from what I have said so far about Schumpeter's book that its contents consisted wholly or overwhelmingly of reproduction of and reasoned appraisal of specific analytic performances. Measured in pages, however, I am sure that much less than half of the book fits these specifications. The remainder consists of a very miscellaneous collection of matter, much of it having only the most tenuous or even no visible connection with economic analysis.

In the first place, the book is badly name-ridden. There is a tremendous parading of names associated with meager and casual bibliographical information, names of all kinds of persons, some listed for commendation as economic analysts, others listed for commendation of their work in other phases of economics, or in other fields, others listed for disapproval, or as uninteresting, and others just listed. There is frequent ranking, and awards of grades for merit of one kind or another, and comparisons as to merit of men whose connection with each other is scarcely indicated. The index of names, on a rough count, lists well over a thousand names, and from a sample check I gather that probably well over a hundred names have not won admission to the index.[2]

In this respect the book follows only too closely the model of Schumpeter's earlier (1924) *Epochen der Dogmen und Methodengeschichte*, which in turn followed too closely the model of Cossa's *Guida allo Studio dell'Economia Politica* in its various editions and translations. An orderly annotated bibliography would have served much better than this clutter of names. It would not be difficult, I think, to enrich the book by adding fifty or so additional names at a prescribed ratio of, say, one new name to ten names dropped. The additions I would propose would be mainly of scholastics, of contemporary commentators on Ricardo, of members of the Trinity College, Dublin, school, and, surprisingly enough given

---

[2] The major service which this book will perform will be as a book of reference rather than as a book for continuous reading. The index, therefore, is all important. I happen to know that Mrs. Schumpeter, who, before her death, put so much effort, devotion, and skill into the preparation of the manuscript for publication, was at one stage at least acutely dissatisfied with the quality of an earlier index which had not been prepared by her or under her direction. I have no criticism of the present index except that it is incomplete, both in its subject part and in its names part. In both cases the incompleteness is serious enough to detract significantly from the potential usefulness of a very important book.

Schumpeter's command and my lack of command of the mathematical literature, of pioneer users of the mathematical, including the graphic, method in their analysis. Much as I would like to, however, I am unable to add to Schumpeter's list the name of a single non-living author for whom I would claim that as economic analyst he was in or near the first rank.

There is, second, a good deal of general intellectual history, not visibly related to economic analysis and frequently described as having no such relation. There is, third, some economic history, sometimes of supreme quality, but often with no demonstrated relation to economic analysis or its history. There are, fourth, references to or accounts of specifically economic writings, and biographical material concerning their authors, with respect to which there is reported the absence of analytic content, or the absence of meritorious analytic content, or the presence of analytic achievement without description of its nature.

These four categories of material account for the great bulk of the first two hundred pages, for perhaps half of the next three hundred pages, and for a much smaller but still substantial fraction of the remainder of the book. It seems to me a great pity that Schumpeter did not concentrate more on the reporting and reasoned appraisal of important analytical work, which he did so exceedingly well, and did not leave the *Kulturgeschichte* to the encyclopedias and the reporting on the great areas barren of economic analysis to the mythical author of the chapter on snakes in the book on the flora and fauna of Ireland.

On the display of bias in this book I will say little. Schumpeter was not simple-minded nor naive, and I would have to know more about him and to know better than I do the corpus of his other writings to be sure that I had correctly identified the patterns it took. His biases could take the form of exaggerated enthusiasm and praise as well as of undue disdain and contempt. He was basically generous, moreover, and there is much evidence of his disciplining himself to give appropriate praise to analytical work which was of a high quality even when executed by men who used it to support conclusions he did not like. The fact remains that in the case of some authors he emphasizes their defects as analysts and admits their merits only grudgingly whereas with others he draws attention only to their strong points and leaves unmentioned or strains himself to find some sort of defense for the weak points in their analysis.

It is when Schumpeter is dealing with authors whose analytical quality he rates highly and whose economic analysis constituted a complex and coordinated system that he rises to his highest level in his book. His reports of these systems are magnificent feats of summarization. In outlining the analytical framework of these systems, moreover, he brings clearly into the light the fullness of their achievement and enables us to read these authors henceforth with deeper understanding and appreciation. It is the substantial portions of the book which he devotes to exposition, appraisal, and praise, of the economic analysis of Cantillon, Quesnay, Marx, Jevons, Menger and Böhm-Bawerk, Cournot, and Walras—and less enthusiastically, Adam Smith, Marshall, and Fisher—which constitute its most valuable contribution. Nowhere else, I think, in the literature of our discipline, can one find, within comparable limitations of space, as brilliant, and as self-effacing, exposition by one economist, himself a master, of the analytical achievements of other economists. Since I have raised the issue of bias, it is incumbent on me to add that there are hints throughout of disagreement with the conclusions even of the economists he praises most highly, that the basis of this disagreement is often some line of analysis more or less special to Schumpeter himself, that his own special doctrine is never obtruded on the reader or even clearly exposed, and that he never makes any claims to priority on his own account or ever refers to any of his own original work.

The remainder of this review will consist mostly of objections of one sort or another, minor and major, to specific positions taken by Schumpeter. It will be a mechanical consequence that the amount of space in this review as a whole given to adverse criticism exceeds the amount given to praise. I would ask the reader to bear in mind, however, that my praise is in general terms and my criticisms are mostly of specific points, and that criticism both calls more for support by appeal to argument and detailed evidence than does praise and is more susceptible of such support than is praise.

Schumpeter's display of command of intellectual history is most impressive in its range and in its apparent depth. My major reaction to it is one of humble and respectful admiration. It may none the less be useful to point out a few instances where I am more or less certain that he has gone astray.

In signaling Petty's pioneer work in introducing "figures" into economic analysis, Schumpeter fails to point out that some of these "figures" were the products of a rather undisciplined imagination or of arbitrary manipulations of data. Partly in consequence of such procedure on the part of Petty, and of other early political arithmeticians, not only was it not true of Political Arithmetic that "nobody attacked" it (p. 211), but it was a frequent subject of satire from the late seventeenth well into the eighteenth century. Among those who made it the butt of their satire were Shaftesbury, Swift, Defoe, Richard Steele, and Mandeville, although it had among its many defenders men who, for our purposes at least, had even greater distinction.

In referring to Tooke and Newmarch's *History of Prices*, excessively factual for the purposes for which it was written, as *"histoire raisonnée"* (p. 690) Schumpeter mistakes the meaning of the term, which was the French equivalent of "conjectural history," or history not factual enough for its purposes.

Schumpeter expresses amusement at the use of the term "experimental" by utilitarians to describe their procedure, and interprets it as an illegitimate attempt at appropriation of a term that, through the successes of physical experimentation, had acquired an eulogistic connotation. Such attempt he says, "runs through the whole history of economics from the seventeenth century" (p. 432; see also pp. 493, 537). "Experimental," however, was commonly used, with no intent to deceive, not only to mean "learning from experiment" but also to mean "learning from experience." This latter is still given as an acceptable meaning by the *Oxford Dictionary*.

Terms like "individualism," "rationalism," "empiricism," "romanticism," the fiat currency of intellectual history, are conceded by Schumpeter not to have stable and uniform meaning, but he nevertheless uses them freely as if they did and without attempt at definition. He states his "strong personal aversion to utilitarianism" (p. 1153). All his references to it, and especially to its Benthamite version, are hostile and abusive. It is associated not only with hedonism, but with a hedonism of "stable and barn" (p. 429). It ruled out, "as contrary to reason, all that really matters to man"; it was "the shallowest of all conceivable philosophies of life" (p. 133). It was "boisterous and vulgar" (p. 66). There is no definition, however, and no argument, and there is, I think, sufficient evidence in this book to show that, surprisingly for him, he had no direct acquaintance with the complex early history of the quite respectable body of doctrine to which, late in its history, was given the name of "utilitarianism."

Schumpeter wrongly identifies Hobbes' "social contract,"—which he explains correctly—with Locke's (p. 119). There is an important difference between them: the monarch is not a party to Hobbes' contract and therefore acquires no obligations to his subjects; the monarch is a party to Locke's contract, and his lawful authority is confined within the limits of the obligations to the citizens which he assumes in entering into that contract.

Schumpeter says of Montesquieu's famous definition of "natural laws" that it is one which "cannot be commended too highly" (p. 232), but quotes only a fragment of it as if it were all of it. High authorities, early and recent, have pointed to Montesquieu's definition as an outstanding example of the survival of confusion between "natural law" as a declaratory statement of observed regularities in the behavior of phenomena and as comprising normative rules of conduct as revealed by "right reason" or as proclaimed by divinely ordained civil authorities.[3]

There follow comments on specific passages in Schumpeter's book more closely related to economic analysis.

On Plato's treatment of division of labor, Schumpeter comments as follows:

---

[3] Cf. André Lalande, *Vocabulaire technique et critique de la philosophie* (Paris, 1926), I, 435.

He elaborates on this eternal commonplace of economics with unusual care. If there is anything interesting in this, it is that he (and following him, Aristotle) puts the emphasis not upon the increase of efficiency that results from division of labor per se but upon the increase of efficiency that results from allowing everyone to specialize in what he is by nature best fitted for; this recognition of innate differences in abilities is worth mentioning because it was so completely lost later on (p. 56).

The importance of innate differences of abilities was one of Schumpeter's strongest convictions. I know of no one of consequence except Adam Smith who failed to point out as one of the services of division of labor that it enabled tasks to be assigned in accordance with aptitudes. (Even Adam Smith's failure was not a complete one.)

There no doubt has been "commonplace" treatment of division of labor in economic writings, but this has by no means been the invariable rule. I know of no study of the history of discussion of the idea, but such a study would reveal that division of labor was at times made the starting point for pioneer exploration of the technological foundations of economic process, of the role of physical capital, especially machinery, in economic progress, and of the relations between occupational and class differentiations of populations.

Schumpeter finds very little economic analysis in the ancient Greeks and Romans. I am not qualified to dispute this judgment, although I think it would be possible to add a little to what he has culled.

On the basis of a passage from his *Ethics*, Schumpeter interprets Aristotle as "groping for some labor-cost theory of price" (pp. 60–61). Commentators on and translators of Aristotle have always had a tendency to find in his texts whatever theory of value was fashionable at the time they were writing. The first attribution to Aristotle of a labor-cost theory of value that I have been able to find was by John Gillies, a classical scholar, in 1797, who in fact charged Adam Smith with plagiarizing Aristotle in this respect.[4] In recent years, when an Austrian-type, or a utility- or demand-type of value theory has been dominant, commentators have found in Aristotle an anticipator of such theory.[5] I have failed myself to acquire any conviction as to what Aristotle was driving at, except that, if modern translations are at all adequate, there is nothing in his texts to justify

[4] John Gillies, *Aristotle's Ethics and Politics* (London, 1797), I, 270–71. Gillies, in addition to the passages on value which are commonly cited today from *Ethics* and from *Politics*, refers to Metaphysics, Bk. 1, ch. 9; 1050A-28ff. (Bekker).

[5] See, e.g., O. Kraus, "Die Aristotelische Werttheorie in ihren Beziehungen zu den Lehren der moderner Psychologenschule." *Zeitschr. f. die gesamte Staatswiss.* (1905), LXI (4), 573–592, and Josef Soudek, "Aristotle's Theory of Exchange," *Proceedings of the American Philosophical Society*, XCVI, February 1952, pp. 45–75.

attributing to him any labor theory of value beyond what is involved in the explicit recognition only of labor as a factor of production.

Schumpeter deals with the economic doctrines of the scholastics throughout in a strongly apologetic way, and as if they still stood in urgent need of defense against the neglect or biased attack which was common generations ago. In the process he praises their value and monetary theorizing not only as basically sound, but as innovating and as superior in many respects to later accepted doctrine. The late schoolmen had all the elements for "a full-fledged theory of demand and supply . . . the technical apparatus of schedules and of marginal concepts that developed during the nineteenth century is really all that had to be added to them" (p. 98). He insists in particular that the subjection of the schoolmen to Church authority did not in any way restrict their resort to scientific analysis of economic phenomena. Only where revelation was involved was Church authority of decisive importance, but "in everything else (and this includes, of course, the whole field of economics) any argument from authority was 'extremely weak' " (pp. 76–77; citing Aquinas).

My direct knowledge of the writings of the schoolmen is fragmentary, but I have read widely the secondary sources, old and recent. On the basis of this reading, my general impression is that Schumpeter is substantially correct in his account of their monetary and value doctrines and that his praise of them, while exaggerated, is largely justified. His selection of particular writers for laudation seems to me rather arbitrary and, despite the profusion of names which he provides, there are some notable omissions.[6]

When it comes, however, to the analytic merits of the scholastic doctrine of usury (interest), it seems to me that Schumpeter carries his apologetics to wholly unreasonable lengths. Here, unlike the question of just price, Church authority, in the form of official interpretations (and translations) of Biblical texts, decisions of Church Councils, Papal Bulls, Church tradition, resolutions of theological faculties, etc., had decisive importance as to what it was permissible not only to practice but to say.

That money capital was sterile—or alternatively that its offspring was illegitimate—was standard doctrine of the Church. All that is of legitimate interest in the present connection is that the prohibition of interest was supported not only on dogmatic grounds but also on economic and utilitarian grounds. In the process

---

[6] Among the secondary sources not referred to by Schumpeter that, I think, provide ample support for this opinion are: Charles Jourdain, "Mémoire sur les commencements de l'économie politique dans les écoles du Moyen Age," Institut National de France, Académie des Inscriptions et Belles Lettres, *Mémoires* (Paris, 1874), XXVIII, Pt. I; Joseph Höffner, *Wirtschaftsethik und Monopole im fünfzehnten und sechzehnten Jahrhundert* (Jena, 1941); A. Sandoz, "La notion de juste prix," *Rev. Thomiste* (Apr.–June 1939), XLV, pp. 285–305; Raymond de Roover, "Monopoly Theory Prior to Adam Smith," *Quart. Jour. Econ.* (Nov. 1951), LXV, pp. 492–524.

of distinguishing between what was licit and what illicit, the doctrine grew progressively in complexity and in subtlety and the arguments supporting the lawfulness of some kinds of transactions were often marked by analytical insight and development. The fact remains that a large part of the scholastic literature on usury consisted of an attempt to demonstrate that there was a sufficiently sharp *economic* difference between the money-loan, or *mutuum*, where if interest was charged it would be (approximately) pure interest only, on the one hand, and transactions in which the interest element was implicit and tied-up with other elements (business ventures involving some participation by the investor in the risks of loss of the enterprise, purchases of annuities and of perpetual bonds, leases of durable property, and so forth) on the other hand, to make reasonable on ethical and economic grounds, as well as necessary on grounds of religious dogma, the condemnation to eternal damnation of those who practiced the former without repentance and restitution, and the sanction, as altogether legitimate, of the latter. In so far as I understand it, the equivalent with reference to English common law would be to hold that a "loan" at interest was illegal, socially injurious, and scandalous, whereas a transaction approaching it as closely as possible in every respect except that it was given the form of a "bailment" would be completely legal, socially beneficial, and without any odor of scandal. The common argument of apologists, which Schumpeter accepts, that the historical economic circumstances were such that this distinction had economic and welfare merit then which it later lost seems to me unsubstantiated, highly questionable, and without *raison d'être* except its services to apologetics.

Schumpeter's defense seems to be in part motivated by the fact that his own theory of interest has some affinity to that of the scholastics in that, like the latter, it sharply distinguishes between interest on money-loans and direct return to durable physical capital. Schumpeter, apparently, would reject the proposition that even an "idle" cash balance, if held in rational amount in relation to the circumstances of the holder, would be no less productive—of product, or of consumer's utility—than an inventory of materials awaiting processing or of goods awaiting sale, than a second plough held in reserve by a farmer, or than the contents of a housewife's deep freeze, when each of these was of rational dimensions. As far as this book is concerned, however, no light is afforded to the reader as to the analytical grounds for such rejection, and I find it difficult even to conjecture what they are, even with the aid of such acquaintance—far from complete—as I have with Schumpeter's handling elsewhere of the problem of interest.

Schumpeter comes equally vehemently to the defense of the mercantilist doctrines against later criticism—including that of the present writer. His defense consists of an acceptance, as reasonable in the historical circumstances, of the national objectives of the mercantilists, including the indefinite accumulation—

apparently at whatever economic cost—of hard money or "treasure" and the pursuit of self-sufficiency with regard to all products except raw materials, and of a justification of the appropriateness (or effectiveness) of the specific means whereby they thought these ends could be promoted. There are no novelties in Schumpeter's treatment of the issue, and there would be no point in joining debate on it here. I make only one comment. Schumpeter asks whether I would condemn modern arguments and practices of a "mercantilist" character as vigorously as I have criticized those of the past (p. 336). The best answer I can give that would be extremely brief is that the events of recent decades have only strengthened rather than weakened my conviction of the faults, analytical, practical, utilitarian, of the mercantilist approach to international economic problems.

Schumpeter's "Reader's Guide" to Adam Smith's *Wealth of Nations*, although unfinished, is an admirable outline of such theoretical structure of "system" as there is in that book, and would make an extremely useful introduction to any new edition of it. Schumpeter does not like Smith, however, as theorist, as man, or with respect to his social views. The *Wealth of Nations*, although in some unexplained way it was "a great analytic achievement" (p. 38), completely lacks originality. It "does not contain a single *analytic* idea, principle, or method that was entirely new in 1776" (p. 184). Many of his predecessors excelled him as analysts. Verri's concept of economic equilibrium was "as far as this goes, rather above than below A. Smith" (p. 178). It is "not without interest to observe how little, if anything, [Campomanes] stood to learn from the *Wealth of Nations*" (p. 173). Most references to Adam Smith are hostile. He suggests that Smith's criticism of Mandeville's (two-volume!) "pamphlet," *The Fable of the Bees*, may have been due to jealousy of Mandeville as the anticipator of the argument for "Smith's own pure Natural Liberty" (p. 184).[7] "The wooden hands of the Scottish professor" and "the safe side that was so congenial to him" (p. 212), his "feelings of resentful distrust" and his "narrow views" with respect to big business (pp. 150, 545), these are representative of Schumpeter's reaction to Smith. Smith was writing "in bad faith" when he claimed that the mercantilists "confused" wealth with money (p. 361). It is not, I think, necessary to accept Adam Smith as a hero of our profession to conclude that Schumpeter's objectivity was somewhat undermined here by the conflict between Smith's and his own "ideologies."

It is a major element in Schumpeter's almost complete rejection of Ricardo's analysis that Ricardo accepted the demand-and-supply explanation of the deter-

---

[7] This conforms with the standard interpretation of Mandeville. It is, nevertheless, about as wrong as it could be, because it overlooks the vital role Mandeville assigns to "the dexterous management of the skillful politician." *Cf.* my introduction to the reprint by the Augustan Reprint Society of Mandeville's *A Letter to Dion* [1732] (Los Angeles, 1953).

mination of market price but rejected it for "natural" or long-run normal (competitive) price. (See pp. 220, 482, 569–70, 604, 611, 684, 921.)

Two comments which Schumpeter makes in connection with other matters have some relevance for this matter also: first, one should distinguish between "the markets of real life" and "markets that are . . . nothing but highly abstract creations of the observer's mind" (p. 1008); second, "with economists' loose ways of expressing themselves, I find it very difficult to arraign individuals whose statements might be amenable to more favorable interpretations" (p. 1052). In using demand-and-supply *terminology* for the determination of "market price," that is, actual price, or temporary price, or instantaneous price, but rejecting it in his explanation of "natural price," Ricardo was not innovating. This practice goes back to the seventeenth century at least. It can be justified on the ground that it was semantically unfortunate that it later on became common to use the same term "demand" (and correspondingly for "supply") both for *the* quantity that would *actually* be taken in a given historical market at a given *actual* price in a given *actual* moment of time and for "that highly abstract creation of the observer's mind," the long-run normal demand function.

The only evidence that Schumpeter offers—and I am unable to add to it—that the issue is more than a semantic one, is the statement with a reference to Ricardo's *Principles*, Chapter 30, that "in the Ricardian system prices can fall to cost level directly, that is, in a way other than by increase of output" (p. 684). The only thing in this chapter which can conceivably be interpreted as supporting this is the use by Ricardo, presumably as a limiting case, of an illustration where, in modern terminology, a demand curve of zero elasticity intersects a (constant-cost) supply curve of infinite elasticity.

In his *Notes on Malthus*, Ricardo refers to a page of Malthus' *Principles* in which the following propositions are laid down: (1) that an alteration in cost without alteration in output would not result in an alteration of price; (2) that "the relation of the supply to the demand . . . is the dominant principle in the determination of prices whether market or natural, and that the cost of production can do nothing but in subordination to it, that is, merely as this cost affects . . . the relation which the supply bears to the demand." Ricardo comments: "These positions those which have preceded them and those which follow are not that I know of disputed by any body." A few lines earlier, Ricardo had said that in a case where hats are produced at constant cost, "their market price will depend on supply and demand—the supply will be finally determined by the natural price—that is to say by the cost of production."[8] Terminology aside, there did

---

[8] David Ricardo, *Notes on Malthus' Principles of Political Economy*, in *The Works and Correspondence of David Ricardo*, Piero Sraffa, ed. (Cambridge, 1951), II, 44–47.

not exist that dual line of price analysis, Ricardian and Malthusian, which Schumpeter insists upon. If there was any significant difference between the two, it was that Ricardo's concentration on constant-cost cases kept him inadvertently from working out an adequate apparatus for explaining the determination of long-run price where both quantity demanded and quantity offered were variables dependent on price. It does not follow, in the absence of supporting evidence, that if such a case were presented to Ricardo, or to any one of his followers, he would have handled it any differently than would Malthus.

Many of Schumpeter's other critical comments on Ricardo's analysis lose their point if Ricardo's major concern in his value theorizing was not the explanation of how a given structure of prices had come to be what it was but the explanation of (a) the effect on a given structure of prices of divergent changes in the amounts of the respective factors, and (b) the effect on the relative amounts of the factors of changes in the structure of prices. This interpretation of Ricardo involves the question of the role of the supply functions of the factors in "Ricardian" as contrasted with "Austrian" theory, to be commented on later. It makes possible, I think, a better explanation of the ability of the Ricardian theory of rent to survive than that offered by Schumpeter (p. 934). It makes Ricardo's rent theory perform a function in his system more fundamental than that of an ingenious device by which Ricardo could offset his inability to handle simultaneous equations by arbitrarily reducing the number of variables in his model (see p. 569).

Schumpeter does not make clear which of four (or more?) possible explanations of Ricardo's stress on the role of labor costs in the determination of relative prices he accepts: as a device to simplify analysis and with no further intended implications; as providing for most (or for some) purposes an adequate approximation to the truth because of the predominance in fact of labor costs in total costs; as having, per unit of cost, more value-determining significance than other costs; as having, per unit of cost, more welfare or ethical significance than other kinds of costs. (See especially pp. 594–96.)

On the strength of a statement by Ricardo in a letter (to McCulloch, June 13, 1820) that "the great questions of Rent, Wages and Profits . . . are not essentially connected with the doctrine of value," Schumpeter agrees "that there is some truth in Professor Knight's indictment that [in Ricardo's *Principles*] the problem of distribution . . . was not approached as a problem of valuation at all." Schumpeter concedes that there is material in Ricardo which refutes it (he could have found some in the very letter in question) but concludes that "it does show that the full implications of the fact that capitalist distribution is a value phenomenon were not clearly seen even by Ricardo" (p. 543; *cf.* p. 568). It all depends on what Ricardo meant by "the doctrine of value." It seems clear to me from the context that what Ricardo here meant by these words was not the explanation of the determination of relative prices but the problem of finding a "measure of value" through time which itself had stable value.

I question whether it is true that Ricardo held "that 'real values' of commodities are 'regulated' by the 'real difficulties' encountered by the least-favored firm" (p. 1032). To confirm this it would be necessary to establish that for Ricardo the intensive margin played no or little part and the producers who were on the extensive margin were always or generally the least efficient and lowest-income farmers.

The repeated association by Schumpeter of the Ricardian theory of rent with a "monopoly theory of rent" puts undue weight on what for the most part represents only a change in usage of the word "monopoly" by economists (pp. 264, 592, 672, 934). In Ricardo's time the term was widely used to cover: (1) ownership of a scarce commodity by a single holder; (2) ownership by a few; and (3) scarcity of a commodity which, because of zero elasticity of supply, a rise in price would not ameliorate. Land was believed to belong to this third class. I think it more correct to say that Ricardo had an inadequate theory for the determination of price in any of these three classes than to say that he had one theory, and that a definable one, for all three classes. The common element for Ricardo with respect to the determination of prices of all three classes was that demand would determine price in these cases irrespective of costs. We would not today call this a "monopoly theory of value."

Schumpeter maintains that the Malthusian population theory dealt with a fictitious problem and dealt with it in a trivial manner (pp. 578 ff.; see also p. 446). Botero's "path-breaking performance" of 1589 was "the only performance in the whole history of the theory of population to deserve any credit at all" (p. 255). From the seventeenth to the first decades of the nineteenth century, "with unimportant exceptions," it was manifestly correct that "under prevailing conditions, increase in heads would increase real income per head" (pp. 251–52).

A look at eighteenth-century England serves, I think, to bring things into truer proportions. English society was then organized so as to check growth of population by "artificial" means. Compulsory poor relief on a parochial basis and financed by local real property taxes together with the settlement laws gave a powerful incentive to the ruling classes to discourage local growth of population. There were in effect deliberate deterrents to marriage of various kinds. There was organized public custody of foundlings and of children of persons on poor relief, and it was common knowledge that this operated so as to ensure that most of them would not survive long. There was nevertheless rapid growth of population and deep and pervasive poverty. If one were to accept Schumpeter's argument, the trouble must have been that there was not enough population.

I am not sure that I grasp Schumpeter's point when he argues that it is wrong to criticize the classical theory of the international mechanism "on the ground that it put an altogether unjustifiable burden upon the price mechanism" since "price variations of the kind the 'classic' theory visualizes imply shifts of demand curves which in turn imply variations in income" (p. 733). A few pages earlier, he had rightly stressed the importance of the distinction between what may be implied in an author's statement and what the author understood by it. Moreover, changes in prices, even when they do imply variations in income, do not account for the nonprice effects of variations in income. Reference to price changes is even more obviously inadequate for the analysis of cases where variations in income are unassociated with any changes in prices, or, as Schumpeter himself puts it, "in patterns in which prices are rigid."

On the question of the validity of the substitution by Jevons, Menger, Böhm-Bawerk, and others of a demand or utility explanation of the determination of price for the Ricardian explanation, Schumpeter, like almost all modern theorists, lines up firmly on the "Austrian" side; the Austrian theory in effect added to the English classical theory what needed to be added and rejected what called for rejection, or, less clearly, what could be rejected without serious loss. Let me distinguish two propositions: first, the need for the introduction into value theory of something like the marginal utility analysis to constitute *a* fundamental or "ultimate" regulator of value; second, the need, or the permissibility, of rejecting costs in the sense either of disutilities or negative utilities, or of the surrender of leisure, of immediate for future consumption, or of more attractive for less attractive employment, as a second fundamental or "ultimate" regulator or determinant of value. After Jevons, etc., had written, scarcely an economist raised any question about proposition one above. It is only on the second proposition that controversy has not altogether expired, and it is only this second proposition which I question.

Marshall, while adopting, and incorporating into his system, marginal utility analysis, rejected proposition two, as did Edgeworth, Taussig, and others, and as do I. It seems to me impossible logically to accept proposition two and at the same time to grant that the quantities of some or all of the factors of production are not given, but are functions of their rates of remuneration. It also seems to me that this difference in the treatment of the amounts of the factors is the only important difference between the Marshallian and the "Austrian" systems, but it is an important difference.

I present some of Schumpeter's comments on Marshall's system which are relevant to this issue:

Marshall's theoretical structure, . . . is fundamentally the same as that of Jevons, Menger, and especially Walras, but . . . the rooms in this new house are unnecessarily cluttered up with Ricardian heirlooms, which receive emphasis quite out of proportion to their operational importance (p. 837).

Thus, we return from this excursion with the same result that we always get when inquiring into the nature and importance of Marshall's deviations, in what purport to be fundamentals, from the Jevons-Menger-Walras analysis: they are negligible (p. 924).

. . . note XXI in the Appendix to Marshall's *Principles* is conclusive proof of the fundamental sameness of his and Walras' models (p. 952).

It is important here to make another distinction: between questions of formal validity and questions of "emphasis," or of practical significance. I confine myself to the former. Marshall's "note XXI" to which Schumpeter refers includes, as one of a list of assumptions: "(iii) m supply equations, each of which connects the price of a factor with its amount."[9] In a corresponding Jevonian, or Austrian, or Walrasian listing of assumptions, the amounts of the factors would be listed as constants. In formal analysis, there is surely nothing more "fundamental" than whether a specific quantity whose importance is not questioned is a constant or a variable. When the quantities of the factors are treated as variables, as functions of their prices, a wide area of analytical development is opened up for and demands exploration. This area Ricardo and Marshall did explore and the "Austrians" did not, except as a side issue, under pressure of criticism, belatedly, and, I believe, incorrectly.

Schumpeter adduces what he calls "the Principle of the Negligibility of Indirect Effects" in support of Marshall's treatment of consumer's surplus (pp. 990 ff.). It seems to me that for some at least of Marshall's analysis it is necessary, for the correctness of his findings, not only that particular indirect effects of the change in a particular price shall be negligible, or of a lower order of size than the (total) direct effect, but that the *sum* of all the indirect effects shall be of a lower order of size, and that Marshall fails to give any reason why this should necessarily or ordinarily be the case.

I can see why, for what I understand to be Schumpeter's own version of static equilibrium under perfect competition, there needs to be atomistic as well as over-all perfect equilibrium and every entrepreneur needs to be a zero-profit entrepreneur. But I cannot see why he thinks this is a necessary condition also for a Marshallian or a Walrasian static equilibrium (pp. 674, 893, 1011). For their systems, I would think, all that is requisite is over-all equilibrium of the balanced

---

[9] Alfred Marshall, *Principles of Economics*, 8th ed. (London, 1920), "Mathematical Appendix," p. 855.

aquarium type, in which firms (fish) and factors (plants) come into being, grow and die, and only aggregates remain the same. In such an equilibrium there could be risks for the individual firm. Such a model would be more realistic, and for some purposes at least more useful, than one in which equilibrium is required to be present not only over all but for each unit.

In a Walrasian system, constant coefficients of production need not involve "that there is, for each product, only one technologically possible way of producing it" (p. 1011; *cf*. p. 1027). All that the Walrasian system requires in this connection is that there always shall be available one way of producing each product such that some of its technical coefficients are smaller and none is greater than for any other technologically possible way of producing it.

Pointing out that first-order homogeneity of the production function means that there are constant returns to scale, Schumpeter comments: "In itself this implies nothing, of course, about what happens when only one of the 'factors' is increased, the others remaining constant, i.e., about the shape of each 'factor's' marginal productivity curve" (p. 1034). I would see nothing to question in this if all that was intended was to deny that first-order homogeneity of the production function either sufficed to prescribe the shape of any particular marginal production curve, or was inconsistent with almost any conceivable shape for any one (not too important) marginal productivity curve. It does seem to me, however, that acceptance of first-order homogeneity of the production function imposes important restrictions on the general pattern of marginal productivity functions and that these are such as to support *a priori* belief in the predominantly decreasing-productivity shape of the marginal productivity curves. I say this after giving due consideration to Schumpeter's warning that there are logical pitfalls in deciding what properties of production functions are "obvious" or "evident" (p. 1037), but quite probably without giving adequate weight to unperceived mathematical pitfalls.

As I see it, there cannot be both first-order homogeneity of the production function and, for each or most of the factors, constant marginal productivity, *i.e.,* independence of the marginal productivity of the factor from the quantity of that factor, unless there is also, for each or most of these factors, independence of the marginal productivity of the factor from the quantities of the other factors with which it is associated. Similarly, as I see it, there cannot be both first-order homogeneity of the production function and increasing productivities for each or most of the factors unless there is also over-all net rivalry, instead of complementarity, in production between the factors.

As I find it difficult to believe either that the particular marginal productivities of the factors are ever independent of the quantities of the other factors associated with them, or that there ever is or can be net over-all rivalry in production between the factors, acceptance of the first-order homogeneity hypothesis does carry for me a strong implication of diminishing marginal productivity of the particular factors.

Schumpeter says that "if there were any sense in speaking of a national production function at all, first-order homogeneity of this function would supply a very simple explanation of a remarkable fact, namely, the relative constancy of the main relative shares of 'factors,' in the national dividend" (p. 1040). But first-order homogeneity presumably is a property attributable only to *static* production functions. There is moreover a big step, analytical and presumably also factual, from the properties of the production function to the characteristics of the distribution pattern. If unmanipulated historical data do in fact show anything like a close approximation to constancy through historical time of the relative shares of factors in the national dividend, the existence of first-order homogeneity in the production function would not suffice to remove the mystery for me, even if the data were indisputably accurate and comprehensive. I am not certain whether Schumpeter relies wholly, or largely, for the validity of the "fact" of constancy of relative shares on the Cobb-Douglas statistical findings. If he does, then there becomes pertinent the additional difficulty that these findings were based, unavoidably, on historical data of incomplete coverage and highly doubtful accuracy, and therefore should not be regarded as providing strong confirmation of any valid static hypothesis.

It does not seem to me that most exponents of what they regarded as a quantity theory of the value of money would have accepted as a necessary condition for the validity of their theory "that velocity of circulation is an institutional datum that varies slowly or not at all, but in any case is independent of prices and volume of transactions" (p. 703). Most of them, I think, would not find variability of velocity disturbing for their theory, provided the variations in velocity were not inverse to those in quantity—or, perhaps, even if they were, provided the amplitude of variation of velocity was less than that of quantity.

I am not convinced that Schumpeter says anything (pp. 1095–1110) which bears strongly against the validity of the quantity theory of money if the latter is understood as holding only: (1) that an authority powerful enough to make the quantity of money what it pleases can so regulate that quantity as to make the price level approximate to what it pleases, and (2) that the possibility of existence of such power is not inconceivable *a priori*.

15

HAYEK ON FREEDOM AND COERCION

THIS IMPORTANT and challenging book presents a learned and powerfully argued brief on behalf of the propositions, that, in general, the maximum possible amount of "liberty" or of "freedom" from "coercion" is both practicable and urgently to be desired, and that the encroachments on freedom which prevail even in the western world are a major evil, in their actual and prospective consequences, if not in themselves. Hayek is, of course, an economist of the first rank. But he also commands a variety of skills belonging to other disciplines, and this work is primarily a treatise on a major problem of political or social philosophy, namely, the desirable pattern of relations between the state and the individual. If there is special emphasis on economic matters, it is because it is in this area that Hayek sees the gravest dangers from undue exercise by government of its power to coerce individuals.

The economist who writes *qua* economist on social policy issues presents his conclusions as a rule on a contingent or "ceteris paribus" basis, even when he neglects to make this clear to his noneconomist audience. He knows, or should know, that his proficiency as an economist is a certificate of the possession of the requisite knowledge and analytical skill only with respect to a part of the range of relevant instrumental and final values, and that deliberately or from ignorance he is abstracting from or ignoring non-economic considerations which may be of over-riding significance.

It seems clear to me that Hayek in this book is not operating in this manner. He writes with every appearance that he is convinced that in reaching his conclusions he has taken adequately into consideration all the values that are relevant, and all the conjunctures that are actually or potentially important except major emergency situations such as war or danger of war. He manages also to reach his conclusions without giving evidence that to do so he had found it necessary to labor with the weighing and measuring of competing values. Great as are the merits of his case, they are not overwhelming enough, I think, to explain how

Review of F. A. Hayek, *The Constitution of Liberty* (Chicago: University of Chicago Press, 1960). Reprinted from the *Southern Economic Journal* 27 (January 1961): 230–36.

Hayek succeeded in reaching substantially unconditional conclusions and in avoiding what is, in social thought, the generally unavoidable and troublesome necessity of coping with major conflicts between values. I suggest, as reasonable speculation and inference, that the conspicuous absence in Hayek's argument of *ifs* and *buts* and of painful wrestling with the task of weighing *pros* and *cons* in the light of a complex pattern of values and of a supply of information which points in various directions is largely the result of two factors: first, that he selects as his targets extremist forms of opposing doctrine and, second, that for the purposes of his argument he works from an extremely limited set of values. With each of these procedures there is associated a particular logical peril. To attack an extreme position when it is not clear that a more moderate position is open to the same *kind* of objections may be, depending on the historical context, to attack a straw man, while to reach final conclusions upon the basis of consideration of a single value, or of a very limited set of values, is liable to result in what has been called "the fallacy of the unexplored remainder."

Hayek, incidentally, does not even include explicitly as a final value that freedom from coercion by other men for which this book is a massive plea. It is as a means to value, as an instrumental value, not as a value in itself, that Hayek presents his case for freedom. "If we knew how freedom would be used, the case for it would largely disappear." Men, however, often support as a means what in fact commands their full loyalty as an end, and I feel fairly confident that freedom from coercion by other individuals is for Hayek, as for me, a goddess in her own right as well as a serving angel.

To follow Hayek's argument, it is necessary to give the closest attention to his use of four key terms, "freedom," "coercion," "discretionary," and "arbitrary." In the case of both "freedom" and "coercion" Hayek makes every effort to present definitions which are precise and clear, but "discretionary" and "arbitrary" are not defined, are used interchangeably, and seem to connote departure from "equal" treatment. Both "freedom" and "coercion" are expressly stated to be matters of degree (pp. 12, 138, 146), but there is no formal analysis of the meaning of "degree" in the context of "freedom" and "coercion." At what point "freedom" disappears as "coercion" manifests itself seems, for some phases at least of Hayek's argument, to depend on whose ox is being gored, and the form of Hayek's general argument is such that some of his conclusions turn on whether "freedom" is or is not present in the maximum possible degree, and on correspondingly formulated propositions with respect to "coercion" and "discretion."

"Freedom" is defined as "that condition of men in which coercion of some by others is reduced as much as is possible in society" (p. 11), as "independence of the arbitrary will of another'' (p. 12), as a relation of men to men ''the only infringement on which is coercion by men'' (p. 12), (that is, which can be infringed upon only by or through the coercion of men), as ''the absence of coercion'' (pp. 421, 422). ''Freedom does mean and can mean only that what we may do is not dependent on the approval of any person or authority and is limited only by the same abstract rules that apply equally to all'' (p. 155).

Of ''coercion,'' Hayek says that it ''is nearly as troublesome a concept as liberty itself, and for much the same reason; we do not clearly distinguish between what other men do to us and the effects on us of physical circumstances'' (p. 133). He insists that we should regard as coercion only the restraint on what an individual may do which is the result of the will of other individuals (or groups of men acting in a unified manner), and that we should not regard as coercion the restraint on what an individual can do imposed upon him by ''physical circumstances.''

''Freedom'' is thus defined as freedom *from* subjection to the will of others, and not as freedom *to do* anything in particular, or for that matter to do anything at all, in the sense of power or ability or opportunity to do it. Whether a man is free or not ''does not depend on the range of choice'' open to him (p. 13). ''It is true that to be free may mean freedom to starve'' (p. 18). ''Coercion,'' says Hayek, ''occurs [only?] when one man's actions are made to serve another man's will, not for his own but for the other's purpose'' (p. 133). It is to enable him to maintain a sharp distinction between ''coercion'' as meaning willed restraints on others and the restraints which result from ''physical circumstances'' that Hayek puts so much stress on what A ''wills'' with respect to B as distinguished from what impact A's behavior has on B regardless of whether A had B in mind or not. As he operates his concepts, what results is that a social pattern in which the poor are miserably poor and the rich splendidly rich can be one in which the poor have unimpaired freedom while the rich have none at all.

> The courtier living in the lap of luxury but at the beck and call of his prince may be much less free than a poor peasant or artisan, less able to live his own life and to choose his own opportunities for usefulness. Similarly, the general in charge of an army or the director of a large construction project may wield enormous powers . . . and yet may well be less free, more liable to have to change all his intentions and plans at a word from a superior, less able to change his own life or to decide what to him is most important, than the poorest farmer or shepherd. (P. 17.)

Here the test as to whether one is free or not seems to be how wide one's range of choice in fact is, although I find it difficult to picture a situation in which the courtier, the general, and the director of a large construction project cannot throw off the chains associated with their status and acquire the freedom of the poorest farmer by choosing to be poor farmers themselves.

In other situations where the question is, or may be, whether the rich and the powerful are coercing the poor and the weak, Hayek rejects as a criterion of the existence of freedom the impact of another's action on one's range of choice as long as one is not reduced to the choice between submission or death. If an employer refuses me employment or a near-monopolist refuses to sell to me except on the employer's or seller's terms this does not constitute coercion "so long as the services of [that] particular person are not crucial to my existence or the preservation of what I most value." Even a complete monopolist does not have any power to coerce unless, as in the case of the owner of the only spring in an oasis, his customers have "no choice but to do whatever the owner of the spring demanded of them if they were to survive." Even in that case the power of the owner of the spring to coerce (profitably?) would be removed if he were required to treat all customers alike (p. 136).

So far, it has been private coercion, of the poor by the rich, which has been in question. Where what is in question is public coercion, say, of a rich minority by a poor majority, Hayek seems to me to change his criterion of coercion. If government applies pressure on individuals, as by taxation, but by "general and impersonal rules" or by rules "so framed as to apply equally to all people in similar circumstances," this is either not coercion or, if it is, it is free "largely of the evil nature of coercion" (p. 143). Progressive taxation is condemned in principle as not applying equally to all in similar circumstances. "Outside the field of taxation, it is probably desirable that we should accept only the prevention of more severe [private] coercion as the justification for the use of coercion by government" (p. 144).

Hayek presents against progressive taxation a number of objections, whose validity I for the moment do not challenge. But insofar as he objects to progressive taxation on the ground that it constitutes invalid coercion of the rich, I do not see how he reconciles this with his refusal to acknowledge coercion by employers or monopolists of employees and customers unless the latter are left with "no choice but to do whatever the owner of the spring [or the monopolist] demanded of them if they were to survive." I am sure that even in its most extreme manifestations progressive taxation has never been carried so far that "survival" has become more difficult for the pre-taxation rich than for the poor.

To practically everyone "freedom" is a laudatory term, and practically everyone tends to make exclusive claim to its use for the kind of "freedom" he likes. But one man's "freedom" is another man's "license," and it seems to me that in learned discourse if one wants to discuss "freedom" without becoming confused or confusing others, one should label the different kinds of "freedom" one is friendly to or hostile to or indifferent to by neutral designations such as *c, k,* or *x*. But Hayek is fighting for the label as well as the idea, and he claims some measure of historical, etymological, and logical authority for his particular definitions. His use conforms to "liberty in its original meaning" (p. 17). "We land into anarchy when we equate liberty with lack of any restraint" (p. 425, note 25, where this is quoted approvingly from Malinowski; incidentally, this is the most portentous warning of the dire consequences of using terminology in other than a prescribed manner that I have ever encountered). "It is questionable whether the use of the word 'liberty' in the sense of 'power' should be tolerated [by whom?]" (p. 18). Hayek does demonstrate that other men good and true have used the sacred words "freedom" and "liberty" in substantially the same manner as he does, but there is no difficulty whatsoever in demonstrating that a host of other men presumptively equally good and true have used them in a different manner. What does matter, it seems to me, is that while it may very well be important to use different terms for "freedom from" and "power to" and not to confuse one with the other, to discuss "freedom from" in abstraction from "power to" is futile, since the extent and practical significance of "freedom from" is highly dependent on the extent and location of "power to." As a rule, what other men can and cannot do to us depends on their and our "physical circumstances," which may be acts of God or the product of laws of nature, like volcanic eruptions, but often are very much man-made creations, and often are the means whereby men find it possible to coerce other men or find it possible to resist the attempts of others to coerce them.

Hayek argues that if citizens are to be secure against evil coercion by government it is necessary that authorities shall act only according to "the rule of law"; that is, by rule instead of in a discretionary manner and that legal rules shall conform to the principle of "equality before the law"; which at one point he expresses as the principle "that the people should be treated alike in spite of the fact that they are different" (p. 86), although elsewhere he concedes that a severely limited measure of classification of persons may be necessary for some legitimate purposes.

There is a vast literature on the issue of "rules versus authorities," in which the case for "rules" is argued on the basis of the certainty and predictability they provide, as well as on the protection they provide against judicial and administrative arbitrariness. A dictum of Lord Camden in a 1705 case was apparently once a standard citation for opponents of judicial discretion:

> The discretion of a judge is the law of tyrants; it is always unknown; it is different in different men; it is casual and depends upon constitution, temper, and passion.

In the best it is oftentimes caprice; in the worst, it is every vice, folly, and passion to which human nature is liable.[1]

As against this it has been asserted from the earliest times that the letter of the law killeth. As a match in one sidedness for Lord Camden's dictum, but on the other side, I cite Benedetto Croce's statement:

> There is no justice under the sun except the justice which is done in individual cases, with the proverbial regard for time, place, and the circumstances by which cases are altered.[2]

Somewhere between these two extremes lies the area of balance and of practicality. Judging from the abundant literature, the experts in many sectors of law and administration are struggling with far from complete success as yet to reduce to rule the departures from rule which are desirable in principle in the interest of "equity" or "justice" or "efficiency" or are simply unavoidable in many instances. To adapt an eighteenth-century saying by Abraham Tucker, "it would be a masterpiece of moral science to know when a fundamental rule may be dispensed with."

It seems to me that we are in the same boat with respect to the principle of "equality before the law." I have already quoted Hayek as saying: "It is of the essence of the demand for equality before the law that the people should be treated alike in spite of the fact that they are different," (p. 86) and he elsewhere says that "rules should be general, even if some are thereby hurt" (p. 159). But this is too strong meat to be taken as a steady diet, and Hayek for some purposes would at least classify persons according as they are idiots or responsible beings. In the fiscal field, he finds "equality before the law" in proportional taxation, and cites in support McCulloch's dictum: "The moment you abandon the cardinal principle of exacting from all individuals the same proportion of their income or of their property, you are at sea without rudder or compass, and there is no amount of injustice and folly you may not commit" (p. 308). But proportional taxation of income means regressive taxation of property, and proportional taxation of property means progressive taxation of income, and at present levels of taxation proportional taxation of income rigorously adhered to would mean starvation for many. The closest possible approach to "equality" in taxation as an objective arithmetical concept would be the poll tax, and the minute one begins to read into the term "equality" more than a bare arithmetical equivalence, there

---

[1] Cited from Roscoe Pound, "Discretion, Dispensation and Mitigation, the Problem of the Individual Special Case," *New York University Law Review*, April 1960, p. 926.

[2] *My Philosophy*, London, 1949, p. 30.

will still be a rudder if the legislators are reasonably sane and reasonably intelligent, but the compass will be lost. Perhaps what is wrong here is the notion that in the field of social relations there are or can be the equivalent of compasses.

Hayek does at one point concede that special rules applicable to different classes of people do not violate the requirement that the rules of true law be general "if they refer to properties that only some people possess." This would be a true concession, an important one, and a fatal one for much of his argument, if the "properties" referred to meant, say, material possessions, or had reference to differences in power, status, needs, desires, deserts, and so forth. But he has effectively safeguarded himself against this concession having appreciable practical significance.

> Such distinctions will not be arbitrary, will not subject one group to the will of others, if they are all recognized as justified by those inside and those outside the group. . . . When . . . only those inside the group favor the distinction, it is clearly privilege; while if only those outside favor it, it is discrimination. (P. 154.)

I don't think that in practice it would often be a simple matter to identify the relevant groupings, and I don't think that in the abstract it would be easy to accept majority rule within the groups as defined, which is what I presume to be the case here, while rejecting it for the aggregate assembly. It seems to me also that this kind of argument not only must start from the premise that members of a society have only property claims on and property obligations to their fellow members in the legitimate area of political relations but must also presume that it is incumbent on all of us to accept the same premise as a categorical one.

Hayek states that the "political philosopher" will often encounter a conflict of values, and in such case he "must choose which he should accept and which reject" in order to attain "that comprehensive outline which must then be judged as a whole" (p. 115). I don't find in this book that "comprehensive outline" in which conflicts and rivalries between a wide range of values have been resolved. The economist within his own limited field does not resolve the rivalries between, say, the values of food, shelter, and clothing, by the acceptance of one and the rejection of the others; in comparable situations in their fields neither does the legislator, the jurist, or the ordinary individual trying to behave like a good citizen. In political philosophy and still more in moral philosophy and in moral theology, rivalry of values—as distinguished from opposition of values—is recognized also, but the method of resolution most often proposed, explicitly or by implication, is to rank the values by classes or categories in a hierarchical "scale of values" dogmatically or intuitively identified and to assign priority for any fragment of value belonging to a higher category over any aggregate of value belonging to a lower category. Even in terms of abstract philosophizing this can lead to fantastic results, and in this respect at least it seems to me that the naive practice of the practical man and of the man on the street is superior even intellectually to the sophisticated nonsense of the philosopher.

Hayek as "political philosopher" does not fall into this age-hallowed intellectual trap. But neither does he adopt, in his wider field, the method of resolution which he would surely follow if he were dealing with the problem of choice between bread and jam. As best I can make out, his procedure consists of narrowing the range of final positive values which he recognizes as entitled to consideration in the sector of political behavior, and of finding only complementarity, instead of rivalry, among the accepted values.

On the level of final values, Hayek recognizes only the values of growth, of change in a desirable direction, economic, intellectual, cultural. Freedom is supported because it best promotes all kinds of desirable growth. Democracy is, after a weighing of *pros* and *cons*, unenthusiastically supported as a means, not as an end. Society is to be left substantially to its own spontaneous forces except for the enforcement of a justice which is substantially the equivalent of "commutative justice," the justice of the competitive market place, where the essential "equality" is in the objective values of the things voluntarily exchanged between honest persons unbound to each other by any other ties than those of fair exchange of considerations. These spontaneous forces will best promote the various types of growth, all of them, which are desirable.

Hayek does not say in so many words that growth-values are the only final values entitled to be taken into consideration in deciding the proper scope of government action, and I attribute this position to him only on the basis of my understanding of the general drift of his argument and of scattered dicta of his in which he relegates to the category of instrumental values what to others are final ends or else rejects as irrelevant to government what are or may be final values. As in the case of democracy, so also "civil liberty" is supported on the strength of its serviceability to growth. So-called "distributive justice" is rejected as a legitimate end of government. "The desire of making people more alike in their condition cannot be accepted in a free society as a justification for further and discriminating coercion" (p. 87). As I have already noted, freedom from coercion is supported for its instrumental value as serving growth, not as an end in itself, although when Hayek states that "It is at least not obvious that coercing people to contribute to the achievement of ends in which they are not interested can be *morally* justified" (p. 144; italics mine) he perhaps justifies the inference that if his attack on coercion for its instrumental defects were to fail he would be willing to attack it as also an evil in itself.

•

Criticizing the "militant antireligionism" of nineteenth-century Continental "liberals," Hayek says that for the true liberal, "the spiritual and the temporal are different spheres which ought not to be confused" (p. 407). The intellectual history of the nineteenth-century relations between secular "liberalism," "Catholic liberalism," and "social Catholicism," is an interesting one which has many points of contact and of contrast with Hayek's treatment, and one in particular which is especially relevant at this point. The secular liberals objected to the injection of "spiritual" considerations into any temporal field; the Catholic "liberals," few in number, opposed the acceptance by government of "spiritual" ends as coming within its framework of reference, but insisted on the importance of the role of the socioethical teaching of the Church for the private ethics of the individual; the "social Catholics" and, still more, the "Catholic socialists" insisted upon the duty of government to impose a moral code upon social behavior, and gave priority to considerations of "distributive justice" and of other "spiritual" values over considerations of economic efficiency and material prosperity. Hayek criticizes the Continental secular liberals for "confusing" the "spiritual" and the "temporal"; I presume he would also criticize the "social Catholics" for their different pattern of "confusion" of the two. As long, however, as "spiritual" values have power over the minds of men, it is probably a mistake to think that it is at all possible to keep in strictly separate compartments "spiritual" and "temporal" values except by arbitrarily downgrading the one or the other. Once they are both recognized, however, the problem presented by rivalry of values has to be faced, whereas Hayek fails to face it.

Hayek's argument for freedom as essential to economic and intellectual growth rests in the first instance on the claim that free private enterprise and the free market, with its rewards for service rather than for "merit," is more efficient in generating income than any alternative system of economic organization, and secondarily, on the claim that economic freedom, despite or rather because of the inequalities of wealth and income that result from it, is the sole possible nursery and protection for the innovating initiative of the gifted individual, for scientific discovery, and for aesthetic achievement. One of the freedoms that Hayek supports is freedom of association, and he characterizes the possibly serious evil consequences of monopoly as so much exaggerated that they are brushed aside in a brief section headed "Monopoly and Other Minor Problems" (pp. 264–266). Trade union monopoly, however, is not treated as a "minor problem."

Hayek insists that government is inherently incapable of exercising an important planning role in the development of desirable institutions, and that institutional development should be left to the play of "spontaneous" (that is, individual or private) forces. This can be relied upon to produce good results. "No institution will continue to survive unless it performs some useful function" (p. 433, note 21). "It is in the pursuit of man's aims of the moment that all the devices of civilization have to prove themselves; the ineffective will be discarded and the effective retained" (p. 36). "All that we know is that the ultimate decision about what is good or bad will be made not by individual human wisdom but by the decline of the groups that have adhered to the 'wrong' beliefs" (p. 36).

I do not see how this doctrine can be distinguished from "social Darwinism," or from that "historicism" which Hayek has elsewhere so persuasively warned us against. I miss a discussion of the rate of speed at which institutions of the past, like serfdom, slavery, caste, trial by torture, latifundia, religious persecution, head-hunting, and so on, which at least today many regard as *never* having been "useful," got displaced, through spontaneous forces, by "useful" institutions. It seems feasible to me to apply Hayek's method of speculative history to government itself, and to treat it, with all its defects and such merits as Hayek may be willing to concede to it, as itself an institution which is in large degree a spontaneous growth, inherently decentralized, experimental, innovating, subject not only to tendencies for costly meddling but also to propensities for inertia and costly inaction.

Hayek ends his book with a long section of eight chapters under the heading "Freedom in the Welfare State," in which he applies his political philosophy as well as high-level technical economic theory to, among other topics, trade unionism, social security, taxation, urban planning, agriculture, which I do not have the space to examine here, and much of which I do not feel informed enough or competent enough to appraise in detail. With much of it I am in substantial agreement; with some of it I am in full agreement. These chapters certainly deserve the careful and objective study of enthusiasts for particular "welfare" measures involving massive intervention by government, even if they find them in some respects unduly subject to quite opposed enthusiasms.

Included in these chapters is a set of positive proposals for government action in the "welfare" field. This is a substantial enough program to destroy any claims Hayek may have to the laissez faire label, or perhaps I should say, to acquit him from the charge of being an exponent of laissez faire, as traditionally understood. I am sure that it is far-going enough to trouble many of the "libertarians" with whom he is commonly associated. I am not at all satisfied that he has shown that his program has any practical possibilities of realization consistent with the principles of "rule of law," of "equality before the law," and of "freedom from coercion" as he expounds them in the earlier portions of his book. His support for the program is largely in terms of "There is no reason why not" or "There is little reason why not" and there is scanty, perhaps no, indication of the nature of the thinking which led Hayek to give support to a program which, with all its limitations and qualifications, does involve a measure of redistribution of income through governmental "coercion." If Hayek were to move a few degrees further in this direction, the possibility would arise of having reasoned debate between those who may in the recent past have gone somewhat too far in their advocacy of the "welfare state" and those who may in the recent past have gone much too far in their hostility to it. To such a debate Hayek could, if he would, make a major contribution, by virtue of his learning, his analytical skills, and his dialectical virtuosity. From such a debate could come that type of enlightenment which the social sciences and social philosophy seem to me in our present age to need more urgently than anything else.

16

"POSSESSIVE INDIVIDUALISM" AS ORIGINAL SIN

PROFESSOR MACPHERSON'S book[1] is essentially a treatise on political theory, written from the point of view of a special socio-economic and ethical ideology, in an intellectual-history setting. I am merely an economist and am further handicapped as a reviewer of this book by an incurable scepticism about the meaningfulness of either dogmatic or "rationalistic" exposition of moral principles. I am not much better circumstanced so far as political theory and its history are concerned, although I have been moved by "idle curiosity" to do what for an outsider is perhaps a fairly extensive amount of reading in this area. All intellectual history outside the fields of pure literature and the natural sciences is in large part written under the pressure of a complex of social, ethical, mystical and ecclesiastical biases, rather than for the satisfaction of idle curiosity unless the latter is a curiosity about the mode of operation of such biases—which is where I come in. I do not except the history of economic thought from these comments. There is this significant difference, however, between the history of economic thought and the history of political thought, that for the typical economist, as for the typical natural scientist, the history of his discipline is either a minor interest, a marginal link with "culture," or, if he is a philistine—as he not rarely is—a boring and futile assembly of dead texts, recording mainly past errors. My own interest in the history of economic thought, intense though it is, is mainly of the "idle curiosity" variety, and I try to refrain from claiming for it much more than curiosity–satisfying power. The prevailing attitude of political scientists to the history of political theory, I gather, is different. They still find important and direct present-day relevance in what Aristotle, Hobbes, Locke, and Marx said. This seems, in any case, to be true of the author of the book under review, and it is one of the aspects of the book to which I find it difficult to adjust myself. I find

Reprinted from the *Canadian Journal of Economics and Political Science* 29 (November 1963): 548–59.

[1] C. B. Macpherson, *The Political Theory of Possessive Individualism: Hobbes to Locke* (Oxford: Clarendon Press, 1962).

the book interesting, stimulating, sophisticated, full to the brim with insights and challenging interpretations. The claims it explicitly or implicitly makes, however, to relevance to present-day problems seem to me somewhat forced. I found the book, moreover, so subtly and at the same time so systematically saturated with an ideology which I happen both to dislike and to fear that as I read it I felt myself repeatedly summoning my wits to protect myself from undergoing on sub-rational grounds an unsought conversion to a dangerous heresy.

The author claims that none of the seventeenth-century writers he examines were full-fledged anticipators of liberal-democratic theory as we know it today, and that those many liberals who in the past century or so have hailed them as such have misunderstood them. On two specific issues which he closely investigates, attitudes towards universal suffrage and attitudes towards class-stratification, I accept his conclusions at once subject only to reservations on details which he might conceivably accept. I have failed in the past, after some effort, to find a single substantial affirmation of belief, before the 1770's, in the desirability of immediate or early universal or near-universal (male) adult suffrage. I am sure that if a careful study were made of the history of the usage of the word "people" in England, this alone would suffice to show that until the nineteenth century most of the upper and middle classes regarded the working classes as substantially constituting a different "race," not qualified to have a share in politics, or otherwise to be treated as equals except before the law and in church, and even here with reservations. What did come to me as somewhat of a revelation, however, was how large a portion of the population would have had the right to vote withheld from them by even such "liberals" as Harrington and the Levellers, and how nearly completely devoid of spokesmen on their behalf were the workers for pay and the small tenant farmers who, with their families, constituted much over half the population of England, when what was at issue was the right to vote or the right to a dignified human status in society.

I wonder, however, whether there may not have been a preparedness on the part of the Levellers and others to extend the franchise beyond the limits specified in their then proposals, if and when those excluded had acquired more settled habits or had become literate, and whether also "property" was insisted upon as a qualification for the vote not because property in itself constituted an inherent or "natural" qualification, but because it was in the circumstances of the time highly associated with degree of literacy, stability of local residence, and so forth.

It was not merely the possession of property, nor the extent of one's wealth, that was presented by writers of all political complexions as constituting valid claims to a share in political power, but some specific personal qualities, of char-

acter, or capacity, or responsibility, or loyalty, which were associated with specific kinds of property ownership. The landed proprietor was held, for example,
to be a more reliable patriot than the urban moneyed man because he and his land
were bound to their loyalty by ties which did not apply at all to the mobile assets
of the financier and did not apply in anything like the same degree to the person
of the banker or the merchant. The farm-tenant, the artisan, the labourer for
wages, were for similar reasons held to be less eligible than the landlord for a
share in political power. The merchant or banker would not be eligible merely
because he was richer than many a landlord, nor would the landlord lose his
eligibility merely because his debts and financial obligations exceeded the value
of the land he owned and occupied.

Rainsboro, the Leveller, made unqualified statements in favour of the principle of universal male suffrage. But he also indicated that he might accept a
landed-property qualification for voting if it was set at a very low minimum level.
Was he here departing from the general Leveller position that, as Macpherson
puts it (p. 134), the line to be drawn "was not between poverty and wealth, but
between dependence [on employers] and independence" or was it the Leveller
position that while all "free men" should in principle have a vote, this was subject to the limitation that they were not in such a condition, such as being on the
margin of their class, that in a radical assault of the propertyless on property
rights they would vote with the propertyless? While concern for property rights
was general among all except the propertyless, who were mostly inarticulate, it
seems plausible to me that throughout the seventeenth century and during most
of the eighteenth century, those who advocated only an extension of the suffrage
within the propertied class, as well as in a lesser degree those who opposed any
extension whatsoever, were not simply setting up property rights against other
"human rights," but were relying upon property qualifications roughly to separate those generally qualified, by literacy, personal character, reputation for responsibility, intelligence, and so forth, to use voting power well from the point
of view of the public interest in general, from those not so qualified. In this way
a link can be drawn between the debate as to qualifications for electoral suffrage
and the historically more important debate before the nineteenth century about
the proper allocation of power between Church and State, Lords and Commons,
Monarch and Parliament, Parliament and the individual citizen.

Macpherson tries to fit the seventeenth-century theorizing into a model built
around the concepts of a "possessive market society," of market processes which
involve systematic "appropriation" of part of the wage-earner's "product," of
"alienation" of the labourer who is not working with some amount of his own
capital. These are all treated as ethically defective institutions, but only hints are

given as to what institutions they are being compared with, retrospectively or prospectively. This is obviously a (partially) new terminology for Marxian and post-Marxian socialist doctrine. Whether a competitive market inherently involves "appropriation" of the "product" of wage-labour by capitalist employers is a matter either of definition, or, semantic problems being resolved, of economic analysis, or of a body of dogma acquired by some process of revelation. Which of these, and in what proportions, the author is relying on for his conclusions I have no way of knowing, and in any case this is not the most appropriate occasion for entering into a discussion as to whether employers "exploit" labour, or, horrible idea, labour "exploits" employers, or as to whether there is such a thing as a "product" of labour which is distinguishable in a causal sense, or in a moral sense, or in a market-determination sense, from the economist's "operational" concept of the multiplicand of (*a*) what happens when an increment of labour is added to a working-combination of factors of production, and (*b*) the number of units of labour at work.

The "alienation" theme of the author, according to which there is "alienation" of a part of the personality of the worker, his labour, if he sells it for wages, is, I suppose, related to the "estrangement" or *Entfremdung* theme in Marx's writings. It is, I gather, a "freedom" concept: the worker is not "free" if, without a real option, he is obliged to sell his labour to a capitalist to live. In the spirit of semantic freedom, I can understand and even accept this language, but for my purposes I need to know more about other possible ways, if any, in which labour can lose its freedom, and to know what are the circumstances, realizable or ideal, necessary to prevail if labour is to be "free." Marx himself described two different types of community in which labour would escape capitalist wage-slavery, in one of which, however, he would continue to suffer "estrangement" or deprivation of personality. One of these community types was a society organized under the dictatorship of a proletarian party. This would still be a coercive society, marked by the fact that a disciplined division of labour would prevail. This society, however, could evolve into a stateless "communist" society, "where nobody has one exclusive sphere of activity, but each can become accomplished in any branch he wishes, society regulates the general production and thus makes it possible for me to do one thing to-day and another tomorrow, to hunt in the morning, fish in the afternoon, rear cattle in the evening, criticize after dinner, just as I have a mind, without ever becoming hunter, fisherman, shepherd or critic."[2]

Macpherson, it seems, has pondered over the problem of what non-Utopian

[2] K. Marx and F. Engels, *The German Ideology* [written in 1846], R. Pascal ed. (London, 1938), 22, 24.

way there might be to get a society in which wage-alienation would be eliminated without substituting another type of alienation, perhaps even a worse one from an ethical or from a utilitarian point of view, and thinks he has found a solution in principle. In a "possessive market society" a liberal-democratic state does not suffice to establish a base for "a valid theory of obligation" to the community, so that state coercion of the individual continues to be necessary. Eliminate, however, "the centrifugal force of market relations," and presumably also economic "classes," and a spontaneous "cohesion" could develop, with a general acceptance as valid of the authority of a central state, that state presumably being set up and maintained by some democratic process (pp. 276–7). Obedience to such a state, even if it involved working for wages under the direction of a bureaucratic boss, would presumably not involve any encroachment on the worker's personality, any "alienation."

This seems to me an arbitrary blend of Marx's two stages of socialization: the coercive but egalitarian state and the stateless paradise where no one needs to be an expert and no one needs to clean sewers if what he prefers to do is to gather violets. It is built on the belief that the market is the sole source of "centrifugal" forces,[3] and apparently also on the thesis that in a society "where individuals are capable of seeing themselves as equal in some respect more important than all respects in which they are unequal," they can deduce, from the facts alone, morally binding obligation to the community and presumably to its state-machinery. I would agree that there is a valid path from factual assumptions to moral conclusions. I would insist, however, that the path is not a "deductive" path, but a "persuasive" one of a different kind, leading legitimately from "is" to "ought," but by "moral demonstration,"[4] not logical demonstration, if one insists upon using the word "demonstration" at all. But let me grant for the moment all that Macpherson says about the "centrifugal" operation of "possessive individualism." Unless it be also granted, what I am not in the slightest degree persuaded to do even after having read this book, that the institution of private property is the sole cause of "centrifugal" forces, there would be no ground whatsoever for assurance that the path, whatever its appropriate label, would be

---

[3] This seems to be essentially the same theory as that expounded by L. S. Feuer, in "Ethical Theories and Historical Materialism," *Science and Society*, VI (1942), 242–72, where it is argued, I presume seriously, that in a socialist world, because "inner strife" and "latent hostility" would be absent, there would be no need for "ethics."

[4] The term "moral demonstration" to mean essentially effective and rational persuasion short of logical demonstration is Joseph Glanvil's. See Jackson I. Cope, *Joseph Glanvil Anglican Apologist*, Washington University Studies (St. Louis, 1956), 61. Plato seems to me to be expounding the same idea when he reports Socrates as asking: "Shall we, then, assume two kinds of persuasion, the one producing belief without certainty, the other knowledge?" and Gorgias replying: "Yes, of course." Plato, *Gorgias*, W. C. Helmbold, tr. (New York, 1952), 13.

generally followed even in Macphersonia. This, it would seem to me, would be the real problem for the political theorist, not the problem the author struggles with, as to whether the political philosopher can find a way of persuading *himself* that his own ideology can be demonstrated to be a demonstrably true dogma. The key element in this ideology is "equality," not defined, which, if it is subjectively recognized to prevail, or to be present to a greater extent than the sum of all inequalities, makes "the deduction of obligation from fact politically unobjectionable." Given the variety of kinds of concepts of "equality," including that kind which holds that it is morally, politically, and economically wrong to treat unequals with respect to "merit" as equals, it seems to me that to make any headway with his thesis the author needed to survey the array of kinds of "equality," to find some communicable way of appraising their relative merits, and to show how general acceptance of his appraisal could be obtained, so that the pursuit of "equality" should not itself be social dynamite rather than a cohesive force.

As for the market processes which serve "possessive individualism" operating as "centrifugal forces," this is a proposition on which the economic theorist—as well as the economic historian—has a special licence to say something. I confine myself here to the flat proposition that it would be extremely difficult to provide either a logical or a "moral" demonstration that there has been in some "traditional" past or that there could be in some realizable future a workable system of economic organization less "centrifugal" in the absence of coercive institutions other than those required to enforce competition than the free competitive market.

In the remaining pages, I will deal with Macpherson's attempt to show that at the heart of Hobbes's and of Locke's political theories was the acceptance as dominant in society, and desirably so, of a "possessive individualism" ("possessive" meaning property-minded), which exclusively presented society with the problem of attaining "cohesion."

I accept most of Macpherson's interpretation of Hobbes's political theory not only as persuasive but as superlatively perceptive. On matters relevant here, there are only two points on which I am impelled to express dissent. I concede that much of Hobbes's argument follows the pattern, as Hobbes sees it, of a competitive economic market, and that although he attributes to man as *ultimate* objectives honour (glory) and power, as well as riches, he also treats honour and power as in a high degree dependent upon the possession of riches and as important means of attaining riches. It does not at all follow from all of this, however, assuming it to be completely valid, that Hobbes thought that the elimination of economic competition would eliminate, or even substantially moderate, the need for strong and coercive government if there was to be peace in society. The desire for power for its own sake, and for honour for its own sake, shut off from exercising itself in the market place, could conceivably operate with more strength and with more disruptive force than would in a competitive society the desires for honour and power *and* riches. I find no evidence that Hobbes would not agree. As for myself, I would contend that it is at least plausible that economic competition, aside from its contribution to economic productivity, is the most effective means man has ever discovered or utilized to channel into directions where they serve civil peace and human happiness instead of breeding communal strife and human misery the propensities of man to seek power and prestige.

My second dissent is less important and less confident, because, like Macpherson, I find apparently contradictory passages in Hobbes's texts bearing on the issue. Macpherson summarizes Hobbes's position with reference to the relationship of human psychology as it is in civil society to human psychology in the "state of nature" in the neat statement that "Natural man is civilized man with only the restraint of law removed" (p. 209). I am inclined to argue that a less summary statement of Hobbes's position but one closer to the truth would be that it is a function or consequence of the restraint of law to "civilize" in a significant degree not only man's patterns of overt behaviour but also his psychology or "nature"; the elimination of the intense fear of one's neighbour which the introduction of civil power to enforce order brings about causes man's co-operative propensities either first to come into being or first to find an arena for safe and pleasurable exercise. Man would not develop a craving for the approval and companionship of his neighbours (or for alcohol) if any effort to satisfy it would result in immediate disaster, as in Hobbes's "state of nature" (or as in the case of alcohol available only in its wood-alcohol form).

In any case, when Hobbes is speaking of human nature as it is in civil society, while he does not throw overboard its original-sin elements, and while he always attributes to the gentler passions a self-interest foundation, he does frequently attribute to them an active and important role which is not merely a response to the new opportunity of profiting in honour, riches, or power through their exercise. There is some love of neighbours in civil society, there is charity, there is gratitude, there is "the dominion of reason, peace, security, riches, decency, society, elegancy, sciences, and benevolence."[5] There are social passions, as well as the evil ones which Hobbes calls "perturbations of the mind." The latter operate in both the state of nature and civil society, but with lesser intensity in civil society; the former play no role in the state of nature except within the family. "Men have no pleasure, (but on the contrary a great deale of griefe) in keep-

---

[5] *Philosophical Rudiments, The English Works* (London, 1841), II, 127.

ing company, where there is no power able to overawe them all.''[6] In civil society, however, there is the ''pleasure [men] take in one another's company; and by which nature, men are said to be sociable.''[7]

Hobbes was even capable of giving a utopian turn to his description of civil society:

> If the moral philosophers had as happily discharged their duty [as the geometers], I know not what could have been added by human industry to the completion of that happiness which is consistent with human life. For were the nature of human actions as distinctly known as the nature of quantity in geometrical figures, the strength of avarice and ambition, which is sustained by the erroneous opinions of the vulgar as touching the nature of right and wrong, would presently faint and languish.[8]

It would be reason, enlightened self-interest, not the social passions, which would be the major instruments of happiness even then, but the disruptive passions would have so shrunk in strength as to cease to be formidable obstructions to happiness.

To fit John Locke into the pattern of a philosophy intellectually and emotionally tied exclusively to private-property considerations, Macpherson had to overcome the special obstacle that Locke repeatedly and emphatically and explicitly proclaimed (or otherwise demonstrated) that he was not so tied. For the most part, previous political philosophers with reasons for depicting Locke as operating from an obsessive and exclusive attachment to private property have simply completely shut their eyes to material in his writings which contradicted such an interpretation. Macpherson shuts only one eye. On the same line, many of these others have pictured Locke as an opponent, along extreme nineteenth-century laissez-faire principles, of any regulation by civil authority of private property and its mode of use. Since Locke was a fairly routine seventeenth-century mercantilist, and the Manchester School had no genuine seventeenth-century anticipators that anyone has brought to light, this is an outright historical anachronism. It is much to his credit that in this respect Macpherson separates himself from his colleagues among the neo-Marxians and ''social Christians'' in the popular game of picturing Locke as the prophet of rugged capitalist-individualism.

As a part of his assault on the ''liberalism'' of Locke, Macpherson charges him with finding in the need for protecting property rights the origin of civil government and in such protection its major and even its sole function. This is,

---

[6] *Leviathan* (Everyman ed.), Part 1, chap. 13, 64.

[7] *Human Nature, The English Works*, IV, 48.

[8] *Philosophical Rudiments, The English Works*, II, Epistle Dedicatory, iv.

of course, now standard doctrine, originated mostly by socialists and social Christians, who regard Locke as the prophet of modern capitalism and find their ideological profit in spattering that prophet with what they are convinced is mud. From them it has spread to the political science texts, where it is a product mostly of shoddy scholarship rather than of anti-capitalist or other pious biases.

If every time Locke used the term "property" he meant by it what we ordinarily mean by it today, namely, possessions, things with a price in the market (or the rights with respect to these things of their owners), the case is made against Locke without more ado. Unfortunately, however, Locke uses the term property in two different senses, which I will distinguish as the narrow (or present-day) sense, meaning things salable for money (including real property and personal property, with the latter still further divisible into tangible and intangible), and the broad sense, where it means an individual's rights to anything (not merely to any *thing*), as in the stock phrase of ancient origin: "life, liberty, and estate," with "possessions," "dower," "fortune" and corresponding terms often substituted for "estate." Further to complicate things, the comprehensive phrase is most often today worded: "life, liberty, and property," where "property" in its narrow sense is a constituent item in the "property" of the broad sense. This last usage also goes far back, and on at least one occasion Locke resorts to it.

When a writer uses in a particular passage the phrase "life, liberty, and estate" without at the same time using the term "property," or when he uses the phrase, "life, liberty, and property," he is reasonably safe against misinterpretation arising out of failure to recognize the existence of two meanings, a narrow and a broad one, for the term "property." But when, as in the case of Locke, he uses the term "property" in both senses we now know that he is going to be misinterpreted even if he repeatedly and carefully defines the two divergent uses. It would have been better for Locke if he had never used the term "property" in both senses, and it would have been better also for the scholarly repute of the vast literature of modern commentary on Locke. But it cannot be charged against Locke that he was innovating in his terminological usage. Take Hobbes, for example. He writes at one place: "Of things held in propriety, those that are dearest to a man are his own life, and limbs; and in the next degree (in most men), those that concern conjugall affection; and after them riches and means of living."[9]

At another place, however, Hobbes refers to a declaration of the Rump Parliament that it was resolved to support the "lives, liberties, and proprieties of the

[9] *Leviathan* (Everyman ed.), chap. 30, 182. It is characteristic of Hobbes that he omits "liberty" from the traditional list; it is also characteristic of him that he adds "conjugall affection," for to Hobbes it was the family, not the individual, that was the social unit or cell.

people," without giving any sign that this was in his opinion out-of-the way usage.[10]

Another illustration of use prior to Locke of the term "property" in its broad sense and this time in fully Lockean application to political doctrine, is by Baxter: "that propriety in his life and faculties, and children, and estate, and honour [which] each man hath and no rulers may unjustly take from him.[11]

Most of the critics of Locke on anti-capitalist grounds simply ignore Locke's repeated definition of "property" in its broad sense, his frequent use of the words "life, liberty, and estate" without further definition, his occasional warning that at a particular point he is using "property" in its narrow sense, and point with horror to Locke's brazen doctrine that government originated (solely) in the desire to protect wealth and that once established its (sole) function was to protect it. A minority of the critics of this school acknowledge the existence in Locke's texts of a definition of "property" which makes it embrace life, liberty, freedom of conscience, that is, human interests to serve which it would not be patently disgraceful for government to be established and to be operated. They find this an intolerable nuisance and in one unbelievably clumsy way or another they brush the offensive definition under the carpet. The broad definition (and also presumably the phrase "life, liberty, and estate") allegedly does not appear in (or near?) the passages they rely upon; the fact that many other scholars of repute refuse to give any weight to what Locke says he means is sufficient justification for their also doing so; that Locke should have ever given the term "property" so comprehensive a meaning was "revealing." What it revealed they do not reveal, but it seems clear to me that they suspected that Locke was deliberately trying to confuse them. In any case, he succeeded eminently in doing so for an astonishingly long list of modern writers of repute and standing.

Macpherson, I regret to have to say, has aligned himself with this group, who, eminent as they are, are, *as scholars*, unworthy companions for a man with his gifts. He complains that Locke's terminological usage was "confusing," and that Locke thereby "somewhat confused matters," but gives no evidence that it confused Locke himself, or any of his contemporaries, or any of his successors in the eighteenth century. Unlike any other member of the group as far as I know, Macpherson, perhaps with indebtedness to Laslett, is aware that Locke was not completely an innovator in using "property" to mean "life, liberty, and estate" and thus to embrace types of human "rights" which it might be wrong but it would not be patently disgraceful to cherish. Nevertheless, he had earlier char-

---

[10] *Behemoth, The English Works*, VI, 361.

[11] Cited from Richard Baxter, *A Holy Commonwealth* (1659), 69, by John W. Gough, *Fundamental Law in English Constitutional History* (Oxford, 1955), 134.

acterized Locke's usage in this connection as "curious." More important, he claims that in the "crucial" passages where Locke is assigning to government a special role vis-à-vis property he is using property in the narrow sense. Let us examine the evidence he presents.

Macpherson cites five sections in the *Second Treatise* where Locke admittedly uses "property" in the broad sense: §§ 87, 123, 131, 137, and 173. He gives references to six sections, 94, 124, 134, 138, 139, and 222, which contain passages which he states to be important for his interpretation of Locke on the relation of government to property, and in which the term "property" is used in the narrow sense. (I would put it in the negative way: where Locke is not explicitly warning his readers that he is using it in the broad sense. He could and at times did so use it without more warning to the reader than the context gave.)

Of the five sections which are alleged to use the narrow meaning, two are linked to immediately preceding sections in which "property" is expressly defined in the broad way, § 124 and § 123, § 138 and § 137; and a third, § 139, is admittedly closely linked to § 138. The section immediately following § 134, i.e. § 135, contains the phrase "life, liberty, and possession"; § 222 opens with the sentence: "The reason why men enter into society is the preservation of their property," but later in the same section Locke speaks of "lives, liberties, and estates of the people," and the preceding section, i.e. § 221, ends with the words "the lives, liberties, or fortunes of the people." Therefore, of the six passages cited by Macpherson as supporting his thesis, five are contaminated by proximity to the broad usage, leaving § 94 alone in unsullied purity, or perhaps with its impurity unexposed.

Let us take a look at this crucial section (which is too long to quote in entirety). The section explains the origin of the shift from personal government to representative government, and the only words in it relevant to the immediate issue are as follows: "the people finding their properties not secure under the government, as then it was (whereas government has no other end but the preservation of property). . . ." I concede only that this section does not expressly contradict Macpherson's thesis. I would hate, however, to have to depend on it alone for sustaining it.[12]

Macpherson ridicules Locke's "famous" Chapter v, "Of Property." In this chapter, "property" unquestionably is used in the "narrow" sense, except for

---

[12] I hesitate to introduce into the argument a further semantic complication. Locke in this passage uses the plural term "properties." I have noticed his use of it on other occasions, but I have not noticed whether its context did or did not imply that it was being used in the broad meaning. The properties may be merely the equivalent of "estates." On the other hand, they may be "life, liberty, and estate." Except for §94, however, I have not noticed any use of the plural term "proprieties" in a "crucial" passage.

the complication that it is made to include ''a property in his own person'' meaning his labour, an extension of the narrow meaning which Macpherson approves
of and makes heavy use of in his own positive theorizing. On the ground that
''labour'' is a part of personality, that it is alienable through sale in the market,
that individuals without some measure of material property are compelled so to
alienate it, and that the market which provides the mechanism for such alienation
is an exploitative one, Macpherson builds his moral, political, and economic case
against capitalism. I think Chapter v is legitimately open to a good deal of ridicule, including much of that which Macpherson directs against it. I cannot accept, however, Macpherson's interpretation of the role of the chapter in Locke's
book, or his appraisal of its historical importance.

Locke's *Treatise* had as its main goal the establishment of claims against unlimited interference by government with personal interests or ''rights.'' ''Property'' in the narrow sense was undeniably one of these ''rights'' to which Locke
attached great importance. It was essential for him to establish its claim to stand
in the same category as ''life'' and ''liberty,'' not as ''inalienable'' rights but as
rights which government could legitimately interfere with only for the public
good, only by ''due process'' or standard procedures,[13] and only by ''consent,''
which by long-standing usage, dating apparently as far back as ancient Roman
times, was a ''legal fiction,'' a term of art, meaning approval by a representative
or other assembly or council of government, as distinguished from an arbitrary
monarch or dictator.

Macpherson finds Locke's use of the term consent as in the phrase ''his own
consent'' for a requirement for legitimate taxation a manifestation of ''extreme
individualism.'' When he finds Locke defining ''his own consent'' as ''the consent of the majority, giving it either by themselves, or their Representatives chosen by them,'' he finds this ''curious'' and difficult to reconcile. Once more,
attention to the history of a term would have facilitated understanding of Locke's
text. To repeat, Locke's usage was standard usage, and the few critics of the time
who pointed out the gap between universal consent literally construed and a majority decision in Parliament (the minority in Parliament, the minority among the
voters, the failure of members of Parliament accurately to express by their votes
the wishes of their constituents, the voteless—that is, most of the propertied, the
great mass of the unpropertied, all women, all minors), did so to reject the claims
of Parliamentary sovereignty over monarchical prerogative and not to support
claims against Parliament of franchised minorities and the unfranchised.[14]

---

[13] Locke claimed ''inalienability'' only for the right to freedom of conscience in religious matters.
Most of the modern critics characterize Locke as an exponent of laissez-faire, but to his credit Macpherson rejects this interpretation. It is only with respect to religion that Locke is a non-intervention-
ist. In most respects, he is a routine, moderate mercantilist.

[14] On the history of usage with respect to the term ''consent,'' see for Roman law usage, F. H.

The function of Locke's Chapter v is to establish two propositions: first, that property in the narrow sense belongs properly to the "life, liberty, and estate" trinity, and second, that like the other members of this trinity property in the narrow sense should be free from interference by an arbitrary and absolute monarch. The latter proposition is in essence a response to Hobbes's position that it is a doctrine "opposite to government" that "each subject hath an absolute dominion over the goods he is in possession of, that is to say, such a propriety as excludes not only the right of all the rest of his fellow-subjects to the same goods, *but also of the magistrate himself.''*[15]

This is radically different from Macpherson's interpretation of Chapter v. My own interpretation, however, does not exempt the chapter from legitimate ridicule but, in some measure, finds different grounds for the ridicule. Its attempt to find a "natural right" basis for the defence of private property—or of life, or of liberty, or of freedom of conscience—is part of an ancient tradition still honoured in important quarters, but which has meagre appeal to me. The utilitarian defence of private property, broadly conceived, satisfies me. The economics in Chapter v is naive and fumbling, although it does include a few valuable insights. Chapter v is not "famous" to economists. There are few references to it in economic literature, and these for the most part are not laudatory. It was not important in the eighteenth-century literature of apologetics for private property—which was not then in urgent need of apologetics—and the references to it in that literature, to the best of my knowledge, are invariably unfavourable. The jurists especially found it objectionable because of the weak case it made for private property and especially because linking the defence of property to its alleged origin in labour undermined rather than helped the status of all that property for which such linkage was specially tenuous. The chief historical function of Chapter v has been to impose an additional burden on the defenders of private property of freeing themselves from the suspicion that they relied on Locke's fragile case.

Macpherson, as I have already said, uses in his case against private property the appeal both to a superior prior tradition and to a superior present-day ideal—

Strube de Piermont, *Ebauche des Loix Naturelles et du Droit Primitif* (new ed., Amsterdam, 1744), 145. For medieval usage, see Maude Violet Clarke, *Medieval Representation and Consent* (London, 1936). For one English example, from the unlimited number readily available, cf. T. Smith, *The Commonwealth of England* [written 1565] (London, 1583), bk. II, chap. II: ". . . the Parliament of England, which representeth and hath the power of the whole realm, both the head and body. For every Englishman is intended to be there present either in person or by procuration and attorney, of what preeminence, state, dignity, or quality soever he be, from the prince . . . to the lowest person of England. And the consent of the Parliament is taken to be every man's consent."

[15] *Philosophical Rudiments*, chap. xii, 7, *English Works*, II, 157–8. Italics mine. Locke claimed "absolute dominion" for the individual only over his religious conscience. What he was contesting, with respect to other personal rights, was "absolute dominion" by government, and especially by an absolute monarch.

or practice elsewhere than in the capitalist world? The prior tradition is much too mixed a one to provide Macpherson with substantial support, and Locke could have drawn from it, if he had been appropriately selective, material which would have strengthened his own case. In one instance, noted by Macpherson, where Locke participates in what was in his time and for more than a century after standard denigration of the political role of the working classes, Macpherson fails to note that Locke was drawing on a very ancient tradition indeed. Macpherson cites from Locke's *The Reasonableness of Christianity*: ''The greatest part of mankind have not leisure for learning and logick, and superfine distinctions of the schools. Where the hand is used to the plough and the spade, the head is seldom elevated to sublime notions, or exercised in mysterious reasoning.'' This is a faithful echo of *Ecclesiasticus* xxxviii (Jesus ben Sirach) in the King James Version of the Apocrypha. Note especially from the latter:

> How can he get wisdom that holdeth the plow . . . ?
> Without these cannot a citie be inhabited,
> And they shall not dwell where they will, nor goe up and downe
> They shall not be sought for in publick counsaile,
> Nor sit high in the congregation.

I have been sharply critical in this review. Let me in conclusion make it clear that I have also found much in the book under review worthy of very high praise indeed, and that I have learned much from it which I am happy to know. My understanding of all the authors he gives major attention to has been greatly improved, I am sure, by my reading of this book, more, so I think, by appreciation of Macpherson's perceptive reading of the texts and his insights than by my hostile reactions to what seemed to me as assuredly or probably or possibly perversions of the texts and drove me to a rereading of them, with a new awareness of what were significant and interesting questions to be directed to these texts. If only the author had not tightly integrated his scholarly endeavour with his apostolic mission I am sure that this book could have been a superlative manifestation of top-level intellectual history. To my biased mind, the procedure he has chosen to follow has resulted in a greater loss to learning than contribution to social salvation.

[EDITOR'S NOTE: A reply by C. B. Macpherson was carried immediately following Viner's review. In it, Macpherson objected to Viner's "misconception of the
book's purpose." Macpherson reiterated that "in Locke's crucial argument on
the limitation of the power of government he is clearly using property in the
narrow sense," denying Viner's charge that he cited sections 94, 124, 134, and
222 in favor of this view (as only sections 138–39, 140, and 193 were cited by
Macpherson for Locke's narrow use of the term property). Macpherson insisted
that Locke's double usage of the term property may have reflected a confusion in
his mind but that Locke was not deliberately trying to confuse anyone. Macpherson said that his book merely offered a "diagnosis of the moral and political
inadequacy of the possessive market society" and that he had no alternative to
offer. He concluded by chiding Viner for his resistance to the "Marxian cast" of
the analysis. See C. B. Macpherson, "Scholars and Spectres: A Rejoinder to
Viner," *Canadian Journal of Economics and Political Science* 29 (November
1963): 559–62.]

THE PERILS OF REVIEWING: A COUNTER-REJOINDER

I will not dispute Professor Macpherson's prerogative to reject my interpretations of the intent of specific portions of his text, or of the book as a whole. I
claim only for my interpretations, however erroneous they may be, that they were
reasonable ones in the light of what I had to go on, which was the book itself and
two earlier articles on Locke, largely incorporated in the book and of which he
says in his Preface (p. vii): "I have not found it necessary to alter or add substantially to what I then said, though I have added references to some subsequent
work on Locke."

On the issue where specific texts are most involved, the debate between us
turns mainly on the significance of Locke's use of the word "property" for the
interpretation of his views on the relation of government to property. The fact is
not in dispute between us, that Locke uses the word "property" in two quite
different meanings, a broad one, to signify "life, liberty, and estate," and a narrow one, to mean, as it ordinarily does today, material possessions. It is Macpherson's thesis that the two usages are tied up with two different and clashing

Reprinted from the *Canadian Journal of Economics and Political Science* 29 (November 1963):
562–66.

doctrines, impossible to reconcile, and reflecting a split, an incoherence, in Locke's mental processes, which "may be ascribed to the confusion in his mind between the remnant of traditional values and the new bourgeois values" (p. 220). It is my position that this alleged dichotomy in Locke's thinking is a myth, that the evidence specifically cited by Macpherson to support it fails to do so, and that there is no other evidence of any weight available in any of Locke's writings to support it. The "traditional values" which Macpherson cites as a contrast to Locke's "new bourgeois values," moreover, seem to me also either largely to be mythical or to be *one* "tradition" which had lived in more or less peaceful co-existence for over a century before Locke with the "new bougeois values." This is a separate story, however, and though relevant I cannot pursue it here.

Macpherson treats the "life, liberty, and estate" passages in Locke as reflecting the "remnant of traditional values" in Locke's thought and treats passages in which "property" is defined or can be inferred to mean material possessions as reflecting the "new bourgeois values." The use by Locke of "property" to embrace life and liberty our author regards as providing a link of a kind between the status of property (meaning material possessions) in Locke's bourgeois or capitalist thinking and the morally superior traditional social values which Locke still in some degree clung to.

In my review, the presentation of my interpretation of Macpherson's account of Locke's views on property and government is marred by at least two defects: I went too far in absolving him from a common failure to consider the history of usage with respect to "property" when reading Locke; I gave an erroneous list of the passages in Locke in which Macpherson claimed to find evidence that Locke had two different and conflicting doctrines of the relation of government to property (in the narrow and now ordinary sense).

In my review, I say: "Macpherson, perhaps with indebtedness to Laslett, is aware that Locke was not completely an innovator in using 'property' to mean 'life, liberty, and estate' and thus to embrace types of human 'rights' which it might be wrong but it would not be patently disgraceful to cherish." In his rejoinder Macpherson comments on this: "Much of what Viner says on this is directed against those who have ignored Locke's broad definition of property or who *have been unaware* that the broad definition was common usage in the seventeenth century, and he acknowledges that I am not to be criticized on either of these grounds" (italics mine). I do acknowledge that Macpherson did not by any means ignore Locke's broad definition of property; unlike the "others" to whom I referred Macpherson relies upon it to support his thesis that Locke was torn between a "traditional" and a "bourgeois" view of the relation of government to property in the narrow sense. As to "awareness" by him of the common usage character of the "broad" meaning of "property," however, what I acknowledged was that he *is* aware of this, not that he *had been* aware of it at all the stages of his development of his interpretation of Locke. In fact, the only evidence I have, even now, that our author was aware even when his book was finished that the "broad" usage was common in Locke's time, and before (and after), is his note 3 on page 143 of his book, where it is the Levellers, not Locke, who are being discussed: "It was of course quite usual in the seventeenth century to speak of a right or a liberty as a property." To the best of my knowledge recognition, in discussions of Locke in print, that the "broad" usage was ever common began, with only one exception, with Laslett's 1960 edition of Locke's *Two Treatises*, which Macpherson used. Laslett's own awareness came only after his book was already in press.[1] In his 1951 article on Locke, Macpherson called the broad usage on Locke's part "peculiar" and "curious." In his book he draws no connection between the occurrence in Locke's writing of two different usages of "property" and common usage in his time, and offers "the confusion in his mind" as the only explanation (see p. 220). He even writes: "It is true that Locke somewhat confused matters by sometimes defining that property whose preservation is the reason for entering civil society *in unusually wide terms*" (p. 198, italics mine). I am still unconvinced that the emphasis he puts on an alleged dichotomy in Locke's views on property does not have its origin in part on insufficient awareness of how general in his time was Locke's double usage with respect to the word "property." It is, of course, open to Macpherson to argue that the double usage by others than Locke was, or may have been, associated with a similar confusion of thought on their part, but from what I know of the relevant literature of the period this would seem to be a random stab in the dark, with the chances very low that further research would turn up any support for it.

I confess unreservedly that I identified incorrectly the set of passages in Locke to which Macpherson appealed in support of his thesis that in Locke's mind two conflicting doctrines as to the relations of government to property lived in unharmonized coexistence. Aside from inadvertence, I slipped into this error because he opened his discussion of Locke's text with a paragraph in which the term "property" was used, without warning and without quotes, as he now says, "simply to show the fundamental political importance Locke gave to 'property' in a sense not yet specified as broad or narrow." Given Macpherson's general attitude of amazement at and hostility to Locke's resort to the "broad" usage, I had no reason to suppose that he would even partially or tentatively embrace it on his own behalf. I thus inferred, wrongly though reasonably, that when I found

[1] See Peter Laslett, ed., John Locke, *Two Treatises of Government* (Cambridge, 1960), 101n, 226n, 368n.

in the passages in Locke referred to by Macpherson in the paragraph in question that Locke was there using "property" in the broad sense, I was correcting Macpherson.

I think, however, I can use the correct list of the passages in Locke by which Macpherson supports his thesis of two clashing and unreconcilable doctrines as to the relation of government to property to support my thesis that such a dichotomy of doctrine is not to be found in Locke. I add that I could also appeal in support of my thesis to many other passages in Locke, including other works of Locke than the *Second Treatise*, did space limits permit, without prejudice of course to the possibility that Macpherson could do likewise in support of his thesis.

The passages specifically appealed to by Macpherson (§§ 138–140; 193) do suffice to show that Locke held that property in its narrow sense originated in the state of nature, that its protection was *an* objective of the establishment of civil government, and that its preservation was *a* function of government once established. No commentator on Locke has ever disputed this; it is equally established in, and fully consistent with, the passages in Locke, of which there are many more, in which he attributes the origin and maintenance of government to the desire to protect life, liberty, and estate; unlike Macpherson, I am not concerned with whether either proposition, the narrow one or the broad one, has any validity, historically, economically, politically, or ethically, or even with whether it has meaningfulness. My issue here with Macpherson turns on whether the "narrow" passages he cites can be reasonably interpreted to hold that it is *only* property in the narrow sense which constitutes the objective of the formation and the maintenance of government. Only then would there be the dichotomy, the "confusion," between these passages and the "life, liberty, and estate" passages, which Macpherson postulates.

That I am correctly identifying what is at issue between Macpherson and me in this connection is shown most clearly, I think, by his statements with reference to "Locke's crucial argument on the limitation of the powers of government": "The property for the protection of which men oblige themselves to civil society is [according to Locke] sometimes . . . clearly *only* goods or land" (pp. 247–8, italics mine); "when the property for the protection of which men enter into civil society . . . is taken to be goods or estates *only*" (p. 248, italics mine). I can find no "only" or equivalent qualifier in the passages Macpherson cites in support of his thesis. I can find no evidence which would justify or even make plausible reading "only" into the relevant texts. I know of only one passage in all of Locke's writings where he does use a qualifier equivalent to "only" in a statement concerning the relation of government to "property" but without clear immediate or proximate explanation that he is using ''property'' in the broad sense (§ 94 of the *Second Treatise*). But Macpherson is not willing to take advantage of this passage.

If there were inner contradiction in Locke's exposition of his doctrine, it could be the result not of confusion on his part but of cunning. Macpherson complains that I aligned him with a group of writers who do attribute to Locke resort to cunning. I had in mind not this point but other doctrinal matters when I found much similarity of pattern between Macpherson and them. I recognize that Macpherson's dichotomy-of-doctrine thesis is an original contribution, regardless of whether it is a correct one, and that it is on this thesis that he puts major emphasis in explaining Locke's alleged self-contradiction. I do not, however, acknowledge that Macpherson wholly and unqualifiedly abstains from the ''concealment hypothesis'': ''The possibility, and in Locke's case the probability, of some measure of concealment of assumptions, cannot be neglected. But it has seemed to me that the concealment hypothesis cannot, even in Locke's case, explain all that has to be explained, and that it is an unsatisfactory alternative to'' the, in effect, dichotomy hypothesis (p. 7); ''Locke did not *care to* recognize that the continual alienation of labour for a bare subsistence wage . . . is in effect an alienation of life and liberty'' (p. 220, italics mine).

Macpherson writes of my ''one specific criticism of [his] handling of the evidence.'' I call his attention, and that of our readers, to what I say in my review of his handling of Locke's texts with respect to the role of ''consent'' in the relations between citizens and their government.

On the other issues that Macpherson raises, I do not think that I can comment fruitfully without more use of space than I could expect to be permitted by the already generous editors. I repeat that I do not claim that I have correctly interpreted Macpherson in all particulars. That would be a major achievement for almost any review; for a book of the subtlety, complexity, and somewhat original terminology of the one here reviewed that would be a supererogatory performance. All I claim, I repeat, is that given the material that I had to work with, my interpretation, though possibly wrong, was reasonable. I repeat also, in conclusion, that I meant sincerely and humbly the praise I gave to the book, and to its author, in my review. May I add that some of the analysis in the book which I admire, and perhaps even accept, seems to me to have Marxian foundations, and perhaps to be none the worse for that.

17

THE EARLIER LETTERS OF JOHN STUART MILL

MASSIVE COLLECTIONS aiming at completeness of the formal writings of particular great or near-great men are in themselves no novelty. More novel, and indeed a phenomenon confined to the last two decades or so and to a handful of countries, is the application by editors of such collections of exact, strictly objective and unobtrusive scholarship, of helpful annotation, and of a wide range of devices for indexing, cross-referencing, and collating of variant texts, all with the purpose of making the path of the serious scholar smoother and freer from hazards and traps. Most novel of all is the application by qualified humanists of all of these types of solicitous attention to the writings of men whose fame rests primarily on other than their contributions to *belles-lettres*, of men who were primarily statesmen, or social philosophers, or economists, or political thinkers, or some combination of these: men like Turgot, Leibnitz, Ricardo, Jefferson, the Adamses, Madison, or Franklin. It is relevant that of these projects that come first to my mind, only one is fully complete as of to-day, and most of the rest still have a long way to go, while still others, Adam Smith and Jeremy Bentham for example, have not yet advanced visibly beyond the planning and organization stage. In these new areas for the application of technically qualified scholarship on a large scale and usually by *teams* of scholars and helpers rather than as individual enterprises, the plans are for magnificent cathedrals to rise out of rather flat country. Like cathedrals, they are liable to take many years to complete, perhaps even more years than are contemplated. They involve great risks, therefore, and make great demands on courage, endurance, and financial resources. But like beautiful cathedrals, they endow generations of mankind with treasures more precious than things purchasable on the market place.

It is not only specialized scholars anxious to know the subjects of such projects whole and to know them as accurately and understandingly as existing knowledge

Review of Francis E. Mineka, ed., *The Earlier Letters of John Stuart Mill*, Vols. XII and XIII (Toronto: University of Toronto Press, 1963). Reprinted from the *University of Toronto Quarterly* 34 (October 1964): 98–103.

permits who profit from them. The editorial services enable scholars of more specialized interest, and the general reader as well, to find easy access to the particular texts or information they are seeking, presented in as authentic form as possible and free from tendentious arrangement, or citation away from context, or manipulation in support of an editor's personal hobby or ideology. The combination in one unified project of "works," "papers," and correspondence, and ideally also of "life," with as comprehensive indexing and cross-referencing as proves practicable, facilitates access to the relevant material on a scale which otherwise would be far beyond the reach, not only of the ordinary reader, but even of the specialized and skilled and industrious scholar. In all such projects, moreover, one of the major contributions is the discovery and assembly in readily usable form of material hitherto not known to exist, or of unknown location, or resting untouched and untouchable in private attics and the locked storerooms of libraries. It is, incidentally, important to understand that no matter how dedicated and energetic the editors of such projects may be, they cannot ordinarily by their own efforts alone locate and make available in printed and edited form, such out-of-the-way material, but must depend largely on the goodwill and co-operation of a host of librarians, scholars, collectors, and owners of attics in locating and making accessible to the editors such manuscripts, printed matter, or knowledge as are, or may conceivably be, helpful for their projects.

The John Stuart Mill project of which these two volumes of correspondence are the first fruits has been planned and is being directed by an editorial committee appointed from the faculty of the University of Toronto and the University of Toronto Press. These volumes are a splendid sample of book-making and printing. Despite close inspection, I have not found a single lapse from impeccability in the press-editing. I congratulate the editorial committee and the University of Toronto Press on this admirable contribution to scholarly publication, which in kind, scale, and quality is, I imagine, a Canadian first. I hope that it will be successfully completed within my time, and since such projects are in their nature little more self-financing than cathedrals, I hope also that no one goes broke in the process.

Aside from the two volumes under review, eleven specific volumes are announced as in preparation. There will be also at least one additional volume of correspondence and probably more, and there will have to be an additional over-all index volume. I presume also that there will be a volume of speeches. This makes at least sixteen volumes in all, and still leaves a substantial amount of miscellaneous material unprovided for: identifiable contributions by Mill to other men's books, submissions to and testimony before official bodies, letters to newspapers, of which there were a good many, and perhaps also, although here, on the basis of what I have seen of this material, samples, I think, would suffice, of Mill's reports of his botanical and other tours, and his dispatches as an East India Company official. The editors will have some difficult decisions to make with reference to such of Mill's letters to his wife as Hayek has not published. I sampled them some years ago, and they are for the most part dull and, to an outsider, depressing beyond belief. It would be excessive editorial rigorism to print them in full, but I think it would be a proper compromise to print a few of the uninteresting letters as the most persuasive justification for not printing them all. No matter, however, what corners are cut, the project will run to major dimensions.

That John Stuart Mill's writings are eminently appropriate for a project of this kind seems to me beyond dispute. Only a small fraction of his writings is available in recent and scholarly editions. The great bulk of his writings can be read today only in out-of-print editions or in extinct periodicals or other out-of-the-way sources, or still await their first appearance in print. Even the greatest libraries do not have files of all the periodicals to which Mill contributed. Even aside from his correspondence, some of his writings may still await discovery, and one of the contributions, no doubt, of this project will be the first complete bibliography of his printed writings. It is, of course, not the mere bulk of his writings which makes their collection and scholarly editing worthwhile, but their quality, their historical importance, and their present-day vitality as influencing current thought whether as guides or as challenges. Throughout the Western world, Mill's ideas still play a major role in the thinking of moral philosophers, of logicians, of political theorists, and of economists. In terms of present-day significance, I can think of no other social philosopher of the nineteenth century who wrote in English, except Bentham, whose works stand in greater need and will more fully repay collection and scholarly editing on the highest modern standards.

The two volumes of correspondence now presented to us are a splendid product of discovery, assembly, and scrupulously scholarly editing. The task of discovery and assembly was begun, as an individual enterprise, by Friedrich Hayek over twenty years ago, with concentration on the correspondence before 1848. For various good reasons, however, he could not complete it or carry it to the publication stage and it was with his consent and co-operation that the enterprise was taken over by Francis E. Mineka, the editor of these two volumes, an authority of high standing on English nineteenth-century intellectual history, whose editorial craftsmanship is in these two volumes made manifest.

Mineka makes graceful acknowledgment to Hayek for his part in the location and assembly of the pre-1849 correspondence, and Hayek in a helpful introduction to these volumes, as well as elsewhere, gives an account, too modest by far, of what it took in effort, in strategems, in surmounting of special obstacles, to attain a collection of the correspondence as close to substantial completeness as this present one seems to be. But a more detailed account would be of interest and use to scholars in general, even if they have no special interest in Mill. I hope that Hayek, or Mineka, or both, will some day take time off to tell the whole story, most appropriately perhaps in a library journal, for what struck me particularly in that part of the story I know most about is the extent to which, where manuscript material is concerned, even great libraries can be unaware of what riches they possess. It is wholly probable in the nature of things that letters of Mill in the pre-1849 period that are not included in the present collection still survive in the papers of recipients thereof, or in collectors' hands, or in strange places. The only suggestion I can make in this connection is that where it is known or can be conjectured that Mill wrote to particular persons but no such letters have been found, publication of a list of such persons might act as a stimulus to the search for such letters or even to the discovery by persons knowing of the existence of such letters that they were being sought for. Some notes I have indicate that in the Yale collection of Mill's papers there is a list in Mill's hand of some of his early correspondence, and that it includes a reference to three letters to Antoine Jerome Balard, his "first friend" (see *The Earlier Letters*, I. xxiii) sent in 1822, 1824, and 1831. Even as meagre a clue as this can conceivably lead to the discovery of these missing letters.

Mineka's editorial handling of the correspondence is excellent. If there were no limitation of time and space, the reader would often like to have before him the texts of the letters to which Mill was replying or which he received in reply to his own. This problem has no complete solution in a finite world, but given all the circumstances, I think that Mineka in his annotations provides as much relevant information about this and other matters as the reader can reasonably demand. I have not found any outright mistakes, and I submit the sum total of the queries I have about the editor's notes, not at all because they are worth presenting for their own sake, but as indicative by their unimportance in number and kind how fully his editing has withstood my search for flaws. An editorial "[?]" is added to the address "Dumfries, N.B." of a letter from Mill to Carlyle (102, n. 1). The "N.B." is here surely the common nineteenth-century abbreviation for "North Britain," a then common appellation for Scotland. On p. 448, there is a note to a letter to George H. Lewes, the first letter to him in this collection, which reads: "Published in Kitchel, p. 29." Such sources of letters are not included in any of Mineka's indexes, and I am not clear as to what he intends the reader to do if he wishes further information. The reference by Mill in Letter 475,

Nov. 1845 to "*Revue des Economistes*" was, I feel sure, a slip on his part for "*Journal des Economistes.*" The modern advocates of bibliographical rigorism will be unhappy, I fear, about the absence of systematic and precise information about the procedures followed by the editor in moving from his source material to final copy for the printer, and perhaps would be even unhappier with the information if it had been supplied. In the case of manuscript material, for instance, did the editor in specific instances work directly from the holograph, or from photographs, or from typed transcripts supplied by others? I have not found, however, a single instance of editor's errors in transcription, or of typographical errors for which the Press or the editor could be scolded. On my standards at least, the editorial task has been fulfilled with as near an approach to absolute perfection as it is reasonable for mortals to expect to encounter, or even to aspire to.

The correspondence here published, a substantial fraction of which here makes its first appearance in print, is for the most part interesting reading, even if taken by itself. I would suggest, however, that both specialists and general readers would add to their enjoyment and profit if they read the correspondence along with Mill's *Autobiography* for the corresponding years. The letters and the *Autobiography* throw light on each other, and provide context for each other, in many instances. Mill had an excellent prose style, and his correspondence rivals his more formal writing for lucidity, economy of verbiage, and precision. Laughter was not for Mill, perhaps even in his youth, and there is comparatively little of a personal note, or of lightness of tone, in his letters. There is scant supply of correspondence with his parents or brothers and sisters. Most of the correspondence is about writing, or ideas, or politics, or publishing. The two love letters to Harriet Taylor clash violently with the austerity of the correspondence as a whole, and even the quite disciplined warmth of his letters to the Foxes of Falmouth and to his "Mutterlein" Sarah Austin strikes the reader as breaching an otherwise solid wall of reserve. There is little hint of play or of joy in these letters. I do not recall that there is explicit evidence in this correspondence that during the period it covers he ever went to the theatre, or read any English novels, or attended concerts—or, when in England, church. He did read German novels, perhaps to learn the language, and on the Continent at least he did look at pictures in the galleries. He did play the piano, apparently for hours at a time, but it may have been spontaneous composition without benefit of training. Poetry he did read, but with deadly seriousness, as medicine for his mental crises.

In the writings of his precocious period, Mill displayed to the full the intellectual self-assurance of his father, who once in a letter to Francis Place declared that: "If I had time to write a book, I would make the human mind as plain as the road from Charing Cross to St. Pauls," an achievement which he perhaps felt he had reached when years later he published his *Analysis of the Human Mind*. But John Mill for a time after his intellectual crisis displayed as he himself expressed it in his *Autobiography* a new "many-sidedness," a "willingness and ability to learn from everybody," although it was an extremely restricted "everybody" whose influence he expressly acknowledged and made fairly manifest in his writings. Chief among these were Wordsworth, Carlyle, the Saint Simonians, Comte. If one looks for what these men had in common, there does not seem to be an obvious answer. Apparently all of these, for a time at least, provided Mill with some release from the logical rigour, the narrowness of interest, the anti-aestheticism and anti-romanticism of his father and of Bentham. All of them placed great emphasis upon leadership by an élite of merit, and were decidedly not believers in the maxim that the voice of the people was the voice of God. With respect to Wordsworth and Carlyle, what appealed most strongly to Mill was apparently the important role which emotions and feelings played in their social gospels. In any case, Mill swung strongly away for a time from the strict Benthamite doctrines. From disparagement of the role of feelings in the good life and of intuition in the intellectual life, he turned to emphasis on their importance. From philosophical radicalism in politics he moved toward a fairly pronounced doctrine of rule by the persons qualified by intellect and character to be rulers. The doctrine that all that was significant in actions was their consequences he did not abandon in so many words. But he came to place strong emphasis on taking "all" the consequences into account, including in the "all" much that he insisted Bentham did not take into account, not only the feelings and the aesthetic and emotional ingredients of "happiness," but also the effects on "character" with respect to both the active agent and the persons affected by his action.

It seems to me that while the impact on Mill of these new ideas weakened in time, and with respect to Saint Simonians and Comte became negligible or even turned to dislike, the influence of Wordsworth, and via Carlyle, of the German romantics, had a lasting effect on his over-all system of thought. It enabled him for the rest of his life to retain, without any sense of basic inconsistency or internal tension, a happiness ethic which gave weight to degrees of quality as well as of quantity, which stressed consequences of action more than motives and feelings but included as "consequences" pleasures of different kinds and qualities and effects as "character," with an intellectual élite and moral élite as the ultimate judge of degree of quality and of character. It enabled him to remain, or again to become, a political liberal without committing himself to an electoral system in which the intellectually superior person would stand as voter on an absolutely even level with the ordinary run of mankind. It enabled him to carry on a sustained liaison with socialist ideas and interventionist economic programmes while conducting economic analysis which on a theoretical level remained almost wholly within the classical school boundaries of *laissez-faire* and economic individualism. The chief harmonizing device here was not the routine one of the distinction between theory and practice or between abstraction and realism, for Mill essentially identified the standard-classical economic doctrine and the dominance of individualism with the best that would be practicable until the character and quality of mankind had been greatly improved, and he reserved the socialism and statism (or perhaps more accurately, voluntary co-operativism) as proper goals for a happier but distant future.

While the correspondence in the two volumes under review extends only to 1848, these various tendencies in Mill's thinking and in his system of values and feelings received full development only after 1848. All of them, however, can be perceived, at least in germ, in the earlier correspondence, and some of them more clearly than in any of his more formal writings, early or later. Many varying interpretations are available of the pattern of Mill's intellectual development, of which Mill's own interpretation does not have an undebatably superior claim to acceptance. When this project as a whole has been completed, there will be for the first time an opportunity to reappraise these interpretations and perhaps to discover a generally persuasive new one on the basis of a full presentation of the relevant data. And this opportunity will not be by any means the least to be cherished of the contributions to learning which this project will make.

PART IV

Commencement Addresses

18

A MODEST PROPOSAL FOR SOME STRESS ON SCHOLARSHIP IN GRADUATE TRAINING

THE TITLE I HAVE CHOSEN for my talk may possibly recall to some of you the somewhat similar form of title which eighteenth-century writers used ironically for brutally satiric essays. Jonathan Swift in his "A Modest Proposal for Preventing the Children of Poor People from being a Burden to their Parents or the Country" recommended that the problem of the starving children be solved by serving the children as food to the rich. Philip Skelton made his irony obvious by the very title of his essay, which read: "Some Proposals for the Revival of Christianity." If, however, there is any irony in the title or satire in the contents of my talk, I would like you to believe that, like M. Jourdain's prose, they are unplanned and unconscious.

My proposal is both sincere and modest. I give also only an old-fashioned and modest meaning to the term "scholarship." I mean by it nothing more than the pursuit of broad and exact knowledge of the history of the working of the human mind as revealed in written records. I exclude from it, as belonging to a higher order of human endeavour, the creative arts and scientific discovery.

What I propose, stated briefly and simply, is that our graduate schools shall assume more responsibility than they ordinarily do, so that the philosophers, economists, mathematicians, physicists, and theologians they turn out as finished teachers, technicians, and practitioners shall have been put under some pressure or seduction to be also scholars.

I do not ask that before economists are turned out from the graduate school assembly line bearing the Ph.D. as a stamp of completion of the training process they be required to have shown that they are finished scholars as well as finished economists. True scholarship is always an unfinished and an unfinishable process. Scholarship is a commitment to the pursuit of knowledge and understanding, but it can never provide guarantees that these have been attained. A great

Address before the Graduate Convocation, Brown University, June 3, 1950.

part of true learning, in fact, takes the form of negative knowledge, of increasing awareness of the range and depth of our unconquered ignorance, and it is one of the major virtues of scholarship that only by means of it, one's own or someone else's, can one know when it is safe to dispense with it. Learned ignorance, therefore, is often praiseworthy, although ignorant learning, about which I will say something later, never is.

There is so much that needs to be known, and so little time in one's student days for learning it, that it is not a depreciation of the doctor's degree to regard it as merely marking the termination of one advanced stage in one's education, the last stage in which the responsibility is shared with others, to be followed by another stage lasting to the end of one's life in which one is intellectually wholly on one's own. The University of Avignon, in 1650, found itself faced by a candidate for the doctorate who had capacity but who had applied himself less closely to the pursuit of knowledge than to less exacting and more exciting extracurricular activities. After some hesitation, it conferred the doctoral degree upon him with the notation *sub spe futuri studii*, which I am told can be translated as "in the hope of future study." May I suggest that our doctoral degrees should be granted, and accepted, in this spirit even when there is not occasion to spell it out in the letter of the parchment?

I do not claim much for the pursuit of scholarship for its own sake, either in material rewards to the scholar or in tangible benefit to the community. We live in perilous times, with crucial problems of life and death, of riches and poverty, of freedom and tyranny, awaiting solution. In the social sciences, as in the natural sciences, students tend to seek first for solutions to these problems, or for skills by aid of which they may be attacked. This is as it should be. These are first, and probably also second, and third, and fourth. It is not as an escape from the burning problems of the world that I speak a word for scholarship. Not for me, and not recommended to any of you, is the plea of Joseph Hall during the British civil and religious contentions in the late sixteenth century:

> 'Mongst all these stirs of discontented strife,
> O let me lead an academic life.
> To know much and to think we nothing know;
> Nothing to have, yet think we have enow.[1]

Nor do I wish to suggest that scholarship loses merit of any kind, even as scholarship, as it gains in utility, in relevance to major current problems. Such doctrine

---

[1] Virgidemiarum, Bk. IV. Satire VI [1599], *The Works of the Right Reverend Joseph Hall, D.D., Bishop of Exeter*, new edition (Oxford, 1863), IX, 649.

was once standard among the learned, but it today smacks of priggishness, of absence of a sense of proportion. A great mathematician, Jacobi, for instance, in a letter to another great mathematician, Legendre, wrote in 1830 of a third great mathematician, Fourier, as follows:

> It is true that M. Fourier had the opinion that the principal purpose of mathematics was public utility and the explanation of natural phenomena; but a philosopher such as he was should have known that the sole end of science was the honor of the human mind, and that by this criterion a question in the theory of numbers was as important as a question of the nature of the universe.[2]

Although I have a sneaking admiration for Jacobi's doctrine of scholarship for scholarship's sake *alone*, judgment and discretion master inclination, and I refrain—not without effort—from subscribing to it. I certainly do not venture to preach it. Given the strength, however, of the prevailing pressures against expenditure of time and thought on learning which cannot demonstrate its relevance to increasing the yield of cotton or winning the cold war, the doctrine is scarcely to be regarded as a dangerous one. It is at least not a doctrine dictated by or approved by Moscow.

The modest proposal I make is that graduate schools make a place in their programs, a modest place, but one not confined to the Humanities departments, for scholarship, and that they require or at least plead with their students, especially those who are destined to be college teachers, to devote to that part of the graduate school program a fraction, a modest fraction, of their attention.

A small place once given to scholarship, moreover, I would not object if it were then confined to its allotted space, or at least not permitted to spread without restraint into areas beyond its proper jurisdiction, where if it intrudes it steals time and other less valuable resources from what are generally acknowledged to be more important activities. A verger of a church, reproved for locking the doors of the church, replied that when they were left open it often resulted in people praying all over the place. I concede that we don't want students and faculty unrestrainedly pursuing scholarship all over our universities while they have so much more urgent business to attend to.

Scholarship may be misplaced, moreover, not only because it distracts attention from more vital matters, but also because the scholar tends to inject himself, his techniques, his values, and his lack of impatience for quick results into problem areas where his contributions are regarded as irrelevant or as not prompt

---

[2] J. T. Merz, *A History of European Thought in the Nineteenth Century* (Edinburgh, 1903), II, 657.

enough to be serviceable. Scholarship out of place brings nothing but embarrassment to the scholar and irritation to his clients—if any. A woman in a shop asked for a drinking bowl for her dog. When the clerk replied that he had no drinking bowls especially for dogs, the woman said that any drinking bowl would do. The clerk, having found one for her, then suggested that he have the word ''dog'' painted on it. ''No, thanks,'' said the women. ''It is not necessary. My husband doesn't drink water and my dog can't read.'' Learning should be kept in its place. A university is today many things, very, very many things. As one of these many things, not too low on the list, it should strive to continue to be, or again to become, a place of and for scholarship. But it cannot be expected, and it will not be permitted, to be a place for scholarship only or predominantly.

Aware of the fact that scholarship does not necessarily yield even to the scholar the limited rewards, spiritual or material, sought from it, I thought for a time of choosing for my title: ''Lo, the Poor Scholar!'' In one of his sermons, Robert South, an eighteenth-century Anglican clergyman, expounds at length, and with traces of complacency, the woes that beset the scholar. He takes as his text, Ecclesiastes I. 18: ''In much wisdom there is much grief; and he that increaseth knowledge increaseth sorrow.'' Among the many perils of learning he lays special emphasis on its hazards for health and prosperity: ''Knowledge,'' he remarks, ''rewards its followers with the miseries of poverty, and clothes them with rags. Reading of books consumes the body, and buying of them the estate.''[3]

Accumulation of knowledge moreover leads by a fatal association to desire to communicate it, and this in turn leads to the desire to write books, and this in turn to additional woes and pains. Rousseau once said, as reported by David Hume, that ''one half of a man's life is too little to write a book and the other half to correct it.'' Rousseau must have meant a scholarly book, for he himself wrote many books, and never corrected any of them, as far as I have been able to discover. The modern scholar spends much more time in correcting the books of non-scholars which, unfortunately, took much less than half a lifetime to write, than in writing his own books. For the writing of books there is little time left to scholars by their other inescapable tasks. It is still true that of the writing of books there is no end, but it is also true that most scholarly manuscripts have no ending. If the scholar does complete his *opus majus*, there is often too little conversion of even university presses to the virtues of deficit financing to make its publication possible. If, nevertheless, the scholar does manage to complete his manuscript and to find an unworldly publisher, he still reaps little reward of any sort, except to his vanity if the reviewers are kind. But the kindness of reviewers, or even the hope of it, let scholars be frank about it, is often a sufficient reward.

---

[3] Robert South, D.D., *Sermons Preached upon Several Occasions* (Library of Old English Divines edition, New York, 1871), V, 11.

Consider the confession of Pascal, who made it his practice not to conceal from others his own weaknesses, or theirs:

> Vanity is so anchored in the heart of man, that a soldier, a soldier's servant, a cook, a porter, brags and seeks admirers; and even philosophers wish for them. And those who write against vanity wish to have the glory of having written well; and those who read what the latter have written wish to have the glory of having read it; and I, who write this attack on vanity, perhaps also have a yearning for this glory; and perhaps also those who will read this.[4]

Nor is yielding to vanity the only reproach which can be levelled against the motives of the scholar. Curiosity is an even more prevalent, and, of course, more serious vice of the true scholar than vanity. Bernard Mandeville, who read human nature the way an editor reads proof-sheets or a professor a doctoral thesis, looking only for errors, faults, and deviations from the standard proprieties, added avarice to vanity and curiosity as the faults of the scholar. Book royalties must have been larger in those days! But Mandeville maintained that private vices are public benefits, and in his *Fable of the Bees* he found illustration for his doctrine in the operations of scholars:

> There is no Part of Learning but some Body or other will look into it, and labour at it, from no better Principles, than some Men are Fox-hunters, and others take delight in Angling. Look upon the mighty Labours of Antiquaries, Botanists, and the Vertuosos in Butterflies, Cockle-shells, and other odd Productions of Nature; and mind the magnificent Terms they all make use of in their respective Provinces, and the pompous Names they often give, to what others, who have no Taste that way, would not think worth any Mortal's Notice. Curiosity is often as bewitching to the Rich, as Lucre is to the Poor; and what Interest does in some, Vanity does in others; and great Wonders are often produced from a happy Mixture of both.[5]

David Hume, perhaps with Mandeville in mind, gave a somewhat different and more realistic, thought not obviously more flattering, account of the motivation of authorship. In his account, avarice was not a supplement but a rival to curiosity, and acted as a barrier to the writing of books, presumably because more profitable activities were usually available:

> . . . it is more easy to account for the rise and progress of commerce in any kingdom, than for that of learning. . . . Avarice, or the desire of gain, is an universal passion, which operates at all times, in all places, and upon all persons. But curi-

---

[4] *Pensées*, 150.
[5] *Fable of the Bees, Part II* [1729], F. B. Kaye, ed. (Oxford, 1924), II, 342.

osity, or the love of knowledge, has a very limited influence, and requires youth, leisure, education, genius, and example, to make it govern any person. You will never want booksellers, while there are buyers of books. But there may frequently be readers where there are no authors.[6]

Hume, in attributing specially to youth a yearning for knowledge, for scholarship, was generalizing from his own experience. As he wrote to a friend, in 1764:

I repent heartily my ever having committed anything to Print. Had I a Son I shou'd warn him as carefully against the dangerous Allurements of Literature as K James did his Son against those of women; tho' if his Inclination was as strong as mine in my Youth, it is likely, that the warning would be to as little Purpose in the one Case as it usually is in the other.[7]

My role today is, of course, the reverse of Hume's. I am pleading for planned increase of the allurements of scholarship rather than for increased protection against them. And I plead on behalf of scholarship, not that it will save the world, although this has conceivably happened in the past and may happen again; not that it brings material rewards to the scholar, although this also may have occurred, to the scandal of his academic superiors; not that it is an invariably exciting activity, for it generally involves a great deal of drudgery, and, like diplomacy for Charles G. Dawes, is often indeed harder on the feet than on the head. All that I plead on behalf of scholarship, at least upon this occasion, is that, once the taste for it has been aroused, it gives a sense of largeness even to one's small quests, and a sense of fullness even to the small answers to problems large or small which it yields, a sense which can never in any other way be attained, for which no other source of human gratification can, to the addict, be a satisfying substitute, which gains instead of loses in quality and quantity and in pleasure-yielding capacity by being shared with others—and which, unlike golf, improves with age.

To the objection that other needs are so pressing that we can't afford the time which scholarship calls for, I fear the answer which Robert Browning gave in his *A Grammarian's Funeral* would not now be acceptable:

What's time? Leave *Now* for dogs and apes!
Man has Forever.

[6] *Essays Moral, Political, and Literary*, Green and Grose, eds. (London, 1898), I, 176.
[7] *The Letters of David Hume*, J. Y. T. Greig, ed. (Oxford, 1932), I, 461.

It is not as easy today as in the good old days of Queen Victoria to believe that Man has Forever. But suppose we do steal from what time we do have some few hours for this less urgent business, surely no clear and present danger to our security or our prosperity or even the prosperity of our universities will result from such larceny.

Not that I would make an unqualified plea for all that is associated with the pursuit of scholarship, even when it is indulged in in only minor doses. So modestly stocked as a rule are the closets of scholars—unless they are of the medical profession—that despite the smallness of these closets there is still room in them to conceal a few skeletons. I propose to say a few words on the skeletons of the scholars. But let those of the fraternity in our midst rest tranquil, for I will speak only of those of our skeletons which we parade before the reading public's gaze.

First, the lay public complains, with something short of complete lack of justification, that scholars have a tendency to pass off obscurity for profundity. A scholar of a kind and poet of a comparable kind, Sir Richard Blackmore, once published an ungenerous couplet on this theme:

> Let idle Students on their Volumes pore
> To cloud with Learning, what was clear before.[8]

To this I can make on behalf of the scholar only this feeble reply in kind:

> Let unlearned laymen not be too sure,
> That what seems simple, is not obscure.

Second, for some reason which I have never quite fathomed, laymen object to footnotes and quotations as if they were always blots ostentatiously or capriciously sprinkled on texts. Perhaps scholars should dispense with footnotes when writing for laymen. They should, of course, dispense with them when they are superfluous or can conveniently to the reader be incorporated in the text. There have been some extraordinary manifestations of what a non-scholar has diagnosed as "foot-and-note-disease," and not all the redundant *infras, op. cits.*, and *loc. cits.* have fallen under the vigilant eye of Frank Sullivan of "A Garland of *Ibids*" fame. Hugo Grotius, for instance, was meticulously careful to append heavy documentation to such propositions of common notoriety as that man embraces woman; the author of "Mother Goose's Melody," said to be Oliver Goldsmith, was poking fun at him when he attached as a footnote to his melody, as

---

[8] "Solomon's Irony" [1714], in *A Collection of Poems on Various Subjects* (London, 1718), p. 468.

an alleged quotation from Grotius, the statement that "It is a mean and scandalous practice in authors to put notes to things that deserve no notice." There is also that somewhat famous footnote in an English book published in 1854, inserted "as a relief to the uniformity and matter of these pages," a footnote to end all footnotes, which extends from page 334 of the book to page 628.[9]

I wish I could persuade laymen, nevertheless, that footnotes and quotations in texts often perform useful functions, and not only for scholars. Footnotes are frequently the only anchor of text to fact, the only obstacle to flights of imagination where what is called for is merely soberly accurate reporting. As for quotations, they are often the only tasty plums in the author's pudding, as I would not have to depart far from my present text to provide an illustration. What irritates the laymen, I suspect, is frequently not the presence of the quotations but of the quotation *marks*. But scholars, and especially writers of doctoral dissertations, can omit these little marks only subject to great professional peril, for they are required to enable the reader to distinguish mere scholarship from creative writing.

Third, there is a special product of scholarship for which it is hard to find an excuse except that it is an occupational disease of the scholar which it often requires severe self-discipline, constant vigilance, and the aid of hostile critics completely to avoid. This is what Jeremy Bentham called "nonsense-on-stilts," a type of sophisticated nonsense, of ignorant learning, which only educated men are capable of perpetrating. An eighteenth-century French wit has distinguished two types of learned balderdash, of "galimatias," the simple type, where the author believes he understands what he is saying but cannot make it intelligible to his readers, and the compound type, where neither author nor readers can make anything of the text. It would not be difficult to extend this classification so as to cover still other types, as, for example, where the readers think they understand but the author knows he doesn't, and it would not be difficult to find illustrations, even in the "Great Books," and especially in the commentaries upon them, for all the types distinguished. Even with respect to highly technical subjects the layman can here make his own contribution to good scholarship by keeping his modesty under control; if after due application he fails to find a text addressed to laymen intelligible, he should hold in mind the bare possibility that the fault lies not with him but with the absence of meaningfulness in the text.

With the impatience of the layman or of the members of other disciplines with a particular discipline's technical terms, however, I have only limited patience. True it is that the scholar needs to be watched lest he use technical jargon to

[9] [Christopher Walton], *Notes and Materials for an Adequate Biography of the Celebrated Divine and Theosopher, William Law* (London, 1854).

conceal the absence of precision, rather than in its service. But technical language, though never a sufficient condition of precision of thought, and sometimes a substitute for it, is often its necessary condition. I have friends who inadequately conceal their incredulity when I plead that to explain to them, for example, my belief that it is sometimes to a country's advantage to have an unfavorable balance of trade, I would have to resort to technical terms. These same friends, however, on the slightest provocation, or even with no provocation at all, will blandly break into a very rash of technical jargon, totally incomprehensible to me, if it is a question of why the runner was out at second base, or how to knit a baby sweater, or how to tell a yellow warbler from a canary.

I come now to the fourth and last of those of the scholar's skeletons which are fit matter for public discussion, at least among friends, to what I regard as the major barrier to the promotion of true scholarship in our graduate schools. This is the ever-growing specialization not only as between departments but even within departments, a specialization carried so far that very often professors within even the same department can scarcely communicate with each other on intellectual matters except through the mediation at seminars and doctoral examinations of their as yet incompletely specialized students. This development has not been capricious or without function. The growth in the accumulation of data, in the refinement and delicacy of tools for their analysis so that great application and concentration are necessary for mastery of their use, has not only ended the day of the polymath with all knowledge for his province, but seems steadily to be cutting down the number of those who would sacrifice even an inch of depth of knowledge for a mile of breadth.

I am told, and do not disbelieve, that this intensive specialization is frequently necessary for discovery, and especially for the improvement of techniques of discovery. To be able to keep on discovering things not known before it seems often to be necessary to work in a narrow groove, and to look always straight ahead in that groove without even glances at the once delectable knowledge in one's scholarly neighbor's rival garden. For our liberal colleges we preach synthesis of disciplines, breadth of view, and historical perspective, and in our liberal colleges there are still teachers who practice it. But when, by fellowships or other blandishments, we have enticed the college graduate into our graduate schools, we at once encourage him to grow the professional blinders which will confine his vision to the narrow research track, and we endeavor—often successfully— to make out of him a trufflehound, or, if you prefer, a race-horse, finely trained for a single small purpose and not much good for any other. We then let him loose on the undergraduates.

There may be a real dilemma here. It may really be true that at least in many cases there is a genuine and sharp conflict between, on the one hand, effective training for discovery, which requires narrow specialization, and, on the other hand, training for broad scholarship, which requires more time, less concentration of interest, less exclusive infatuation with laboratory models whose charms are the product of art rather than of nature, than progress in research can afford.

I yield to no one in recognition of the importance to mankind of the training for research which our graduate schools administer. If in the last generation or so American research over a wide range of fields has come of age, I would claim for the American graduate schools a great share of the credit. if the only relationship between graduate schools and colleges consisted in the recruiting from the colleges of the students for the graduate schools, I could even reconcile myself, though reluctantly, to the existence under modern conditions of an inherent conflict between research and scholarship, between narrowly-specialized skills and broad learning, and I would let the graduate schools go on in their present course, and encourage scholarship to seek refuge elsewhere.

The graduate schools, however, train our college teachers as well as our researchers, and the graduate school faculties also teach in the colleges. The graduate schools, I repeat, tend to mould their students into narrow specialists, who see only from the point of view of their subject, or of a special branch of their special subject, and fail to recognize the importance of looking even at their own subject from other than its own point of view. These students then acquire their doctoral degrees on the strength of these which have demonstrated to the satisfaction of their supervisors that they have adequately decontaminated their minds from any influences surviving from their undergraduate training in other fields than those occupied by their chosen discipline. They then find their way back to the colleges to transmit to the next generation the graduate school version of a liberal education, or how to see the world through the eye of a needle. I would not pause to emphasize that mechanical shuffling of college curricula or verbal relabeling of courses is not an effective antidote to aggravated specialism in college teaching, were it not for my conviction that we often underestimate how very true, how very important, and how very much neglected, truisms can be.

Men are not narrow in their intellectual interests by nature; it takes special and rigorous training to accomplish that end. And men who have been trained to think only within the limits of one subject, or only from the point of view of one subject, will never make good teachers at the college level even in that subject. They may know exceedingly well the possibilities of that subject, but they will never be conscious of its limitations, or if conscious of them will never have an adequate motive or a good basis for judging as to their consequence or extent.

Samuel Johnson once said, before the urgent need of saying it had become obvious: "the rights of nations and of kings sink into questions of grammar, if grammarians discuss them." Samuel Johnson certainly had no prejudice against grammar. I don't think, therefore, that I am being unduly generous to him, and I am at least making my quotation from him more relevant to my present purposes, if I interpret it as intended only as a warning to specialists not to reduce all issues to *mere* applications of their specialty. Pride in one's special subject matter is a virtue, not a vice. It is right and proper, and good to look upon, to see a tanner in love with leather and a carpenter in love with wood. But what a meager portion of the realm of the mind is covered even by the proudest single subject! If only there is the will, how much of the rich realm of the human mind lies open for invasion, for the physicist beyond, beside, and behind nuclear fission, and for the economist in regions where the circulating medium is of more precious metal than even under the gold standard.

Robert Browning began his *A Grammarian's Funeral* with a dirge for scholarship:

> Let us begin and carry up this Corpse,
> Singing together,
>
> .   .   .   .   .   .
>
> This is our master, famous calm and dead,
> Borne on our shoulders.

Browning did not end on a mournful note, however, and neither will I. Ways can be found to harmonize training in professional skills with training in scholarship. They must be found. They will be found. They need not involve any change in the declared objectives of our graduate schools. They will involve, however, changes in their actual practice. What the required changes are is a matter for exploration and experimentation.

Our graduate schools are now turning out large new crops of doctors of learning, whose primary task it will be to rescue the world from the perils of war, of disease, of poverty, and of sin. May they be given moments of leisure, and may they use some of these moments to give a little thought to the ways by which scholarship, as an ornament of the peace and the prosperity they will be winning for us, might also be promoted.

19

ADDRESS AT THE UNIVERSITY OF TORONTO CONVOCATION

PRESIDENT BISSELL HAS GIVEN me no instructions as to what my mission is this evening beyond asking me to speak and imploring me to get it over with as quickly as possible. I will therefore, by my lights, although perhaps not by yours, be brief. I will address myself to today's graduates. You have just completed your education, and I am the last obstacle to your receipt of official certification to that effect. It has, I am sure, been an excellent education, and your teachers and your great University are, I am sure, justly proud of the diligence and ability with which you have absorbed it. Tomorrow you step into a world of promise and of peril to embark on your active careers, crammed to the brim with knowledge, letters, and professional skills, and eager to serve and to achieve. I wish you all possible luck and I hope the world will reward your merits generously and will deal kindly with the occasional lapses from perfection which experience suggests are probable. I suspect it is my intended function on this occasion to impart to you from the stock of wisdom which one is supposed automatically to accumulate with age some words of advice which, as a top-dressing to what your professors have already bestowed on you from their own stock, will complete your preparation for your careers. But if that is my assignment, a belatedly acquired sense of modesty restrains me from accepting it. Like many others, I had supposed that when one's active career as a teacher had reached its allotted end, one was still subject to the obligation of dispensing advice generously and freely to the young and the not-so-young. This seemed in prospect to be an ideal program for retirement. Leisure, Bernard Mandeville once explained, ''is an aversion to business, generally attended with a desire of being inactive.'' If one added to this, to ward off ennui, the lavish giving of advice, what more could one ask? Since my retirement, however, it has been made clear to me that my proper role henceforth is to be a recipient rather than a dispenser of advice. I have been warned that when a man of years gives advice based on his own experience, it tends to degenerate

Address at the University of Toronto Convocation, November 24, 1961.

into the repetition of stale maxims which are either trite or false. After forty-five years, therefore, in which giving advice, good, bad, and irrelevant, earned me my living, I now find that I have regained a sort of second youth, in which I receive advice, mainly on the perils of leisure, but no longer have the courage and self-assurance to give it. I am reminded also of the moribund ex-dean of a divinity school whose conscience drove him to inflict on his successor so prolonged a course of detailed advice that the latter's patience gave out and he besought his predecessor "to stop talking and get on with the dying."

There is one recommendation, however, that I can bring myself to give, especially on an occasion like this, as possibly useful for graduates as they face the task of applying what they have been taught in the every-day pursuit of their careers, in their callings as citizens and good neighbors, and above all in their intellectual life. You have listened to great teachers; you have read great books. Take what they said most seriously. Go back to them if the opportunity offers; listen to them again and read them again. Ponder as deeply as you can what they endeavored to transmit to you. Even when your occupational designation is no longer that of a student, continue to seek great teachers, and continue to read great books, old ones and new ones. But pass their lessons through the filter of your own minds, absorb them discriminatingly, in the light of your own reason, and, at least if they are in the realm of temporal affairs, accept them not because they come from an authority, but because you have been reasonably persuaded by their arguments. Beware of rhetoric that is effective by other means than reasonable and reasoning persuasion. Be yourself, but be a reasonable and a reasoning self. In matters for which your training and your capacities provide you with no criteria for judgment, you must perforce depend mainly or wholly on authority. But if it is *human* authority that is in question, be aware that this is a reasonable *de*pendence only because reasonable *inde*pendence is foreclosed to you. Even in such cases, do not make Gods out of men, do not be a disciple. Bethink you constantly that the authority you are following may be wrong, and keep your mind open always to the possibility that new knowledge, new insights, new values may before long make his error evident.

There are dangers, I concede, intellectual, moral, even material, in this procedure, and it needs to be pursued with measure and balance. The independence I am recommending is for adults, not children, and it must not be carried to the length where it becomes intellectual pride, arrogance, the substitution of yourself as an authority for the authority of a great man or a great tradition.

In 1621, a Puritan opponent of James I, George Wither, published a poem whose central and sole theme, extended over many pages, is adequately stated in the following lines:

My mind's my kingdom, and I will permit
No other's will to have the rule of it;
For I am free, and no man's power, I know,
Did make me thus, nor shall unmake me now.
But through a spirit none can quench in me,
This mind I got; and this my mind shall be.

Should we cry, "Bravo!"? I am not sure. Wither was protesting against an absolute monarch who was encroaching on what he regarded as inalienable and
private, his religious conscience. The absolute monarch promptly put him in
prison for the offense of publishing this declaration of intellectual independence.
As against James I, I am too much a Whig and too much an individualist not to
decide for Wither. But I am not at all sure that Wither was not substituting himself
as absolute monarch over his own mind for the absolute sovereignty which James
I was trying to exercise over it. If every adult in full possession of the normal
range of mental capacities has a natural right to sovereignty over his own mind,
it is a sovereignty which should be exercised constitutionally, reasonably, with
openness to argument, openness to the influence of new knowledge and understanding. It is a sovereignty which has only a distant resemblance to the absolute
sovereignty which the mule exercises over his own mind.

Nor am I recommending unlimited scepticism, or negativism, or aversion to
attaining strong convictions whether from outside sources or from the workings
of one's own reasoning capacity. I have long regretted that we have abandoned
the distinction which was made by David Hume, and by John Stuart Mill following him, between a "proof" and a "demonstration," or at least that we have
failed to see the ever-recurrent need for the distinction which they made, although
it would have been better if they had expressed it in terms less liable to general
misinterpretation. For Hume and Mill a demonstration was an argument whose
refutation would be inconceivable to a reasonable man, where as a proof was an
argument falling short of demonstration, but so persuasive that if there was sufficient motive to a decision one way or the other a reasonable man would feel
bound to accept it, subject, however, to amendment or rejection upon the appearance of new evidence or new reasoning to the contrary. Neither Hume nor
Mill would have much commerce with "demonstrations" outside the fields of
pure logic and pure mathematics. But Hume, the supposedly extreme sceptic,
was a believer in the availability of "proofs" even in the fields of politics, and
economics, and the philosophy of history, while Mill is still being subjected to
jeering refutation of his attempt to "prove" the validity of utilitarianism by philosophers who think that Mill meant "demonstration" when he said "proof." Be
highly sceptical of the availability of "demonstrations," but be only duly cau-

tious, retain only the right to reconsider, to reappraise, to search, to ponder, and to consult other doctors, when it is a question of "proofs" in Hume's and John Stuart Mill's sense. This is a design for dangerous intellectual living I recommend to you. It is a design which if followed will constantly keep your intellectual muscles stretched, and may at times strain them. But if you accept the principle that it is often obligatory to act on mere "proofs," and that it is sometimes obligatory to act on even much weaker claims to persuasive influence, it will not lead you to a life of negativistic indecision and irresolution, and it will enable you to render full honor to the dignity and the responsibility of being a University graduate.

INDEX